CANNAE

CANNAE

The experience of battle in the Second Punic War

Gregory Daly

London and New York

FOR MAM AND DAD

First published 2002
by Routledge
11 New Fetter Lane, London EC4P 4EE

Simultaneously published in the USA and Canada
by Routledge
29 West 35th Street, New York, NY 10001

Routledge is an imprint of the Taylor & Francis Group

Typeset in Garamond by Florence Production Ltd, Stoodleigh,
Devon
Printed and bound in Great Britain by MPG Books Ltd, Bodmin

British Library Cataloguing in Publication Data
A catalogue record for this book is available from the British
Library

Library of Congress Cataloging in Publication Data
Daly, Gregory, 1975–
Cannae: the experience of battle in the Second Punic War /
Gregory Daly.
p. cm.
Includes bibliographical references and index.
1. Cannae, Battle of, 216 B.C. 2. Hannibal, 247–182 B.C.—
Military leadership. 3. Punic War, 2nd, 218–201 B.C.—
Campaigns—Italy. 4. Strategy. I. Title.

DG247.3 .D35 2002
937'.04—dc21   2001048415

ISBN 0–415–26147–3

CONTENTS

MAPS AND FIGURES

Maps

Figures

PREFACE

According to Cicero, when Hannibal was in exile in Ephesus, long after his victory over the Romans at Cannae and eventual defeat at Zama, he attended a talk given by a famous philosopher called Phormio, who apparently 'held forth for several hours upon the functions of a commander-in-chief and military matters in general'. After the speaker had finished, a delighted audience asked Hannibal what he thought of Phormio's ideas. He did not share their enthusiasm, and declared that time and again he had seen many old madmen but never one madder than Phormio' (Cicero, *De Oratore* 2.18.74–6).

This story may well be apocryphal, but it should certainly cause students of military history to pause for thought. Since the publication of John Keegan's *The Face of Battle* (1976), it has become almost commonplace to find books on warfare prefaced by suitably modest admissions of ignorance, with historians quietly admitting that since they themselves have never experienced battle, they ultimately cannot be certain of its nature. Such admissions are refreshingly and admirably honest, and if they are desirable when considering such recent battles as Waterloo and Edge Hill, they ought to be obligatory when attempting to discuss ancient warfare.

Humility is absolutely necessary when analysing the nature of battle in antiquity, since warfare has changed so much in the meantime. In fact, one might wonder whether modern military experience would help analyses of ancient battles. Paul Fussell has doubts about whether the battles of the First World War ought to be called battles at all, since they have no real resemblance even to the battles of a century earlier (Fussell, 2000, p. 9). It could equally be said that they have no real resemblance to more recent warfare. Veterans of the recent NATO bombing campaign against Serbia, carried out to protect the Kosovar Albanians, could hardly be said to have a specially pertinent insight into the events at the Somme in AD 1916 or at Cannae in 216 BC.

> The Kosovo conflict looked and sounded like a war: jets took off, buildings were destroyed and people died. For the civilians and

soldiers killed in air strikes and the Kosovar Albanians murdered by Serb police and paramilitaries the war was as real – and as fraught with horror – as war can be.

For the citizens of the NATO countries, on the other hand, the war was virtual. They were mobilized, not as combatants but as spectators. The war was a spectacle: it aroused emotions in the intense but shallow way that sports do. The events in question were as remote from their essential concerns as a football game, and even though the game was in deadly earnest, the deaths were mostly hidden, and above all, they were someone else's.

. . . Although the war galvanized opinion across the planet, the number of people who actually went to war was small: 1500 members of NATO air-crews and thirty thousand technicians, support staff and officers at headquarters. On the opposite side were the air-defense specialists of Serbia, numbering less than a thousand, and forty thousand soldiers, dug into redoubts and bunkers in Kosovo and Serbia. Face to face combat occurred rarely and then only between KLA guerrillas and Serbian forces on the Kosovo–Albanian border. For NATO combatants the experience of war was less visceral than calculative, a set of split-second decisions made through the lens of a gun camera or over a video-conferencing system. Those who struck from the air seldom saw those they killed.

. . . It was fought without ground troops, in the hope and expectation that there would be no casualties at all. And so it proved.

(Ignatieff, 2000, pp. 3–5)

The contrast with the Second Punic War, and the battle of Cannae in particular, could hardly be greater. Despite being heavily outnumbered, Hannibal's multinational horde of mercenary troops and subject and allied levies were able to surround and virtually annihilate at close quarters the largest Roman army ever assembled. It is possible that more than 50,000 Romans and Italians fell at Cannae, in what Victor Hanson aptly describes as 'a battlefield Armageddon [sic] unrivalled until the twentieth century' (Hanson, 1995b, p. 49). If the ancient casualty figures are even remotely accurate, and no ancient author believed that less than 48,200 Romans and Italians were killed at Cannae, it is likely that no European army has ever suffered as heavily in a single day's fighting as the Roman forces did on that day in 216 BC. Even more striking, perhaps, is the fact that there were more Romans and Italians killed in one day of fighting at Cannae than Americans killed in combat during the whole Vietnam War.[1]

The battle of Cannae may be the most studied battle in history; it has almost certainly had the most important effect on the development of military tactics. Scipio, later surnamed Africanus, a survivor of Cannae, seems to have had the lessons of Cannae in mind when he devised the tactics that brought him victory at Baecula, Ilipa, and the Great Plains.[2] In fact, Vegetius indicates that the use of an offensive reserve by Roman armies was adopted from the Carthaginians, who, he claims, had in turn learned it from the Spartans (Veg. 3.17). The influence of Cannae did not end with the Romans, however. The rise of the musket in the late sixteenth and early seventeenth centuries, a military revolution which effectively gave birth to modern warfare, was largely facilitated by the tactical innovations of the Counts of Nassau, whose 'linear battle order' was to some extent modelled upon Hannibal's outflanking manoeuvre at Cannae (Parker, 1995, pp. 154–5). In the twentieth century alone, Cannae was the inspiration behind the Schlieffen Plan, Germany's invasion of France and Belgium in 1914, their victorious tactics at Tannenberg that same year, and the unsuccessful German assault on the Kursk salient in 1943. Eisenhower's lifelong dream seems to have been to emulate Hannibal's victory at Cannae, while more recently General Schwarzkopf, apparently an ardent admirer of Hannibal, was expected by many to attempt a double envelopment in the Gulf War of early 1991.[3]

The importance of the battle of Cannae is therefore incontestable, both for the ongoing influence of Hannibal's tactics upon military thought, and for the sheer scale of the Roman defeat on what was one of the bloodiest days in the history of warfare. Academics have not been slow to recognise this, and there is an immense amount of literature about Cannae. So why another attempt to analyse it?

Most previous work on Cannae has been concerned with such matters as tactics, the topography of the battlefield, and the strategic role of the battle in the context of the Second Punic War as a whole. Since the publication of *The Face of Battle*, John Keegan's groundbreaking study of Agincourt, Waterloo, and the Somme, military historians have begun to pay attention to the experience of battle for the individuals who did the fighting. Recent studies of Cannae in this mould include articles by Victor Hanson and Martin Samuels, as well as Philip Sabin's important study of battle mechanics in the Second Punic War (Hanson, 1992; Samuels, 1990; Sabin, 1996).

While useful, these articles are all lacking in some way. Hanson's article is mainly concerned with recreating the experience of Cannae for individual soldiers, and, being extremely short, does not make a serious attempt at analysing the battle's manoeuvres in any broader sense. Samuels recognises the fact that it is impossible even to begin to understand what happened at Cannae without a solid understanding of the opposing armies; unfortunately, his analyses of the respective armies are fraught with problems, which in turn devalue his conclusions. Sabin's article is a very useful investigation of battle mechanics in the Second Punic War as a whole, skilfully blending the broad Grand Tactical perspective with the more immediate Keegan-style approach, but owing to brevity does not deal with Cannae or any other battle in detail, instead emphasising features common to the war's many battles.

This book tries to examine the 'reality of Cannae' as experienced by the individual soldiers who took part in the battle, without losing sight of the 'big picture', the battle as a whole. It begins, therefore, by considering the battle in terms of such conventional criteria as strategic significance, Grand Tactics, topography, and manpower. Having done this, it digresses to study the Roman and Carthaginian armies, a complicated but necessary task, in order to comprehend how they fought at Cannae, and why they fought at all. Armed with reasonably complete pictures of the opposing forces, it is possible to focus specifically once more on the battle itself, first by investigating the part played by the opposing commanders, in order to see how far and in what ways they influenced the battle's outcome. After this, the 'Keegan Model' can be used to analyse the battle in an attempt to recover the individual experience of battle at Cannae.

In preparing this book and the thesis upon which it is based, I have incurred many debts which are a pleasure to acknowledge, above all to my supervisor, Dr Andrew Erskine, whose advice and encouragement ensured, among other things, that my thesis made infinitely more sense than if I had been left to my own devices, and to Victor Connerty, for his help and support when Dr Erskine was abroad. I am also grateful to Professor Andrew Smith, and to Carine O'Grady, whose assistance I called upon with embarrassing frequency. My thanks are due to Dr Louis Rawlings and Matthew O'Brien, of the University of Wales Cardiff, who were obliging enough to meet me for an afternoon in August 1998; several of the ideas expressed here were first discussed then. Paul Hunt, of University College London, provided many helpful suggestions about Polybius. Professor Tim Cornell, of the University of Manchester, examined my thesis, and encouraged its publication. The initial interest and constant support of Richard Stoneman and his team at Routledge proved invaluable, as did the many useful criticisms of Routledge's two anonymous readers. Needless to say, all errors remain my own.

I must also thank UCD Faculty of Arts for providing me with a Postgraduate Scholarship and a Travel Scholarship, enabling me to continue my studies and to visit Cannae and Lake Trasimene. While in Italy, Professor Andrew Wallace-Hadrill gave me access to the library of the British School at Rome as well as useful advice on maps and other matters. I have made constant use of the libraries of University College Dublin and Trinity College, Dublin, and occasional use of that of the Institute of Classical Studies in London; the librarians of all three institutions were unfailingly helpful.

Thanks are due to all those of my friends who helped in too many ways to describe: Ambrogio Caiani, Lucy Corcoran, Beulah Croker, Jim Darcy, Colin De Paor, Eva Dunne, Peggy Harris, Aidan Higgins, Daron Higgins, Colum Keating, Malcolm Latham, Tony Marnell, Elaine Murphy, Claire O'Brien, Sandra O'Reilly, John Rafferty, Geraldine Scott, and Charlotte Steiner. It may seem rude to single some out, but I am especially grateful to Heinrich Hall, Alison Moore, David Delaney, and the Delaney family.

Finally, I would like to thank those of my family who helped in any way, especially my sister Elaine, and my parents to whom this book is dedicated, since it was only through their constant support that it was made possible.

ACKNOWLEDGEMENTS

All translated extracts in this book (unless otherwise cited) are from:

Livy: History of Rome, Volume V reprinted by permission of the publishers and the Trustees of the Loeb Classsical Library, Loeb Classsical Library Volume 233, translated by B.O. Foster, Cambridge, Mass.: Harvard University Press, 1929.

Polybius: The Histories, Volume II reprinted with permission of the publishers and the Trustees of the Loeb Classsical Library, Loeb Classsical Library Volume 137, translated by W.R. Paton, Cambridge, Mass.: Harvard University Press, 1922.

Polybius: The Histories, Volume III reprinted with permission of the publishers and the Trustees of the Loeb Classsical Library, Loeb Classsical Library Volume 138, translated by W.R. Paton, Cambridge, Mass.: Harvard University Press, 1923.

The Loeb Classical Library ® is a trademark of the President and Fellows of Harvard College.

ABBREVIATIONS

AHB	*Ancient History Bulletin*
AJA	*American Journal of Archaeology*
AJP	*American Journal of Philology*
Amm.	Ammianus Marcellinus
ANRW	*Aufstieg und Niedergang der Römischen Welt*
App., *Hann.*	Appian, *Hannibalic War*
—, *Iber.*	*Spanish Wars*
—, *Pun.*	*Punic Wars*
Arist., *Eth. Nic.*	Aristotle, *Nicomachean Ethics*
Arr., *Anab.*	Arrian, *Anabasis*
—, *Tact.*	*Tactics*
Asclep.	Asclepiodotus
Caes., *B Afr*	Caesar, *African War*
—, *B Civ*	*Civil War*
—, *B Gall*	*Gallic War*
CAH	*Cambridge Ancient History*
Cass. Dio	Cassius Dio
CJ	*Classical Journal*
CP	*Classical Philology*
CQ	*Classical Quarterly*
Diod.	Diodorus Siculus
Dion. Hal.	Dionysius of Halicarnassus
Enn., *Ann.*	Ennius, *Annales*
Eutrop.	Eutropius
Flor.	Florus
Frontin., *Strat.*	Frontinus, *Strategemata*
GRBS	*Greek, Roman, and Byzantine Studies*
Hdt.	Herodotus
HSCP	*Harvard Studies in Classical Philology*
JHS	*Journal of Hellenic Studies*
JRS	*Journal of Roman Studies*
LCL	Loeb Classical Library

Liv.	Livy
LSJ	Liddell and Scott, *Greek–English Lexicon* (ninth edition, 1940)
Macrob., *Sat.*	Macrobius, *Saturnalia*
Nep., *Hann.*	Cornelius Nepos, *Hannibal*
OCD	*Oxford Classical Dictionary* (third edition, 1996)
Onas.	Onasander
Oros.	Orosius
PBSR	*Papers of the British School at Rome*
Plat., *Leg.*	Plato, *Laws*
Plaut., *Poen.*	Plautus, *Poenulus*
Plin., *Nat. Hist.*	Pliny, *Natural History*
Plut., *Vit. Aem.*	Plutarch, *Life of Aemilius Paullus*
— , Vit. *Alex.*	*Life of Alexander*
— , Vit. *Cleom.*	*Life of Cleomenes*
— , Vit. *Crass.*	*Life of Crassus*
— , Vit. *Eum.*	*Life of Eumenes*
— , Vit. *Fab. Max.*	*Life of Fabius Maximus*
— , Vit. *Marc.*	*Life of Marcellus*
— , Vit. *Philop.*	*Life of Philopoemen*
— , Vit. *Pomp.*	*Life of Pompey*
— , Vit. *Pyrrh.*	*Life of Pyrrhus*
— , Vit. *Tim.*	*Life of Timoleon*
Polyaen.	Polyaenus
Polyb.	Polybius
RhM	*Rheinisches Museum für Philologie*
Sall., *Cat.*	Sallust, *Catiline War*
Str.	Strabo
Thuc.	Thucydides
Val. Max.	Valerius Maximus
Varro, *Ling.*	Varro, *De Lingua Latina*
Veg.	Vegetius
Xen., *Anab.*	Xenophon, *Anabasis*
—, *Cyn.*	*On Hunting*
—, *Cyr.*	*Cyropaedia*
—, *Eq.*	*On Horsemanship*
—, *Hell.*	*Hellenica*
—, *Mem.*	*Memorabilia*
Zon.	Zonaras

GLOSSARY

Accensi Light-armed troops in the mid-Republican Roman army, later military servants.

Aediles Roman magistrates in charge of public works and buildings, markets, and festivals. They were of two types, curule and plebian.

Ala A unit of allied troops approximately the same size as a legion, here usually translated 'brigade'.

Auspices Natural phenomena thought to reveal the will of the gods.

Caetra Small, round, Spanish shield.

Caetrati Spanish light infantry, who used a *caetra*.

Centurion Commander of a century.

Century In a military context, a unit of sixty or more men making up half a maniple; alternatively a voting unit.

Classis A division of the Roman army in the reform attributed to Servius Tullius.

Cohort A unit of about 500 allied troops; during the Second Punic War the term began to be used for units composed of a maniple each of *hastati*, *principes*, and *triarii* acting together.

Consuls The most important magistrates of the Roman Republic; two were elected each year, with the primary function of leading the state in war.

Decurion One of three commanders of a *turma* of Roman cavalry.

Dictator A Roman magistrate elected during an emergency, without any colleagues and with authority exceeding all other magistrates.

Dilectus The Roman procedure for levying troops.

Equites The Roman cavalry, selected from Rome's wealthiest citizens.

Extraordinarii A special unit of allied troops in a Roman army, consisting of a third of the cavalry and a fifth of the infantry.

Falarica A Spanish incendiary spear, similar to the Roman *pilum*, but with the metal shaft wrapped in tow smeared with pitch which would be set on fire before being thrown.

Falcata A curved Spanish sword, similar to the Greek *kopis*, and the Gurkha *kukri*, especially suited for cavalry combat.

Gens A group of Roman families sharing a name and certain religious rites.

Gladius The Roman sword, possibly based on a Spanish design, suitable for both cutting and thrusting.

Hasta The long spear used by the *triarii*.

Hastati The first line of Roman heavy infantry.

Hoplite An infantryman armed with a large round shield and a thrusting spear, fighting in a phalanx.

The 'Hundred' One of Carthage's most important governing bodies, composed of 104 aristocrats, to whom officials had to account for their actions on leaving office.

Iuniores Male Roman citizens of military age, between 17 and 46.

Legion The largest units of the Roman army, composed of thirty maniples of *hastati*, *principes*, and *triarii*, along with *velites* and *equites*.

Longche A javelin or throwing spear of some sort.

Longchophoroi The skirmishers in Hannibal's army, armed with javelins of various sorts.

Lorica Mail cuirass worn by Roman infantry.

Maniple The basic tactical unit of the Roman heavy infantry; there were thirty per legion, each composed of two centuries, one termed *prior* and the other *posterior.*

Master of Horse Assistant to a Dictator, normally appointed by him.

New man A Roman who achieved high office, usually the consulship, none of whose ancestors had held such a position.

Noble A Roman whose ancestors in a direct male line had achieved high office, usually the consulship.

Optio A rear-rank officer, assistant to a centurion or decurion.

Ovation A lesser triumph, where the victorious Roman general entered the city on foot or on horseback, rather than in a four-horse chariot.

Peltast Lightly armed infantryman, originally equipped with a wicker shield.

Phalanx The line of battle formed by hoplites.

Praetors Roman magistrates, second only to the consuls in prestige, whose original functions were mainly judicial, but who could command in war.

Prefect of the Allies Roman official in charge of allied troops.

Pilum The heavy Roman throwing spear.

Primus pilus The highest-ranking centurion in a legion, commanding the first century of *triarii*.

Principes The second line of Roman heavy infantry.

Pugio The short dagger carried by Roman troops.

Quaestors Roman magistrates with financial responsibilities who accompanied consuls on campaign.

Quincunx Modern term for the Roman legion's 'chequerboard' formation.

Rorarii Light armed troops of the mid-Republican Roman army, probably identical to *velites*.

Saunion   A Spanish throwing spear, made entirely of iron.

Scutarii   Spanish line infantry armed with large oval shields like the Roman *scutum*.

Scutum   The long, curved, oval or oblong Roman shield.

Senate   The main Roman deliberative body, composed of former magistrates. In theory it was an advisory body, but in practice it ran the state.

Signifer   A Roman standard-bearer.

Suffete   One of Carthage's chief administrative officials.

Triarii   The third line of Roman heavy infantry.

Tribune, military   One of six junior officers in a legion.

Triumph   A parade by a victorious Roman general.

Turma   A squadron of Roman cavalry.

Velites   The standard term for Roman light infantry during the Second Punic War.

1

INTRODUCTION

Rome and Carthage[1]

Carthage was probably founded at some point in the late ninth century BC,[2] as a trading colony established by the Phoenician city of Tyre. She maintained close links with her mother-city, but eventually outgrew her, and by 264, more than half a century after Tyre's destruction at the hands of Alexander the Great, Carthage was the greatest power in the western Mediterranean. Her wealth was proverbial, with Polybius claiming that Carthage was the richest city in the Mediterranean world even when she fell in 146, despite the fact that this was long after she was deprived of her overseas territories (Polyb. 18.35.9).

Such territories had been extensive. As a primarily commercial city, Carthage had close connections with the older Phoenician colonies in Spain, cities such as Gades, Malaga, Abdera, and Sexi. A Phoenician colony on the island of Ibiza may have been originally Carthaginian, but even if not, was clearly within Carthage's sphere of influence by the fifth century, as were the other Balearic islands and the island of Malta. Phoenician colonies had long existed in Sardinia, and by the late sixth century the island was obviously under Carthaginian control. Corsica also appears to have been largely under Carthaginian influence. Carthaginian expansion in Sicily had brought her into conflict with the western Greeks, who decisively defeated a Carthaginian army at Himera in 480. Despite this setback, Carthage did not give up, so the Greeks continued to fight under such men as Timoleon, who was victorious at the river Crimesus in 341, and Agathocles, who led an invasion of Africa in 310. Agathocles' invasion was initially successful, but he failed to take Carthage itself, and eventually returned to Syracuse. By 277 Carthage had lost virtually all of Sicily aside from Lilybaeum to Pyrrhus of Epirus, but her position improved rapidly after his departure and by the outbreak of the First Punic War in 264 Carthage dominated western and southern Sicily. In addition to her overseas territories Carthage controlled the coast of North Africa from Cyrenaica to the Atlantic, past the Pillars of Hercules, founding colonies of her own or taking over other Phoenician settlements such as Utica and Hadrumentum. This network of colonies gave Carthage a virtual monopoly over trade routes in the western Mediterranean, effectively turning the area into a Carthaginian lake.

1

Apart from the coastal colonies, Carthage had a substantial influence on the interior of northern Africa. Alliances existed with the various Numidian and Moorish tribes who lived in what are now Algeria and Morocco; the Numidian and Moorish rulers appear to have been client kings, who were obliged to send troops to fight in Carthage's armies. From the fifth century, shortly after her defeat at Himera, Carthage expanded southwards, eventually conquering about half of what is now Tunisia. The highly fertile land thus acquired, coupled with scientific farming techniques, brought Carthage a vast amount of agricultural wealth. Large country estates belonging to Carthaginian aristocrats occupied the city's immediate hinterland, while land further south was worked by the indigenous population, known as Libyans. They were obliged to serve in Carthage's armies, and perhaps a quarter of the grain they grew went to Carthage as tribute.[3]

Carthage was essentially ruled by an oligarchy based on wealth, although it had what was known to ancient writers on politics as a 'mixed constitution', one involving elements of monarchy, aristocracy, and democracy. Carthage had originally had kings of some sort, but by the time of the Punic Wars the 'monarchic' element in the state was represented by the two suffetes, the most powerful officials, who were elected on an annual basis. These supreme magistrates had civil, judicial, and religious roles, but lacked a military function, a highly unusual situation in antiquity. Most administrative decisions were made by a council of several hundred notables, each of whom was appointed for life; the procedure for their appointment is unknown. Thirty councillors formed an inner council, the precise function of which is uncertain, although it is likely that they prepared business for the larger body, making them highly influential. Another important instrument of the state was the 'Hundred', a court of 104 judges chosen from the main council. The court's function was to control the magistrates, especially the generals, who would have to answer for their actions during their time in office. Wealth, as well as merit, was required for appointment to any public office in Carthage, and it appears that bribery was commonplace (Polyb. 6.56.1–4). Finally, the popular assembly was theoretically supreme, and Polybius records that its power grew over time (Polyb. 6.51.3–8). The real extent of its powers is uncertain, however, and it seems that a small number of families dominated both the council and the important magistracies.

Rome was traditionally thought to have been founded in 753, becoming a republic in 509. Like Carthage, Rome also had a 'mixed constitution' but was in practice an oligarchy, timocratic rather than plutocratic in character; what counted was military glory, not commercial success. The 'monarchic' element in the state was provided by the two annually elected consuls; these were the most important magistrates, whose chief function was to lead the state in war. Other magistrates included praetors, quaestors, and aediles. All these offices were filled by annual elections. The senate was the state's 'aristocratic' element, comprising about 300 former magistrates. Technically, the senate was only an advisory body, but in practice it tended to control Roman foreign policy, receiving and sending embassies, and advising the magistrates, to whom it also allocated tasks and resources. The senate's decrees did not have the force of law, and had to be ratified by the people, who could meet in assemblies, the 'democratic' element in Rome's consti-tution. These assemblies were not forums for discussion, but merely voted on proposals. The three main assemblies were the *comitia centuriata*, the *comitia tributa*, and the *concilium plebis*. The wealthier citizens held sway in all three assemblies, especially the *comitia centuriata*, which elected the senior magistrates and could vote to declare war or accept peace.

Rome was ruled by Etruscan monarchs prior to the foundation of the Republic, and had consequently had good relations with Carthage, since both the Etruscans and the Carthaginians were opposed to the western Greeks. These good relations were evidently maintained, as Polybius records three treaties between Rome and Carthage (Polyb. 3.22–6), the first being negotiated in the first year of the Republic, which he dates to 507; this may have in fact been a renewal of a treaty originally conducted between Carthage and regal Rome. Under the terms of this treaty Rome and Carthage swore to remain friends and not to act against each other's interests. Rome's interests were clearly territorial, as Carthage was barred from interfering in Latium, while Carthage's interests were primarily commercial, with Roman trade in Libya and Sardinia being strictly regulated. A second treaty is of uncertain date, but probably dates to 348.[4] This imposed stricter limits on Roman trade with Africa, requiring it to be channelled through Carthage itself, as well as blocking Roman commercial access to Spain. At the same time, it recognised Roman control in Latium, and also seemed to envisage the possibility of Romans plundering and colonising overseas.

This second treaty may have been renewed, or at least informally re-affirmed, in 343, since Livy records that in that year the Carthaginians congratulated the Romans on their victory over the Samnites, and offered a gold crown to Capitoline Jupiter (Liv. 7.38.2). Both states were soon to survive major challenges, with Carthaginian expansion in Sicily being halted by Timoleon at the river Crimesus, while Rome's allies revolted in 341. The Romano-Latin War resulted in the settlement of 338, under which Rome would henceforth have separate alliances with each individual commu-nity, rather than dealing with leagues or confederations. Each community had a clear legal relationship with Rome, and was obliged to send troops to serve in Rome's armies. This settlement provided the pattern for Rome's conquest of the rest of Italy, and can rightly be regarded as one of the major turning points of Roman history.

The Second Samnite War broke out in 328, and over the following half-century Roman power spread with phenomenal speed. Constant campaigning on an almost annual basis brought Rome victory over Samnites, Etruscans, and Celts, giving her control of much of the Italian peninsula. Livy claims that Rome and Carthage conducted another treaty in 306 (Liv. 9.43.26). Polybius mentions no such treaty, although he goes to great pains to deny the existence of a treaty recorded by the Sicilian historian Philinus, which recognised Italy and Sicily as respectively Roman and Carthaginian spheres of influence (Polyb. 3.26). If Polybius was mistaken and the so-called 'Philinus treaty' was genuine, it may well correspond to Livy's treaty of 306.[5]

Thurii and other Greek cities in southern Italy appealed to Rome for help against the depredations of their Lucanian neighbours, but Roman involvement in Greek Italy was opposed by Tarentum, the most powerful of the Greek cities there. In 282 the Tarentines attacked a squadron of Roman ships, and cast out the Roman garrison at Thurii, replacing its oligarchic government with a democratic one. Rome understandably declared war, and the Tarentines, realising that they could hardly resist Rome without help, turned to Pyrrhus of Epirus, the powerful Greek monarch. It appears that Pyrrhus was only too glad of the opportunity to build a new empire in the west, an empire that would include not merely Italy, but also Sicily and Carthage, if Plutarch is to be believed (Plut., *Vit. Pyrrh.* 14.3–5). He arrived in Italy in 280, leading an army of over 25,000 men and twenty war elephants, counting on the support of the western Greeks as well as that of the Samnites, Lucanians, Bruttians, and Messapians. Pyrrhus was twice victorious over the Romans at the battles of Heraclea and Ausculum, but he suffered enormous losses which he could ill afford. None of Rome's allies defected to him, and Rome fought on, refusing to negotiate while he was still on Italian soil, ignoring the unwritten conventions of Hellenistic warfare by not suing for peace despite having been beaten. Realising that the war in Italy was a lost cause, Pyrrhus answered Syracuse's appeal for help against Carthage, and set out for Sicily.

At some point while Pyrrhus was in Italy, probably just after his victory at Ausculum, the Carthaginian admiral Mago arrived at the Tiber with a fleet of 120 ships, offering assistance (Justin 18.2). It was most likely at this point that Rome and Carthage negotiated another treaty. This confirmed previous agreements and added that should either state conduct an alliance with Pyrrhus, it would do so with the proviso that it would be permitted to go to the assistance of the other should it be attacked; in such an eventuality the Carthaginians would provide ships for transport or war (Polyb. 3.25.2–5) (see Walbank, 1957, pp. 349–52). The treaty did not oblige Rome to come to Carthage's assistance in Sicily, it merely permitted it. Pyrrhus was initially very successful against Carthage in Sicily, but failed to take Lilybaeum, and in late 276 he returned to Italy, losing a sea battle to the Carthaginians on the way. Following a defeat at Malventum, the future Beneventum, he lost heart, withdrawing to Tarentum and sailing back to Greece.

When he left Sicily Pyrrhus is reputed to have declared 'what a wrestling ground we are leaving behind us for the Romans and the Carthaginians'

(Plut., *Vit. Pyrrh.* 23.8). Such a remark, if true, was to prove prophetic. Rome continued the war against the western Greeks after Pyrrhus' departure from Italy, eventually compelling Tarentum to surrender. However, while the Romans were besieging the city in 272 an ominous event occurred: a Carthaginian fleet appeared in Tarentum's harbour. The Romans protested, and the Carthaginians claimed that the fleet had actually only come to offer assistance to the Romans in accordance with the terms of their recent treaty. Nevertheless, this event must have provoked much suspicion in Rome (Lazenby, 1996a, pp. 34–5). In Pyrrhus' absence the Carthaginians had an almost entirely free hand in Sicily, being opposed only by Hiero of Syracuse. Messana, opposite Rhegium on the Straits of Messina, had been occupied by a group of Campanian mercenaries called 'Mamertines' since 288; these came into conflict with the Syracusans, who defeated the Mamertines in battle at the river Longanus (Polyb. 1.9.7–8). Realising the weakness of their position, the Mamertines appealed to both Rome and Carthage for help (Polyb. 1.10.1–2). The Carthaginians were the first to respond, sending a garrison to protect the town.

In an unprecedented move, Rome also responded to the Mamertine appeal, sending troops outside the Italian peninsula for the first time in their history. Such an action, which was in contravention of the 'Philinus treaty', assuming that the treaty actually existed, was bound to bring Rome into conflict with Carthage. The reasons for Rome's decision are unclear, but the strategic value of Messana must have been obvious. Control of Messana could have enabled Carthage to take control of all Sicily, and Messana itself was perilously close – only 10 miles – from Roman Rhegium. The senate was split on the issue so the matter was taken to the people. Perhaps driven by that desire for military glory which was the hallmark of Rome's aristocrats, the consuls advocated alliance with Messana, tempting the people with the prospect of plunder in the subsequent war; the people agreed, and appointed Appius Claudius Caudex, one of the consuls, to the Sicilian command (Polyb. 1.10.3–11.3) (Lazenby, 1996a, pp. 37–41; Walbank, 1957, pp. 57–61; Scullard, 1989a, pp. 539–43; Harris, 1979, pp. 182–90).

The Mamertines expelled their Carthaginian garrison, and invited the Romans into the city. The Carthaginian officer was then executed by his own men, and the Carthaginians made a fresh and highly unlikely alliance with the Syracusans, with the aim of driving the Mamertines, and by implication the Romans, from Sicily. The Carthaginians sent troops to garrison Agrigentum and lay siege to Messana, near where the Syracusans were also encamped. Claudius was nevertheless able to transport his army across the Straits of Messina, and then sent embassies to Hiero and to Hanno, the Carthaginian commander, demanding that they lift their siege of a city which was allied to Rome. They refused, and war was declared. The First Punic War lasted for twenty-three years, from 264 to 241, and was probably the longest continuous war in ancient history.

Hiero soon switched sides, and henceforth proved a loyal ally of Rome. Agrigentum was besieged for seven months in 262, but although the town fell to the Romans the Carthaginian commander and most of his men escaped. Several other Carthaginian-controlled towns defected to Rome, and Carthage instead decided to fortify several points in Sicily and, while holding these, to harry the Roman supply lines in Sicily and use their naval supremacy to plunder the Italian coast. In order to deal with this the Romans quickly expanded their navy, building twenty triremes and 100 quinqueremes, and equipping these ships with a strange device called a *corvus*, or 'crow'. This was a boarding-bridge with a hook on one end which could be dropped onto the deck of a hostile ship, pinning it into position and allowing Roman troops to board it. After an impressive naval victory off Mylae in 260, Rome mounted small-scale expeditions with some success to Corsica and Sardinia, and in 256 achieved another immense naval victory at Cape Ecnomus. This cleared the way for the launching of an invasion of Africa, which was initially very successful, until one of the consuls, Lucius Manlius Vulso, was withdrawn, leaving Marcus Atilius Regulus in command of a reduced army. The following year Regulus was defeated by a Carthaginian army commanded by a Spartan-trained mercenary called Xanthippus. In 254 the Romans were again victorious at sea, but most of their fleet was soon destroyed in a storm off Camerina, with further disasters in subsequent years. On land, the fortunes of both sides varied. The Romans captured Carthaginian Palermo in 254, but failed to take their stronghold at Lilybaeum. Hamilcar Barca, a young Carthaginian general, was sent to help Himilco defend Lilybaeum in 247 or 246. He based himself on Mount Eryx, raiding the Italian coast as far north as Cumae and harassing the Romans in Sicily itself. Rome raised another fleet which attempted to blockade the Carthaginians in Lilybaeum and Drepanum, and when a Carthaginian fleet arrived it was decisively defeated at the Aegates islands. Hamilcar was instructed to negotiate a peace treaty with Rome.

This treaty dictated that the Carthaginians evacuate Sicily and not attack Syracuse. All prisoners of war were to be returned, and Carthage would have to pay war reparations of 2,200 talents of silver over twenty years (Polyb. 1.62.8–9). However, when these terms were put before the Roman people they were rejected, and so a ten-man commission modified the treaty, making it much harsher: they demanded war reparations of 3,200 talents of silver, to be repaid over only ten years, and insisted that Carthage also evacuate all islands between Sicily and Italy (Polyb. 1.63.1–3).

Carthage's woes were far from over, as an army of about 20,000 mercenaries, which she could not afford to pay, rose against her and based themselves at Tunis. Their numbers were soon swollen by the subject Libyans, glad of a chance to try to shake off the Carthaginian yoke. Carthage was cut off from its territory, with rebel armies besieging Utica and Hippo. Hanno failed to relieve Utica, and was replaced by Hamilcar Barca, who defeated the insurgents at the battle of the Bagradas. He destroyed another insurgent army at a spot called the Gorge of the Saw, and the rebels were again defeated decisively in 237. After this, the occupied Hippo and Utica quickly surrendered to Hanno and Hamilcar. This 'Truceless War' had been a real life-or-death struggle for Carthage, and was notable for the remarkable cruelty with which it was conducted on both sides.

Unfortunately for Carthage, her mercenaries in Sardinia had also revolted. Rome behaved impeccably towards Carthage during the war, and refused to accept the insurgents as allies, despite appeals from the mercenaries in Sardinia and Utica. However, the native Sardinians managed to expel the mercenaries, who again asked Rome for help. Despite Carthaginian protests, the Romans proceeded to occupy the island. They threatened Carthage with a renewed war, and when Carthage submitted, a further 1,200 talents were added to the reparations she was to pay Rome (Polyb. 1.88.8–12). Carthage may not have fought to keep the Romans out of Sardinia, but the island's inhabitants did not submit so readily, and Rome appears to have campaigned constantly in Sardinia and Corsica up to 231, at which point she turned her interests further east, to the Celts of Cisalpine Gaul and to Illyria (Harris, 1979, pp. 190–200).

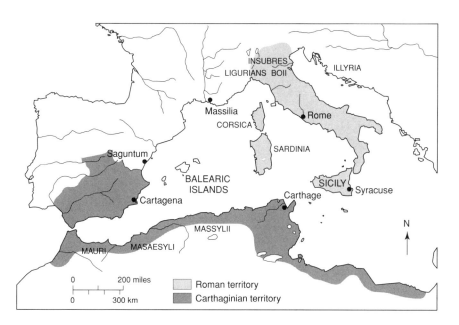

Map 1 The Western Mediterranean at the outbreak of the Second Punic War.

2

THE ROAD TO CANNAE

Introduction: the origins of the Second Punic War

Having achieved victory over their rebellious former mercenaries, the Carthaginians sent Hamilcar Barca to Spain in 237, in order to develop a Carthaginian empire as a compensation for the recent losses to Rome of Carthaginian territory in Sicily and Sardinia; these losses had deprived Carthage of valuable wealth and endangered her mercantile hegemony in the western Mediterranean.[1] Carthage may have wished to exploit Spanish resources directly, rather than relying on native trading partners, in order to facilitate the repayments of the war indemnities imposed by Rome in 241 and increased when Rome annexed Sardinia, and it is not inconceivable that a further reason for this newly aggressive phase in Carthaginian imperialism was to boost popular support for Carthage's government. Following his death eight years later, Hamilcar was succeeded in this Spanish command by his son-in-law Hasdrubal, who was in turn succeeded by Hamilcar's son Hannibal in 221. Between them, the Barcids carved out for Carthage a sizeable province, particularly valuable as a source of metal ore and manpower (Wagner, 1989, p. 156; Lancel, 1998, pp. 29–30; Scullard, 1989b, p. 41).[2]

The growth of Carthaginian power in Spain was a cause of concern to Rome, which was probably egged on by her ally Massilia. Massilia, modern Marseilles, was a powerful Greek city in southern Gaul, whose colonies and commercial interests in Spain were threatened by the Carthaginian expansion. In 231 Rome sent an embassy to Hamilcar, enquiring after the motives for this new aggressive phase of Carthaginian expansionism. Hamilcar's claim that its purpose was to enable Carthage to pay off her war indemnities towards Rome apparently satisfied the embassy, which withdrew, having demonstrated that Rome was fully aware of Carthage's empire-building in Spain (Cass. Dio, fr. 48).[3]

A further embassy was sent to Hasdrubal in 226 (Sumner, 1967, p. 217; Walbank, 1957, p. 168),[4] again probably at Massilian instigation; Hasdrubal's establishment of a large coastal base at Cartagena further threatened the

Map 2 Spain.

interests of Massilia (Sumner, 1967, pp. 217–18; Walbank, 1957, p. 169), which would have been able to persuade Rome to send an embassy to Spain by raising the spectre of a potential, albeit unlikely, alliance between the Carthaginians in Spain and the Celts of Transalpine and Cisalpine Gaul (Kramer, 1948, pp. 14 ff.; Kagan, 1995, pp. 259–60). This embassy led to a treaty which barred the Carthaginians from campaigning north of the Iber river, probably the modern Ebro. The treaty, which apparently gave the Carthaginians a licence to treat all Spain south of the river as their sphere of influence, was not really a concession on Rome's part as Spain was so far away (Errington, 1970, p. 38). The treaty was evidently flawed, recognising Carthaginian domination in Spain and not really restraining it, while being couched in insulting terms; by insisting that Carthage not campaign north of the Iber, Rome was ensuring that she herself should be recognised as the greater power with a right to intervene in Carthaginian affairs (Kagan, 1995, p. 260).[5]

Roman interference in 220 on behalf of Saguntum, a Spanish town south of the river and a recent ally of Rome,[6] pushed Hannibal into asserting the independence of Carthage from Rome by laying siege to Saguntum, regardless of Roman demands, making war inevitable. The sequence of events concerning Saguntum which led to the outbreak of the Second Punic War is not entirely clear, owing to later distortions in the Roman annalistic tradition; it seems safest to follow Polybius' account, in the main. An embassy was sent to Hannibal in late 220, warning him neither to attack Saguntum nor cross the Iber; Hannibal's response made it clear that he would not tolerate further Roman interference (Polyb. 3.15). It is likely that the Romans thought that Hannibal was bluffing, and that aggressive diplomacy would once again serve to restrain Carthaginian imperialism, despite Polybius' claim that they believed Hannibal yet took no direct action to deal with him as they saw no immediate threat (Polyb. 3.15.12–16.1). They were wrong. After requesting support from Carthage, Hannibal set out for Saguntum, beginning a siege which probably lasted from May 219 to late December or early January 218 (Polyb. 3.15.8, 17.1–9; Rich, 1996, p. 29). Rome took no action until after the new consuls took office in March 218, some weeks after news of Saguntum's fall would have reached Rome (Kagan, 1995, p. 268; Rich, 1996, p. 29). An embassy was sent to Carthage to deliver the ultimatum that Rome would declare war on Carthage unless Hannibal and his advisers surrendered to Rome; the ultimatum was rejected.[7]

The Second Punic War was not the result of Carthaginian hatred of Rome; rather, constant Roman interference in Spain attempted to restrict Carthage's efforts to make up for her losses in the First Punic War, hurting Carthage's pride and provoking resentment. Rome's failure to support her aggressive diplomacy with military force encouraged Carthage to strike first, enabling Hannibal to fight the war on his own terms.

Initial strategies

Rome's initial troop dispositions for 218 clearly indicate that the Romans did not intend to fight a defensive war; rather they planned an aggressive 'pincer strategy' where one army would be sent to Spain and another to Africa (Polyb. 3.40.2, 41.2; Liv. 21.17.5, 17.8; Adcock, 1940, p. 79; Briscoe, 1989, p. 46). The Spanish army, under Publius Cornelius Scipio, was apparently composed of 22,000 infantry, 2,200 cavalry, and sixty ships (Liv. 21.17.8); its function was probably to intercept Hannibal's army, possibly at the Rhone, before launching an offensive against the Carthaginians in northern Spain, where the Romans could hope for local support (Scullard, 1980, p. 203; Connolly, 1998, p. 147). Tiberius Sempronius Longus commanded the other army, which would be first stationed in Sicily, and consisted of about 24,000 infantry, 2,400 cavalry, and 160 warships (Liv. 21.17.5). This army would carry the war to Africa, in emulation of Agathocles of Syracuse and Marcus Atilius Regulus in the late fourth century and First Punic War respectively, but would do so only if Scipio's army succeeded in keeping Hannibal out of Italy; the invasion was probably intended to serve as a show of strength to incite Carthage's

Libyan subjects to revolt (Scullard, 1980, p. 80; Bernstein, 1994, p. 79). It is likely that the Romans expected the impending war to be fought along the lines of the First Punic War, with most of the fighting being centred on Spain, rather than Sicily; with Hannibal contained in Spain, a Roman expeditionary force in Africa could, if supported by insurgent Libyans, strike a decisive blow against the Carthaginians (Adcock, 1940, p. 79; Bernstein, 1994, p. 76).

Ultimately, Spain was to prove the most important theatre of the Second Punic War, and a Roman expedition to Africa under Scipio's son, later styled Scipio Africanus, did indeed strike the decisive blow against Carthage at Zama in 202, but this was a long way off. Roman plans for a two-pronged pincer strategy were not to be realised in 218.

Hannibal's aim in the war was not to destroy Rome, but to reduce it to the status of just another Italian power. This is indicated by the text of the treaty made by Hannibal with Philip V of Macedon in 215, which clearly anticipates the future existence of Rome (Polyb. 7.9.12–15), and is perhaps supported by Livy's statement that after Cannae, Hannibal declared himself to be fighting Rome for honour and for empire (Liv. 22.58.3; Briscoe, 1989, p. 46; Lazenby, 1996b, p. 42). With Rome reduced to the status of a secondary power, Carthage would have been able to regain Sicily, Sardinia, and her other lost territories, as well as having a free hand in Spain.

In order to achieve this, Hannibal's strategic options were limited: he could remain in Spain and fight any Roman forces on his own terms, or he could take the war to Italy itself (Lazenby, 1978, p. 29). Despite Santosuosso's claim to the contrary, it seems unlikely that Hannibal ever seriously favoured the former option, as Roman troops in Spain would doubtless have received support from local tribes opposed to the Carthaginian presence in Spain (Santosuosso, 1997, p. 170; Connolly, 1998, p. 147). Instead, on the principle that 'attack is the best form of defence', an invasion of Italy was planned (Errington, 1971, p. 62). Hannibal must have realised that he lacked the resources to conquer Italy, for Roman manpower had been the deciding factor in the First Punic War, which had essentially became a naval war of attrition won by Rome's seemingly inexhaustible reserves (Delbrück, 1990 [1920], p. 337; Bagnall, 1990, p. 168; Strauss and Ober, 1992, p. 139). On paper, Rome's resources stretched to over 770,000 men, according to Polybius, and although this figure is doubtless an overestimation, it nevertheless indicates the scale of the task Hannibal was to perform, as he invaded Italy with an army of fewer than 35,000 men.[8]

Hannibal's strategy was basically to bring the Roman field army to battle on his own terms; defeat in battle would prove Rome incapable of defending her allies and cause them to defect to the side of Carthage (Errington, 1971, p. 62; Connolly, 1998, p. 147; Bernstein, 1994, p. 77). As the allies made up more than half of Rome's potential manpower, this would have the dual effect of depriving Rome of troops while boosting Carthaginian numbers.[9]

According to Livy, Hannibal pointed out this very fact to Antiochus in 193, when the Seleucid monarch faced war with Rome (Liv. 34.60.3; Lazenby, 1996b, p. 44):

> Hannibal's opinion never varied; the war should be fought in Italy. Italy, he said, would provide both food supplies and troops for a foreign enemy; whereas if no movement was made in Italy, and the Roman people were allowed to use the manpower and resources of Italy for a war in foreign parts, then neither the king nor any nation would be a match for the Romans.

This strategy was probably inspired by the Libyan revolts against Carthage after the First Punic War, and by the fact that the Celts of the Po valley, only recently suppressed by Rome, were bound to support the Carthaginians (Strauss and Ober, 1992, p. 141). To implement his strategy, Hannibal first had to get his own army to Italy; an overland route was the only real option as ancient warships tended to stay close to the coast and the Romans effectively controlled the coastal approach from Spain to Italy.[10]

The Carthaginian invasion of Italy

The speed of Hannibal's advance from the Iber to the Po valley derailed the Roman pincer strategy (Adcock, 1940, p. 79; Strauss and Ober, 1992, p. 144; Polyb. 3.33–59; Liv. 21.21–38; Lazenby, 1978, pp. 29–48; Scullard, 1980, pp. 204–6; Connolly, 1998, pp. 153–66; Bagnall, 1990, pp. 155–67; Peddie, 1997, pp. 9–32; Lancel, 1998, pp. 57–80). Having failed to intercept the main body of Hannibal's army at the Rhone, Publius Cornelius Scipio had sent his brother Gnaeus on to attack Spain as planned with Publius' consular army, while Scipio himself hurried back to Italy to take command of the two legions, with allied complements, in the Po valley (Polyb. 3.49.1–4; Liv. 21.32.1–5). Tiberius Sempronius Longus was recalled from Sicily with his consular army, aborting plans to take the war directly to Africa, in order to join Scipio in defending the north of Italy. He was probably recalled once Scipio reached Pisa, with news of how close Hannibal was to Italy (Polyb. 3.61.9–10; Liv. 21.51; Lazenby, 1978, pp. 54–5; Lancel, 1998, p. 82).

Hannibal descended from the Alps into the territory of the Taurini, enemies of his allies the Insubres; when they rejected his advances he attacked and took their principal city. Atrocities committed there persuaded neighbouring tribes to join him, but the other tribes in the Po valley were cut off from Hannibal by Scipio's legions, which were near Placentia (Polyb. 3.60.8–12; Liv. 21.39.1–6). Battle was inevitable, as neither commander could allow the other to hold his position, thereby potentially controlling the entire plain, the gateway to Roman Italy (Bagnall, 1990, p. 171). The

Map 3 Italy.

battle of the Ticinus is thought to have taken place somewhere near modern Lomello, north of the Po, roughly halfway between the Ticino, the ancient Ticinus, and the Sesia (Walbank, 1957, p. 399; Lancel, 1998, p. 83; Connolly, 1998, p. 168). Rather than being a pitched battle, it was effectively a large-scale skirmish, where the two armies initially sent their cavalry out to reconnoitre each other, the Roman force also including light infantry (Polyb. 3.65.3; Liv. 21.46.3). Scipio's cavalry and light infantry were pinned down by Hannibal's heavier cavalry, allowing his nimbler Numidian cavalry to outflank the Romans and attack their rear; Scipio himself was wounded, and the Romans scattered (Polyb. 3.65.4–11, 66.9; Liv. 21.46.4–10; Santosuosso, 1997, p. 172; Lazenby, 1978, p. 53).[11]

Scipio withdrew to Placentia, while Hannibal organised his army's crossing of the Po and met envoys from the neighbouring Celts who wished to ally themselves with him, before making for Placentia himself, offering battle and then setting up camp nearby; over 2,000 Celts soon defected from Scipio's army and the powerful tribal federation of the Boii formally allied themselves with the Carthaginians (Polyb. 3.66.1–3, 67.7; Liv. 21.47.2–48.3). Immediately after the Celtic defection, Scipio led his army across the river Trebia and set up camp on the nearby hills to await Sempronius and his forces (Polyb. 3.67.8–68.6; Liv. 21.48.3–7). Hannibal again followed and set up camp close to the Roman base, relying on his Celtic allies for supplies (Polyb. 3.68.7–8). When Sempronius arrived he encamped near Scipio, and the two consuls discussed their situation (Polyb. 3.68.14–15). Apparently Sempronius favoured facing Hannibal as soon as possible, while Scipio argued that time was on the Romans' side, as if they waited until the winter was over the troops would be better trained, while Hannibal's Celtic allies would have grown disenchanted with him (Polyb. 3.70.1–4). Hindsight may be playing a part in this analysis, which also smacks of Polybius' pro-Scipionic bias, but, despite Walbank's protestations (1957, p. 404), it is not unlikely that there was some dissent between the consuls over when to fight Hannibal. Scipio, being wounded, would be deprived of a chance to win prestige and glory by defeating Hannibal if the battle was fought soon, but if they delayed, the new consuls would replace Scipio and Sempronius, depriving Sempronius of his chance for honour (Polyb. 3.70.5–7).[12]

The battle of the Trebia, the first major battle of the war, took place in late December 218 or perhaps early January 217.[13] Hannibal had a force of 1,000 cavalry and 1,000 infantry under his brother Mago lie in ambush at a nearby watercourse while he used his Numidians to goad the Romans into offering battle early in the morning, without having breakfasted or prepared (Polyb. 3.71.1–10). Crossing the cold river took its toll on the already tired and hungry Romans; the Carthaginian army, on the other hand, were well prepared; after eating they had anointed their bodies to protect themselves from the cold (Polyb. 3.72.3–6; Liv. 21.54.8–55.1). The Roman army consisted of 16,000 Roman and 20,000 allied infantry, with about 4,000 cavalry, and deployed as usual, with line infantry in the centre, cavalry on the wings, and skirmishers in front. Hannibal placed his 20,000 line infantry in the centre, with 10,000 cavalry divided between the wings, 8,000 skirmishers in front, and his elephants in front of both wings (Polyb. 3.72.7–13).[14] The battle, the tactical manoeuvres of which will be discussed later, was a decisive victory for the Carthaginians; about 10,000 Roman troops escaped in a body, but the bulk of the remainder were killed or captured (Polyb. 3.74.6–8; Liv. 21.56.2–5; Lazenby, 1978, p. 57; Lancel, 1998, p. 87; Bagnall, 1990, p. 176; Santosuosso, 1997, p. 175; Connolly, 1998, p. 171).

Hannibal was now master of northern Italy, and that winter released his non-Roman captives, claiming that he had come to fight on their behalf; this was in accordance with his strategy as outlined above and echoes traditional Greek liberation propaganda (Polyb. 3.77.3–7).[15] The new consuls marched north in early spring, Gaius Flaminius to Arretium and Gnaeus Servilius to Ariminum, in an attempt to cut Hannibal off from the most obvious routes into central Italy (Polyb. 3.77.1–2; Lancel, 1998, p. 91). Hannibal's route into central Italy is uncertain, but he probably crossed the Apennines through the Colline pass before braving the Arno swamps and reaching the vicinity of Faesulae, modern Fiesole (Lazenby, 1978, pp. 60–1; Lancel, 1998, pp. 91–2; Connolly, 1998, p. 172; Bagnall, 1990, p. 178; Walbank, 1957, p. 413). The passage through the swamps was particularly arduous, and Hannibal himself developed ophthalmia, leading to the loss of sight in one eye (Polyb. 3.79; Liv. 22.2–3.1).[16] Travelling southwards through Etruria from Faesulae, he passed the Roman camp, goading Flaminius into pursuing him (Polyb. 3.82).[17]

According to Ovid, the battle of Lake Trasimene took place on 21 June (Ovid, *Fasti* 6.767–8); the Roman calendar seems to have been running about a month ahead of time at this point, so it is likely that the battle took place in early May.[18] The precise location of the battle is a matter of some dispute, as the lake may have been substantially higher in Roman times than it is now; if this was so, the battle was probably fought on the northern shore of the lake, east of modern Tuoro.[19] In any case, it was another decisive victory for Hannibal, who concealed most of his troops on the hills along the shore of the lake; the following morning Flaminius led his army along the shore, unable to see the Carthaginian forces hidden by the early morning mist and thinking that the troops which could be seen in the distance were the rear units of Hannibal's army (Polyb. 3.83.2–7; Liv. 22.4.2–4). When Flaminius reached these, the concealed units charged down at the Romans, throwing them into disarray; about 15,000 were killed, including Flaminius (Polyb. 3.84; Liv. 22.4.5–7.5).[20]

The disaster at Trasimene, followed by Maharbal's subsequent defeat of Servilius' 4,000 cavalry under Gaius Centenius (Polyb. 3.86.1–5; Liv. 22.8.1), led the Romans to change their strategy. Quintus Fabius Maximus was elected dictator, with Marcus Minucius as his master of horse (Polyb. 3.87.6–9; Liv. 22.8.6–7; Walbank, 1957, p. 422; Lazenby, 1978, p. 67; Lancel, 1998, p. 98). Fabius' strategy involved avoiding direct battle with Hannibal. Traditional interpretations, based primarily on Livy's account, argue that by constant skirmishing and by restricting Hannibal's ability to forage and move freely, Fabius hoped to defeat the invading force through

15

attrition (Bagnall, 1990, pp. 184–5; Lazenby, 1978, pp. 68–9; Shean, 1996, p. 181; Strauss and Ober, 1992, p. 146; Peddie, 1997, p. 76). However, Fabius' army was too weak in cavalry to skirmish effectively against Hannibal's forces, and Polybius' account gives no real evidence of food shortages in Hannibal's army. It is perhaps more likely that Fabius was shadowing Hannibal without offering battle simply because he was waiting for the best possible circumstances to do so. His troops lacked experience, especially when compared to Hannibal's men (Polyb. 3.89.5–9); it therefore would have made no sense to rush into an engagement. In any case, he would obviously want battle on terrain where his own troops could manoeuvre, but where Hannibal's cavalry advantage would be neutralised.[21] Hannibal had led his army to the Adriatic coast, giving his men and horses an opportunity to recover from their recent campaigning; Fabius followed him to Apulia, into Samnium, and then the Falernian fields in northern Campania. Seemingly cornered in Campania, the Carthaginians were nevertheless able to escape back to Apulia, where the army would be quartered for the winter (Polyb. 3.88–94.6; Liv. 22.9.1–5, 11–17; Connolly, 1998, pp. 178–9; Lazenby, 1978, pp. 68–71). Fabius followed, but when he temporarily returned to Rome, Minucius won a minor victory over the Carthaginians, and as Fabius' policy of attrition and avoiding battle was unpopular the people took the unprecedented step of granting Minucius the same powers as Fabius (Polyb. 3.94.7–10, 100.1–103.4; Liv. 22.18, 22.23–26; Walbank, 1957, p. 434). The two commanders then split their forces between them, only reuniting their armies after Fabius rescued Minucius from a Carthaginian ambush (Polyb. 3.103.6–105.11; Liv. 22.27.8–30.6).

When Fabius' six-month term of office ended, probably in December, Servilius resumed command of his forces, while Marcus Atilius Regulus, Flaminius' replacement, took over the other army (Liv. 22.31.7, 22.32.1–3).[22] These two continued the Fabian strategy of avoiding battle, and led the armies in a proconsular capacity until they were joined by the new consuls, Lucius Aemilius Paullus and Gaius Terentius Varro. The consuls were elected in March, apparently under an *interrex*, after much political turmoil, and seem to have spent the next few months raising fresh troops, only joining the army in Apulia about a week before the battle of Cannae (Polyb. 3.106.3–5, 106.9–108.1).[23]

Hannibal had moved his forces from their winter quarters near Geronium once the corn harvest was ripe, and marched about 96 km (60 miles) to the small fortified town of Cannae. Although the town itself had been destroyed, the Romans were using it as a grain depot (Polyb. 3.107.1–3). It also had an important strategic position, commanding Apulia's fertile coastal plain and the valley of the Aufidus, which linked Apulia with Campania.[24] If the senate had not already decided to abandon the Fabian strategy by this point, the capture of Cannae appears to have compelled them to do so; the new

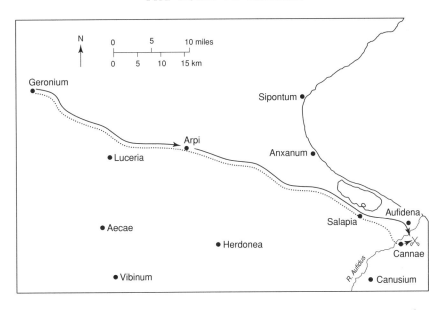

Map 4 Apulia, showing the routes of the Roman and Carthaginian armies from Geronium to Cannae.

consuls were despatched with orders to give battle (Polyb. 3.107.7–108.1; Lazenby, 1978, pp. 74–5; Bagnall, 1990, p. 191; Scullard, 1973, pp. 51–3). According to Macrobius, working from the *Annales* of Claudius Quadrigarius, the battle took place on 2 August (Macrob., *Sat.* 1.16.26; Walbank, 1957, p. 438; Derow, 1976, p. 277).[25] Although Walbank argues that the calendar was accurate in the early years of the war, Derow suggests that the battle took place instead on 1 July. This earlier date makes sense since the battle seems to have been fought within about a month of Hannibal's departure from Geronium, and Polybius apparently regards this as having happened in early summer, certainly by the end of May (Walbank, 1957, pp. 412–13; Derow, 1976, pp. 277–8; see Polyb. 3.107.1). In any case, the precise date of the battle is largely irrelevant to this book, although the fact that it evidently happened in midsummer doubtless had some bearing on the physical conditions. The intense summer heat must have made the fighting even more exhausting for the participants.

Sources

There is no contemporary evidence for the battle of Cannae, and any reconstruction of the battle must rely on later writers. Polybius, a Greek writing in the mid-second century, perhaps slightly more than fifty years after the events of 216, is the earliest such source. All other accounts were written considerably later; Livy, writing in the Augustan period, effectively follows the 'Polybian' model of the battle, as does Plutarch, a Greek biographer of the late first or early second century AD. Appian, a Greek historian of the second century, wrote an account of the battle that is distinctive by having virtually nothing in common with other accounts. There are numerous references to the battle in other writers, but there is little to be gained from them.[26] In the main, Polybius is to be regarded as the most important and accurate source for the battle of Cannae, but it is important to realise that his account is not to be taken at face value; his sources were far from perfect, and his use of them seems to have been somewhat naive.

Polybius

Polybius had access to quite a wide range of sources for his account of the Second Punic War as a whole: he claimed to have interviewed eyewitnesses of the war's events (Polyb. 3.48.2), presumably also interviewing the relations of dead participants, who would have heard anecdotes about the war from those who took part in it; he read earlier accounts of the war by historians who wrote from both Roman and Carthaginian viewpoints; and he examined whatever documentary evidence was available.[27] Polybius evidently deemed himself an able critic of this material. He argued that personal experience was the most important qualification for a historian, as without personal experience of warfare or politics, historians could not even hope to write accurately about these subjects (Polyb. 12.28.3–7, 25f.1–25h.6). He clearly believed himself to have been exceptionally well qualified in this regard, having had an active political career in Greece prior to his deportation to Rome after Rome's Third Macedonian War, while his time in Rome had given him opportunities for study and debate with intellectual peers from Rome's leading families. Furthermore, he had travelled widely, visiting many of the places about which he wrote (Walbank, 1957, pp. 1–6; 1972, pp. 6–13; Astin, 1989b, pp. 3–4; Derow, 1996, pp. 1209–11). Since he regarded making personal investigation as the historian's most important duty (Polyb. 12.4c.4–5), this was important.

It seems, however, that Polybius' military experience was rather limited, as a cursory examination of his career makes clear. Born at the very end of the third century in Megalopolis, the son of a prominent Achaean, he seems to have lived through a relatively peaceful period of Achaean history. He was almost certainly too young to have taken part in the suppression of Messene's secession from the Achaean League in 183,[28] and although he served as the League's *Hipparchos*, or cavalry commander, in 170/169, this position was more a political than a military one in Polybius' day. There is no evidence that the Achaean League was involved in any significant military activity between 183 and Polybius' exile, and Polybius does not seem to have witnessed any of the major events of Rome's war with Perseus of Macedon; he does appear to have witnessed the capture of Heracleium

"PHILIP THE QUEER"

by Q. Marcius Philippus,[29] but was sent back to the Peloponnese shortly afterwards (Polyb. 28.13.6–7), and does not seem to have returned north at any point. If this was so, he could not have witnessed the battle of Pydna in 168, the decisive battle of the war. It is difficult to tell what sort of military activity Polybius would have seen while a Roman internee, but, even if he was present at any point in any of Rome's wars during his internment, he is unlikely to have seen much that would have aided him in criticising his sources for the battle of Cannae, as these wars tended to be relatively low-key affairs (Harris, 1979, p. 233).

Against this, it should be remembered that Polybius had clearly read a lot of military history, as is shown by his frequent digressions to discuss other historians, especially Timaeus and Callisthenes (Polyb. 12.3–28a; Walbank, 1957, pp. 2–3). He believed that generalship could be learned through studying military accounts (Polyb. 11.8.1), which seems somewhat ironic, considering that he deemed personal experience necessary for historians, and evidently regarded himself as accomplished in this field, even going so far as to write a handbook on tactics.[30]

What sort of problems was Polybius likely to have encountered during his investigations? In the first place, even the youngest surviving participants in the battle of Cannae must have been in their late sixties, if not considerably older, by the time he interviewed them. After all, he had almost certainly not commenced researching his work until some time after his deportation to Rome, fifty-one years after Hannibal's passage through the Alps. It is unlikely that their recollection of events would have been as clear as Polybius would have wished. In addition, old soldiers with reputations to uphold are notoriously prone to glamorise their own actions, something which Keegan terms 'the Bullfrog Effect' (1976, p. 33). Any Roman survivors of the battle, for instance, must have been extremely keen to justify their survival, when so many of their fellows had fallen, while surviving relatives of other participants would have been inclined to paint their ancestors in as illustrious a light as possible, making them very unreliable as sources.

Aside from bad memories and dishonesty, a more fundamental problem must have been that virtually nobody who participated in the battle knew what was going on outside their immediate surroundings. Discussing night-fighting outside Syracuse in 413, Thucydides notes that:

> In daylight those who take part in an action have a clearer idea of it [than those who fight at night], though even then they cannot see everything, and in fact no one knows much more than what is going on around himself.
>
> (Thuc. 7.44.1)

Clearly, this inability of participants to observe the overall course of any military action inevitably hinders all attempts to reconstruct such events;

Wellington famously compared the futility of writing the history of a battle to the similar impracticality of doing so for a society ball (Keegan, 1976, p. 117; Holmes, 1985, p. 9). As a result of this failure in the sources, battle narratives by Polybius and all other historians of antiquity must be treated with extreme caution.

Polybius' main Roman literary source was probably Fabius Pictor, a Roman senator who had been sent on a mission to Delphi following the defeat at Cannae (Liv. 22.57.5); Polybius used him as a source for the First Punic War, and at least the early part of the Hannibalic War (Polyb. 1.14.1–3, 15.12, 58.5, 3.8.1). Fabius wrote in Greek, which was common among the Roman aristocracy and was the traditional language of literary prose, at a time when Rome was becoming heavily involved in the Greek world; presumably his work was on the whole 'a senator's attempt to explain Roman institutions and policies to the Greeks' (Badian, 1966, p. 4). Badian argues (p. 5) that the general theme of Fabius' history must have been the wisdom of the Roman senate compared to the folly of the people. Traces of this can be discerned in Polybius' attitude to 'popular' leaders such as Flaminius and Minucius (Polyb. 3.80.3, 90.6, 103.5–9).

Other pro-Roman sources would have included the works of Lucius Cincius Alimentus, the praetor of 210/209 who served in Sicily and was captured by Hannibal (Liv. 21.38.3; Badian, 1966, pp. 6–7), and of Aulus Postumius Albinus, who served as consul in 151. Gaius Acilius' work was probably not published until about 142, and the later books of Marcus Porcius Cato's *Origines* appear to have been published after Cato's death in 149, meaning that neither could have been used for Polybius' account of the battle of Cannae.[31]

Polybius mentions Chaereas and Sosylos as pro-Carthaginian sources for the war, scorning them as mere gossips and citing their accounts of senate debates on the issue of war with Carthage as evidence for their worthlessness (Polyb. 3.20.5). Nothing more is known of Chaereas, but Sosylos was a Spartan who taught Hannibal Greek and who accompanied him on his expedition, writing a seven-book history of his campaigns (Nep., *Hann.* 13.3). A surviving fragment of his work competently describes a naval battle early in the war, suggesting that Polybius' criticism may have been unfounded, something which is supported by the fact that the debates Sosylos described seem to have been genuine.[32] Walbank mentions several other possible pro-Carthaginian sources, notably Silenos of Kaleakte, who also accompanied Hannibal and wrote an official history of the war (Nep., *Hann.* 13.3; Walbank, 1957, pp. 28–9).

The description of the battle itself seems to be almost entirely Carthaginian in origin, noting how events take place in accordance with Hannibal's plans (Polyb. 3.115.11) or Hasdrubal's ingenuity (Polyb. 3.116.7), while avoiding any analysis of the Roman tactics. Polybius makes no attempt to explain why the Romans adopted their peculiarly deep formation, and is content simply to narrate how the Romans blundered unthinkingly into the Carthaginian trap. This is not surprising as most of the Roman combatants were either killed in the battle or unaware of what exactly was going on around them. The Carthaginian source is uncertain. Sosylos and Silenos are obvious possibilities, while Delbrück suggests that Polybius may have relied on Fabius, who could in turn have derived his material from Carthaginian prisoners or deserters, perhaps even the Liby-Phoenician commander *THE* Muttines (Delbrück, 1990 [1920], p. 32). The latter theory is supported *μTT* by the fact that even though Polybius describes the quantity and skill of the Carthaginian cavalry as the deciding factor in the battle, he pays more attention to the role of the Libyan infantry, something which would be understandable if the ultimate source for the battle's Grand Tactical manoeuvres was an infantry officer, keen to praise his own unit. Walbank suggests that Fabius was Polybius' source for the quarrels between Paullus and Varro, but as Polybius was a close friend of Scipio Aemilianus, who was both Paullus' grandson and the adoptive son of Scipio Africanus, who had served at Cannae as a military tribune, it is equally possible that this element in the narrative derived from a non-literary source (Walbank, 1957, p. 440).

In any case, Polybius' description of the battle, deriving either from one of Hannibal's official historians or from a high-ranking officer, probably reflects Hannibal's tactical plans more accurately than it does the reality of the battle. Polybius gives a highly formalised, 'bird's eye' view of the battle, recording the movements of large, homogenous masses: Iberians, Libyans, Celts, etc. In effect, he was trying to simplify the course of the battle, to instil order upon chaos.[33] He considered himself to be writing 'pragmatic history' and his intended audience of future soldier-statesmen would have found a straightforward description of the battle's grand-tactical manoeuvres far more useful than an analysis of the experience of battle on an individual level.[34]

Not only is Polybius' account of the battle highly simplified; it seems also to have been consciously designed to portray the Romans at their most vulnerable, and exaggerates the scale of the disaster accordingly. Polybius was writing his *Histories* in order to show:

> by what means and under what system of polity the Romans in less than fifty-three years [220–167] have succeeded in subjecting nearly the whole inhabited world to their sole government – a thing unique in history.
>
> (Polyb. 1.1.5)

The events covered in Polybius' first two books serve as a prologue to the work as a whole. Book 1 concentrates on Rome's first war with Carthage, a war which Polybius described as 'the longest, most continuous, and greatest war we know of' (Polyb. 1.63.4). In his analysis, Rome and Carthage were well matched, and although Rome's soldiers tended to be braver than their Carthaginian counterparts, the finest general of the war was the Carthaginian commander Hamilcar Barca (Polyb. 1.64.5–6; Schepens, 1989, p. 323). Rome's war with the Celts in the 220s is the centrepiece of Polybius' second book and is described as follows:

> a war which, if we look to the desperation and daring of the combat-ants and the numbers who took part and perished in the battles, is second to no war in history, but is quite contemptible as regards the plan of the campaigns, and the judgements shown in executing it, not most steps but every single step that the Gauls took being commended to them rather by the heat of passion than by cool calculation.
>
> (Polyb. 2.35.2–3)

In other words, prior to his account of Rome's rise to supreme power, Polybius describes Rome successfully facing two enormous threats, Carthage and the Celts.

Polybius' third book, the beginning of his *Histories* proper, shows Rome facing the greatest possible threat, as her mightiest foes combine in an attempt to avenge their previous defeats; revenge is explicitly identified as the driving force behind both Carthaginians and Celts.[35] The third book concludes with an account of the Roman defeat at Cannae and the battle's immediate consequences. Polybius then turns to affairs in the eastern half of his world, before returning to western matters with a discussion of Rome's constitutional and military systems in his sixth book. This serves the thematic purpose of showing how:

> though the Romans were now incontestably beaten and their mili-tary reputation shattered, yet by the peculiar virtues of their constitution and by wise counsel they not only recovered their supremacy in Italy and afterwards defeated the Carthaginians, but in a few years made themselves masters of the whole world.
>
> (Polyb. 3.118.8–9)

It is instructive to compare the pre-battle speeches of Paullus at Cannae and Scipio at Zama, the battle which Polybius effectively presents as a 'rematch' between the two powers.[36] Scipio's speech, as recorded by Polybius, features the first occasion that Polybius presents the concept of world rule as a Roman aim in a historical context. Polybius has him say that a Roman victory would make them not merely masters of Africa, but of the whole world (Polyb. 15.10.2; Derow, 1979, pp. 3–4). According to Polybius, Paullus, addressing the Roman troops some days before Cannae, told them that Rome had no more resources to use against Carthage, and that they were the state's sole hope of safety (Polyb. 3.109.10–11). Polybius' casualty figures are self-contradictory and clearly exaggerated, as will be shown later, but serve to present Cannae as the nadir of Roman fortunes, with virtually the entire army, so recently described as Rome's last hope, dead or captured (Polyb. 3.117.2–4).

Florus says that it was as if the Romans rose from the dead after Cannae (Flor. 1.22.23), and it certainly seems as if Polybius is behaving here like the chroniclers of the medieval period, using numbers as 'a device of literary art to amaze or appall the reader'.[37] The defeat at Cannae was indeed a catastrophe for the Romans, but the casualty figures which Polybius gives for the battle are more symbolic than factual. He makes Cannae seem an even greater disaster than it really was in order to enhance the remarkable resurgence in Roman fortunes in the years following. As will be seen below, his account of the battle tallies remarkably well with his inflated casualty figures; as these figures are surely wrong, it is clear that Polybius' battle narrative is by no means above suspicion.

Livy

Livy, the other major source for the Second Punic War, born at Patavium in northern Italy, is generally thought to have lived from 59 to AD 17, and seems to have devoted his life to literary matters. His major work was a history of Rome in 142 books, entitled *Ab urbe condita libri*.[38] Books 21 to 30 covered the Second Punic War, with the battle of Cannae being described at the end of book 22. The military details covered in Livy's account of the battle essentially follow the Polybian pattern, although Livy includes some details unmentioned by Polybius, in particular explaining why the cavalry mêleé by the river developed as it did, and describing the effects of the dust blown into the Romans' faces by the local wind, the Volturnus (Liv. 22.46.9, 47.2). Although Livy was familiar with Polybius' work, he probably based his description of Cannae on that of Lucius Coelius Antipater, his main source for the early years of the Second Punic War (Luce, 1977, p. 178; Walsh, 1961, pp. 124–32; Burck, 1971, p. 27).[39] Coelius completed a history of the war in seven books at some point after 121, and seems to have used the same sources as Polybius, especially the works of Fabius Pictor and Silenos of Kaleakte. These common sources probably account for the similarities between Livy's and Polybius' accounts (*OCD*, p. 355; Burck, 1971, p. 27; Walsh, 1961, pp. 124–5). The other main literary sources used by Livy in the composition of his third decade seem to have been the late annalists Valerius Antias and Claudius Quadrigarius. Their histories were largely based upon official Roman records and consequently were natural choices for Livy when he required information on politics and administration in Rome itself (Walsh, 1961, pp. 119–22, 127; Burck, 1971, p. 28; *OCD*, p. 1577: Valerius Antias; *OCD*, p. 342: Claudius

Quadrigarius). There is no evidence that Livy consulted them for his account of the battle of Cannae.

Walsh describes Livy as 'unique amongst the greater Roman historians in having no personal experience in politics and warfare', and points out that Livy seems neither to have visited the places he wrote about nor consulted any documentary evidence, but apparently relied entirely on literary evidence (Walsh, 1961, pp. ix, 110 ff., 138 ff.). He was not uncritical of his sources (Luce, 1977, pp. 140–1; Burck, 1971, p. 37; Lazenby, 1978, p. 260),[40] but his lack of personal experience clearly hampered his use of them. He is particularly poor on military affairs, and his accounts of battles are largely schematic, as he was not a soldier and did not envisage his work as being a textbook for soldiers; rather he wrote for a general readership with clarity as his primary aim (Walsh, 1961, p. 197; Burck, 1971, p. 38). Livy's battle narratives are notable for being described in terms of a number of clear chronological stages, with the action at each of the two wings and the centre being sharply defined (Walsh, 1961, pp. 161–3; Burck, 1971, p. 39). Considering the chaotic nature of the battles, this approach must be seen as highly artificial, but necessary if the battles are to be comprehensible to a layman. Livy tends to suppress specific technical details which would obscure the clarity of his accounts, while frequently attempting to introduce an element of surprise into the narratives by featuring sudden interventions by ambush or relief forces (Walsh, 1961, pp. 201–3). Emphasis is usually placed upon the parts played by the commanders, and on the psychological aspects of the battles (Walsh, 1961, pp. 168–72, 198–9, 203–4; Burck, 1971, pp. 39–40).

It is also important to realise that Livy's account is not unbiased. The senate is the hero of his history, and consequently 'popular' leaders such as Flaminius, Minucius, and Varro are portrayed in a poor light.[41] In Livy's account, Flaminius' impatience clearly results in the Roman defeat at Lake Trasimene (Liv. 22.3.8–13, 4.4), although his valiant behaviour in the battle itself is remarked upon (Liv. 22.5.1, 6.1–4), while Minucius is seen as impatient and foolish, until he learns to follow the lead of the more sensible and cautious Fabius Maximus (Liv. 22.27.1–30.6). Aemilius Paullus is entirely exonerated from the defeat at Cannae, while his consular colleague Terentius Varro is scorned for his lowly origins, and is held wholly responsible, even though in the aftermath of the battle he was commended by the senate for 'not having despaired of the republic' (Liv. 22.61.14).[42] Furthermore, by blaming commanders in this fashion, Livy removes some of the responsibility for Rome's defeat from the troops, the behaviour of whom he is prone to idealising.[43]

Livy's account of Cannae is therefore to be treated with even more caution than that of Polybius. Where Polybius did not have much experience of warfare, Livy had none at all and so was forced to accept his sources at their word, even though they would have faced similar problems to Polybius.

Livy's account of the battle is highly formalised in order to ensure clarity, and is modified to heighten its dramatic quality. The passages describing the attack by Numidian 'deserters' on the Roman rear and the death of Paullus (Liv. 22.48.1–4, 49.1–12), the former being absent from Polybius' account, the latter being mentioned rather than described (Polyb. 3.116.9), are ingredients typical of Livy's battle narratives, and are thus of dubious authenticity. Against this, Livy's descriptions of the actual fighting rather than the tactical manoeuvres may be of some benefit; in attempting to portray the horror of battle, he goes beyond Polybius' somewhat dry tactical analyses.[44] It is difficult to tell, however, whether such descriptions are realistic reconstructions of the experience of battle rather than simply being fine examples of Livy's literary talent.

Appian

Appian, an Alexandrine Greek writing in the second century AD, is the most important of the remaining sources for the Second Punic War, but unfortunately his battle narratives leave much to be desired. His account of the battle of Zama, for example, implausibly features single combats between Hannibal and Scipio, and later between Hannibal and Masinissa (App., *Pun.* 45–6). Delbrück goes so far as to quote the entire text of Appian's account of Cannae, which he dismisses as based on 'some Roman account or other', in order to show how fortunate we are to have the accounts of Polybius and Livy, as it would be otherwise impossible even to approach the truth of what happened at the battle (Delbrück, 1990 [1920], pp. 328–31). Lazenby notes that Appian's account is not to be trusted as it has virtually no similarity to the Polybian model of the battle, claiming also that it makes very little sense (Lazenby, 1978, p. 261). It is difficult to identify Appian's sources: he certainly drew on Polybius for his account of the Third Punic War (App., *Pun.* 132), and presumably used him as a source for the Second Punic War, but his account of the battle of Cannae is clearly not Polybian in origin, probably being derived from the patriotic annalistic tradition.

Manpower

Rome

According to Polybius, the Roman army at Cannae consisted of 80,000 infantry, 10,000 of whom served as a camp garrison rather than on the battlefield, and over 6,000 cavalry (Polyb. 3.113.5, 117.8). This was the largest Roman force ever assembled:

> They decided to bring eight legions into the field, a thing which had never been done before by the Romans, each legion consisting

of about five thousand men apart from the allies. . . . On occasions of exceptional gravity they raise the number of foot in each legion to five thousand and that of the cavalry to three hundred. They make the number of the allied infantry equal to the Roman legions, but, as a rule, the allied cavalry are three times as numerous as the Roman. . . . Most of their wars are decided by one consul with two legions and the above number of allies, it being only on rare occasions that they employ all their forces at one time and in one battle. But now they were so alarmed and anxious as to their future that they decided to bring into action not four legions but eight.

(Polyb. 3.107.9–15)

Appian and Plutarch support these figures, the former claiming that four new legions were raised and that the army deployed at Cannae consisted of 70,000 infantry and 6,000 cavalry excluding camp garrisons (App., *Hann.* 17), while the latter notes that the combined Roman forces at Cannae came to 88,000 men (Plut., *Vit. Fab. Max.* 14.2).[45]

Livy records two broad traditions regarding the size of the army at Cannae:

Some say that ten thousand new soldiers were enlisted as replacements; others that four new legions were enrolled, so that they took the field with eight. Some assert that the legions were also increased in the numbers of their infantry and cavalry, and that each received an additional thousand foot and a hundred horse, bringing the total of every one to five thousand foot and three hundred horse; and that double the number of horse and an equal number of foot were furnished by the allies.

(Liv. 22.36.2–4)

Most of this generally supports Polybius, barring the reference to 10,000 new recruits, which is dealt with below. If there were eight legions of 5,000 infantry and 300 cavalry each, and eight allied brigades of 5,000 infantry and 600 cavalry each, there would have been 87,200 troops in the Roman forces at Cannae.

It is difficult to decide what to make of the rather nebulous reference to 10,000 new recruits. Were these troops used to bring existing legions up to strength, as a supplement to legions already at full strength, or formed into fresh legions? Furthermore, were they a combination of citizens and allies, as Brunt believes (Brunt, 1971, p. 672), or purely a citizen force, in which case 10,000 allies were presumably also enrolled? Given these uncertainties, this tradition merely indicates that the Roman army at Cannae was somewhere between 45,000 and 60,000 strong, including camp garrisons (Dorey and Dudley, 1968, p. 63).

De Sanctis believed that Polybius' figures derived from a biased 'Carthaginian' source, which had evidently inflated the size of the Roman forces to make Hannibal's victory seem more glorious. The alternative tradition of 10,000 new recruits was more convincing, he argued, for several reasons, which are explained below. All of these reasons are speculative in nature, and not one of them is strong enough to warrant the rejection of the relatively precise Polybian tradition in favour of the rather ambiguous one cited by Livy.[46]

The most obvious reason put forward for rejecting the 'Polybian' tradition in favour of a mere 10,000 new recruits, whatever that means, is that smaller estimates of army sizes are inherently more probable. However, while perhaps generally true, this principle is hardly a universal rule, to be automatically applied whenever we have conflicting figures for army sizes. Each case ought to be considered individually.

It has also been objected that 6,000 cavalry seems too few for an army of eight legions with allies, especially since Livy claims that in 219 the Roman army which Sempronius was to take to Sicily included 300 citizen cavalry attached to each legion and 900 allied cavalry attached to each allied brigade (Liv. 21.17.5). On this basis, one would expect a Roman army of eight legions and eight brigades to have no less than 9,600 cavalry. This argument is extremely weak. In the first place, the 1,800 allied cavalry in Sempronius' forces apparently accompanied no less than 16,000 infantry. Polybius' figures give 40,000 allied infantry. Thus if there were 900 cavalry for every 8,000 infantry, there would have been 4,500 allied cavalry, which, when added to the 2,400 citizen cavalry, would have given a combined cavalry force of 6,900, not much larger than the 6,000 cavalry reported by Polybius. Secondly, it may simply have been the case that far fewer allied cavalry were available in 216 than had been available in 219.

A stronger argument against Polybius' figures is based on the fact that the term he uses for a legion, *stratopedon*, is more generally translated as 'army' and is applied inconsistently by him. If his source had mentioned eight *stratopedoi* being used, Polybius might have taken this to mean specifically eight legions apart from the allies, rather than four legions and four allied brigades. This is certainly possible; at one point, Polybius describes an army as consisting of two Roman *stratopedoi* and two allied *stratopedoi* (Polyb. 10.16.4). Nevertheless, it seems a spurious foundation upon which to reject Polybius' claim that the Roman forces at Cannae consisted of eight legions and eight brigades. Polybius elsewhere uses the term *stratopedon* to refer to an entire consular army of two legions, possibly with allies (Polyb. 8.1.4, 11.26.6). On this basis, it could equally be argued, that if Polybius had come upon a reference to the Romans having raised eight *stratopedoi* in 216, he could well have interpreted it to mean sixteen legions and sixteen brigades!

In addition to the reasons given above, Brunt has also claimed that Hannibal's tactics would not have been adopted against an army much larger than his own, as they could not have worked. This seems an odd claim. In the first place, Polybius was surely in a far better position than we are to comment on whether or not the Carthaginian tactics were feasible in the circumstances he described. Even if he lacked personal experience of battle, his readers might not have done, and would surely have realised the impossibility of an army of over 80,000 men being defeated by a much smaller force using the tactics described, if such an achievement was in fact impossible. It would be strange for the ancient sources to have been almost unanimous in their belief that the Romans greatly outnumbered the victorious Carthaginians at Cannae, if the tactics ascribed to Hannibal by Polybius simply could not have worked.

Furthermore, Livy's account contains circumstantial evidence, unmentioned by Polybius but supporting his manpower figures, which indicates that there was a combined total of over 80,000 casualties, prisoners, and fugitives from the battle.[47] These figures are almost certainly Roman in origin, further discrediting any notion that Polybius' manpower figures derive from a biased 'Carthaginian' source. While it must be admitted that casualty figures are notoriously unreliable, the fact that Livy does not mention any alternative traditions regarding the fate of the Roman forces at Cannae must be significant. His figures are the lowest casualty figures we possess, and even then they still support Polybius' emphatic claim that the Roman forces at Cannae included over 80,000 men.

Despite this, De Sanctis and Brunt maintain that the Roman army which took the field at Cannae was composed of perhaps 45,000–50,000. In itself, this is bizarre, as it presumes that the Romans were willing to face the Carthaginians with an army only slightly superior in infantry and significantly outnumbered in cavalry, which implies that they had learned nothing from the defeat at the Trebia. Perhaps more striking is the fact that De Sanctis and Brunt's manpower figures require casualty figures radically different from those reported by the ancient sources: approximately 30,000 dead and captured, and about 15,000 survivors. The significance of this relatively low estimate of Roman losses can be seen by contrasting it with the losses at the Trebia, where the greater part of 30,000 Roman citizens and allies appear to have been killed or captured (Polyb. 3.74.6–8; Liv. 21.56.2–5). It is difficult to conceive how the defeat at Cannae could have become the incarnation of all horror to the Romans, if its consequences, however terrible, were not significantly worse than previous defeats.[48]

The Polybian tradition should almost certainly be followed, but the possible origins of Livy's alternative tradition are worth considering. Whether or not Livy used Polybius as a source for his account of the battle of Cannae is uncertain, but his main source for the first two books of his third decade was probably Lucius Coelius Antipater, who wrote in the late second century, and used essentially the same sources as Polybius, notably Fabius Pictor and Silenos of Kaleakte. It is possible that Livy was unfamiliar with writers such

28

as Pictor and Lucius Cincius Alimentus at first hand, being acquainted with them only through Coelius (Burck, 1971, pp. 26–7; *OCD*, pp. 332, 355, 583). It seems unlikely that Coelius would have known of a tradition which was unavailable to Polybius, although unlike Polybius he had access to the histories of Gaius Acilius for the early part of the Hannibalic War.[49] It is equally difficult to see how Acilius would have had access to reliable information which was unavailable to Polybius. Valerius Antias, a first-century annalist, was also used by Livy, but being apparently prone to exaggeration (Liv. 26.49.3; Burck, 1971, p. 28) he would seem an unlikely suspect for the claim that only 10,000 new recruits were sent to Apulia in 216. How then could Livy have come by this detail, apparently unknown to all other extant ancient writers? It may be significant that *murioi*, the Greek term for 10,000, is merely the plural form of *murios,* countless, which often appears in plural form (LSJ, s.v.). Although ancient historians almost always use the word in the context of a definite figure, Diodorus Siculus sometimes gives it in its more general sense (Diod. 24.1.3, 1.4). It is quite possible, if unprovable, that an early historian of the Hannibalic War, ignorant of how many recruits were raised in 216, claimed that the Romans recruited 'countless' fresh troops, this claim being misinterpreted as '10,000' new recruits in the course of translation from Greek into Latin.[50]

It seems quite safe to conclude that the Roman army in Apulia was indeed about 86,000 strong.[51] It is unlikely that the entire army was available for battle at Cannae, as some troops were doubtless sick or injured, for instance.[52] Of those troops available to fight, Polybius claims that 10,000 troops were left behind as a garrison in the main Roman camp (Polyb. 3.117.8).[53] It seems more likely that the camp garrison consisted of a Roman legion and an allied brigade, rather than the entire complement of *triarii*, the legions' most experienced troops, as some modern writers think.[54] Appian's claim that 5,000 men were left to guard the smaller Roman camp (App., *Hann.* 4.26) is unconvincing, however, as the camp would have needed no more than a token garrison, situated as it was behind the Roman line of battle. It would therefore seem that the Roman army which took the field at Cannae consisted of perhaps slightly under 70,000 infantry and slightly over 6,000 cavalry.

Carthage

Polybius and Livy state that Hannibal's army at Cannae was made up of 40,000 infantry and 10,000 cavalry, but these figures are not entirely trustworthy.[55] Apart from the fact that the total of 50,000 troops looks suspiciously like an estimate, this figure, like the Roman one, almost certainly includes the troops who were left behind as a camp garrison (Lazenby, 1978, pp. 80–1; Walbank, 1957, p. 439). The size of this garrison is indeterminable, but a figure of 8,000 has been plausibly suggested,[56] which would mean that the Carthaginian line of battle consisted of about 32,000 infantry and 10,000 cavalry. Livy's account suggests that these figures refer only to troops stationed in the line of battle (Liv. 22.46.6); if this is indeed the case the light infantry, or skirmishers, who were stationed ahead of the main part of the army as a covering force (Polyb. 3.113.6; Liv. 22.46.1), are excluded from the figures given.

It is useful to consider where these figures originated. Polybius' account of the battle, which Livy largely agrees with, combines Roman and Carthaginian sources into a single narrative of mainly Carthaginian origin (Walbank, 1957, p. 440). The figures given for the Carthaginian army must be from Polybius' Carthaginian source, whose identity is uncertain, although Silenos of Kaleakte and Sosylos of Sparta are obvious candidates as both accompanied Hannibal on his campaigns (Nep., *Hann.* 13.3).[57]

In the summer of 205 Hannibal erected an inscription in Greek and Punic, commemorating his achievements, at the temple of Hera Lacinia near Croton in southern Italy (Liv. 28.46.16). Polybius claimed to have personally seen this inscription, and cites it twice in support of his figures for Hannibal's army (Polyb. 3.33.18, 56.4). His failure to mention it with regard to the army of Cannae suggests that his figure of 40,000 infantry and 10,000 cavalry does not derive from this source, but an examination of the information he does cite from the Lacinian inscription can prove enlightening. On reaching the Po, Hannibal's army was as follows:

> Twelve thousand African and eight thousand Iberian foot, and not more than six thousand horse in all, as he himself states in the inscription on the column at Lacinium relating to the number of these forces.
>
> (Polyb. 3.56.4)

Polybius clearly accepts these figures at face value, remarking at one point that Hannibal arrived in Italy with fewer than 20,000 men (Polyb. 2.24.17), but it is interesting to note that Livy was not convinced by Polybius' claim, which was apparently the lowest recorded estimate of the size of Hannibal's army on descending from the Alps (Liv. 21.38.2). In fact, Livy favours the figures cited by L. Cincius Alimentus, a one-time prisoner of Hannibal, of 80,000 infantry and 10,000 cavalry, although he qualifies this by pointing out that these figures include the Celtic troops who joined Hannibal in Italy (Liv. 21.38.3–4). It is possible that Livy simply finds Polybius' relatively low figures incredible, believing that such a small army could hardly have inflicted such damage on Rome; it would have been natural for Roman writers to exaggerate the size of Hannibal's army in order to explain their own defeats. In practice, Polybius' figures, when based on the Lacinian inscription, must be regarded as generally reliable but by no means infallible, as Alimentus' figures could to some extent have been derived from Hannibal himself.

Delbrück has convincingly argued that Polybius' figures for the army at the Po are too low; they appear to exclude the 8,000 light infantry, many of whom were Balearians and Moors, who fought at the Trebia (Polyb. 3.72.7; Delbrück, 1990 [1920], pp. 361–2). These troops evidently did not feature in the Lacinian inscription, for Polybius does not mention them in the context of the army which arrived in Italy, yet it seems unlikely that Hannibal would have attempted to cross the Alps without a substantial number of troops skilled in skirmishing and missile combat. Heavy infantry were trained to fight *en masse* as close-order infantry and would have been of little use on rugged terrain against hostile mountain tribes. Furthermore, the 8,000 light infantry can surely not have been included in the 20,000 infantry who arrived at the Po in 218, as this would mean that the total number of Spanish and African heavy infantry in 218 was 12,000, of whom it is unlikely that more than 10,000 would have been left by the time of the battle of Cannae; Delbrück sensibly points out that neither the Spaniards nor the Africans would have been able to carry out their roles effectively in such small numbers.

It has been argued that the Lacinian inscription dealt in terms of nationalities rather than army sections, and consequently would have had no reason to mention light troops specifically (Walbank, 1957, p. 366). However, while Polybius indeed identifies the troops sent to Africa and Spain in 218 by nationality, this is in the context of showing how Hannibal ensured the loyalty of particular allied tribes (Polyb. 3.33.9–16), something which was largely irrelevant to the composition of the army which arrived in Italy. Describing the invasion force, Polybius, working from the Lacinian inscription, gives no details of the precise nationalities of the various African and Spanish troops, and deals with the cavalry as a homogenous mass, failing even to distinguish between Spaniards and Numidians (Polyb. 3.56.4). It should perhaps also be borne in mind that the *longchophoroi*, henceforth translated as 'spearmen', are the only unit in Hannibal's army which Polybius never identifies by nationality (e.g., Polyb. 3.72.7, 73.7, 82.2–3, 84.14, 94.6), which may indicate that they were a multiracial force incapable of being categorised in this manner.

Polybius' terminology strongly supports Delbrück's thesis. Describing the battle of the Trebia, Polybius notes that:

> Hannibal ... threw forward as a covering force his pikemen [spearmen] and slingers, about eight thousand in number, and led out his army. After advancing for about eight stades he drew up his infantry, about twenty thousand in number, and consisting of Spaniards, Celts, and Africans, in a single line.
>
> (Polyb. 3.72.7–8)

At Cannae, Polybius notes that Hannibal stationed his spearmen and slingers ahead of the main body of troops, yet claims that Hannibal drew up his entire army in a single line (Polyb. 3.113.8). On each of these occasions the light-armed troops, termed *euzdonoi*, are clearly distinguished not simply from the army as a whole, but from the heavy or line infantry, *pezdoi*. It is specifically as the latter that the 20,000 Spanish and African infantry who arrived at the Po are identified (Polyb. 3.56.4).

Delbrück's thesis and Polybius' terminology evidently support the suggestion in Livy's account, noted above, that the light infantry are not included in the 40,000 infantry, from whom the camp garrison must be deducted, who reportedly fought at Cannae. On this basis, a reasonable estimate can be made of the size of the individual contingents at Cannae. Assuming that there were 32,000 heavy infantry, about 10,000, divided into two equal-sized units, would have been African, with about 6,000 being Spanish, allowing for 4,000 casualties since Hannibal's arrival in Italy.[58] The remaining 16,000 troops would have been Celts, deployed in alternate units with the Spaniards, probably in groups of about 250 and 100 men respectively (Connolly, 1998, p. 187). There were probably still almost 8,000 skirmishers because the bulk of Hannibal's losses had been borne by his new Celtic recruits (Polyb. 3.74.10, 79.8, 85.5, 117.6), and in any case, the loose formations adopted by skirmishers would have made them tricky targets (Holmes, 1985, p. 159). It is difficult to estimate how many Spanish, Celtic, and Numidian horse there were respectively, though round figures of 2,000, 4,000, and 4,000 seem plausible.[59]

It is vital to bear in mind at all times that these figures are far from certain, and are by no means precise. The Roman total of about 86,000 men including cavalry is largely based upon theoretical unit-strengths, something which is in reality subject to much variation, although it is to some extent confirmed by Livy's casualty figures. The Carthaginian figures, on the other hand, are entirely without confirmation and rely wholly upon the figures explicitly stated by Polybius and Livy. Considering the unreliability of even modern writers on matters such as this,[60] the figures for both armies as presented by the ancient sources must be treated with a great deal of caution.

Topography

The battle of Cannae took place on level ground, ideal for cavalry, next to the river Aufidus, the modern Ofanto, near the town of Cannae; unsurprisingly, the precise site of the battle is uncertain, and has been a matter of much debate.[61] The main factors to be borne in mind in trying to determine the location are Polybius' claims that the Roman army faced south, with its right flank on the river, while the Carthaginians were deployed facing north in such a way that the rising sun bothered neither side (Polyb. 3.113.2–3, 114.8). Some later writers record that the Romans were bothered by dust blown in their faces by the Volturnus, a south-east wind (Liv. 22.46.9; App. *Hann.* 20; Zon. 9.1). Attempts to reconcile these claims have led writers to

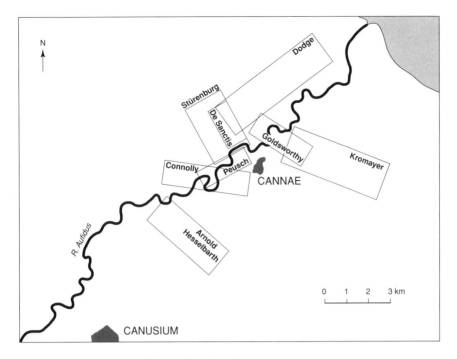

Map 5 Cannae: proposed sites of the battle.

place the battle in diverse locations around the hill of Cannae (Map 5 illustrates where various authors have located the initial deployments).

Historians of Cannae in the early nineteenth century tended to believe
that the battle had taken place on the left, or north-west, bank of the river,
for the simple reason that this plain was clearly visible from the hill of
Cannae itself.[62] However, this expressly contradicts Polybius' unequivocal
statement that the Romans faced south with their right flank on the river,
as well as implying that Hannibal first foolishly offered battle on rough
terrain, ill-suited to his cavalry, and that the Romans not only rejected such
a perfect opportunity, but the following day offered battle on level terrain
where Hannibal's cavalry would have had the advantage.[63] In addition, if it
did take place on the far side of the river, it seems odd that ancient writers
refer to the battle as happening at Cannae, rather than on the Aufidus.[64]

Realising these difficulties, other authors placed the battle on the right
bank of the river, but a few kilometres south-west of the hill of Cannae.
This idea is perverse; the ground upstream is hilly and could not have
accommodated a setpiece battle such as took place.[65]

The most common modern view, originated by Kromayer (see Map 6),
places the battle on the right bank of the modern Ofanto, on virtually level
terrain east of Monte di Canne, the hill of Cannae, with the Roman forces
facing south-south-west and the Carthaginians north-north-east (Kromayer

33

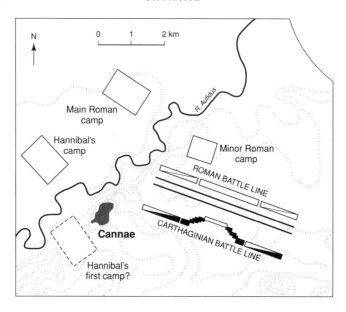

Map 6 Cannae: Kromayer's theory.

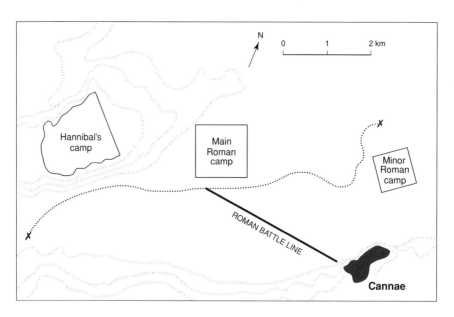

Map 7 Cannae: Connolly's theory. The modern course of the river is not shown; instead the line xx represents the old course of the river as suggested by Connolly.

and Veith, 1912, pp. 295ff.; Walbank, 1957, pp. 435–8; Dorey and Dudley, 1968, pp. 63–4; Lazenby, 1978, pp. 77–9; Scullard, 1980, p. 495; Lancel, 1998, p. 106). This area is a fairly broad plain with an almost imperceptible slope, which Kromayer calculates as on average a mere 66 cm per 100 m.

Connolly, however, makes the valid point that the Ofanto has changed its course many times since 216, and assumes that the most natural location for the main Carthaginian camp would have been the low ridge on which the modern town of San Ferdinando now stands; on this basis he argues that the battle was fought on flat ground, west of Monte di Canne, straddling the course of the modern Ofanto (see Map 7).[66] However, Kromayer's theory allows for a line of battle at least 1 km wider than is possible with Connolly's theory, and this extra space may well have been necessary considering the large numbers of both men and horses fighting at Cannae. Also, the main Roman camp seems uncomfortably close to that of the Carthaginians, being less 2 km away, and downhill. Perhaps most importantly, Polybius states that on the day before the battle, Hannibal deployed his army along the river to offer battle, an offer that the Romans declined (Polyb. 3.112.1–2). Unlike the following day, neither army had crossed the river, implying that the Carthaginians had deployed for battle on the left bank of the river, between their camp and the main Roman camp. Connolly's hypothesis, unlike Kromayer's, does not allow either army room to deploy in that position.

Although Kromayer's hypothesis seems by far the most plausible theory put forward on the site of the battlefield at Cannae, it must be admitted that without conclusive archaeological evidence it remains unproved. Nevertheless, it accords with the sources, throws up no topographical difficulties, and makes the battle's manoeuvres easily comprehensible. The following analysis assumes Kromayer's theory to be true.

Tactics

The Polybian model of the battle, followed in the main by Livy and Plutarch, must be treated as being substantially correct in terms of the grand-tactical manoeuvres which took place; it is therefore necessary basically to disregard Appian's account of the battle, which is clearly incompatible with the principal elements of the Polybian tradition. It must be remembered also that Polybius says virtually nothing about the opposing generals' tactical plans, so that to a great extent these have to be extrapolated from the way their troops were deployed and the eventual course of the battle.

According to Polybius, Hannibal's army deployed for battle along the river on the day before the actual battle, but the Romans, that day commanded by Paullus, did not take up the Carthaginian challenge (Polyb. 3.112; Liv. 22.44.4–45.4). The following day, however, the Romans opted to face the Carthaginians and crossed the river to offer battle; the Carthaginians followed them and deployed to accept the challenge (Polyb. 3.113; Liv. 22.45.5–46.7).

According to the sources the initial Roman rejection of Hannibal's challenge was due to Paullus' caution, whereas the giving of battle on the following day was a result of the impetuousness of Varro, whose turn it was to command. However, if the consuls appear to have been of one mind in terms of how to deal with Hannibal, as seems to have been the case, some other reason for this apparent change of mind must be sought.

It is impossible to be certain why Paullus declined battle that first day, but it is perhaps likely that he simply did not wish to give Hannibal the psychological advantage of being able to pick the battlefield. Polybius claims that Paullus did not like the terrain on which Hannibal had chosen to face him (Polyb. 3.112.2), and this may be substantially correct. Hannibal had picked his ground well, for by deploying his army along the river he prevented the much larger Roman army from enveloping his forces and falling upon the Carthaginian rear, while the flat ground on the left bank of the river was good terrain for his cavalry.[67] Goldsworthy argues that battle was declined most often in antiquity when one or both armies had adopted positions which were particularly strong. The Roman refusal to accept battle must have given the Carthaginian army the impression that the Romans were lacking in courage, giving them a psychological edge (Goldsworthy, 1996, pp. 144–5; Pritchett, 1974, p. 152). The Romans would have been aware of this and the troops probably eager for battle (Polyb. 3.112.4–5). It is hardly surprising then that the Roman commanders offered battle on ground of their own choosing the following day.

Just after sunrise, Varro led his troops across the river, where they linked up with their counterparts in the small Roman camp. Crossing the river made sense from a Roman perspective since offering battle on the left bank would have meant facing Hannibal on terrain on which he had deployed his forces the previous day and this could have given the Carthaginian forces a psychological edge. Furthermore, Varro may have wished to weaken Hannibal's forces by compelling him to leave a sizeable force to protect his camp from the 10,000 troops the Romans were leaving behind; giving battle across the river from the camps would have facilitated this (Kromayer and Veith, 1912, p. 307). Lazenby also points out that since the ground on the right bank of the river was marginally less regular than on the left bank, the threat posed by Hannibal's cavalry may have been slightly diminished (Lazenby, 1978, p. 79). The army deployed as was normal, with cavalry on the wings, line infantry in the centre, and the skirmishers being placed some distance ahead of the whole force. The only innovation in this arrangement was that the individual maniples, the tactical sub-units of the Roman line infantry, were deployed closer together than normal and were formed up in such a way that the depth of each maniple was much greater than its width (Polyb. 3.113.3–4).

The effect of this deep formation was to nullify the flexibility of the Roman manipular system, which required a certain amount of space for each maniple to operate efficiently. Had the Romans deployed along a wider front the individual maniples would have been able to fight in their customary manner. Furthermore, in order to face them Hannibal would have been virtually compelled to draw up his smaller army in a very thin line which the Romans, operating in their usual flexible formation, could probably have penetrated without too much difficulty.

Why then did the Romans adopt such a formation? Perhaps the most obvious possible reason is that Varro believed that by massing his infantry deep along a narrow formation he could take advantage of his numerical superiority by turning his army into what was virtually a giant phalanx, which would, he hoped, drive straight through the Carthaginian line (Bagnall, 1990, p. 192; Hanson, 1992, p. 43). Santosuosso argues that Varro had learned from the Roman defeat at the Trebia, and presumably from that at Lake Trasimene too, since on both those occasions Roman troops had pierced the Carthaginian line 'even in a losing cause' (Santosuosso, 1997, p. 177; see Polyb. 3.74.4, 84.11; Liv. 21.41.2–3, 22.6.8).

Another possibility is that this relatively narrow formation was used since wide formations in general can be very unstable, especially in armies not trained to march in step. If even one unit fails to march in a perfectly straight line it can cause confusion, opening a gap on one side while crowding the unit on the other, creating a situation which enemy troops can exploit. Wide formations could thus have been very dangerous except for well-trained troops, and even if not dangerous could have slowed the advance, with constant pauses being necessary to correct irregularities (Muir, 1998, p. 70). It is all too easy to overstate the lack of experience in the Roman army at Cannae, but it must be admitted that a sizeable portion at least of the Roman forces were very inexperienced, and the army as a whole was certainly not used to working as a unit.[68] A relatively narrow formation would have enabled the enormous Roman army to advance fairly quickly without losing formation. Furthermore, Goldsworthy notes that deep formations are especially useful with new or unreliable troops, as the presence of so many men behind them compels the front ranks to advance and fight.[69]

Even this might be looking at the problem the wrong way. The Roman deployment at Cannae was indeed unusually deep, but it was certainly not unusually narrow. Kromayer points out that even ignoring the issue of gaps between maniples, if the maniples were half their normal width the total length of the Roman battle line would have been no longer than that of a 'normal' double-consular army, such as that which fought at the Trebia (Kromayer and Veith, 1912, p. 323). It should be remembered that none of the officers in the Roman army had any experience in commanding an army of the size of that deployed at Cannae. Such an unprecedentedly large force must have posed unprecedented problems, especially regarding communication (Sabin, 1996, p. 68), and the Roman commanders may simply have been reluctant to adopt a formation far wider than any previously used.

Whatever the reason for the Roman formation, Hannibal's plans were tailor-made to deal with it. Sending his skirmishers forward, he deployed his heavier cavalry, Celts and Iberians in the main, on his left wing, opposite the Roman citizen cavalry, with his infantry in the centre and the Numidian cavalry on the right wing, facing the Roman allies (Polyb. 3.113.6–7; Liv. 22.46.1–3). Such a formation, with cavalry on the wings and skirmishers in front of the main infantry line, was normal in antiquity, but Hannibal's deployment of his infantry was most unorthodox. He made his centre weak, by placing his Libyan infantry, his best troops, at either end of the infantry line, with the less reliable Celts and Iberians arrayed in alternate companies in the centre. Polybius then describes a remarkable manoeuvre:

> After thus drawing up his whole army in a straight line, he took the central companies of the Iberians and Celts and advanced with them, keeping the rest of them in contact with these companies, but gradually falling off, so as to produce a crescent shaped formation, the line of the flanking companies growing thinner as it was prolonged, his object being to employ the Libyans as a reserve force and to begin the action with the Iberians and Celts.
>
> (Polyb. 3.113.8–9)

The exact nature of this formation has been a source of some controversy, Kromayer arguing that it was in reality a formation in echelon, i.e., a type of wedge, where the units were deployed in depth, each unit being stepped back with its front clear of the units on either side, while Delbrück thinks that the centre was in fact a straight line of Celts and Iberians, with the Libyans deployed in column at the wings, at a right angle to the centre. In this case the forward curve which Polybius refers to must have been unintentional, being caused simply by the central companies of the line advancing more quickly than the extremities. However, Polybius, as quoted above, is quite clear that the formation was crescent-shaped, rather than simply curved, and entirely intentional on Hannibal's part.[70]

Before attempting to analyse Hannibal's tactics at Cannae it is necessary briefly to describe the main Grand Tactical manoeuvres of the battle. The following account, based almost wholly upon Polybius and illustrated below, does not presume to represent in any way the complex realities of the battle; rather, it seeks to simplify so that the major movements can be readily understood (Fig. 1).

The fighting was begun by the light infantry, who were placed some distance ahead of the main lines of battle; their skirmishing seems to have had no great tactical significance, giving neither side an advantage over the other (Polyb. 3.115.1). The Celtic and Iberian cavalry then engaged with the Roman citizen cavalry next to the river, while on the far side of the battlefield Hannibal's Numidians skirmished with Rome's allied cavalry. The latter action was not decisive, but as the allied cavalry were pinned down they could not effectively protect the left flank of the infantry while the defeat of the citizen cavalry by the Carthaginian heavy cavalry exposed the infantry's right flank. At some point the skirmishers withdrew and the line infantry joined battle, the Romans quickly gaining the advantage and pushing the Celts and Iberians back. The fighting at first took place along a very narrow front, owing to the peculiar crescent-shaped formation of the Celts and Iberians, and the Roman maniples began to crowd inward from the wings in order to share in the anticipated victory. However, as the crescent slowly but steadily began to collapse under pressure the Romans pushed too far ahead. The Libyan units, deployed in column at either end of the Carthaginian infantry line, turned inwards to face the Romans, who suddenly found themselves under attack from both flanks.[71] Livy claims that the Libyan units altered their formation in order also to attack the Roman rear (Liv. 22.47.8). Whatever the case, the Roman rear was indeed soon to come under attack. Once the Roman citizen cavalry had been decisively beaten, the Carthaginian heavy cavalry rode across the battlefield behind the Roman infantry to assist the Numidians, who were still skirmishing with Rome's allied cavalry. On seeing the advancing cavalry force the allies fled. Hasdrubal, commanding Carthage's heavy cavalry, left the pursuit of the fugitives to the Numidians, and turned to harass the Roman rear. The Romans were surrounded on all sides, and it was only a matter of time, in Polybius' analysis, before they were annihilated (Polyb. 3.115.1–116.12).

The essence of Hannibal's plan therefore appears to have been to use a weak centre to draw the Romans into a trap, allowing the stronger infantry and faster cavalry on the wings to envelop them from both sides. Similar tactics had been used, whether by accident or design, by the Athenians at Marathon, where in an effort to match the length of the Persian line, the outnumbered Athenians kept their wings strong but deployed their centre only a few ranks deep; this allowed them to attack the Persian centre from both sides once it penetrated their own shallow centre (Hdt. 6.111–13).

The Carthaginians appear to have adopted this tactic and refined it considerably. In 255, led by the Spartan-trained mercenary Xanthippus, they defeated a Roman army under M. Atilius Regulus by surrounding it. Their cavalry had routed the numerically inferior Roman cavalry and then attacked the flanks and rear of the infantry, who were already under pressure from Carthaginian elephants supported by heavy infantry in front of them (Polyb. 1.33.6–34.9). Some years later, at the battle of the Bagradas, the Carthaginians under Hamilcar defeated an army of insurgent Libyans and mercenaries by feigning retreat to tempt the enemy troops into a reckless attack, before turning to face them.[72] The subsequent panic among the rebels allowed the Carthaginian elephants and cavalry to run amok amongst them with devastating effect (Polyb. 1.76.1–9). Hamilcar apparently had a

Figure 1 Grand Tactical manoeuvres at Cannae.

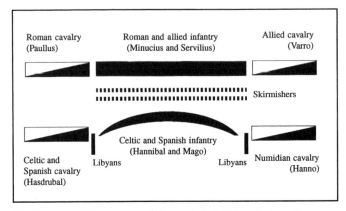

(a) The Roman and Punic forces deploy with their light infantry acting as covering forces by skirmishing in front of the main bodies of men.

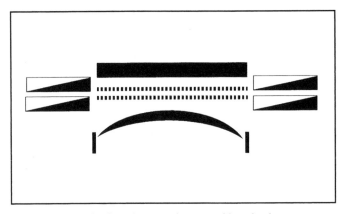

(b) The cavalry on each wing advance and engage with each other.

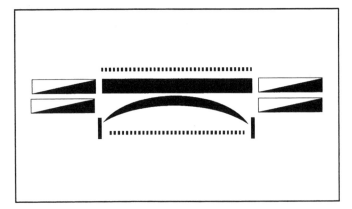

(c) The skirmishers withdraw and the line infantry advance and engage with each other, initially on a narrow front owing to the peculiar crescent formation used by the Carthaginian centre.

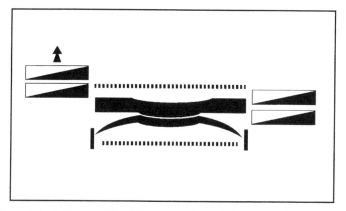

(d) Hasdrubal's Celtic and Spanish cavalry drive back the Roman citizen cavalry. The Roman infantry gradually force the Carthaginian centre back. The Romans begin to lose their formation as they push forwards along what is still quite a narrow front.

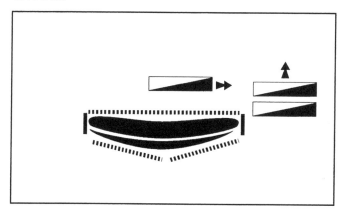

(e) Rome's allied cavalry, busy skirmishing with the Numidians, flee when Hasdrubal approaches. Hannibal's Libyans turn in to attack the exposed flanks of the Roman infantry, who have lost formation through advancing in an uncontrolled manner.

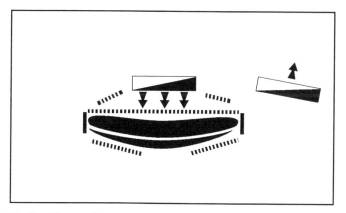

(f) The Numidian cavalry pursue the Roman fugitives, while Hasdrubal's cavalry return to complete the envelopment of the Romans, harassing the Roman rear.

penchant for feigned retreats (Polyb. 1.74.9), and at the Bagradas he supported this tactic with the combination of elephants and cavalry which had proved so destructive against Regulus (Thompson, 1986, p. 117).

Walbank (1957, p. 143) tentatively suggests that 'the last stages of the battle of the Bagradas may have contained the germs of the tactics Hamilcar's son later perfected', which seems very likely as Carthaginian tactics at the Ticinus, the Trebia, Cannae, and Ibera display apparent similarities to those at the Bagradas, insofar as these latter can be reconstructed.

Although the battle of the Ticinus was really a large-scale skirmish rather than a pitched battle, it clearly demonstrates the Carthaginian principle of double envelopment. Hannibal advanced to face the Romans with his heavier cavalry, having stationed his Numidian light cavalry on the wings in order to outflank the Romans, which they succeeded in doing while the heavier cavalry engaged the Romans head on. Attacking the Romans in the rear caused them to scatter and flee (Polyb. 3.65.6–11; Liv. 21.46.5–9).[73]

The battle of the Trebia was a formal battle which displayed the same characteristics, albeit with extra refinement, notably the planting of a large ambush force nearby under Hannibal's brother Mago (Polyb. 3.71.9). After the usual preliminary skirmishing, Hannibal's line infantry pinned the Roman infantry in place while his cavalry drove back the Roman cavalry from the wings, exposing the flanks of the Roman infantry and allowing the Carthaginian light infantry and Numidian cavalry to harass them (Polyb. 3.73). At a prearranged time the ambush force launched themselves on the Roman rear, throwing them into disarray; as the wings collapsed and fled, about 10,000 Romans managed to escape by punching their way through the weak centre of the Carthaginian line (Polyb. 3.74.1–6).

The Grand Tactical manoeuvres of Cannae, according to Polybius at any rate, have been described above, and it is clear that at Cannae Hannibal used his relatively weak centre, making it advance in a crescent shape, as bait to draw the Romans into a trap; his cavalry cleared the Roman cavalry from the battlefield and enabled the Libyan infantry to attack the flanks of the Roman infantry while the heavy cavalry turned on the Roman rear as the Numidian cavalry pursued the Roman fugitives.

In Spain in early 215, Hannibal's brother Hasdrubal used similar tactics at Ibera, placing his Iberian infantry in the centre, flanked by Libyans and mercenaries on the left, and *Poeni* (presumably levies from the nearby Phoenician colony at Gades) on the right, with cavalry on either wing (Liv. 23.29.4). On this occasion the weak centre was quickly routed by the Roman legions; as at Cannae, the advancing Romans then came under pressure from stronger Carthaginian troops on both flanks, but this time were able to deal with the challenge, almost certainly helped by the fact that after the central collapse the Carthaginian cavalry had panicked and fled (Liv. 23.29.9–14). Bagnall (1990, p. 204) and Head (1982, p. 77) both argue that Hasdrubal's tactics here were modelled on Hannibal's at Cannae, but the failure to advance the central troops, as Hannibal had done, suggests that Hasdrubal's plan was not in fact based on his brother's tactics. It is more likely that both brothers were inspired by the tactical ideas of their father, Hamilcar Barca, but that Hasdrubal perhaps lacked the imagination to refine and develop these principles as effectively as his brother.

Later writers do not attribute Hannibal's success at Cannae solely to the tactics analysed above. Livy and others describe the devastating effects of the local wind, the Volturnus, which rose about midday and blew dust into the faces of the Romans, blinding them and weakening the force of their missiles, while simultaneously aiding those of the Carthaginians.[74] The authenticity of this story has been doubted, as Polybius never mentions it, but it is possible that a reference to dust in the eighth book of Ennius' *Annales* refers to the battle of Cannae.[75] Ennius was born in Calabria in 239, and died in 169 or perhaps a little later. He had served in the Roman army, presumably in an allied brigade, and so is likely to have fought in the Second Punic War. If so, he may well have been acquainted with other veterans of the war, including, perhaps, survivors of Cannae. If the reference to dust genuinely refers to Cannae, it ought therefore to be accepted as authentic. It should be remembered though that the Romans deployed first on the day of the battle and are unlikely to have deployed to face a wind which would have more or less blinded them. Moreover, Hannibal had deployed his troops the previous day along the river, almost at a right angle to the direction of their line of battle the following day; had the Romans accepted their challenge, both sides would have suffered equally from the wind-blown dust. It seems probable then that even if the Romans were genuinely troubled by dust blown in their eyes by the Volturnus, their troubles were surely not as dire as Livy and other writers make out.

In addition to exaggerating the effects of the Volturnus on the Romans, Livy and other later writers also claim that Hannibal ambushed the Romans at Cannae, something Polybius never mentions. Apparently a party of 500 troops, either Numidians or Celtiberians, pretended to desert to the Roman side and, having surrendered their weapons, were placed behind the Roman lines. However, at an appropriate moment they drew weapons which had hitherto been concealed and attacked the Romans from behind (Liv. 22.48.1–4; App., *Hann.* 20, 22; Flor. 1.22; Zon. 9.1). Furthermore, Appian and Zonaras both refer to ambuscades being planted in advance in nearby ravines, these forces launching themselves on the Roman rear at an appropriate moment (App., *Hann.* 20, 22; Zon. 9.1). Hannibal was certainly fond of ambushes, Polybius recording that he used such tactics at the Rhone (Polyb. 3.42.6, 43.1–10) and the Trebia (Polyb. 3.71.1–9, 74.1–3), with the battle at Lake Trasimene basically being an enormous ambush (Polyb. 3.83.1–84.5), and it would be perverse to believe that Polybius had ignored evidence for such tactics being used at Cannae, had this been

*HAROLD
LAMB .*

available. It seems more likely that the feigned surrender and ambuscades described by later writers are merely annalistic fictions, designed to explain away the defeat of Rome's largest ever field army by a significantly smaller force. In the ancient world, 'Punic Faith' was a byword for treachery, and patriotic Roman writers may simply have invented the deceitful tactics they ascribed to Hannibal at Cannae to contrast with the straightforward and transparent tactics used by the 'honourable' Romans.

Where Polybius' account of the battle breaks down is in its final stages. He describes how the Romans were surrounded, but fails to describe in any detail what happened then. In his analysis, Hasdrubal's cavalry closed the trap by constantly charging the Roman rear, after which there was nothing but slaughter:

> The Romans, as long as they could turn and present a front on every side to the enemy, held out, but as the outer ranks continued to fall, and the rest were gradually huddled in and surrounded, they finally were all killed where they stood.
>
> (Polyb. 3.116.10–11)

This neatly wraps up his account of the battle, swiftly summarising something which must have taken several hours if the Romans held out as tenaciously as he claims. A cursory analysis of the reported casualty figures suggests that this was not the case.

These casualty figures are extremely problematic and will be discussed in more detail later. For now, it is important only to note the following hyperbolic claim:

> Of the infantry, about ten thousand were captured fighting but not in the actual battle, while only perhaps three thousand escaped from the field to neighbouring towns. All the rest, numbering about seventy thousand, died bravely.
>
> (Polyb. 3.117.3–4)

In other words, in Polybius' analysis virtually none of the infantry who fought at Cannae survived the battle. This certainly accords with his account of the Romans being surrounded and fighting until the last man fell, and indeed it would be bizarre if it were otherwise. It is clear, however, that his figures are too high as there were surely more survivors of Cannae than he allows for. It is unnecessary at this point to analyse the other sources, save to note that Livy's figures, which allow for 14,550 fugitives (Liv. 22.50.3, 54.1, 4), are supported by his later references to the *legiones Cannenses*. According to Livy, the survivors of Cannae were sent to Sicily, where they made up two legions and were later reinforced by the defeated survivors of the first battle of Herdonea. These troops were not to be released from service and were forbidden to return to Italy until the war was over, consequently becoming perhaps the most experienced troops in the entire Roman army, and serving as the backbone of Scipio's African expeditionary force in 204.[76] These 'legions' may in reality have been irregular hybrids, incorporating large numbers of Latin and Italian allies, rather than being exclusively Roman. As Livy points out, the fact that many of the troops which were transferred to Sicily were allies rather than citizens caused unrest among the allied communities (Liv. 27.9.1–4). Against this, Livy claims that when Scipio was organising his army to invade Africa, he brigaded the survivors of Cannae into two legions, each of 6,200 infantry and 300 cavalry, with the allied troops being brigaded separately (Liv. 29.24.14). In any case, even if the legions included allies and cavalry and were only 4,500-strong each, there must have been no fewer than 9,000 survivors of Cannae who were not captured by the Carthaginian forces. This is obviously a very conservative estimate, but it clearly demonstrates the inaccuracy of Polybius' casualty figures.

These figures, however, though clearly wrong, yet make perfect sense in the context of Polybius' analysis of Cannae, in which the Romans were completely surrounded and, with no way out, fought, in effect, to the last man. The fact that two legions could be assembled from the survivors who fled the battle proves that Polybius is wrong, and that in reality the Romans did not by any means fight to the last man. The final chapter of this book attempts to explain what really happened at Cannae, insofar as that is possible, by going beyond tactics to look at the mechanics of battle.

Conclusion: the consequences of Cannae

The catastrophe at Cannae was Rome's third major defeat at Hannibal's hands, and it is likely that Rome had lost something approaching 120,000 men since Hannibal arrived in Italy.[77] Nevertheless, Rome continued to resist and eventually proved victorious when Publius Cornelius Scipio, later surnamed Africanus, the son of that Scipio who had been defeated at the Ticinus, in command of an army built around the veteran survivors of Cannae, decisively defeated Hannibal on African soil at the battle of Zama in 202. It is worth briefly considering how Rome managed to ride out the storm after Cannae.

Livy and Plutarch claim that in the immediate aftermath of victory at Cannae, one of Hannibal's cavalry officers encouraged him to head straight for Rome itself, claiming that in five days he could be dining on the Capitol![78] Hannibal refused, to the officer's dismay, and Livy claimed that this failure to follow up the victory saved Rome (Liv. 22.51.4). Although Montgomery (1968, p. 97) has argued that the officer was right, it would have been virtually impossible for Hannibal to take Rome so quickly. In the first place, Hannibal's army must have been physically and emotionally exhausted after a long, hot day of slaughter on an unprecedented scale, and would not have been in any condition for the long march to Rome. Second, Hannibal's army seems to have moved quite slowly, covering perhaps 20 km (12.5 miles) a day on average during the march from Spain to Italy. It was over 400 km (250 miles) from Cannae to Rome,[79] meaning that it would take about twenty days, rather than five, to reach Rome. Twenty days would have given the Romans ample time to prepare for the Carthaginian attack, for the city was well fortified, and there was no shortage of men to defend it. Even in the improbable event of the walls being breached, it is far from certain that Hannibal would have been able to hold the city, considering that the Carthaginian army could then have become involved in street-fighting with the far more numerous inhabitants of the city.[80]

In any case, it is unlikely that Hannibal could have realistically considered marching on Rome from Cannae. Shean (1996, pp. 175–85) convincingly argues that Hannibal's campaigns were largely dictated by his logistical situation, and that after Cannae his army scarcely had supplies for a few days, let alone a three-week march. If he had made it to Rome the subsequent siege could have lasted for months, if not years, posing a logistical nightmare since his army's opportunities for foraging would have been limited by being permanently stationed at one point. Even if Hannibal had wanted to follow up his victory at Cannae by marching on Rome, it is incredibly unlikely that he would have been able to do so.

It is possible that Hannibal expected Roman resistance to collapse after such a devastating defeat. Nicolet (1980, p. 91) points out that the unwritten rules of Hellenistic warfare dictated that Rome ought to have capitulated after such a crushing blow as Hannibal had dealt her. The treaty between Hannibal and Philip V of Macedon in 215 clearly envisaged the survival of Rome, albeit without her Illyrian possessions (Polyb. 7.9.12–15), and it is likely that Hannibal's aim would have been to reduce Rome to the rank of an average Italian power, rather than a major Mediterranean one. The first stage in negotiations would normally have been the ransoming of prisoners, but when Hannibal gave the senate the opportunity to do so, it declined (Liv. 22.58–61).[81] According to Livy, Hannibal had been behaving more like a victorious conqueror than one who was still waging war in the days after Cannae (Liv. 22.58.1). If Livy's account is accurate, Hannibal had been fighting this war like a typical Hellenistic general, and naively expected Rome to do likewise. If this was the case the strategy was indeed a complete failure (Nicolet, 1980, p. 91; Shean, 1996, pp. 186–7; Montgomery, 1968, p. 97), as Hannibal did not realise that the Romans would not 'play the game' by yielding after their defeat at Cannae.

Perhaps it is more realistic to say that Hannibal hoped, rather than expected, that the Romans would surrender after Cannae. Carthage's first war with Rome had taken twenty-three years; Hannibal would have been aware of this and probably did not automatically expect Rome to submit after a handful of quick victories (Lazenby, 1996b, p. 43). The basic principles of Hannibal's strategy of detaching Rome's allies have been discussed above, and it seems that this strategy nearly worked in the long term. Lazenby calculates that the majority of the Campanians and 40 per cent of Rome's other allies had defected to the Carthaginian cause by 212, after which the Etruscans and Umbrians also began to waver.[82] Even the Latin allies were not immune to this strategy, and in 209 twelve of the thirty Latin colonies refused to send men to serve in Rome's allied brigades (Liv. 27.9–10). Nevertheless, the heart of Italy held relatively firm, giving Rome the benefit of short internal lines of communication and cutting Hannibal off from his Celtic allies in the Po valley.

What Hannibal needed to ensure that this strategy worked in the long term was more major victories on Italian soil. Paradoxically, the sheer scale of his victory at Cannae prevented this. Fabius' strategy of *cunctatio*, avoiding battle unless circumstances were ideal, was wholeheartedly adopted by the senate after the catastrophe at Cannae. This senate was a much reduced version of that which had began the war in 218; numerous losses at the hands of Hannibal and the Celts of northern Italy had seen to that. Since these losses had been filled in the main by young and inexperienced *equites*, the most prominent senators were men who were in their late fifties, if not older, whose experience gave them an importance out of all proportion to their numbers.[83] The renewed Fabian strategy certainly paid dividends, as restricting Hannibal's movements limited his ability to plunder and forage, to the benefit of Rome and her allies and the detriment of Hannibal. Unable to attack either Rome or her armies, Hannibal was forced to fall back on a defensive strategy in Italy, relying on proxy wars in Spain, Sicily, Sardinia, and Illyria to damage Rome in ways that he was unable to do in Italy itself (Fuller, 1954, pp. 128–9).

The new strategy did not work, as Rome proved victorious on all the new fronts. Having been successful in Spain, Publius Cornelius Scipio, the son of that Scipio who had been defeated at the Ticinus, revived Rome's original plan of taking the war to Carthage itself, and in 204 took an army composed of volunteers and veterans of Rome's defeats at Cannae and Herdonea to Africa, where they were joined by the excellent light cavalry of the Numidian king Masinissa. The following year Scipio was victorious over the Carthaginians, led by Hasdrubal son of Gisgo, at the battle of the Great Plains, and Carthage sued for peace. Hannibal then returned from Italy and hostilities were soon renewed. In late summer or early autumn 202, Scipio and Hannibal finally faced each other at Zama. Scipio's victory there signalled the end of the Second Punic War.

3

THE ROMAN ARMY

Introduction

In a landmark paper first delivered in 1920, Whatley (1964, pp. 119–39) identified five 'aids' which could be used in attempting to reconstruct what happened in ancient battles. These aids were: the study of geography and topography; deductions from universal strategic and tactical principles; use of logic, generally to rule out impossibilities; the combination of the three earlier principles and statements from ancient authors from other periods, interpreted appropriately; and 'the most thorough study from all sources of the armies engaged, their strategy and tactics, their weapons and methods of using them, their systems of recruiting and organisation, their officers and staff' (p. 130). Whatley believed that this fifth aid, the study of the armies themselves, was generally neglected to a greater or lesser degree, something which he believed to be inexcusable, realising that the study of ancient armies was as important for an understanding of ancient military history as the study of the Roman constitution was necessary to understand the political history of the age of the Gracchi.

Interestingly, Samuels' 1990 article on Cannae emphasised this particular 'fifth element', concentrating on 'the study of internal characteristics . . . the purposes of the institution, the functions necessary to achieve them and the internal structures and procedures which are directed towards this aim. Parallel to this, the study of the evolution of the institutions concerned allows those factors which have the greatest impact on the operations of each army to be examined' (Samuels, 1990, p. 10). Samuels' conclusions are rarely convincing, frequently relying on careless use of primary sources and questionable assumptions about the nature of the relevant armies, as will be shown below. However, their very improbability is demonstrative of the importance of this approach. His attempt to portray the reality of Cannae is entirely dependent upon his analyses of the opposing armies, and as his analyses are flawed, so too is his reconstruction of the battle.

Whatley's point is a valid one. All armies are different, reflecting the societies from which they issue, and fighting for their objectives in accordance with their own values. As cultures differ, so too do both their conceptions of warfare and their armies, the instruments by which they wage war (Keegan, 1993, pp. 3–60). The purpose of this chapter and the next is to analyse the nature of the Roman and Carthaginian armies which fought at Cannae, stressing what was distinctive about them in order to reconstruct their experience at that battle. It is useful to go beyond quantifiable features, like training and equipment, by taking into account such intangible factors as morale. The importance of maintaining morale has been recognised throughout history, and the state of morale of the opposing armies deserves to be considered in this context (MacMullen, 1984, p. 440).

Rome's militia and the 'Servian' constitution

Armies differ widely in nature and can be classified in various ways. Keegan (1993, pp. 221–34) identifies six broad categories of military organisation: warrior; mercenary; slave; regular; conscript; and militia. These categories are not rigidly defined, and armies can occupy 'grey areas' spanning more than one category. An example of this, discussed in greater detail in the following chapter (pp. 102–6), is the Celts who served in the Carthaginian army, since they were both mercenaries and warriors. Dealing with this, Rawlings (1996, pp. 81–95) prefers a simpler binary distinction between 'soldiers' and 'warriors', the former being defined by their relationship to the state, the latter by their ties to individual chieftains. By Rawlings' definition, the Roman army was made up of soldiers, but Keegan would more precisely define it as a militia. At least half of Rome's armed forces in any given campaign were supplied by her allies; these will be dealt with later on, as their status is not quite as clear-cut as that of the Roman citizens with whom they served.

In a traditional militia system, all free men of property were required to train for war and serve in time of danger, providing their own arms, as a condition of citizenship. Indeed, in the ancient world citizens were almost by definition soldiers (Keegan, 1993, p. 232; Nicolet, 1980, p. 90; Garlan, 1975, p. 87). Mid-Republican Rome was in theory a timocratic society where the wealthiest and most politically influential citizens had the most onerous military obligations (Scullard, 1980, p. 74). According to tradition, this system was instituted by Servius Tullius, the sixth king of Rome, who divided the people up into *classes* and centuries on the basis of wealth and age (Liv. 1.42.5). Although the principles of this system may indeed have originated under Servius in the middle of the sixth century, the system as described in the ancient sources can hardly have been that which Servius created (Liv. 1.43; Dion. Hal. 4.16–18; Scullard, 1980, p. 71; Garlan, 1975, p. 87; Sumner, 1970, p. 76; Ogilvie, 1965, pp. 166–8). His original system was probably based on a *classis* of sixty centuries, made up of those who could afford to arm themselves and fight as hoplites, with the remaining citizens, *infra classem*, fighting as light-armed troops (Cornell, 1995, p. 189). This system seems to have been reformed sometime around the end of the fifth century, probably in tandem with the introduction of pay for military service in 406. The system of five *classes* described by the ancient writers was apparently established to create a popular assembly where the old and wealthy held sway, and was very unlikely still to be linked with the organisation of the field army, the legions being indiscriminately recruited from all those with the necessary property qualification and then organised almost solely on the basis of age (Cornell, 1995, pp. 186–8).

The reformed Servian system, as described by Livy and Dionysius of Halicarnassus, divided the bulk of the population, those who could be called upon to serve as infantry, into five *classes*, a total of 170 centuries. In addition, there were 23 'supernumerary' centuries: 18 centuries of *equites*, the wealthiest citizens who supplied the army's cavalry; 2 centuries of engineers; 2 centuries of musicians; and 1 century of *capite censi*, those who were not permitted to fight as they were too poor to provide their own equipment (Cornell, 1995 p. 179; Keppie, 1998, pp. 16–17). In each *classis* there was an equal number of centuries of *iuniores* (aged between 17 and 45) and *seniores* (aged between 45 and 60), the former forming the field army while the latter formed a kind of 'home guard' in the city. The sources indicate that the first three *classes*, 120 centuries in total, were obliged to serve as heavy infantry, with the remaining two *classes*, 50 centuries in all, supplying the light infantry. Although it seems unlikely that the internal structure of the legions was really based on wealth, it is striking that in a standard legion there were 3,000 heavy infantry and 1,200 light troops, a ratio of 60:24, remarkably close to the proportion of centuries of *iuniores* in the first three *classes* to those in the last two, 60:25 (Cornell, 1995 pp. 181–3).

In Polybius' day, the field army was still composed of *iuniores*. He claims that 'a cavalry soldier must serve for ten years in all and an infantry soldier for sixteen years before reaching the age of forty-six . . . In case of pressing danger twenty years' service is demanded from the infantry' (Polyb. 6.19.2–4).

The actual length of time served by individual soldiers is uncertain. Polybius probably does not mean that all infantry served for the sixteen full years for which they were eligible. In any case, service before the Second Punic War tended to involve seasonal campaigns rather than year-round duty (Harris, 1979, p. 45). It has been suggested that a six-year tour of duty was normal, as Appian records troops in Spain in 140 being replaced, having served for six years (App., *Iber.* 78; Keppie, 1998, pp. 33–4). However, this incident may have been exceptional or may simply indicate that six years was the longest continuous period for which a citizen would have been expected to serve. The total period in service is more important, in which respect it is significant that Polybius stresses that citizens might sometimes be called upon to serve for twenty years. He would hardly have emphasised this if troops usually served for only six years, and it seems improbable that the average recruit would have taken part in fewer than ten or twelve campaigns (Harris, 1979, pp. 44–5; Walbank, 1957, p. 698). It was probably normal for many cavalrymen to serve their full ten campaigns, as ten years' military service was the basic requirement for a political career, it being forbidden to stand for office without this (Polyb. 6.19.4–5).

Citizens were apparently obliged to provide their own equipment, but were paid for their service. This practice seems to have begun in 406 in order to compensate recruits for loss of earnings during long campaigns.[1] According to Polybius, the standard rate of pay for an infantryman was two obols a day, centurions receiving four obols and cavalry a drachma. In Roman terms this probably meant that a legionary earned a denarius every three days, a centurion two denarii every three days, and a cavalryman a denarius a day, the cost of rations, clothes, and extra equipment being deducted from these earnings (Polyb. 6.39.12, 15).[2] Rations were as follows:

> The allowance of corn to a foot soldier is about two thirds of an Attic medimnus a month, a cavalry soldier receives seven medimni of barley and two of wheat.
>
> (Polyb. 6.39.13)

In practice, this meant that infantry received about three *modii* of wheat while cavalry received thirty *modii* of barley, to feed the horse, and nine of wheat, probably including food for the groom.[3]

Although the army was a militia, it is difficult to determine whether the men should be regarded as conscripts or volunteers. The *dilectus*, the recruitment procedure, was backed by compulsion, which would be applied if necessary, but it should not be automatically assumed that recruits were unwilling to serve. Military service was seen as a right as well as a duty, with patriotism doubtless being an important factor, and could offer adventure, the prospect of booty, and opportunities for social advancement.[4]

Military service was particularly important for members of the Roman aristocracy, Polybius noting that the completion of ten annual campaigns was a basic requirement for anyone aspiring to political office (Polyb. 6.19.4).[5] Young aristocrats must almost always have served their ten-year military apprenticeship in the cavalry, drawn as it was from the wealthiest citizens. Having served for five years they would become eligible for election or appointment to the rank of military tribune, although ten of the twenty-four annually elected tribunes had at least ten years' experience (Polyb. 6.19.1–2). Following the conventional *cursus honorum,* rising aristocrats could gain further military experience as quaestors and praetors, before eventually reaching the consulship. The two consuls were in practice the chief officers of the state, and their most important role was as commanders of Rome's armies (Harris, 1979, p. 15). Harris notes that military success was of vital importance to the personal aims of most Roman aristocrats; prestige was essential for them since they exercised their power in Rome indirectly, through elections and assemblies, and success in war allowed them to earn the high esteem of their fellow citizens: 'on one level laus, on a higher level *gloria*' (Harris, 1979, p. 17).

The army as a society

Roman society, particularly at its upper levels, was highly militarised. However, the army should not simply be regarded as an institutional extension of this wider society, for in many respects it was a society in its own right, albeit not nearly to the extent it reached in the late Republic and the Empire.[6]

Each new recruit had to take an oath of loyalty *(sacramentum dicere)* linking him in a special way with the state, his commander, and his fellow soldiers; the oath had religious implications, as those who violated it were 'accursed' (Nicolet, 1980, p. 103). The oath developed over time, apparently being formalised only in 216, just before the battle of Cannae, presumably because the disasters at the Trebia and Lake Trasimene had damaged morale and a formal oath was seen as a way of remedying this:

> An oath was then administered to the soldiers by their tribunes – which was a thing that they had never done before. For until that day there had only been the general oath to assemble at the bidding of the consuls and not depart without their orders; then, after assembling, they would exchange a voluntary pledge amongst themselves – the cavalrymen in their decuries and the infantry in their centuries – that they would not abandon their ranks for flight or fear, but only to take up or seek a weapon, either to smite an enemy or to save a fellow citizen. This voluntary agreement among the men themselves was replaced by an oath administered formally by the tribunes.
>
> (Liv. 22.38.2–5)

The significance of this oath should not be underestimated, forming as it did a pact between the soldier and his gods, state, commander, and comrades. Even in our largely secularised times, such oaths of loyalty are important rituals, vital for the creation of group identity.[7] New recruits to Rome's army also had to take another oath on joining their unit, a less important one than the oath of loyalty, involving among other things a promise not to steal anything from the camp (Polyb. 6.33.1; Nicolet, 1980, p. 105; Walbank, 1957, p. 716). It is worth noting in this context that the standard punishment for crimes against the unit, in particular fleeing one's post or abandoning one's weapons in battle, was the *bastinado*: the beating or stoning of a guilty man, usually to death, by all his comrades. Those who survived this terrible punishment became outcasts (Polyb. 6.37). In other words, crimes against the unit were punished by the unit, reinforcing the idea of the legion as a separate society.[8]

Drill and general training played a vital role in the development of group identity. Along with its obvious practical purposes, drill had a ritualistic role which helped troops to identify themselves as soldiers rather than civilians.[9] As late as the fourth or early fifth century AD, Vegetius attributed the Romans' acquisition of their Empire to their training methods, camp discipline, and military skill (Veg. 1.1). Military attitudes were instilled into Roman citizens from their youth and physical exercises, almost paramilitary in nature, were normal for all male youths (Nicolet, 1980, pp. 95–6). On taking the military oath citizens ceased to be civilians; drill helped them to feel like soldiers.[10] The training scheme instituted by Scipio after his capture of Cartagena in 210 is described by Polybius:

> He ordered the soldiers on the first day to go at the double for thirty stades in their armour. On the second day they were all to polish up, repair, and examine their arms in full view, and the third day to rest and remain idle. On the following day they were to practise, some of them sword fighting with wooden swords covered with leather and with a button on the point, while others practised casting javelins also having a button on the point. On the fifth day they were to begin the same course of exercise again.
>
> (Polyb. 10.20.2–3)

Livy, who significantly stresses the group rather than the individual in his account of this training regime by referring to manoeuvres, parades, and a mock battle, reverses the order of the third and fourth days, which seems reasonable (Liv. 26.51.14; Walbank, 1967, p. 219). This training programme seems to have been specifically devised by Scipio, and was presumably different, in some sense, from that undergone by the army which fought at Cannae.

Nevertheless, training was clearly very important in the army before this point, as Polybius notes that Roman defeats in the early years of the Second Punic War were attributed to the legions being composed of undrilled raw recruits (Polyb. 3.70.10, 106.5, 108.6). The army of Cannae was expected to prove much more resilient, since the new recruits were sent on to join the army in Apulia before being joined by the consuls, so that through training and constant skirmishing with the enemy they would gain the necessary confidence for a general engagement (Polyb. 3.106.3–4). Even a fairly short period of training could be expected to have significant effects, presumably improving both technical skill and *esprit de corps*, as indicated by the elder Scipio's desire to avoid battle at the Trebia in order to spend the winter drilling his troops (Polyb. 3.70.4); it was usual to spend only January and February in winter quarters.[11] Furthermore, many of the troops at Cannae must have had some experience of military service before 216, as suggested by Paullus' supposed, and indeed hyperbolic, declaration that the Roman troops had fought their Carthaginian enemies every day for almost two years (Polyb. 3.109.2). The legions of Cannae must have included veterans not only of the Trebia and numerous skirmishes in the Second Punic War, but also of the Celtic *tumultus* of the mid-220s and Paullus' Illyrian campaign of 219. It is even possible that veterans of the Illyrian war volunteered for service in 216 in order to serve under their former commander.[12]

A high degree of *esprit de corps* was evident at every level of the Roman army. Soldiers felt loyalty not solely to their commander and the legion as a whole, as confirmed by the oath of allegiance taken upon recruitment, but more importantly, to smaller sections of the legion. The century, the legion's basic administrative unit, seems to have had more emotional significance than the larger maniple, the legion's basic tactical unit, each maniple being composed of two centuries.[13] The emotional bond was largely focused on the military standards, of which there was one per maniple. The standards remained a focus of veneration for the troops right up to the Christianisation of the army in the late Imperial period.[14] Perhaps the decisive element in the building of *esprit de corps* was small-group cohesion, created by the *contubernia*, the eight-man mess-units designed for an administrative purpose but with the highly significant side-effect that the men in these units knew each other very well through living together. Such small groups are usually very effective in battle as the men tend to fight hard to earn the respect, or avoid the ridicule, of their comrades (Lee, 1996, p. 209; Holmes, 1985, pp. 293 ff.; MacMullen, 1984, p. 443; Connolly, 1998, p. 142).

Polybius on the Roman army

The most detailed and generally reliable source of information on the army of mid-Republican Rome is the description of it in the sixth book of Polybius' *Histories* (Polyb. 6.19–42). However, although Polybius' description chronologically follows his account of the battle of Cannae, in order to explain how Rome survived such a catastrophe, it was probably composed sometime around 160, perhaps fifty years after the events at Cannae, and it has been argued that, as Polybius was writing 'pragmatic history', his description of the army is more likely to reflect the reality of his own day than that of the Second Punic War (Samuels, 1990, p. 9; Rawson, 1971, pp. 13–14). This certainly makes sense, and it is striking that Polybius uses the present tense to describe the army, suggesting that he is indeed writing about the army of his own day. Whether this is the case or not, it clearly demonstrates the basic problem in attempting to reconstruct the nature of the Roman army at Cannae. The Roman army was not a static entity, but was constantly changing, adopting new tactics and equipment and modifying existing ones. The task for the historian of Cannae is to analyse Polybius' account in order to 'freeze' the army as it stood in 216.

Rawson argues that Polybius seems to have closely modelled his account on a literary source, perhaps an obsolete handbook for military tribunes, rather than simply relying on his own observations. His account occasionally records both obsolete and contemporary practice, suggesting that his written source was at odds with the reality of Polybius' own day.[15] This theory, while very plausible, must be treated with caution, as it is perhaps just as likely that Polybius simply observed the army of his own day and asked people whether it had been different in the past.[16] This method would have resulted in a description of the army of his own day, composed in the present tense and appropriate for his 'pragmatic history', which was also largely applicable to the army which fought at Cannae.

The army as described by Polybius was essentially composed of three lines of 'maniples', the maniple being the basic tactical unit of the mid-Republican Roman army, as discussed below (pp. 55 ff.). The first two lines were armed with heavy javelins, swords, and long shields, the last line having long spears instead of javelins. This army of heavy infantry would have been accompanied by light-armed skirmishers and cavalry. Curiously, Polybius seems unaware of any recent changes in how the infantry were armed and organised, only noting changes in the cavalry. This may reflect the fact that he had been *hipparchos* of the Achaean League, or that at the time of writing he was an associate of the young Scipio Aemilianus who, as a young aristocrat, perhaps in his mid-twenties, would probably have been serving as a cavalry officer or military tribune.[17]

A manipular system of troops armed with throwing spears and oblong shields was almost certainly in use long before Polybius' day, as indicated by Livy's admittedly problematic account of the manipular system during the Latin revolt of 340:

> The Romans had formerly used small round shields; then, after they began to serve for pay, they made oblong shields instead of round ones; and what had before been a phalanx, like the Macedonian phalanxes, came afterwards to be a line of battle formed by maniples.
>
> (Liv. 8.8.3–4)

Although modern writers differ on the authenticity of Livy's account,[18] Diodorus notes that the Romans adopted manipular tactics and equipment when dealing with enemies who fought in such a fashion (Diod. 23.2); the *Ineditum Vaticanum* implies that the enemies in question were Samnites (*Ined. Vat.* 3). The *scutum* was usually regarded as having been Samnite in origin and although the *pilum* was probably adopted from Spanish troops fighting for Carthage in the First Punic War it is likely that the Romans had previously used some sort of heavy javelin.[19] It is impossible to say for certain when the new system was introduced, but Polybius claims that in the early third century Pyrrhus' battle formations involved alternating Italian maniples and Hellenistic phalanx units (Polyb. 18.28.10–11). He also refers to a manipular formation in an account of a battle between Romans and Celts in 223:

> The tribunes therefore distributed amongst the front maniples the spears of the *triarii* who were stationed behind them.
>
> (Polyb. 2.33.4)

It seems reasonably safe, therefore, to take Polybius at his word, and accept his description of the Roman army, even if written about fifty years after its defeat at Cannae, as an essentially accurate description of the army as it existed in 216.

The organisation of the legions

The manipular legion[20]

Rome's citizen legions formed the heart of the army and, in order to comprehend their behaviour at Cannae, it is necessary to understand how they were organised and equipped. The legion was the largest unit by which Rome's citizen militia was organised. The standard complement of the 'Polybian' legion seems to have been 4,200 infantry accompanied by 300 cavalry, in theory if not in practice (Polyb. 6.20.8–9). The legions of Cannae were abnormally large, each one being allocated about 5,000 infantry accompanied by 300 cavalry, owing to Rome's dire predicament (Polyb. 3.107.9–11; Liv. 22.36.4).[21]

To reconstruct the organisation of these 5,300-strong legions, the theoretical structure of the more common 4,500-man legion must be examined. Three hundred men, chosen on grounds of wealth, were selected to serve as cavalry (Polyb. 6.20.9),[22] the remaining recruits serving as infantry, some being light infantry, or skirmishers, called *velites* in Polybius' day, and the rest being heavy infantry, or troops of the line, tactically divided into three lines according to their age:

> They [the military tribunes] choose the youngest and the poorest to become the *velites*; the next to them are made *hastati*; those in the prime of life *principes*; and the oldest of all *triarii*.
>
> (Polyb. 6.21.7)

The number of *triarii* was fixed at 600 per legion, and there were generally 1,200 *principes* and 1,200 *hastati*, with the remaining troops being *velites*, unless the legion was over 4,000 strong, which was apparently normal. In this case any surplus troops were divided among the *principes, hastati*, and *velites* (Polyb. 6.21.9–10). It is generally thought that in an average 4,500-strong legion there were 1,200 *velites* (Keppie, 1998, pp. 34–5; Connolly, 1998, p. 129; Sumner, 1970, p. 67; Walbank, 1957, p. 703).

Each of the 5,300-strong legions at Cannae included 300 cavalry and 600 *triarii*. Of the remaining 4,400 troops, there must have been on average 1,466 men for each of the *velites, hastati*, and *principes*. However, as each line of heavy infantry was tactically subdivided into ten maniples of two centuries each, and assuming that the maniples were equal in size, it is probable that each maniple of *hastati* and *principes* had a paper strength of 144 men, each century being composed of 72 men, as such a century could be easily deployed in a range of formations, allowing the commanders to adopt a wide or deep formation in battle. On this basis, the legions of Cannae were probably made up of 300 cavalry, 1,520 *velites*, 1,440 *hastati*, 1,440 *principes*, and 600 *triarii*. It is, however, impossible to be certain about this.[23]

How were such legions commanded? In a typical Roman army, usually composed of two legions of Roman citizens accompanied by an equal or larger number of allies, a consul would normally be in command, although sometimes a praetor would fulfil this role. Whenever the two consular armies of any given year combined, the two consuls would each command on alternate days (Polyb. 3.110.4; Suolahti, 1955, p. 27). Each consul was aided by a quaestor, who appears to been responsible for the army's finances, perhaps acting as a kind of quartermaster in charge of logistics (Polyb. 6.12.8, 31.2; Suolahti, 1955, p. 44). Owing to the vast size of the army at Cannae, which effectively consisted of four consular armies, a consul of the previous year was also present, along with that year's master of horse, who perhaps commanded one of the armies as a legate (Keppie, 1998, p. 40).

The consuls and quaestors had responsibility for the army as a whole. At divisional level the legions were commanded by military tribunes and the allies by Prefects of the Allies (Polyb. 6.19.1, 6–9, 26.5). Twenty-four military tribunes were elected each year, each legion being allocated six, two or three of whom had at least ten years' service experience, the remainder having served for at least five years. Such experience was almost certainly gained during service as cavalry,[24] where they may have commanded at the lowest tactical levels, as *decuriones* or *optiones*. If more than four legions were employed in any given year, extra military tribunes, nicknamed *Rufuli* (Redheads), would be appointed by the commanding magistrate; presumably these unelected tribunes were generally chosen, at least in principle, on the grounds of proven ability and experience.[25] In the case of the forty-eight tribunes at Cannae, twenty-four were clearly unelected; many of these were probably tribunes of the previous year, while others seem to have been former magistrates, since Livy claims that the dead of Cannae included eighty distinguished individuals, who were members of the senate or had held offices which qualified them as members (Liv. 22.49.17). Although the tribunate was the bottom rung on Rome's aristocratic *cursus* it was a prestigious position which was indeed sometimes filled by established aristocrats.[26] Considering that some of the tribunes who served at Cannae were distinguished aristocrats, while others had at least held their positions before, Samuels' presentation of them (1990, pp. 13–14) as inexperienced and concerned only with personal glory seems simplistic and unfair. Although some of them were doubtless as hotheaded as he claims, many must have been experienced, capable, and responsible.

As noted already, the tribunes were assigned to individual legions rather than to the army as a whole. There they had a wide range of responsibilities, both administrative and tactical. Having been appointed, their job was to enrol new recruits, exact a formal oath of loyalty from them, and divide the infantry into their four categories. They may also have been responsible for the training of recruits, as well as their health and general welfare. Furthermore, they were responsible for the selection of a suitable campsite and the supervision of the camps, and had the ability to punish certain offences. Tribunes worked in pairs, each pair commanding the legion for two months out of every six, while the remaining tribunes served with their commanding consul in a 'staff' capacity, where their duties might have included troop deployment or the relaying of news to the commander.[27]

Individual maniples, the basic tactical sub-units of the legion, were commanded by centurions, experienced infantrymen appointed by the military tribunes, while the cavalry *turmae* were commanded by decurions, also appointed by the tribunes. Both centurions and decurions were aided by rear-rank officers termed *optiones* (Polyb. 6.24.1–2, 25.1–2). The functions and importance of these low-ranking officers are discussed below (pp. 63, 74).

Each of the eight legions at Cannae was composed of about 5,000 infantry and 300 cavalry, the infantry probably being divided up, at least in theory, as follows: 1,520 skirmishers, 1,440 *hastati*, 1,440 *principes*, and 600 *triarii*. Overall command of the combined forces at Cannae was in the hands of the two consuls for 216, assisted by their respective quaestors and a consul and the master of horse from the previous year. Individual legions were thus commanded by military tribunes, six per legion, many of them experienced soldiers, while at a close tactical level infantry and cavalry were commanded by centurions and decurions, men of the same social class as the men they commanded.

Heavy infantry

The manipular legion was very different from the conventional infantry formation of the Hellenistic world, the Macedonian-style phalanx. The phalanx (which is Greek for 'roller') seems to have developed in Greece in the early seventh century and consisted of a single line of infantrymen, deployed in close order, usually eight ranks deep, with their shields overlapping and primarily armed with thrusting spears, generally about 2 metres long. As the hoplites (heavy infantry) lacked missile weapons, the phalanx was useful only for shock tactics based on close combat with a short 'killing zone' (the 'killing zone' being the distance from the user's body in which a weapon can be used to strike the enemy; in the hoplite phalanx this would have been only a metre or two) (Ferrill, 1985, pp. 99–106; Santosuosso, 1997, pp. 7–23; Warry, 1980, pp. 34–9; Connolly, 1998, pp. 37 ff.; Hanson, 1995a, pp. 14–18. For the killing zone: Goldsworthy, 1996, p. 177). The phalanx underwent radical changes during the fourth century after the reforms of Philip II of Macedon, and during the Hellenistic period the standard infantry formation was the Macedonian phalanx. This formed a single line, the basic tactical unit of which was the 256-man *syntagma*, deployed in a square, sixteen men deep. The phalangites had less armour than their classical predecessors and wore a small shield hung from the neck, as this left both hands free to wield the long *sarissa*, or Macedonian pike, which was at least 4.5 m long. This phalanx had a killing zone of at least 3.5 m, and the pikes of the first five ranks were capable of reaching the enemy; the ranks behind the front five would hold their pikes high to ward off missiles. Although the Macedonian phalanx was virtually invincible on perfectly level ground, its tight formation could be easily disrupted on irregular terrain, and it was particularly vulnerable to attacks from the flank and rear, because the length of the pikes reduced the manoeuvrability of individual phalangites (Walbank, 1967, pp. 586–91; Griffith, 1979, pp. 419–24; Hanson, 1995b, p. 36; Ferrill, 1985, pp. 177–9; Santosuosso, 1997; pp. 112–13, 160 ff.; Warry, 1980, pp. 72–3, 124–7; Connolly, 1998, pp. 69–70, 75 ff.).

The manipular legion of the mid-Republic was a far more flexible arrangement, as Polybius makes clear in his famous comparison between the legion and the phalanx (Polyb. 18.28–32). Rather than forming a single deep line, each legion was deployed in three successive, relatively shallow lines: *hastati*, *principes*, and *triarii*. The *hastati*, the youngest of the line infantry, were the front-line troops, being followed by the *principes*, men in their prime, with the oldest troops, the *triarii*, bringing up the rear. Unlike the citizens who were allocated to the light infantry on the grounds of both youth and poverty, the three classes of heavy infantry were distinguished by age alone (Polyb. 6.21.7–8).[28] Differing only in age and experience, the first two lines were armed in the same fashion according to Polybius, each legionary carrying a *scutum*, a large oblong shield, two *pila*, throwing spears or heavy javelins, and a *gladius Hispaniensis*, a short cut-and-thrust sword. For protection, a crested bronze helmet and greaves were worn. In addition, troops with property valued over 10,000 *asses* wore a *lorica*, a coat of chain mail, while the remainder had only a small bronze plate, a *pectorale*, upon their chest (Polyb. 6.23.1–15). Polybius is probably oversimplifying in this respect since it seems more likely that it was simply a case of anyone who

could afford to wearing a *lorica*, while the small *pectorale* was probably standard-issue armour (Connolly, 1989, p. 153; Head, 1982, p. 158; Delbrück,
1990 [1920], p. 280). The *triarii* were equipped in much the same fashion,
albeit with a *hasta*, a long thrusting spear, instead of *pila* (Polyb. 6.23.16).
The purpose of this trilinear pattern of deployment was to ensure a constant
supply of reinforcements in battle – fresh units could filter through those
which had already been involved in the fighting, effectively replacing the
tired line with a new one able to launch a new assault. It is likely that, in
general, the *triarii* simply presented a hedgerow of spears to the enemy,
enabling beaten *hastati* and *principes* to retreat; they had a shorter 'killing
zone' than the *hastati* or *principes* because of their lack of missiles, and so
were more important for defensive than offensive purposes (Connolly, 1989,
p. 163; Head, 1982, p. 59).

Maniples and centuries

Delbrück memorably characterised the Roman legion as a phalanx with
joints, as each line of heavy infantry was composed of ten tactical sub-
units, the maniples; rather than being a solid line, each line of maniples
formed a flexible chain.[29] For administrative purposes, each maniple was
divided into two centuries. These were purely administrative units, and
the maniple was always the basic tactical unit (Connolly, 1989, p. 152;
Walbank, 1957, p. 707; Delbrück, 1990 [1920], pp. 272–5; Fuller, 1965,
p. 78). The centuries were each led by a centurion, assisted by an *optio*, a rear-
rank officer (Polyb. 6.24.1–2). The *centurio prior*, the first of the two to be
appointed, was personally responsible for commanding the right half of the
maniple, the *centurio posterior* being in charge of the left. It was standard
practice in Rome for a unit or army leader to command at the right, and as
the maniple rather than the century was the tactical unit, the *centurio prior*
must have commanded the maniple as a whole in battle, the *centurio posterior*
only taking over if the other was incapacitated.[30] Each maniple had two standard-bearers, but it seems that there was only one standard per maniple, as
discussed elsewhere (p. 214 n. 14), so one of the standard-bearers was evidently a substitute should anything befall the other. Although Polybius mentions neither trumpeters (*tubicines*) nor horn-blowers (*cornices*) in his analysis
of the legion's structure, he was aware of their presence in the army, and
as there were two centuries of musicians in the 'Servian' army it is possible that every maniple in Polybius' day had both a trumpeter and a hornblower.[31]

It is generally thought that the parade-ground formation of the legion
was a chess-board pattern, normally referred to nowadays as a *quincunx* formation, after the pattern formed by the five dots on a die (Keppie, 1998, p.
39; Adcock, 1940, p. 9; Hanson, 1995b, p. 46; Connolly, 1998, p. 128). The
hastati maniples were deployed in a line with large gaps between each

maniple, equal in width to the maniples themselves; the *principes* maniples were deployed in a similar fashion behind the *hastati*, covering the gaps in their line; likewise, the *triarii* covered the gaps in the line of *principes*. The centuries in each maniple were probably not deployed side by side; instead, the *prior* centuries were almost certainly stationed in front of the *posterior* ones, as their names would suggest (Hanson, 1995b, p. 46; Connolly, 1989, p. 162). Presumably there was a gap between each line, although its size can only be guessed at.[32]

Kromayer and Adcock believed that this pattern was maintained in battle, with the intervals between maniples being kept. In order to replace the *hastati* with *principes,* for example, the maniples of the latter would fill the gaps in the former's line, allowing the maniples to fall back intact. This may seem unlikely, but individual units of a pike phalanx could certainly not have advanced into the gaps since this would have exposed their vulnerable flanks; the phalanx was, after all, designed purely to face frontal opposition. Advocates of the 'broken-line' theory maintain that even a more flexible formation would not have penetrated the gaps in the Roman front, since this would endanger the advanced units, who would find themselves facing Romans on both sides, as well as in front, if the covering maniple moved forward.[33]

These attempts to defend the idea of the Romans fighting in a *quincunx* or 'chequerboard' formation underestimate the importance of missiles in ancient warfare.[34] The *pilum,* the heavy Roman throwing spear, probably had a range of about 30 m, which was significantly less than the range of other ancient missiles.[35] Hostile troops facing large gaps in the Roman line would have been able to take advantage this, if they were armed with long-range missiles, since they could threaten the forward maniples without being endangered themselves. In any case, the fact remains that if the intervals were ever successfully penetrated, individual units could easily have become isolated and surrounded by attackers on all sides. It is more probable that the intervals were filled before the Romans met their enemies; presumably the *posterior* century would move to the left and forward, filling the gap and allowing the entire maniple to be commanded from the right by the *centurio prior* (Fig. 2).[36]

If each line did indeed deploy without intervals, how then was it replaced in battle? It is probable that the intervals were reopened to enable line replacement to take place during natural pauses in battle (Sabin, 1996, p. 72). It might be objected that such lulls in the fighting could not be relied upon and that even if they did occur, it is difficult to believe that the opposing forces would have stood idly by, politely waiting for the Romans to replace tired troops with fresh ones. Connolly has argued that if the *hastati* were unable to reopen their intervals safely, the *principes* could themselves have formed a continuous line in open order and then filtered through the *hastati*. This is possible since, according to Polybius, each man had a

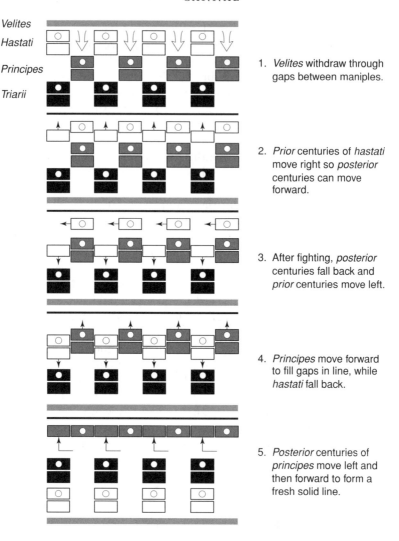

Velites

Hastati

Principes

Triarii

1. *Velites* withdraw through gaps between maniples.

2. *Prior* centuries of *hastati* move right so *posterior* centuries can move forward.

3. After fighting, *posterior* centuries fall back and *prior* centuries move left.

4. *Principes* move forward to fill gaps in line, while *hastati* fall back.

5. *Posterior* centuries of *principes* move left and then forward to form a fresh solid line.

Figure 2 The line replacement system in the mid-Republican Roman army.

frontage of six Roman feet (1.75 m), as well as an equivalent depth (Polyb. 18.30.6–8; Connolly, 1989, p. 163). Goldsworthy and Sabin doubt this figure, as it assumes that Roman troops always fought in an open formation when a closed one would have done as well; however, writing centuries after Polybius, Vegetius appears to have used a Republican source and claims that individual legionaries occupied a three-foot frontage (0.9 m) and one-foot depth (0.3 m) with six feet (nearly 2 m) between ranks (Veg. 3.14–15).[37] This close-order formation could have been adopted by simply having the rear half of each file in the Polybian formation move forward, occupying the gaps between the files; it would have been relatively easy for well-trained troops to revert from this closed formation to an open one to allow replacement troops to filter through.[38] This procedure would have been quite dangerous, and it is perhaps more likely that the Romans would await or precipitate lulls in the fighting to allow them to replace their lines; Sabin argues that these lulls were actually the normal conditions of ancient battle, being periodically broken by outbreaks of actual fighting (Sabin, 1996, p. 72).

The centurions who commanded these units were, unlike the military tribunes, of the same social class as the men they led, and through their experience and ability constituted the backbone of the legions (Adcock, 1940, p. 18; Garlan, 1975, p. 161). Tenacity appears to have been their most prized quality:

> They wish the centurions not so much to be venturesome and dare-devil as to be natural leaders, of a steady and sedate spirit. They do not desire them so much to be men who will initiate attacks and open the battle, but men who will hold their ground when worsted and hard-pressed and be ready to die at their posts.
>
> (Polyb. 6.24.9)

Samuels assumes that men so noted for their steadiness would have been wholly lacking in imagination and initiative, but he is probably overstating his case. The wisdom and intelligence of the centurions were evidently valued, as indicated by the presence of the *centurio primi pili*, the first centurion to be appointed, who served as *centurio prior* in the first maniple of *triarii*, in the consul's war council (Polyb. 6.24.2; Samuels, 1990, p. 14; Keppie, 1998, p. 35; Connolly, 1998, p. 129). Such men could be very experienced; Livy cites the famous early second-century example of Spurius Ligustinus, who worked his way up through the ranks as a standard legionary, being decorated for bravery on numerous occasions and being appointed centurion many times, including being made *centurio primi pili* four times in the course of twenty-two years of service (Liv. 42.34.11). Admittedly such a record was exceptional even in Ligustinus' own day, a period of remarkable expansion in Spain and the Hellenistic world which had led to the gradual professionalisation of the army (Samuels, 1990, p. 14; Keppie, 1998, p. 53; Connolly, 1989, p. 165), but it seems certain that many of the centurions at Cannae would have had a considerable amount of experience. The centurion's main role in battle was to lead by example at the front (Polyb. 6.24.9), while his *optio* would have been stationed in the rear rank, or possibly just behind it, so as to control and exhort the men in front of him (Connolly, 1998, p. 112; Goldsworthy, 1996, pp. 182, 197, 205).

Legionary equipment

Pilum *HEMONNHOIDS?*

The *hastati* and *principes* hurled *pila* at the enemy before closing with them. According to Polybius, there were two sorts of *pila*, stout and fine:

> Of the stout ones some are round and a palm's length in diameter and others are a palm square. The fine *pila*, which they carry in addition to the stout ones, are like moderate-sized hunting-spears, the length of the haft in all cases being about three cubits. Each is fitted with a barbed iron head of the same length as the haft. This they attach so securely to the haft, carrying the attachment halfway up the latter and fixing it with numerous rivets, that in action the iron will break sooner than become detached, although its thickness at the bottom where it comes into contact with the wood is a finger's breadth and a half; such great care do they take about attaching it firmly.
>
> (Polyb. 6.23.9–11)

It seems unlikely that both types of *pila* were carried into battle at once. The *pilum* was thrown while charging, at a range of about 30 metres, and it would hardly have been possible for a second volley of *pila* to have been delivered immediately afterwards. Furthermore, the horizontal handgrip on the Roman *scutum* would have made it very difficult for the spare *pilum* to be carried into battle (but see Connolly, 1998, p. 142). It seems more likely that the extra *pilum* was carried on the march only, being left behind the lines in battle as an ammunition reserve to be used if retired *hastati* or *principes* were to return to battle.[39]

Pila used during the Second Punic War were probably based on throwing spears used by Spanish mercenaries working for Carthage during the First Punic War, although throwing spears were certainly known in Rome before the First Punic War,[40] and the first authentic reference to the Roman *pilum* is a reference to Roman troops in 251 using a *hyssos* (Polyb. 1.40.12). The heavy *pilum* as described by Polybius would have weighed 8.5 kg, too heavy to throw. It seems more probable that the 'heavy' *pilum* was thicker only where the shaft and head connected, as on this basis a 2.1 m-long 'heavy' *pilum* would have weighed between 3.69 kg and 4.68 kg, while a lighter *pilum* would have weighed about 2 kg (Walbank, 1957, p. 705). The *pilum* was an 'armour-piercing' missile with a barbed pyramidal head which would pierce an enemy's shield and continue on; the head was but the tip of a long, narrow, iron shank which could easily pass through the puncture made by the head, either wounding the enemy himself or rendering the enemy's shield too cumbersome for use. A useful side-effect of this was that the narrow shank would often bend on impact, ensuring that the enemy would not throw the weapon back (Bishop and Coulston, 1993, pp. 48–50; Goldsworthy, 1996, p. 198).

Hasta *LA VISTA, BABY.*

The *triarii*, unlike the first two lines of heavy infantry, were armed with a long thrusting spear rather than a *pilum* (Polyb. 6.23.6); this *hasta* was the same weapon as that used in the days when the Roman army fought as a phalanx. As such it was probably more or less the same as the standard hoplite spear of classical Greece, generally between 2.1 and 2.4 m long with a socketed iron head, often between 20 and 30 cm long, and a bronze butt-spike (Walbank, 1957, p. 706; Bishop and Coulston, 1993, pp. 52–3; Anderson, 1991, pp. 22–4). Samuels (1990, pp. 11–12) claims that the *principes* at Cannae were also armed with the *hasta*, and that the legion was in effect a spear-armed phalanx at that stage in its development. His argument is based on a passage where Polybius claims that in a battle against Celts in 223, the front maniples used the spears of the *triarii* in order to ward off the initial Celtic attack (Polyb. 2.33.4).[41] Samuels perversely claims that Polybius has simply come across a reference to the *principes* using *hastae* and, naively believing that the army of his own day was identical to that of the late third century, assumed that this unorthodox use of weaponry was a once-off innovation. Samuels' reasoning is clearly faulty here, as in the first place *hastati*, rather than *principes*, were front-line troops in 223 (in fact, according to Livy (8.8.6), the *principes* formed the second line more than a hundred years earlier). In any case, Polybius was hardly blind to the fact that the army had changed over time as his references to changes in cavalry enrolment and equipment make clear (Polyb. 6.20.9, 25.3–11).

Scutum *and* gladius *UP YOUR SCROTUM GLADLY*

Having cast their *pila*, Rome's line infantry would advance to close combat with sword and shield. Close fighting with these weapons seems to have been the hallmark of the Roman soldier during the mid-Republican period, as Polybius' comparison of the Roman legion and the Macedonian phalanx makes clear (Polyb. 18.28–32). Polybius describes these weapons in detail:

> The Roman panoply consists firstly of a shield [*scutum*], the convex surface of which measures two and a half feet in width and four feet in length, the thickness at the rim being a palm's breadth. It is made of two planks glued together, the outer surface being then covered first with canvas and then with calf-skin. Its upper and lower rims are strengthened by an iron edging which protects it

65

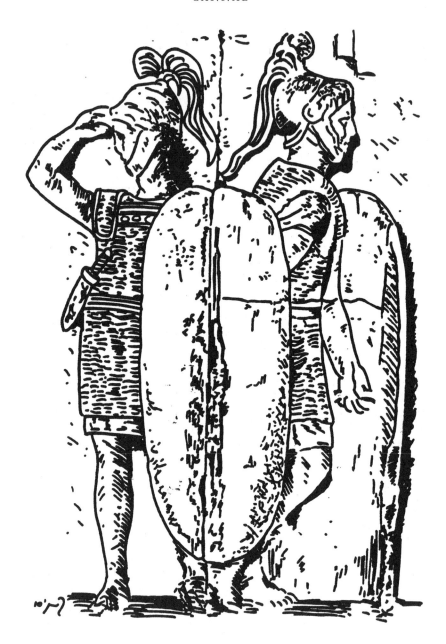

Figure 3 Roman infantrymen represented on the Altar of Domitius Ahenobarbus. Each man is equipped with a *scutum*, and wears a *lorica* of chain mail. The soldier on the left has a *pugio* (dagger) on his right hip. He appears to be wearing a *Montefortino*-type helmet, while the soldier on the right is wearing a slightly different helmet, which may be of Etrusco-Corinthian design.

from descending blows and from injury when rested on the ground. It also has an iron boss [*umbo*] fixed to it which turns aside the more formidable blows of stones, pikes, and heavy missiles in general. Besides the shield they also carry a sword, hanging on the right thigh and called a Spanish sword [*gladius hispaniensis*]. This is excellent for thrusting, and both of its edges cut effectually, as the blade is very strong and firm.

(Polyb. 6.23.2–7)

Like the *pilum*, the *scutum* seems originally to have been a Samnite weapon (Cornell, 1995, p. 170; Walbank, 1957, pp. 703–4). Such shields as Polybius describes, oval or oblong in shape with a long spine and a spindle-shaped boss, are depicted on the Altar of Domitius Ahenobarbus (Fig. 3) and the Aemilius Paullus Monument (Bishop and Coulston, 1993, pp. 49, 20). A curved plywood shield of this type, found in 1900 in Kasr el-Harit in the Egyptian Fayum, was originally regarded as Celtic in origin but is more probably Roman. The shield, 1.28 m long and 0.635 m wide, was made of three layers of wooden strips, the vertical strips in the central layer being wider than the horizontal strips in the central layers; these layers were glued together and both sides were covered with lambs' wool felt. The shield was thickest, and therefore strongest, at the centre where it was about 1.2 cm thick. Its thinner edges gave the shield a certain degree of flexibility. It had a wooden boss and long vertical spine, and its horizontal handgrip was behind the boss. Unlike the shields Polybius describes, the Kasr el-Harit shield lacked an iron boss and metal edging. However, details such as these probably varied according to circumstances. A fragmentary iron boss suited to such a shield has been excavated at Renieblas. This type of shield has been reconstructed by Peter Connolly and weighed slightly over 10 kg. Though this may seem unrealistically heavy, a reconstruction of a similar, though flat rather than curved, first-century shield found at Doncaster weighed almost the same amount, 9 kg (Bishop and Coulston, 1993, pp. 58–9; Connolly, 1998, p. 131).

The origins of the Roman *gladius* are uncertain. Polybius describes it as Spanish and claims that it was adopted during the war against Hannibal (Polyb. fr. 179), but it is perhaps more likely that, like the *pilum*, it was copied from Spanish mercenaries fighting in the First Punic War (Walbank, 1957, p. 704). In any case, the Romans were certainly using a short cut-and-thrust sword of this type during the Celtic *tumultus* of 225 (Polyb. 2.30.8, 33.5). Perhaps the design was merely modified along Spanish lines during the Second Punic War. A short sword matching Polybius' description has been found as Los Cogotes in Avila (Connolly, 1998, p. 130), but the only known Roman Republican *gladius*, excavated at Delos, is dated to 69, when there was piratical destruction on the island; it was 60 cm long, including the tang, which fitted into a wooden pommel, and 5.7 cm wide

Figure 4 Sword (a) is a Spanish sword from the fifth or fourth century, from Atienza about 100 km north-east of Madrid. Sword (b) is a Roman sword from the early first century AD, found at Rheingönheim in Germany.

(Bishop and Coulston, 1993, p. 53). The Mainz type of sword, used in the first century AD, had a slightly tapering blade, 40 to 55 cm long, with a long point (Goldsworthy, 1996, pp. 216–17); it is not known whether this type of *gladius* replaced the model found at Delos, but given the fact that citizens were responsible for providing their own equipment, there were probably several styles of sword in use simultaneously. Short swords such as these, double-edged and with a relatively long point, would have been quite suited to close-order fighting, as they were capable not only of thrusting but also of cutting, while not needing as much room to manoeuvre as a longer Celtic-style sword.[42]

Protective equipment

Rome's line infantry also wore a certain amount of protective equipment: a helmet, body armour, and at least one greave (Polyb. 6.23.8, 12–15). The so-called *Montefortino*-type helmet was the most common variety during the mid-Republican period, probably adopted from a fourth-century Celtic design.[43] The helmet design was basically a hemispherical bowl beaten to shape, with a narrow peaked neck-guard and often a crest knob with a hole in it. Such helmets also frequently had large, triangular cheek-pieces. The helmet was secured by straps attached to a double ring under the neck-guard, crossed beneath the chin, and fastened to the hooks at the bottom of the cheek-pieces. It was decorated, according to Polybius, with:

> a circle of feathers with three upright purple or black feathers about a cubit in height, the addition of which on the head surmounting

Figure 5 The *Montefortino* helmet.

> their other arms is to make every man look twice his real height,
> and to give him a fine appearance, such as will strike terror into
> the enemy.
>
> (Polyb. 6.23.12–13)

Crests like this, or horsehair ones as depicted on the Altar of Domitius
Ahenobarbus, were attached to the crest knob by means of a pin (Bishop
and Coulston, 1993, p. 61; Connolly, 1998, p. 133).

There are no examples of Republican greaves in existence, but it appears
that in practice only one greave was worn, as Polybius uses the singular
form of *proknemis* (Polyb. 6.23.8; Bishop and Coulston, 1993, p. 60;
Walbank, 1957, p. 705). If this was indeed the case, the greave was worn
on the left leg, for according to Arrian it was worn on that shin which was
thrust forward in fighting and in gladiatorial combat, and therefore presumably in battle (Arr., *Tact.* 5.3). It was the left foot that was placed ahead
of the right to enable the combatant to put his weight behind the blows
delivered. The combination of greave, shield, and helmet thus ensured
maximum protection on the soldier's prominent left side (Connolly, 1998,
p. 133; Bishop and Coulston, 1993, p. 60).

In addition to helmet and greaves, body armour was also worn, Polybius
describing two sorts:

The common soldiers wear in addition a breastplate of brass a span square, which they place in front of their heart and call the heart-protector [*pectorale*], thus completing their accoutrements; but those who are rated above 10,000 drachmas wear instead of this a coat of chain mail [*lorica*].

(Polyb. 6.23.14–15)

Although Polybius seems to believe that the *lorica* was worn only by members of the first 'Servian' *classis*, those rated above 100,000 *asses* (Walbank, 1957, p. 706), it is more likely that rather than being an anachronistic regulation, such armour was preferred by anyone who could afford it, the *pectorale* being standard-issue armour for all (Delbrück, 1990 [1920], p. 280; Head, 1982, p. 156; Healy, 1994, pp. 39–40). No known examples of the square *pectorale* described by Polybius are in existence, though a round bronze plate has been found near Numantia, slightly smaller than the Polybian *pectorale*, with a diameter of 17 cm, and fragments of larger plates have been found. Head suggests that the round plate may have been worn by an Italian allied soldier rather than a Roman citizen, but it is equally possible that the square *pectorale* was not the only type, or that the design changed over time (Bishop and Coulston, 1993, p. 59; Head, 1982, p. 158). Ring mail, from which the *lorica* was made, was adopted from the Celts and probably worn over a padded undergarment of some sort (Bishop and Coulston, 1993, p. 59; Walbank, 1957, p. 706). Both the Aemilius Paullus monument and the Altar of Domitius Ahenobarbus show soldiers wearing ring-mail cuirasses: the cuirasses are thigh-length with shoulder-doubling for extra protection against downward sword strokes and are worn with a belt, which would transfer some of the cuirass's weight from the shoulders to the hips. Since such cuirasses weighed about 15 kg, this was an important consideration (Bishop and Coulston, 1993, pp. 60–2; Connolly, 1998, p. 133).

Overall, it seems that Polybius' description of the equipment used by Rome's heavy infantry is to all intents and purposes applicable to the army which fought at Cannae.

Light infantry

The light-armed troops would normally open the battle, by skirmishing in front of the main bodies of men, and so will be dealt with first here. Polybius describes the light troops of his own day, the *velites*, as follows:

The youngest soldiers are ordered to carry a sword, javelins, and a target [*parma*]. The target is strongly made and sufficiently large to afford protection, being circular and measuring three feet in diameter. They also wear a plain helmet, and sometimes cover it

with a wolf's skin or something similar both to protect and to act
as a distinguishing mark by which their officers can recognise them
and judge if they fight pluckily or not. The wooden shaft of the
javelin measures about two cubits in length and is about a finger's
breadth in thickness; its head is a span long hammered out to such
a fine edge that it is necessarily bent by the first impact, and the
enemy unable to return it. If this were not so, the missile would
be available for both sides.

(Polyb. 6.22)

The *velites* Polybius describes were the youngest troops and the poorest ones,
divided for administrative purposes among the maniples, each maniple being
allocated the same number of *velites* (Polyb. 6.21.7, 24.4); on this basis,
each maniple of a standard 4,500-man legion would have had 40 *velites*, in
addition to its 60 or 120 heavy infantry, whereas the legions of Cannae
ought to have had about 56 *velites* attached to each maniple. Although the
velites appear not to have had their own officers, being commanded by the
centurions stationed with the heavy infantry, they were quite effective in
battle. Livy describes them successfully skirmishing from a distance by
throwing their javelins and then fighting at close quarters with their swords,
using their shields to protect themselves (Liv. 31.35.4–6, 38.21.12–13).

It has been argued that the light infantry of 216 were not armed in this
fashion, and that Polybius is simply describing those of his own day
(Samuels, 1990, pp. 12–13). The following problematic passage of Livy has
been interpreted as meaning that light-armed troops were first included in
the heavily armed legions in 211:

Out of all the legions were picked young men who by reason of
strength and lightness of build were the swiftest. These were
furnished with round shields of smaller size than those used by
cavalry, and seven javelins apiece four feet long and having iron heads
such as are on the spears of the light-armed troops. The horsemen
would each of them take one of these men on to their own horses,
and they trained them both to ride behind and to leap down nimbly
when the signal was given. When thanks to daily practice they
seemed to do this with sufficient daring, they advanced into the
plain which was situated between the camp and the city-wall in the
face of the Capuan cavalry in battle-line. And when they had come
within range, at a given signal the light-armed leapt to the ground.
Thereupon an infantry line suddenly dashes out from the cavalry at
the enemy's horsemen, and while attacking they hurl one javelin
after another. . . . Thereafter the Roman side was superior in cavalry
also; it was made the practice to have light-armed in the legions.

(Liv. 26.4.4–7, 9)

Gabba has argued that the passage refers to a complete reorganisation of the light infantry following a reduction in the minimum property qualification for military service from 11,000 to 4,000 *asses* at some point between 214 and 212.[44] This reduction may in fact never have happened, but Samuels accepts its historicity and argues that light infantry before 211 were *accensi*, military servants rather than proper soldiers, equipped simply with a spear and a few javelins. Without a shield they would have been vulnerable to missiles and unsuitable for close combat, and he believes that these were replaced with the better-armed, and more effective, *velites*.[45] Keppie, on the other hand, suggests that the reduction in the property qualification had brought numerous recruits into the legions who could not afford expensive weaponry, which would suggest that the *velites* were less well equipped than previous light infantry (Keppie, 1998, p. 33).

Neither hypothesis is particularly compelling, as apart from anything else, Polybius refers to Roman skirmishers in 255 as *grosphomachoi*, the same term he uses for *velites* (Polyb. 1.33.9, 6.21.7), and Livy mentions *velites* before their supposed creation in 211 (Liv. 21.55.11, 23.29.3, 24.34.5). Furthermore, Livy's account of the reforms of 211 is rife with problems, notably the apparently contradictory statement that the newly established *velites* carried javelins tipped with iron, like the spears of the *velites*, and that these new *velites* rode into battle with the cavalry, even though there were only 300 horse per legion, not nearly enough to carry 1,200 light infantry into battle (Lazenby, 1996a, p. 178). In any case, the latter change ought not to be regarded as a general reform, as it seems to have been a specific tactic adopted for specific circumstances, in order to startle the Campanian cavalry through an unfamiliar mode of attack (Liv. 26.4.8).

It should also be borne in mind that there is scarcely any evidence for how light infantry were armed and organised before Polybius' day, and such evidence as exists is not entirely reliable. According to Livy, the fourth and fifth *classes* in the 'Servian' constitution served as light troops, the former carrying a spear and javelin, the latter just a sling (Liv. 1.43.6–7).[46] By the mid-fourth century, according to Livy's questionable account of a battle during the Latin War, 300 *leves*, armed with just a spear and javelins, were attached to the *hastati*, while *rorarii* and *accensi* were stationed at the back of the legion.[47] Both *rorarii* and *accensi* must have served as light infantry; according to Varro, *accensi* was a second-century term for military servants, whereas *rorarii* remained in use as a term for light-armed troops throughout the second century, long after the supposed establishment of the *velites* in 211.[48]

Even if there were reforms in 211, they would hardly have been on the scale envisaged by Gabba and Samuels. There is no evidence for Samuels' belief that the numbers of light infantry increased in 211; as noted above, in the 'Polybian' army, each 4,500-man legion included 1,200 light troops, whereas in the reformed 'Servian' army there were 60 centuries of heavy infantry and 25 of light infantry, which would in practice have meant two legions, each of 3,000 heavy infantry and about 1,200 light troops.[49] From 311 on two legions were enrolled for each consul, rather than just one as before. There is no reason to believe that the proportion of light troops to heavy infantry changed or that the new legions were smaller than their predecessors (Liv. 9.30.3; Cornell, 1995, pp. 182, 354).

Livy's problematic account of the army of the mid-fourth century can throw some light on the supposed reform of 211. The legions he described had 5,000 infantry and 300 cavalry, but as 900 of the infantry were *accensi*, hastily armed servants rather than soldiers, there were in reality 4,100 infantry,[50] approximately corresponding to the 4,200 infantry of the 'Servian' and 'Polybian' legions. Livy's account therefore gives 1,200 light troops per legion: 300 *leves* and 15 *vexilla* of 60 *rorarii* (Liv. 8.8.5, 7–8). His specific observation that the *leves* lacked shields implies that they were less well equipped than the *rorarii*. It is likely that the reforms of 211, if genuine in any respect, may simply have involved an upgrading of the *leves*, providing them in effect with the same equipment as the *rorarii*. This standardised force of light troops may then have been collectively renamed *velites*. If this was the case, it is understandable that the obsolete term *rorarii* persisted throughout the next century, as the new *velites* were really an enlarged force of *rorarii*. Furthermore, the 300 former *leves* could indeed have ridden into battle as passengers of the 300 cavalry, as Livy describes.[51]

It seems therefore that the light-armed infantry were actually quite well armed in legions such as fought at Cannae, despite Samuels' arguments to the contrary. At least three-quarters of the light infantry were indeed armed as Polybius describes them, being equipped with a fairly large, round shield, several light javelins, a short sword, presumably of the type used by the heavy infantry, and an unadorned helmet (Polyb. 6.22.1–2). The remaining light troops were presumably too poor to afford such equipment and were armed only with a spear and a few javelins. As they apparently lacked their own officers, groups of light troops probably relied on unofficial 'natural leaders' for tactical command of small units. Polybius mentions how certain *velites* would wear a wolf's skin over their helmets so that they would be visible to their officers from a distance (Polyb. 6.22.3); such individuals, being keen to impress their superiors, could well have led by example. The light infantry as a whole were probably commanded by horn signals, which were audible from a distance (Krentz, 1991, p. 110); they may also have been to some extent co-ordinated by military tribunes, who could have ridden amongst them.

Cavalry

Three hundred cavalrymen served in the typical legion of Polybius' day, divided into ten squadrons of thirty men each (Polyb. 6.25.1). These squadrons, called *turmae* (Gr. *ilai*), were commanded by decurions (Gr. *ilarchai*), of whom there were three per *turma*, appointed by the military tribunes and assisted by three rear-rank officers, *optiones* (Gr. *ouragoi*), chosen by the decurions themselves. The first of the three decurions to be selected would command the squadron as a whole (Polyb. 6.25.1–2). This organisation suggests that the squadron was divided into three files of ten, each led by a decurion and closed by an *optio*, or six rows of five.[52] These files were clearly not independent tactical sub units, for the squadron was evidently intended to operate as a single entity, as is indicated by the superiority of one decurion over his two colleagues.[53]

Polybius discusses changes in the Roman cavalry in some detail:

> The cavalry are now armed like that of Greece, but in old times they had no cuirasses but fought in light undergarments, the result of which was that they were able to dismount and mount again at once with great dexterity and facility, but were exposed to great danger in close combat, as they were nearly naked. Their lances too were unserviceable in two respects. In the first place they made them so slender and pliant that it was impossible to take a steady aim, and before they could fix the head in anything, the shaking due to the mere motion of the horse caused most of them to break. Next, as they did not fit the butt ends with spikes, they could only deliver the first stroke with the point and after this if they broke they were of no further service. Their buckler was made of ox-hide, somewhat similar in shape to the round bossed cakes used at sacrifices. They were not of any use for attacking, as they were not firm enough; and when the leather covering peeled off and rotted owing to the rain, unserviceable as they were before, they now became entirely so. Since therefore their arms did not stand the test of experience, they soon took to making them in the Greek fashion.
>
> (Polyb. 6.25.3–8)

The important question here is whether or not the cavalry at Cannae were equipped like the Greek cavalry of Polybius' own day, or whether in 216 they were still using the inferior equipment described above. Rawson believes that the adoption of Hellenistic cavalry equipment took place either during the Second Punic War or else in the early second century, when Rome was becoming deeply entangled in Greek and Macedonian affairs, and Samuels goes so far as to include the cavalry reform in his rather spurious reform package of 211 (Rawson, 1971, pp. 20–1; Samuels, 1990, p. 13). Any of these theories would mean that the cavalry at Cannae were extremely poorly armed light cavalry.

None of these hypotheses are particularly convincing, however. Rome's first encounters with Greek cavalry were in the Pyrrhic Wars of 280–276, which seems the most likely catalyst for Rome improving her own cavalry forces.[54] In any case, it seems bizarre to date the change in Roman cavalry equipment to the early second century, considering that Polybius claims that the inferior equipment had been used in old times, but was soon replaced with Greek-style equipment. Polybius was writing in the mid-second century and would hardly refer to the 190s as old times. Furthermore, Samuels' dating of the reform to 211 is largely based on a belief that Rome's cavalry were ineffective before that date and far more potent after it. Such a belief is largely unfounded, as Polybius' accounts of early encounters between Roman and Numidian cavalry suggest no significant qualitative difference between the two (Polyb. 3.45, 65), while the annihilation of the citizen cavalry at Cannae can be largely explained by their being greatly outnumbered.[55]

It therefore seems almost certain that the cavalry at Cannae were armed in what Polybius describes as 'the Greek fashion'. Polybius implies that they wore cuirasses, which was certainly standard practice in the Hellenistic world from Alexander's day onward.[56] These cuirasses appear to have been very similar to those worn by the infantry, the only significant difference being a split at the thigh to enable the wearer to straddle a horse, as indicated by cavalrymen depicted on the Aemilius Paullus Monument.[57] Like Greek cavalry, the reformed Roman cavalry carried a long, strongly made spear with a butt spike for use as a secondary weapon should the shaft break (Polyb. 6.25.8–9; Bishop and Coulston, 1993, pp. 52–3; Bar-Kochva, 1976, p. 74; Warry, 1980, p. 82).

The nature of the cavalry shield is debatable, as the *parma equestris* carried by officers was clearly round, yet Polybius says that the cavalry used *thureoi*, which were, strictly speaking, oval in shape (Polyb. 6.25.7, 10). Polybius was probably using the term loosely, for cavalry shields were almost certainly round, as appears to have been the case in the Hellenistic world from some point in the third century. These shields were sturdy and quite large, and may occasionally have been faced with bronze (Rawson, 1971, p. 20; Connolly, 1998, p. 133; Snodgrass, 1999, p. 122).

The cavalry also appear to have carried swords, which were used as side-arms when spears were lost or broken; Livy describes the horror felt by Macedonian troops on seeing the hideous wounds inflicted upon their cavalrymen by Roman cavalry armed with the 'Spanish' sword (Liv. 31.34.1–5).[58] The *gladius* used by cavalrymen may well have been a little longer than that of the infantry, but it should not be confused with the long *spatha* of the Imperial period.[59]

It is difficult to estimate how effective such cavalry would actually have been. Cavalry could only manoeuvre properly on level ground (Veg. 3.13), and furthermore, all ancient cavalry lacked stirrups, which do not seem to have been adopted in China, from where they eventually reached Europe, until the fifth century AD (Dixon and Southern, 1992, p. 140; Warry, 1980, p. 82; Keegan, 1993, p. 285). Cavalry without stirrups could hardly have made good shock troops, as it would have been impossible for charging cavalrymen to remain seated once their lance had found its target without the leverage provided by stirrups (Luttwak, 1999 [1976], p. 43; Adcock, 1940, p. 25; Spence, 1993, pp. 44–5). Against this, the Macedonian cavalryman, famous in antiquity, seems to have released his *sarissa* at the moment of impact, or perhaps just before it, in order to avoid being unhorsed (Ferrill, 1985, pp. 176–7); presumably the Roman cavalry would have used their spears in a similar fashion. Even if they made poor shock troops against disciplined infantry, cavalry could be effective against enemy cavalry, and deadly against infantry once the lines had broken and troops were fleeing (Santosuosso, 1997, pp. 118–19).

Samuels argues that most Roman cavalrymen, who were young aristocrats for whom service in ten campaigns was a requirement for public office, would have been in their twenties, and consequently lacking in discipline, even if individual soldiers displayed courage on the battlefield. He even goes so far as to claim that 'with such personnel, it is possible that the spirit would have been more like that of an English public school outing, rather than of a military unit' (Samuels, 1990, p. 13). While this analysis may perhaps contain an element of truth it is overly harsh. Wealth and horsemanship were probably closely linked at Rome, suggesting that the cavalry would have been good riders (Dixon and Southern, 1992, p. 21). As for discipline, it is important to remember that from the age of 17 the most serious education of Roman aristocrats was in 'warfare and military command'; a sense of discipline was almost certainly deeply instilled in the young cavalrymen.[60]

The allies

Rome's allies supplied more than half the paper-strength of her total manpower resources, according to Polybius' account of the Gallic *tumultus* of 225 (Polyb. 2.24; Walbank, 1957, pp. 196 ff.; Brunt, 1971, p. 45). The allies were divided into two broad groups: Latins and Italians. The *socii nominis Latini*, 'Allies of the Latin Name', included a handful of old states which had not been granted citizenship after Rome's defeat of her insurgent allies in 338, as well as thirty Latin colonies, such as Placentia, Cremona, and Brundisium, strategically sited throughout Italy (Lazenby, 1978, p. 10; Badian, 1958, p. 23; Salmon, 1982, p. 64). Their main duty was to supply troops to Rome's army, and the greater part of the army was either Roman or Latin.[61] The other allies were Italians of various nations; Polybius mentions Sabines and Etruscans from central Italy, Umbrians and Sassinates from the Apennines, Veneti and Cenomani from Cisalpine Gaul, Iapygians and Messapians from Apulia, and Samnites, Lucanians, Marsi, Marrucini, Frentani, and Vestini from the southern Apennines (Polyb. 2.24).

The Latin allies were very closely linked to Rome, and have been described as Rome's allies by status rather than by treaty. It is significant that no Latin state abandoned Rome for Carthage during the Second Punic War, despite Hannibal's overtures (Sherwin-White, 1973, p. 96; Lazenby, 1978, p. 10), although in 209 twelve Latin colonies declared that they could no longer supply men or money to Rome (Liv. 27.9.7–14). Many of the Latin colonists were descended from Roman citizens, who had accepted Latin status in place of Roman citizenship in order to make a fresh start.[62] The culture of these colonies was virtually identical to that of Rome, with the same gods, similar institutions, and certain rights in Roman law, and, at least in the second century, Latins could regard themselves as Roman; full citizenship could easily be attained through settling on formal Roman territory (Lazenby, 1978, p. 10; Badian, 1958, p. 23). All the initial settlers in these colonies spoke Latin, even non-Romans, and natives had almost certainly adopted the language within two or three generations (Salmon, 1982, p. 65). In fact, the settlement of 338 did much to create a process by which the concepts of *Romanitas* and *Latinitas* became interchangeable (Badian, 1958, p. 23).

Rome's Italian allies, the *socii* or *foederati* proper, were a diverse lot, being politically, geographically, ethnically, culturally, and often linguistically distinct (Lazenby, 1978, p. 10; Salmon, 1982, p. 66). They were in theory independent, although in practice Rome was clearly the dominant partner in the alliances. Some were linked to Rome by *foedus aequum*, a treaty between equals; these may have been states which voluntarily allied themselves with Rome, rather than being forcibly allied through defeat in war.[63] The allies who did not fall into this category have often been described as tied to Rome by *foedus iniquum*, but there is no evidence for the Romans ever having described these alliances as such. In any case, it would have been diplomatically tactless to proclaim an ally's inferiority in this fashion, and it is more likely that all alliances were, on paper, between equals (Badian, 1958, p. 23; Lazenby, 1978, p. 11).

The common requirement for all of Rome's allies was to supply men for her armies; the Greek allies in southern Italy were probably *socii navales* who supplied ships rather than infantry or cavalry (Lazenby, 1996a, p. 12; Badian, 1958, pp. 28–30). In general, according to Polybius, there were as many allied infantry as Roman citizens in any given Roman army, along with three times as many allied cavalry as citizen cavalry (Polyb. 6.26.7). However, in reality it seems that it was not unusual for allied infantry significantly to outnumber their Roman counterparts, for example at the battle of the Trebia in 218, where the combined consular armies had 16,000 Roman and 20,000 allied infantry (Polyb. 3.72.11; Walbank, 1957, pp. 200, 709). The allied troops were enrolled in their own states and would take the standard oath before setting out to join the assembled citizen forces under their own commander and paymaster (Polyb. 6.21.5). For administrative purposes the allies were enrolled in cohorts which varied in size; Livy cites cohorts of 460, 500, and 600 men (Liv. 23.17.11, 17.8, 28.45.20). This variance in size was probably due to the differing sizes of each settlement's population, rather than annual changes in Rome's manpower requirements.[64]

The organisation and equipment of the *socii* are difficult to ascertain. The allies were divided between the consuls, each group assembling with the consul's two legions at the consul's rendezvous point (Polyb. 6.26.2–5). There they would be organised by the Prefects of the Allies *(praefecti sociorum)*, Roman citizens appointed by the consuls to organise and command the allies. They probably had similar duties to Rome's military tribunes and may have commanded groups of cohorts in battle (Lazenby, 1978, p. 13; Suolahti, 1955, pp. 200–1). Polybius notes that there were twelve such prefects (Polyb. 6.26.5), which is normally interpreted to mean six per consular army, or three per allied brigade (Suolahti, 1955, p. 200; Lazenby, 1978, p. 13); it is possible, however, that Polybius is referring simply to there being twelve prefects at a given rendezvous point, which seems to be the context of his claim. On this basis, there would have been as many prefects as military tribunes, which certainly seems likely, considering that they had at least as many men to look after (Keppie, 1998, p. 23). The allies were divided into three groups: one-third of the cavalry and one-fifth of the infantry were classed as *extraordinarii,* select troops of uncertain function, while the remaining troops were divided into two brigades, termed the left and right wings (Polyb. 6.26.7–9). Each allied brigade, or *ala sociorum,* was divided for administrative purposes into a number of cohorts. Keppie claims (1998, p. 22) that there were usually ten per *ala,* but this number could obviously vary, as Livy mentions the army in Spain being reduced to one legion and fifteen allied cohorts (Liv. 20.41.5). Although the *extraordinarii* had a special place in the order of march and in camp (Polyb. 6.40.4, 8, 31), they do not seem to have had a special role in battle and may have simply served with the rest of the allies.

Like the legions, each *ala sociorum* seems to have been tactically subdivided into maniples. Describing the Roman army at Ilipa in 206, Polybius notes that the term 'cohort' was here used to refer to a combination of skirmishers and three maniples (Polyb. 11.23.1), presumably one each of *hastati*, *principes*, and *triarii*, along with their respective complements of light infantry. In this case he is probably speaking of Roman citizens rather than allies, but it is likely that allied cohorts were organised on similar lines.[65] Livy claims that Latin troops of the mid-fourth century fought in the same manipular system as was used by the Romans themselves (Liv. 8.8.14–16). This claim may, however, be based purely on a retrojection of a story from the first-century Social War, or even be an invention by an annalist or antiquarian (Oakley, 1998, p. 475). Even if Livy's description is incorrect in this regard, it seems that maniples were a standard tactical formation in Italian warfare in the early third century, as Pyrrhus' battle formations involved alternating Italian maniples and Hellenistic phalanx units (Polyb. 18.28.10–11). In any case, Polybius' silence on this subject suggests that the allies were organised and equipped along Roman lines, which would certainly have been desirable as it would have enabled them to interact smoothly with the legions. Presumably their traditional arms and tactics were gradually replaced by Roman methods and weaponry (Keppie, 1998, p. 22; Lazenby, 1978, p. 13).

Lazenby suggests that since neither Polybius nor Livy ever mentions allied light infantry, it is possible that the allies did not actually supply light infantry (Lazenby, 1978, p. 13). However, in the legions the skirmishers were distributed for administrative purposes among the maniples (Polyb. 6.24.4–5), something which may well also have been the case with the allies. It certainly seems plausible that younger or poorer allied troops would have served as light infantry, like the Roman *velites* or *rorarii*. As noted already, the allied cavalry force was generally three times larger than that of the citizens; these cavalry were presumably also from the wealthiest strata of society, as suggested by Livy's reference to young noblemen from Tarentum who served at the battles of Lake Trasimene and Cannae (Liv. 24.13.1). The cavalry were commanded, at least from the second century, by Roman *praefecti equitum*, presumably with local commanders at squadron level (Keppie, 1998, p. 23; Suolahti, 1955, pp. 203–4). As with the citizens, allied cavalry were better paid than infantry (Polyb. 6.39.14–15). The cost of rations was probably borne by Rome, with the allied communities paying their own troops (Walbank, 1967, p. 648).

Syracusan light troops

In addition to the forces supplied by Rome's Latin and Italian allies, the army at Cannae apparently also included a force of light infantry supplied by Hiero of Syracuse. Livy describes them as a 1,000-strong force of archers and slingers, supplied on Hiero's own initiative as he realised that they would be particularly useful against Hannibal's skirmishers (Liv. 22.37.7–9). According to Polybius, however, the Romans had actually appealed to Syracuse for help, and Hiero then provided 500 Cretan troops, presumably archers, and 1,000 shield-bearing (*peltophoroi*) light infantry (Polyb. 3.75.7). Archers would have been very useful as a supplement to Rome's skirmishers, for the ancient bow had a greater range than the javelin (Gabriel and Metz, 1991, p. 59; Goldsworthy, 1996, pp. 183 ff.). No indication is given of these troops' terms of service, but the more or less simultaneous provision by Syracuse of large quantities of grain to Rome (Liv. 22.37.6) probably indicates that the Syracusan light troops received their rations, and perhaps pay, from a centralised Roman source, although both rations and pay may ultimately have been of Syracusan origin.

Conclusion

The Roman army which fought at Cannae was substantially the same as that which Polybius described in his sixth book and contrasted with the

Macedonian phalanx in his eighteenth book. Heavily armed line infantry made up by far the largest and most important element in the army in battle, as light infantry was used primarily for preliminary skirmishing, while cavalry served basically to protect the flanks of the legions. The line infantry were deployed, as a rule, in three clear lines, each line being divided into ten semi-independent tactical sub-units called maniples, which gave the lines a degree of flexibility. The trilinear system served to ensure that the Romans could launch or withstand a series of assaults, by replacing tired and injured men with fresh troops.

The Roman legions operated on the militia principle, whereby all the legionaries were required to serve as a condition of citizenship. Service was in many ways an honour, which would have contributed in no small degree towards morale. *Esprit de corps* would have been extremely high, because of this and because of how the legions presented themselves as a society within a society. New recruits were required to swear oaths of loyalty on joining their units, and constant training would have reinforced the feeling that soldiers were part of a greater whole. The century, the legion's basic administrative unit, seems to have had the most emotional significance for soldiers, who venerated the standards and lived with the men alongside whom they would have fought. The centurions, the experienced commanders of these sub-units, were of the same social class as their men and were prized for their tenacity and reliability, which must have contributed immensely to the effectiveness of their men.

4

THE CARTHAGINIAN ARMY

Introduction

Unfortunately, even less is known about the Carthaginian army which fought at Cannae than about the Roman army commanded by Paullus and Varro. This is not particularly surprising, as Polybius, the most reliable source for the Second Punic War, considered himself to be writing 'pragmatic history' for a mainly Greek audience forced to face the reality of life under Roman rule (Walbank, 1972, chs 1, 3; 1966, pp. 46–9). In practice, this meant that Polybius' main aim was to explain Roman methods and institutions to future Greek politicians:

> the soundest education and training for a life in active politics is the study of history, and . . . the surest and indeed the only method of learning how to bear bravely the vicissitudes of fortune, is to recall the calamities of others. . . . For who is so worthless or indolent as not to wish to know by what means and under what system of polity the Romans in less than fifty-three years have succeeded in subjecting nearly the whole inhabited world to their sole government – a thing unique in history?
>
> (Polyb. 1.1.2–5)

Since Carthage had effectively ceased to be a threat to the Greek world following the loss of her overseas territories in the Second Punic War, a description of Carthaginian institutions would have been largely irrelevant to Polybius' purposes.

Polybius' brief analysis of Carthage's constitution and military system is as a result intended purely as a contrast to what he regards as the far superior Roman system, the subject of his sixth book (Polyb. 6.51–2). His observations on Carthaginian military institutions, which have been described as 'an orgy of rhetorical antithesis' (Griffith, 1935, p. 231), are contemptuously dismissive of the Carthaginian army, stating that the:

Carthaginians entirely neglect their infantry, though they do play some slight attention to their cavalry. The reason for this is that the troops they employ are foreign and mercenary, whereas those of the Romans are native of the soil and citizens. . . . [The Carthaginians] depend for the maintenance of their freedom on the courage of a mercenary force but the Romans on their own valour and on the aid of their allies. . . . Italians in general naturally excel Phoenicians and Africans in bodily strength and personal courage.

(Polyb. 6.52.3–10)

Although heavily biased in favour of the Roman system, and hence against that of Carthage, Polybius nevertheless seems to have been substantially correct in his description of Carthaginian institutions. In the era of the Punic Wars, Carthage did indeed rely almost entirely on allied or mercenary troops under Carthaginian officers, except when the city itself was threatened, in which case a citizen militia would be assembled (e.g. Polyb. 1.33.6, 73.1–2, 15.11.2–5; Lazenby, 1996a, pp. 26–7; 1978, pp. 14–15; Griffith, 1935, pp. 207–33).

It is probably safe to assume that even had he wanted to, Polybius would have been unable to write about the Carthaginian army in the same depth as the Roman system. His internment in Rome between 168 and 150 may have given him some opportunities to observe the Roman army in action, but it is unlikely that he saw any Carthaginian soldiers until the Third Punic War, when he was present with Scipio at the fall of Carthage in 146. He had probably finished his account of the first two Punic Wars by this date, and in any case the Carthaginian army of the mid-second century was strikingly different from that which served under the Barcids, for Carthage's defeat in 202 had effectively ended her employment of mercenaries (Griffiths, 1935, p. 233). In addition, as discussed in the previous chapter, it is possible that Polybius used some sort of handbook for military tribunes as a source for his description of the Roman army, but such a handbook was almost certainly unavailable for Carthaginian officers, given that the composition of Carthaginian armies was so unstable.

The paucity of evidence on Carthage's army has led it to be almost entirely neglected by modern academics.[1] However, enthusiastic wargamers, notably Duncan Head, have gone some way towards filling the gap. Head's research, while admittedly frequently conjectural, is largely based on snippets of information gathered from Polybius and Livy, supported by lengthier passages in the work of later writers such as Strabo, and by what little archaeological evidence is available. It is fairly detailed and emphasises the traditional equipment and combat styles of the various national contingents in Carthage's army. This is probably the best possible approach to the subject, given that Hannibal employed a wide range of foreign troops, such as Libyans, Numidians, Iberians, and Celts (Polyb. 9.19.4).

This multinational character of Carthaginian armies is the key to under-standing the internal dynamics and military effectiveness of Hannibal's army at Cannae. As Polybius realised, Carthaginian citizens made up a very small part of their army, being restricted, as a rule, to positions of authority and not serving in the ranks. The bulk of the army was composed of subject or allied levies and foreign mercenaries.

No attempt appears to have been made to standardise these troops, who were neither armed nor trained to fight in a uniform manner. Instead, they appear to have been equipped and to have fought according to the customs of their respective nations. For example, the Balearians fought as infantry skirmishers armed with slings, while the Numidian cavalry were armed with javelins and fought as skirmishers rather than as shock cavalry (Gsell, 1928, pp. 374–6; Head, 1982, pp. 150, 155–6). Such troops were organised on the basis of nationality, since it would have been impractical to deploy troops together who did not understand each other or lacked similar weapons and combat styles. These national units were not subdivided in a uniform fashion as administrative and tactical subdivisions had to be appropriate for diverse national customs and combat styles. It is possible that standards were used in battle to rally the various units of the army, but there is no proof of this, as such standards are referred to by Livy only when he lists Roman trophies.[2]

For what it is worth, the only known disciplinary rule for Carthaginian armies is to be found in Plato's *Laws*, which notes that the consumption of alcohol is forbidden in Carthage's armies (Plat. *Leg.* 674a4). This law may have slipped by Hannibal's time, however, for according to Polybius, when the Romans had been victorious at the Metaurus in 207 they pillaged the Carthaginian camp, finding numerous drunken and sleeping Celts (Polyb. 11.3.1); against this, the passage looks like another example of the disparagement of 'barbarians' so often found in ancient literature.

The higher-ranking officers in Hannibal's army were almost exclusively Carthaginian, and their duties and characteristics are dealt with in Chapter 5. Lower-ranking officers seem to have shared the nationality of the men who followed them (Connolly, 1998, p. 149; Lancel, 1998, p. 62; Gsell, 1928, pp. 391–2). Accounts of events at Lilybaeum during the First Punic War make this clear, as Polybius records how the mercenary leaders there attempted to betray the town to the Romans (Polyb. 1.43). There are also many references to mercenary officers in his account of the outbreak of the war between Carthage and her mercenaries following the First Punic War (Polyb. 1.66.6, 67.10, 69.1, 11, 70.2). It should be borne in mind, however, that it is likely that the Mercenaries' War of 241 to 237 led Hamilcar and his successors in Spain to reform the Carthaginian army in order to diminish the threat of future revolts, and if this was the case, the command struc-ture might well have been changed. That said, the Celtic elements in Hannibal's army certainly seem to have had their own officers, even if other national groupings did not (Polyb. 8.30.4).

Unlike the Roman army, therefore, which is easily divided into cavalry, line infantry, and infantry skirmishers, it is generally more convenient to analyse Hannibal's army in terms of nationality (Bagnall, 1990, pp. 8–11; Lancel, 1998, pp. 60–1; Connolly, 1998, pp. 148–52; Samuels, 1990, pp. 17–20; Lazenby, 1978, pp. 14–15; 1996a, pp. 26–7). This chapter is thus divided into sections on African, Spanish, and Celtic troops, examining their equipment and combat style in order to aid attempts to reconstruct how they fought at Cannae. It also considers the terms of service of different types of troops, as this can shed light on the army's internal dynamics and *esprit de corps*, which would in turn have affected their morale at Cannae. As the infantry skirmishers seem to have been the only element of Hannibal's army not organised by nationality, or at least not recognised as such by the sources,[3] these are examined separately from the national groupings.

Africans

The term 'Africans' is here used in the modern sense, and refers to any of Hannibal's troops which hailed from the continent of Africa, rather than merely to the native subjects of Carthage, which is how Livy uses the term. There were several African elements in Hannibal's army: Carthaginian citizens, who seem to have served only in a 'staff' capacity and will therefore be dealt with in the following chapter; Libyans; Liby-Phoenicians; Numidians; Moors; and Gaetulians.

Libyans

The native subjects of Carthage, referred to by Polybius and Livy respectively as 'Libyans' (*Libyes*) and 'Africans' (*Afri*), supplied the core of the Carthaginian army; as late as 218, 12,000 of the 20,000 line infantry Hannibal brought to Italy were Libyan, the remainder being of Spanish origin (Polyb. 3.56.4). Libyans had apparently served in Carthaginian armies from a very early date. At some point in the sixth century Carthage had ceased to rely solely on a citizen levy and began to employ mercenaries and allied troops, many of whom must have been Libyan (Griffith, 1935, pp. 207–8). However, the earliest Libyans to fight for Carthage, as at Himera in 480 (Hdt. 7.165), would have been mercenaries rather than subject levies, as Carthage only began to acquire dependent territory in Africa some years after her defeat at Himera (Lancel, 1995, pp. 257a; Warmington, 1960, p. 40).

In general, it seems that 'Libyans' was a term used to refer collectively to the lighter-skinned inhabitants of North Africa, so as to distinguish them from the darker-skinned 'Ethiopians' to the south (Hdt. 4.196; Law, 1978, pp. 140–1). However, whenever Polybius mentions Libyans he specifically means the native subjects of Carthage, rather than the Numidians and Moors to the west of the city (Law, 1978, p. 129). These groups, nowadays described as Libyco-Berbers (Desanges, 1981, p. 428), appear to have been of essentially the same ethnic background – Berber stock, possibly with some Negro admixture – the main difference being that the two western groups primarily practised pastoralism whereas the Carthaginian subjects practised a more settled form of agriculture.[4] Such distinctions are not uncommon in ancient writers, and the truth was doubtless far more complex (Shaw, 1982–3, pp. 13–15; Law, 1978, p. 144). The Libyans, who lived opposite Sicily, south and just east of Carthage, seem to have had relatively fair complexions, much lighter than the swarthy Numidians, and many of the native North Africans had blue eyes and light-coloured hair, differing little from other Mediterranean peoples.[5] Modern Berbers are a very diverse group of peoples, whose main connections are linguistic (Brett and Fentress, 1996, pp. 3–4), and it seems that the Libyans had their own language, for inscriptions from the Roman period, written in a non-Punic local language, have been found throughout North Africa from modern Morocco to Tripolitana (Millar, 1968, pp. 128 ff.). However, this language may have had more than one dialect, as several Libyan alphabets are known, and it is possible that Punic was common among the élite, where it would have been a mark of status (Mattingly and Hitchner, 1995, p. 172).

Although, as has been pointed out, the first Libyans to serve in the Carthaginian army must have been mercenaries, it seems likely that the Libyans were obliged to provide soldiers for Carthage once they had been conquered (Warmington, 1960, p. 40). They evidently supplied a large portion of the army, since Plutarch, writing of the Carthaginian defeat at the Crimesus in 341, remarked that there was no record of so many Carthaginian citizens having been killed in any previous battle as:

> they generally employ Libyans, Iberians, and Numidians to fight their battles, so that when they were defeated the loss was borne by the other nations.
>
> (Plut., *Vit. Tim.* 28.6)

It appears that the Libyans made up a quarter of the Carthaginian infantry which faced the threat posed by Agathocles in 311, supplying 10,000 of a total of 40,000 troops, with possibly two-thirds of the remainder being Greek, Greek soldiers having greatly impressed the Carthaginians in their war against Timoleon (Diod. 19.106; Griffith, 1935, p. 210).

At the outbreak of the Mercenaries' War in 241, when there were over 20,000 mercenaries in Carthaginian employment, the largest portion of the army was Libyan, despite there also being Iberians, Celts, Ligurians, Balearians, and some Greeks (Polyb. 1.67.13, 7). These Libyans were probably mercenaries rather than subject levies, and Polybius certainly identifies them as such by treating them as part of the combined mercenary force. It is possible that during or before the First Punic War the Carthaginians abandoned the practice of levying troops from their native subjects and instead demanded a higher rate of tribute in order to hire more foreign mercenaries (Griffith, 1935, p. 219). The rate of taxation was certainly very high at this time; apparently half of the Libyan crops were demanded as tribute whereas the previous rate was probably 25 per cent, assuming that the peasantry's taxes had, like those of the townsmen, been doubled (Polyb. 1.72.1–2; Law, 1978, p. 130; Warmington, 1960, p. 72; Walbank, 1957, p. 134). The employment of Libyans as mercenaries rather than as subject levies may also explain their apparent absence from the Carthaginian army which Xanthippus commanded against Regulus in 255 (Polyb. 1.33.6–7; Griffith, 1935, pp. 212–13, 219).

It is uncertain whether the Libyans in Hannibal's own army served as mercenaries or levies. Although Polybius distinguishes between the mercenaries and the Libyans deployed at Zama in 202 (Polyb. 15.11.1–2), Livy seems to regard the Libyans as being mercenaries rather than allies or subjects (Liv. 27.4.2, 5.11, 28.44.5, 29.3.13).[6] Whereas it is possible that there was a mixture of subject levies and mercenaries in the Libyan ranks, it is surely equally likely that the mercenary revolt in 241 led the Carthaginians to levy troops from their Libyan subjects rather than hire them as mercenaries. Ultimately the official status of the Libyan troops was probably largely irrelevant; their true loyalty was neither to their homeland nor to the distant paymaster that was Carthage, but rather to each other and to their Barcid commander (Griffith, 1935, p. 232).

Libyans were known for their agility and powers of endurance and traditionally fought as skirmishers (Warmington, 1960, p. 41; Gsell, 1928, p. 359; Lancel, 1998, p. 60); they were armed with javelins (Hdt. 7.71), perhaps used with a small dagger and a small round shield (Lancel, 1998, p. 60; Head, 1982, p. 145; Law, 1978, p. 145; Gsell, 1928, p. 359). However, most Libyans in the Carthaginian army served as line infantry and must have been armed accordingly. They seem to have been armed by the Carthaginian state, rather than being responsible for supplying their own equipment, if the reported surrender of 200,000 Carthaginian cuirasses to Rome during the Third Punic War is historical (Polyb. 36.6.7; App., *Pun.* 80). Carthage would never have required so many cuirasses, as her entire population including non-combatants such as women and children probably never exceeded 400,000 (Warmington, 1960, p. 124), and only 10,000 troops, including mercenaries, could be raised to serve under Hamilcar Barca during the Mercenaries' War (Polyb. 1.75.1–2). It is reasonable to assume that the equipment mentioned must have been intended for the use of Carthage's subject levies.[7] Perhaps Carthage was reluctant to give her subjects the responsibility of providing their own weapons when they served as soldiers – after all, a subject people with the right to bear arms could pose a significant threat to their masters.[8]

Libyan organisation and equipment

How then were these Libyans armed and equipped? At the Crimesus in 341 a 10,000-strong force of heavy infantry, most of whom must have been Libyan levies, were assumed by their Greek enemies to have been a purely Carthaginian force, indicating that the Libyans were armed to some degree in a similar fashion to the Carthaginians. The Carthaginian citizens were armed in a fashion not unlike Greek hoplites, wearing bronze helmets and iron breastplates and using large circular white shields, spears, and swords (Plut., *Vit. Tim.* 27–8). Soldiers armed in this fashion are depicted on Carthaginian stelae (Head, 1982, pp. 140–2). Armed in a pseudo-Greek style, the Libyans and Carthaginian citizens of the mid-fourth century presumably fought in something like a Greek phalanx.

Polybius describes the Carthaginian army under Xanthippus in 255 as a phalanx (Polyb. 1.33.6), a term he also uses for Hannibal's army at Zama in 202 (Polyb. 15.12.7). The fact that Libyans fought side by side with Carthaginian citizens and *Carthaginienses* (presumably citizens of the Phoenician colony at Gades) at Zama and Ilipa respectively suggests that they were still armed in much the same way as their Carthaginian masters (Polyb. 15.11.2; Liv. 28.14.4).

On the basis of the above facts, it is frequently claimed that Hannibal's Libyans fought as some sort of spear-armed phalanx, although the exact nature of their equipment is much disputed.[9] To assume that the Libyans of Hannibal's day normally fought in a phalanx armed with spears of some sort is in any case anachronistic. Considering the developments in warfare throughout the Mediterranean world since the mid-fourth century, it is foolish to assume that Carthaginian and, by implication, Libyan infantry were armed and fought in essentially the same way in 216 as in 341.[10]

Furthermore, it is unwise to place too much emphasis on the fact that Xanthippus' army in 255 and Hannibal's in 202 are described by Polybius as 'phalanxes'. The term 'phalanx' need not mean a formal hoplite or Macedonian-style phalanx, but simply a large body of men fighting *en masse*. Asclepiodotus, for instance, speaks of phalanxes of cavalry and light infantry (Asclep. 1.4). Polybius also refers to the Roman *hastati* and the Carthaginian mercenaries at Zama as phalanxes (Polyb. 15.12.7), even though the former fought in their usual manipular formation, whereas the latter seem to have been a medley of light-armed missile troops and swordsmen (App., *Pun.* 40; Walbank, 1967, pp. 456–7; Lazenby, 1978, p. 222).

In addition, the evidence for the entire Xanthippus episode can be forced too far. Polybius and Philinus, the most probable source for Polybius' account of the affair (Walbank, 1957, p. 65), were both Greek, and Polybius' description of the events of 255 carries a clear subtext about the superiority of the Greek way of war over that of the barbarian Carthaginians, perhaps an indication that his account is not entirely objective (Warmington,

1960, p. 156). Even if Polybius did not intend to present Xanthippus in this light, passages such as the following give little definite information and are thus easily misinterpreted:

> ... on his leading the army out and drawing it up in good order before the city and even beginning to manoeuvre some portions of it correctly and give the word of command in the orthodox military terms, the contrast to the incompetence of the former generals was so striking that the soldiery expressed their approval by cheers and were eager to engage the enemy.
>
> (Polyb. 1.32.7)

This entire incident seems to be the origin of the tradition of somewhat dubious authenticity that the Carthaginians were educated in the art of war by the Greeks (Delbrück, 1990 [1920], p. 303). Vegetius, the late fourth- or early fifth-century AD author of a Latin manual on warfare, claimed that not only did Xanthippus conclude the entire campaign for the Carthaginians, but even more extravagantly, that Hannibal acquired the services of a Spartan tactician to aid him in his Italian campaigns (Veg. 3. *praef.*); presumably he is referring to Sosylos, who, according to Cornelius Nepos, taught Hannibal Greek and wrote an account of his campaigns (Nep. *Hann.* 13.3). There is, however, no evidence to indicate that Sosylos served Hannibal in an advisory capacity, or that, as Lazenby speculates, he served under Xanthippus in 255 (Wheeler, 1983, pp. 2, 16; Lazenby, 1985, p. 170).

What Xanthippus did with the Carthaginian army is unclear. Despite what some modern writers claim, perhaps following Vegetius' lead, there is no evidence that Xanthippus reorganised the Carthaginian army on Greek lines.[11] It is impossible to ascertain what form Xanthippus' 'orthodox' commands took, for instance. Assuming they were oral, rather than visual or horn signals, were they in Greek or Punic? The former might seem more likely in the context of a Spartan officer commanding a Hellenistic-era army,[12] but Greek was at most a 'language of command' in this army. Diodorus records Xanthippus speaking with the Carthaginians through interpreters (Diod. 23.16.1) and, according to Polybius' account of the Mercenaries' War, Punic seems to have been something of a *lingua franca* for the army; he describes the Celtic chief Autaritas rising to prominence in the insurgent mercenary army through his fluency in Punic, a tongue with which all veterans were to some degree familiar (Polyb. 1.80.6). It is also significant that Xanthippus seems to have had no particular difficulty in manoeuvring the Celtic and Spanish elements in the army, neither of which were spear-armed; this perhaps suggests that it was not necessary for the Libyans or Carthaginians to serve as a spear-armed phalanx under him either. It therefore seems that the Carthaginian army was nowhere near as 'Hellenistic' as it might first appear.

The conventional weapons of the Carthaginian infantryman during the Third Punic War in the mid-second century were light spears, a sword, and an oval or oblong shield,[13] and, as is shown below, it is extremely likely that these were the standard weaponry of Hannibal's Libyans over fifty years earlier.

The Libyans at Cannae

According to Polybius and Livy, these Libyans were armed with the best of the Roman equipment that had been looted after the battles of the Trebia and Lake Trasimene (Polyb. 3.87.3, 114.1; Liv. 22.46.4). It is difficult to know quite what this means. Were the Libyans issued only with defensive equipment such as shields, helmets, greaves, and body armour, or did they also receive offensive weapons such as *pila* and *gladii*? Some Carthaginian troops certainly seem to have been equipped with Roman shields, which made it difficult to distinguish them from Roman troops,[14] and Livy notes that the Libyans could easily have been mistaken for actual Romans, armed as they were with mainly Roman equipment (Liv. 22.46.4). The *scutum*, being such a large and distinctive shield, could have created this illusion from a distance, but for the illusion to have been maintained at a close quarters the Libyans probably wore Roman-style greaves and helmets.[15] Whatever Roman body armour was worn probably consisted of the mail cuirasses worn by those Romans who could afford them, rather than the standard issue, and probably rather ineffective, *pectorales*. Linen corselets may have been worn by any Libyans not fully equipped with Roman defensive equipment (Head, 1982, p. 144).

So much for defensive equipment. A thornier issue is whether or not the Libyans were armed with *pila* and *gladii*. If they were, it would seem almost certain that they were used to fighting as swordsmen rather than like Greek or Macedonian-style spearmen, since it is unlikely that Hannibal would have risked retraining his men while on campaign.[16] The absurdity of simply assuming that there had been no significant changes in Libyan equipment since 341, when they certainly were spearmen, has been noted, and the fact that they clearly used the large, heavy, Roman shield at Cannae surely indicates that they had not adopted the Macedonian-style pike – such a weapon could be extremely heavy and required both hands for use, something which would have been impossible while carrying a Roman *scutum*.[17]

Polybius' criticism of the Carthaginian occupation of a hill near Adys in 256, while attempting to relieve the besieged town, rests on his claim that elephants and cavalry were of little use save on level ground (Polyb. 1.30.6–7); his failure to make such an observation about Carthage's infantry might suggest that they were not similarly handicapped, and were probably capable, to some degree, of operating on irregular terrain. In other words, it is unlikely that they were spearmen who served in phalanxes.[18]

After evaluating the situation some months later, the Spartan mercenary Xanthippus concluded that the Carthaginian army would be best suited to fighting on level ground owing to its strength in cavalry and elephants (Polyb. 1.32.2–4), again possibly suggesting that level ground was not absolutely necessary for the infantry to operate effectively, even though by this stage the bulk of the infantry were Carthage's citizen militia.

Polybius' and Livy's accounts of the fighting at Lake Trasimene during the Second Punic War support this hypothesis, as their descriptions are much more convincing if the Libyans are thought of as swordsmen rather than spearmen. According to both writers, the Carthaginian army attacked the Romans from higher ground, charging downhill simultaneously at numerous points to attack the Romans on all sides (Polyb. 3.84.1–4; Liv. 22.4). Although it was not unheard of for a spear-armed phalanx to charge downhill,[19] it is difficult to see how this would have happened in practice. Running with spears was almost certainly hazardous, as their length could have caused individuals to trip, which would have had a 'snowball effect', possibly putting entire sections of the phalanx in disarray. Swords would have been less cumbersome, and, if kept in their scabbards until the last possible moment after javelins were thrown, would have allowed their users to charge downhill relatively unencumbered.

Even if the Libyans did fight as close-order spearmen during Carthage's first war with Rome, it is highly improbable that they did so under Hannibal. As noted above, it is unlikely that their adoption of Roman equipment after the victories at the Trebia and Lake Trasimene included offensive equipment unless they were already used to fighting as swordsmen. Pompeian legionaries under Lucius Afranius at Ilerda in Spain in 49 were described by Caesar as fighting in a very loose order, having adopted the tactics of the Spanish tribes they had grown used to fighting against (Caes., B Civ 1.44); Libyan troops had fought in Spain under the Barcids since 237, and it is very probable that they too had adopted local combat styles. Tactics and weaponry are inextricably linked, and it is therefore likely that the Libyans used Spanish equipment. This is not surprising, considering that the Romans are often thought to have adopted the *gladius* and *pilum* from Spanish mercenaries serving Carthage during the First Punic War; it would be strange if Carthage had not supplied her own troops with such efficient equipment. This equipment generally consisted of large oval or oblong shields, short cut-and-thrust swords, and throwing spears – in other words, the typical panoply of the Spanish footsoldier was essentially the same as that of the Roman legionary. If this was the case, the Libyans at Cannae, accustomed to Spanish equipment, may have worn virtually the entire Roman panoply, for it was not fundamentally different from their former equipment, though perhaps of higher quality.

Liby-Phoenicians

In 218, according to Polybius, Hannibal had a force of 450 Liby-Phoenician and Libyan cavalry stationed in Spain (Polyb. 3.33.15); Livy believes that this force was exclusively Liby-Phoenician (Liv. 21.22.3). There is no record of Liby-Phoenicians having served under Hannibal on his Italian campaign, but considering the fact that so many Liby-Phoenician cavalry were introduced to Spain that year, it seems likely that Hannibal's own expeditionary force included some Liby-Phoenicians.

Livy describes the Liby-Phoenicians as a mixed race, half Punic and half African (Liv. 21.22.3), but this is overly simplistic, as the term generally refers to the inhabitants of the Phoenician colonies along the African coast – Liby-Phoenicians could be people of Phoenician race living in these colonies, or simply native Libyans who had adopted Phoenician culture (Lancel, 1995, p. 288; Walbank, 1957, p. 363; Warmington, 1960, p. 55). They seem to have had the same laws as the Carthaginians, in the main, but despite Warmington's suggestion that they had the same rights as Carthaginian citizens, they were liable to dues on imports and exports, as well as military service on certain occasions when Carthaginians seem to have been exempt (Polyb. 7.9.5; Walbank, 1967, pp. 53–4; Lazenby, 1996a, pp. 24–5; Warmington, 1960, pp. 70–1).

Although certain modern writers believe the African line infantry to have been either Liby-Phoenician or a combination of Libyans and Liby-Phoenicians (Connolly, 1998, p. 148; Healy, 1994, p. 20; Warry, 1980, p. 122), there is no evidence that the Liby-Phoenicians ever served as infantry in Carthaginian armies. The 450 Liby-Phoenician horsemen sent to Spain in 218 are never described by either Polybius or Livy, but since Polybius distinguishes between Numidian and 'bridled and steady' cavalry in his account of the battle of the Trebia (Polyb. 3.65.6), it is probable that any Liby-Phoenician cavalry in his army of Italy were 'heavy' cavalry, unlike the Numidian skirmishers. How they were armed is uncertain, but it was quite possibly in the Hellenistic fashion, wearing a mail coat or plated cuirass and carrying a lance and shield.[20] Livy's reference to Carthaginian cavalry fighting the Vaccaei in 219 from a distance and up close, suggesting that they were armed with javelins and swords, is not evidence to the contrary, as many of these 'Carthaginian' cavalry were doubtless Numidians and Iberians (Liv. 21.5.14). Duncan Head (1982, p. 143) has tentatively identified as Liby-Phoenician a North African figurine of a bare-headed cavalryman wearing a Hellenistic 'muscled' plate cuirass and carrying two light spears or javelins as well as a round shield with a rounded boss and raised rim. If Liby-Phoenician cavalry were indeed equipped in this fashion, they almost certainly also carried some sort of sword for use when their missiles had been thrown – a curved slashing sword like the Greek *kopis* would have been the ideal choice, according to Xenophon (Xen., *Eq.* 12.11; Snodgrass, 1999, pp. 97, 109).

Finally, it is worth noting that there was obviously considerable scope for promotion for Liby-Phoenicians in Hannibal's army. Between 212 and 210, the Numidian cavalry fighting in Sicily were commanded by a Liby-Phoenician referred to by Livy as Muttines (Liv. 25.40.5).[21] He is described as an experienced soldier trained in the art of war by Hannibal, and it is clear that Hannibal trusted him since he assigned such an important role to him.

Numidians

Although it is impossible to ascertain how many Numidian cavalry fought at Cannae, modern writers tend to assume that there were no more than 4,000 of them.[22] The Numidians were of Berber stock, possibly with some Negro admixture, and were generally distinguished from their neighbours by practising a nomadic form of pastoralism rather than a more settled form of agriculture, though this distinction, as already noted, was almost certainly too simplistic. Indeed, the Numidians seem to have been frequent victims of negative stereotyping in the ancient world, for although their powers of endurance were often remarked upon (e.g. Polyb. 3.71.10; App., *Pun.* 11, 71), Polybius describes both Libyans and Numidians as cowardly, with a tendency to flee for up to three days if defeated in battle (Polyb. 1.47.7), while Livy scorns them as untrustworthy, undisciplined, hot-tempered, and with more violent appetites than any other barbarians (Liv. 25.41.4, 28.44.5, 29.23.4, 30.12.18).

Mercenaries or allies?

The Numidians were not a single nation, but consisted instead of two main kingdoms – the Masaesyli in the west and the Massyli in the east, adjacent to Carthage's own territory – as well as many small tribes with their own chieftains and domains, such as the Maccoei and Areacidae.[23] Their exact status in Carthage's armies is uncertain, though Numidians seem normally to have served in an allied, rather than mercenary, capacity. They certainly served as allies whenever they were led by their own princes or chieftains, famous examples being Naravas (Polyb. 1.78.1–11), Tychaeus (Polyb. 15.3.5), and above all Masinissa.[24] There is no direct evidence to suggest that the Numidians at Cannae served under their own commanders, but this may well have been the case. Tellingly, Appian names several Numidian chieftains in the Carthaginian army which fought at Zama (App., *Pun.* 33, 44).

Their official status may not really matter, as it is probable that Hannibal's Numidians at Cannae had previously served under Hannibal, Hasdrubal, and even Hamilcar in Spain, in which case they probably transferred their loyalty over time from their own kings in Numidia to their Barcid commander (Griffith, 1935, p. 227). A similar phenomenon has already been proposed in the case of the Libyan infantry, but for the Numidians the bond between commander and men may have been strengthened by marriage ties – during the Mercenaries' War the Numidian prince Naravas had been betrothed to Hamilcar's daughter (Polyb. 1.78.8–9). Polybius makes no further mention of Naravas, and it is therefore impossible to tell if the marriage ever took place, but if it did it is surely likely that Naravas' own men would have continued to fight under the Barcid banner.[25]

Organisation and equipment

The Numidians at Cannae were apparently led by one of Hannibal's Carthaginian lieutenants, either Hanno (Polyb. 3.114.7) or Maharbal (Liv. 22.46.7), and in Sicily they were led by the Liby-Phoenician Muttines. This may refer to an overall divisional command, with individual units, effectively tribal groups rather than formal administrative sub-units, being commanded by their own leaders.[26] Livy occasionally refers to Numidians operating in *turmae* (Liv. 25.17.3, 27.26.8), and though this probably does not mean a thirty-man squadron, as in the Roman army, it does suggest that the Numidians operated in units significantly smaller than tribal groups of several hundred men.

Numidian horses appear to have been small hardy ponies.[27] The Numidians on Trajan's Column are depicted astride very small mounts. Livy describes their horses as small and lean in a passage which praises the Numidians' horsemanship and ridicules their appearance (Liv. 35.11.6–11), and Strabo comments on the speed and small size of North African horses (Str. 17.3.7). Polybius distinguishes between the heavy cavalry, which he describes as bridled and steady, and the Numidians at the Ticinus (Polyb. 3.65.6), as the Numidians, who rode bareback, used neither bit nor bridle to control their horses, relying instead on a neck strap to steer them (Connolly, 1998, pp. 149–50). Griffith suggests that the Carthaginians, like the Egyptians, supplied their mercenaries with horses, since Polybius clearly regarded as preposterous the mercenaries' demand after the First Punic War that they be compensated for the loss of their mounts (Polyb. 1.68.8–9; Griffith, 1935, pp. 281, 289). A similar arrangement may have existed with the Numidian allies, as Appian records that on arriving in Africa from Italy in late 203 Hannibal set about buying horses and making alliances with local chieftains (App., *Pun.* 33).

Although they lacked armour, wearing instead light tunics fastened at the shoulder, the Numidians were not entirely without protective equipment, despite the fact that Polybius' reference to shield-bearing cavalry crossing the Rhone (Polyb. 3.43.2) almost certainly refers to Hannibal's Spanish cavalry. Numidian cavalry generally carried a light, round, bossless, leather shield, which was slightly convex with a narrow rim.[28] Their basic weapon was the javelin, and each Numidian evidently had several, enabling them to skirmish like mounted peltasts rather than fight as close-order cavalry (Connolly, 1998, p. 150; Bagnall, 1990, p. 8; Caes., *B Civ* 2.41; App., *Pun.* 11). These javelins must have been much the same as those used by Hannibal's infantry skirmishers, the *longchophoroi*, as Polybius refers to the spears which Naravas surrendered before negotiating with Hamilcar during the Mercenaries' War as *longchai* (Polyb. 1.78.5). Knives or short swords may also have been used as secondary weapons – a prince's grave dated to the second century BC held, along with some iron javelin heads, a sword with a blade approximately 60 cm (2 feet) long, and Livy claims that some of the Numidians who fought at Cannae carried concealed swords (Liv. 22.48.2; Connolly, 1998, p. 150).

Moors

The Mauri, or Moors, inhabited the lands to the west of the Numidians; they were of the same racial stock as the Libyans and Numidians, and Polybius evidently regarded them as simply another group of Numidians. During the Second Punic War the Moorish tribes formed a single nation under King Baga (Law, 1978, p. 188), and seem not to have had any formal relationship with Carthage. At any rate, no mention is made of alliances between Carthage and the Moors, and the Moors who fought for Carthage at Zama were deployed in the first line of infantry, classified by Polybius as mercenaries (Polyb. 15.11.1). Moorish infantry were light-armed skirmishers, as is clearly indicated by Livy's statement that in 216 Hiero of Syracuse sent a force of archers to serve in the Roman forces in order to aid the Romans against the threat posed by Hannibal's missile troops, notably the Balearians and Moors (Liv. 22.37.8–9). A more detailed analysis of such troops is to be found below, in the section on 'Skirmishers' (pp. 106–12).

Gaetulians

The Gaetulians lived to the south of the Numidians and Moors, on and to the south of the Atlas mountains, and were also of Libyco-Berber stock. There were three tribal groups of Gaetulians, according to Pliny, who is doubtless simplifying things immensely: the Autoteles in the west; the Baniurae in the east, and the Nesimi in the desert south of the Atlas mountains (Plin., *Nat. Hist.* 5.17; Law, 1978, p. 143). The only mention of Gaetulians in Hannibal's army is a reference by Livy to Hannibal sending an advance party of Gaetulians under an officer called Isalcas to the town of Casilinum in 216 (Liv. 23.18). No indication is given as to the size of this unit, but the fact that he expected it to be able, if necessary, to storm the town, may suggest that there were more Gaetulians in this advance party than their almost complete absence from the sources might otherwise imply. Gaetulian cavalry, which, like their Numidian counterparts, lacked bridles, seem to have been quite effective, if their presence in later Roman armies is anything to go by (e.g. Caes., *B Afr* 32, 56, 61). Presumably they were armed and fought in a fashion almost identical to the Numidians, which would explain why Polybius never mentions them, having simply classed them as Numidians.[29]

Spaniards

Polybius, referring to the inscription on the Lacinian promontory, states that there were 8,000 Spanish infantry in Hannibal's army when it descended from the Alps; he does not specify how many of Hannibal's 6,000 cavalry were from Spain, but seeing that most modern writers believe that there were no more than 4,000 Numidian cavalry in the army, it is reasonable to assume that there were perhaps 2,000 Spanish cavalry (Polyb. 3.56.4). Considering that the greater part of Hannibal's losses prior to Cannae had been borne by his new Celtic allies, it is likely that the majority of these Spanish troops were still alive at this point (Lazenby, 1978, p. 81). 'Spaniards', in the context of this thesis, refers to any of Hannibal's troops from the Iberian peninsula. It is important to bear this in mind since terms like 'Iberian' had no clear meaning in antiquity; Strabo points out that, even in his day, the name 'Iberia' was applied to a number of places (Str. 4.4.19), as Iberia was largely seen as an inaccessible subcontinent on the fringes of the known world (Lancel, 1998, p. 31; Richardson, 1996, p. 2). Hannibal's army included Celtiberians and Lusitanians, peoples of Celtic origin who inhabited the northern half of the peninsula (Richardson, 1996, p. 10). The majority of Hannibal's troops would, however, have been Iberians proper, from the southern half of the peninsula. While they lacked political unity, they appear to have had a common language and culture, possibly developed as a response to Greek and Phoenician settlements (Richardson, 1996, pp. 10–16).

Iberians

Carthage had been employing Iberian troops for a long time before the Punic Wars. Herodotus mentions Iberian troops commanded by Hamilcar in Sicily in 480 (Hdt. 7.165), and Thucydides has Alcibiades describe Iberian mercenaries as being among the best fighting material to be found in the western Mediterranean (Thuc. 6.90.3; Griffith, 1935, pp. 208–9). Carthage's Iberian troops must have served as mercenaries, rather than levies, as Carthaginian involvement in Spain was restricted to alliances and trade agreements, without any element of military control, before the Barcid campaigns which followed the First Punic War.[30] However, by the Second Punic War many of the Iberians in Carthage's armies were indeed allied levies,[31] and it is entirely possible that direct Carthaginian control was extended throughout Spain under the Barcids in order to provide Carthage with a virtually inexhaustible source of manpower, thus giving her an effective platform from which to fight a new war with Rome, but this controversial point is outside the scope of this book.[32]

The Iberian levies came from many different tribes. For example, Spanish troops sent to Africa included Thersitae, Mastiani, Iberian Oretes, and Olcades (Polyb. 3.33.9–10; Walbank, 1957, p. 362). The old Phoenician colonies at Gades, Malaca, Sexi, and Abdera, together with the entire coastal area of lower Andalusia, had long had close links with Carthage, and the native population – sometimes called Blasto-Phoenicians – had adopted the Phoenician language,[33] but the remaining tribes had come under Carthaginian control through the military and diplomatic skill of the Barcids (Polyb. 2.1.5–9, 13, 36, 3.13 ff.; Diod. 25.10–12; Lancel, 1998, pp. 25–56; Bagnall, 1990, pp. 142–51). It is significant that individual settlements, rather than the larger tribes, were the basic political units among the Iberians, who as a result lacked a sense of common identity, which doubtless facilitated their willingness to serve in Carthaginian, and later in Roman, armies.[34]

The Iberians may have been generally willing to serve in Carthaginian armies, but the levy seems to have been an unpopular way of recruiting troops. The Oretani and Carpetani came close to revolting in 218, ill-treating the recruiting officers because of the great demands that Hannibal put upon them (Liv. 21.11.13). In order to keep individual tribes loyal to Carthage, Hannibal granted leave of absence, following the capture of Saguntum, to any Iberian troops who wished to visit their families before setting out for Italy in the spring (Polyb. 3.33.5; Liv. 21.21.5–8). Iberian troops were stationed in Africa in 218 (Polyb. 3.33.7–16; Liv. 21.21.10–13), acting both as garrisons and hostages, and thousands of troops were allowed to return home prior to the passage through the Pyrenees (Polyb. 3.35.6; Liv. 21.23.4–6).[35] Such attempts to ensure loyalty may not have been entirely successful, if Livy's claim that Hannibal's Spaniards were on the brink of desertion shortly before the battle of Cannae because of food shortages is accurate (Liv. 22.40.8). The absence of this detail from Polybius' account of the battle, however, suggests that it may be no more than Roman propaganda.

As a rule, therefore, it seems safe to assume that Hannibal's Iberian troops were loyal to him; in fact, this loyalty may have been of a highly personal nature. According to Diodorus, Hasdrubal was honoured by the Iberians with a title which Diodorus translates as *strategos autokrator*, supreme commander (Diod. 25.12), the same title which Alexander had been given by the League of Corinth (Diod. 17.4.9). This position was probably also held by Hannibal, especially since, like Hasdrubal, he had married a Spanish noblewoman (Lancel, 1998, p. 38; Hoyos, 1994, p. 272). It is striking that Scipio was similarly honoured by Spanish tribes, who had previously been subject to Carthage, in 210; when the Spaniards hailed him as a king, he instead requested that they refer to him as *Imperator*, the term which his troops used (Polyb. 10.38, 40; Liv. 27.19.3–6; Scullard, 1970, p. 76).

Whether the Iberian title which was bestowed upon Hasdrubal, presumably Hannibal, and Scipio is best translated 'King' or 'Supreme Commander' is uncertain, but it seems clear that the Iberian nobles recognised Hannibal as a leader more powerful than themselves.

Iberian organisation

The Iberians in Hannibal's army included skirmishers, line infantry, and cavalry. Iberian skirmishers, the light infantry usually referred to as *caetrati* by modern writers, after the small round shields which they carried, are dealt with elsewhere (pp. 106–12), along with their African, Celtic, and Balearian counterparts, as there is no evidence for them having operated in national corps.

Polybius describes Hannibal's Iberian line infantry at Cannae as having been deployed in *speirai* (Polyb. 3.114.4), which is the same term he uses for maniples (Polyb. 6.24.5, 8). The term is clearly not being used in a precise sense here, but it is nevertheless unlikely to refer to a unit of less than 100 men, while at the same time its upper limit is probably about 500. In practice, the term probably denotes tribal units of some sort, perhaps the levies recruited from individual settlements; if so, they will have been of an irregular size, being proportionate initially to the size of their original settlements, although Connolly suggests that the average size of a Spanish 'maniple' was about 100 men (Connolly, 1998, p. 187). Organisation by political units in this fashion would have contributed to a sense of *esprit de corps*, as soldiers would have lived and fought alongside friends and relatives.[36]

Infantry equipment

How then were these Spanish line infantry armed? Polybius describes them at Cannae:

> The shields of the Spaniards and Celts were very similar, but their swords were entirely different, those of the Spaniards thrusting with as deadly effect as they cut, . . . the Spaniards in short tunics bordered with purple, their national dress.
>
> (Polyb. 3.114.2–4)

These troops were *scutarii*, so called because their large oval shields were like the Roman *scutum*, although flat rather than curved and with the central handgrip parallel to the shield's long axis (Healy, 1994, pp. 26–7; Head, 1982, pp. 146–8; Connolly, 1998, p. 150). Iberian swords were of two basic types. Polybius describes the type of sword upon which the Roman *gladius hispaniensis* was modelled, a straight sword perhaps 60 cm long with two cutting edges and a point (Connolly, 1998, p. 150; Walbank, 1957, pp. 445, 704; Gsell, 1928, p. 372). More common was an elegant

Figure 6 An *espada falcata*.

curved sword, referred to by modern writers as the *espada falcata*, a variation on the Greek *kopis*, most common in the south and south-east of Spain.
This was sharpened on the back edge near the point in order to enable it
to thrust as well as cut, and had a small blade between 35 cm and 52 cm
long (Healy, 1994, pp. 22–4; Head, 1982, pp. 146–7; Connolly, 1998, pp.
150–1; Gsell, 1928, pp. 372–3). A small dagger was probably also carried,
as these were common in Spain, sometimes being worn on the sword's scab-
bard, which itself was worn on the left hip, suspended by a baldric (Head,
1982,   pp.   146–7;   Connolly,   1998,   pp.   150–1).

It is almost certain that Hannibal's Iberian line infantry used javelins
of some sort, presumably using similar tactics to the Romans.[37] Javelins
were common throughout Spain, and several types are known. The *saunion*
or *soliferreum* was a distinctive Spanish weapon, a slim javelin, about
1.6–2.0 m long, made entirely from iron, with a small barbed head and
a pointed butt (Head, 1982, pp. 145–6; Connolly, 1998, pp. 150–1;
Warry, 1980, p. 122; Gsell, 1928, p. 373). Another type of throwing spear
had an iron head, about 25 cm in length, attached to a wooden shaft
(Gsell, 1928, p. 373), whereas other Iberian throwing spears resembled
the Roman *pilum*, and may have served as models for it. Perhaps the most
famous of these Iberian *pilum*-prototypes was the formidable incendiary
spear, the *falarica*:

> The Saguntines had a javelin, called a *falarica*, with a shaft of fir,
> which was round except at the end whence the iron projected; this
> part, four-sided as in the *pilum*, they wrapped with tow and smeared
> with pitch. Now the iron was three feet long, that it might be
> able to go through both shield and body. But what chiefly made
> it terrible, even if it stuck fast in the shield and did not penetrate
> the body, was this, that when it had been lighted at the middle
> and so hurled, the flames were fanned to a fiercer heat by its very
> motion, and it forced the soldier to let go his shield, and left him
> unprotected against the blows that followed.
>
> (Liv. 21.8.10–12)[38]

Figure 7 Relief sculpture of a Spanish *scutarus* found at Osuna. He is wearing a
crested sinew hood and a tunic which appears to have a border, and is
carrying a large shield and what may be a *falcata*.

It seems that the Iberians wore no armour, having only the white linen
tunics with purple borders that Polybius described as their national uniform,
although some may well have also worn looted Roman *pectorales* (Polyb.
3.114.4; Liv. 22.46.6; Warry, 1980, p. 122). Such tunics are depicted on
sculptures of soldiers found at Osuna in southern Spain (Connolly, 1998,
pp. 150–1). It has been suggested that the linen of their tunics was stiff
enough to stand up fairly well to cuts,[39] but this seems unlikely, save
perhaps for extremely light, glancing blows. Unlike the Carthaginians,
Spaniards wore their tunics belted, and although some went barefoot, most
wore shoes or boots of some description. Neither Polybius nor Livy mentions

Iberians wearing helmets, but sinew caps were commonly worn as helmets throughout Spain at the time, some being simple and unadorned, while others were hoods, covering the nape of the neck and with a horsehair crest (Str. 3.3.6, 4.15; Head, 1982, pp. 146–7; Connolly, 1998, pp. 150–2; Warry, 1980, p. 122).

Cavalry

As noted already, there was probably about 2,000 Spanish cavalry in Hannibal's army in 218, and the majority of these were still alive for the battle of Cannae. Unlike the Numidians, the Spaniards were not skirmishers, as their style of fighting indicates. At Cannae they virtually collided with their Roman foes, many men even dismounting and fighting on foot (Polyb. 3.115.2–4; Liv. 22.47.1–3). Livy's description of the fighting there between the Romans and Hannibal's Celts and Spaniards seems to imply that the ferocious mêlée which took place developed only because of a lack of room for more sophisticated outflanking manoeuvres, but the fact that Polybius describes the Spanish cavalry at the Ticinus as 'steady' (Polyb. 3.65.6) probably indicates that they fought *en masse*, unlike the Numidian skirmishers, who fought in a very loose formation, or even as individuals (Lazenby, 1978, p. 15).

The bulk of Hannibal's Spanish cavalry were doubtless allied troops, and probably noblemen. This was certainly the case among the Celtic cavalry, and the Celts and Spaniards appear to have had similar warrior cultures.[40] Spanish cavalry were normally armed much like their infantry, lacking armour but wearing the traditional tunic of white linen with a purple border, as well as a sinew cap. They normally carried the small round *caetra*-type shield, two javelins or light spears with buttspikes, and a *falcata*-type sword (Head, 1982, pp. 149–50; Connolly, 1998, pp. 151–2); this would have been much more useful for cavalry than the straight *gladius hispaniensis*-type sword as a curved blade was perfectly adapted to slashing from a height. Some cavalry appear to have carried large oval or round shields and a single long thrusting spear; these seem to have been genuine shock troops – unlike the other cavalry who basically used their horses as platforms to enable them to slash from a height – and may well have been armoured, possibly wearing the scale cuirasses that were occasionally depicted in Spanish art.[41]

Celtiberians and Lusitanians

Any Celtiberians or Lusitanians in Hannibal's invasion force were there in a mercenary rather than allied capacity, for Carthage had not conquered their territory (Griffith, 1935, p. 226; Lancel, 1998, p. 46). There are not many references to these non-Iberian Spanish troops serving in Hannibal's army of Italy, which may indicate that there were relatively few of them,

100

but since Livy refers to Lusitanian and Celtiberian raiders in the north of Italy in 218 (Liv. 21.57.5), and Appian claims that there were Celtiberians at Cannae (App., *Hann.* 20),[42] it seems safest to describe briefly both Celtiberian and Lusitanian troops here.

Diodorus gives a colourful description of Celtiberian equipment, probably influenced by Poseidonius:

> They wear rough black cloaks, the wool of which resembles the hair of goats. As for their arms, certain of the Celtiberians carry light shields like those of the Gauls, and certain carry circular wicker shields as large as an aspis ... The swords they wear are two-edged and wrought of excellent iron.
>
> (Diod. 5.33)

They apparently wore sinew greaves and bronze helmets, probably of the *Montefortino* type, with crimson crests, and although Celtiberians did indeed use the *falcata*, straight swords like the *gladius hispaniensis* were more common (Head, 1982, p. 148). The Celtiberians at Cannae must have been *scutarii*, rather than armed with round, Greek-style shields, to have blended in with the similarly armed Celtic and Iberian line infantry there. Wearing Roman-style helmets and carrying large oval or oblong shields, they could easily have been mistaken for Romans in the confusion of battle, which might explain Appian's otherwise dubious account of their role at Cannae.

Lusitanian infantry seem to have specialised as skirmishers (Head, 1982, pp. 148–9), and were normally equipped with the *caetra* and carried several javelins – notably the barbed iron *saunion* – and a sword, both the *falcata* and *gladius hispaniensis* sword types being common in Lusitania. Lusitanians usually wore sinew helmets and linen cuirasses. Some were mail shirts, but the fact that the sole reference to Lusitanians in Hannibal's army has them marauding on mountainous ground (Liv. 21.57.5) suggests that they served as light-armed skirmishers, a style of warfare at which they were highly skilled (Str. 3.3.6; Diod. 5.34.4).

If there were any Celtiberian or Lusitanian cavalry in the army at Cannae, it is likely that they wore mail shirts, in addition to the conventional equipment of javelins, slashing swords, and small round shields (Head, 1982, p. 150).

Gauls

The term 'Gauls' is here used in a very general sense, to include both the Gauls of the Po valley proper, here referred to as Celts, and their Ligurian cousins of the northern Apennines and the Italian riviera. As discussed already (p. 32), there were about 16,000 Gallic troops in the main line of battle at Cannae, and there were probably a further 8,000 or so left behind as a camp garrison, assuming that Hannibal deployed all his available Spanish and

African infantry. Hannibal's Celtic troops came from the two largest tribal federations in Cisalpine Gaul, the Insubres and the Boii, respectively from north and south of the Po (Polyb. 2.22.1, 17.4, 7). The Insubres were apparently the larger of the two, and appear to have controlled several other tribes, notably the Ligurian Laevi (Walbank, 1957, p. 182); this might explain why Polybius evidently regards the Ligurians as Celts rather than a distinct national element in Hannibal's army.

Celts

Mercenaries or allies?

The exact status of Hannibal's Celtic troops is worth examining: were they mercenaries or allies? As with the Spaniards, the situation is far from clear. Hannibal certainly had alliances with both Celts and Ligurians,[43] but what these alliances involved is uncertain, and it is quite likely that the initial Celtic recruits in the Carthaginian army under Hannibal were mercenary volunteers (Griffith, 1935, p. 229). The subsequent formal alliances may have involved a levy of some kind, but it should be borne in mind that diplomacy was generally regarded as the most efficient way of recruiting mercenaries in the Hellenistic era (Griffith, 1935, pp. 254, 257).

Organisation

It has been suggested that whereas Hannibal's Libyan troops may have served under Carthaginian officers, the Spaniards were led by their own chieftains (Samuels, 1990, p. 18); this was certainly the case with Hannibal's Celts, as is demonstrated by Polybius' reference to Carthaginian and Celtic officers in Hannibal's army at Tarentum in 212 (Polyb. 8.30.4). Celtic society was tribal, each tribe being divided in turn into a number of clan groups (Samuels, 1990, p. 19). Although there were formal institutions of government, society was in practice dominated by individual nobles around whom warbands of retainers were centred (Goldsworthy, 1996, p. 54). The chieftain's status was based on 'ties of obligation and patronage, or on charisma', while status among retainers was determined partly by their relations with their leaders and partly by their own skill as warriors, which would earn their honour and prestige (Rawlings, 1996, pp. 81–2). Polybius notes that:

> They treated comradeship of the greatest importance, those among them being the most feared and powerful who were thought to have the largest number of attendants and associates.
>
> (Polyb. 2.17.12)

Although this interpretation is probably substantially correct, it must be remembered that Polybius' interest in the Celts is primarily as a cultural contrast to the 'civilised' Romans; his viewpoint is coloured by classical stereotypes of barbarians, causing him to present the Celts as primitive and irrational.[44]

Chieftains and their retainers were mainly to be found among the cavalry, but amongst the infantry, which could be closely packed and where each man was probably surrounded by friends and relations, it is likely that the most distinguished warriors led the charge in battle, as in a society with a heroic ethos the 'bravest and best equipped naturally gravitated to the front rank' (Goldsworthy, 1996, p. 59). As with the Spaniards, Polybius describes the Celtic infantry at Cannae as being deployed in *speirai* (Polyb. 3.114.4), which probably refers to tribal units of irregular size, although Connolly (1998, p. 187) suggests that these units were in the main about 250-strong.

Equipment

Polybius describes the Celts at Cannae as being naked, armed with long slashing swords and oval shields (Polyb. 3.114.2–4), and Livy concurs, although he refers to the Celts as being naked only from the waist up (Liv. 22.46.6).[45] This seems more likely, since at the battle of Telamon in 225 the Insubres and Boii retained their trousers and cloaks, even though their Gaesetae allies fought naked (Polyb. 2.28.7–8). Their nakedness apparently rendered them almost entirely helpless against the Roman javelins, as their bodies were clearly defined targets, not obscured by loose clothing (Polyb. 2.30.1–3). Although fighting naked was not uncommon among the Celts (Diod. 5.30.3; Pleiner and Scott, 1993, p. 25; Walbank, 1957, p. 205), who perhaps entered battle in this fashion to show their courage in the face of death, it seems to have been alien to the Celts of the Italian peninsula in the third century, and would hardly have been adopted following the slaughter of the Gaesetae at Telamon. The Boii and Insubres at Cannae almost certainly wore trousers, tied at the ankles, as well as shoes (Pleiner and Scott, 1993, p. 25; Head, 1982, pp. 150–3; Walbank, 1957, p. 205); the *sagum*, the traditional Celtic cloak, was probably discarded in the late summer heat, although it may have been retained to provide some small measure of protection against the Roman javelins.

Celtic noblemen and chieftains, who mainly fought as cavalry, probably wore mail shirts made from interlinking iron rings; mail armour was invented by the Celts, apparently in the fourth century, and would have been worn over a padded undershirt of some sort (Bishop and Coulston, 1993, p. 59; Head, 1982, pp. 152–3; Connolly, 1998, p. 175). Helmets were also worn by noblemen, and presumably by whatever few regular infantry could afford them, bronze *Montefortino*-style helmets being the most common design, although more elaborate helmets were also worn (Diod. 5.30.2; Head, 1982, p. 152).

Diodorus Siculus gives a vivid description of the Celtic shield:

> For armour they use long shields, as high as a man, which are wrought in a manner peculiar to them, some of them even having the figures of animals embossed on them in bronze, and these are skilfully worked with an eye not only to beauty but also to protection.
>
> (Diod. 5.30.2)

Colourful as this description may be, it is not entirely accurate. Although the Celtic shield was indeed oval or oblong, like the Roman *scutum*, it was flat and rather narrow (Liv. 38.21.4), which may explain why it failed to provide an adequate degree of protection against the Roman javelins at the battle of Telamon (Polyb. 2.30.3). Furthermore, although some ceremonial shields may well have been decoratively embossed in bronze, battle shields were painted (Head, 1982, p. 155). Celtic shields varied both in size, being about a metre high and 55 cm wide on average, and in shape, some being squared off at top and bottom or straight along the sides, rather than simply oval (Head, 1982, p. 152). Such shields were made from oak or linden planks and covered with leather, which may have been doubled over at the rim, since Celtic shields, like Spanish ones, lacked metal reinforcement at the edges. They had long spines with spindle-shaped central bosses, reinforced with a metal boss plate and hollowed out to accommodate the handgrip, which ran horizontally across the long spine (Healy, 1994, pp. 23–5; Head, 1982, p. 152; Warry, 1980, p. 165). The shield was apparently thicker at the centre, where it was about 13 mm thick, than at the edges, where it was only about 6 mm thick, which gave it strength and a certain amount of flexibility. It has been suggested that oaken Celtic shields were significantly stronger than their Roman equivalents (Samuels, 1990, p. 19), but this is difficult to prove. Some indeed may have been so, but if this was the case their weight would quite possibly have been greater than that of Roman shields, which may have weighed over 10 kg. Such a shield was presumably propped up on the ground in battle, allowing its user to fight from behind it in a somewhat crouched position (Bishop and Coulston, 1993, pp. 58–9; Connolly, 1998, p. 131). This would not have been feasible for Celts armed with long slashing swords, who required room to fight. Diodorus mentions Celts armed with light shields, perhaps suggesting that thinner shields or wickerwork shields with hide coverings were common (Diod. 5.33.3; Head, 1982, p. 152).

Polybius makes two main observations about the aforementioned Celtic sword. Firstly, it was unsuited to thrusting, being a slashing weapon requiring a long sweep (Polyb. 2.30.8, 3.114.3). Secondly, it was badly made, tending to buckle easily and quickly becoming useless unless its wielder was able to take the time to straighten it (Polyb. 2.33.3). Later classical writers took both these points for granted (Pleiner and Scott, 1993, pp. 33–5, 157–9). However, most Celtic swords had prominent points and could certainly have been used for thrusting, although slashing would have been a more natural use for the long (75–90 cm) blades which had two cutting edges (Pleiner and Scott, 1993, p. 33; Healy, 1994, pp. 23–5; Head, 1982, pp. 151–3). The majority of such swords would also seem to have been of relatively high quality; Polybius' comments on the flexibility of their blades, possibly derived from Fabius Pictor, his main source for Rome's Celtic wars, may well have its origins in camp rumours put about to reassure nervous soldiers (Walbank, 1957, pp. 184, 209; Delbrück, 1990 [1920], p. 306).

It should also be borne in mind that most Celts were probably armed with throwing spears or javelins of some sort (Diod. 5.30.4). Indeed, Celtic spears were so well known in the classical world that four Celtic terms were adopted as loan-words to denote such weapons: *lancea*, *mataris*, *saunion*, and *gaesum* (Pleiner and Scott, 1993, p. 27).

Cavalry

There were probably about 4,000 Celtic cavalry at Cannae, the bulk of whom would have been noblemen or their retainers for Celtic nobles generally fought as cavalry (Goldsworthy, 1996, p. 58; Samuels, 1990, p. 19). Griffith suggests that the earliest Celtic recruits to Hannibal's army after the descent from the Alps were mercenary volunteers, and as these were mainly cavalry it would seem that most of Hannibal's Celtic cavalry were mercenary noblemen.[46] These would have been paid more than infantry, and would also have been entitled to a greater share of booty.[47]

About two centuries after the Second Punic War, Strabo wrote of the Celts that although they were all natural fighters, they were better as cavalry than as infantry (Str. 4.4.2). Being mainly nobles, Celtic cavalry tended to be well equipped, frequently wearing helmets, and mail shirts, possibly with overhanging shoulder defences, and carrying a shield, usually round, though sometimes oval, in shape (Head, 1982, pp. 152–5). They were normally armed with the traditional Celtic sword and a heavy thrusting spear or lance, the use of either being presumably facilitated by the security provided by the four-horned saddle favoured by the Celts, who also appear to have used short spurs to urge on their horses.[48]

The Celtic warrior ethos was doubtless strongest amongst the noblemen who made up the cavalry, so that although they operated as heavy cavalry they seem not to have acted as a single, centrally co-ordinated unit. There was clearly a tendency for certain troopers to act independently of their comrades, as is demonstrated by Livy's account of how Ducarius, a cavalryman of the Insubres, sought out and killed the Roman consul Flaminius in revenge for Flaminius' campaigns in the Insubrian lands six years earlier (Liv. 22.6.3–4).[49]

Ligurians

Although Polybius does not specifically mention Ligurians in Hannibal's Italian army, he does mention a small force of Ligurians under Hasdrubal's command in Spain in 218 (Polyb. 3.33.16), and notes that the first line of infantry at the battle of Zama in 202 included Ligurians (Polyb. 15.11.1). The treaty between Hannibal and Philip V of Macedon in 215 specifically identified the Ligurians as allies of the Carthaginians (Polyb. 7.9.6), and Livy makes reference on several occasions to Ligurians helping Carthage against Rome, even going so far as to supply men to Hannibal's army (Liv. 21.22.2, 38.3, 58.2, 59.10, 27.39.2, 48.7–49.8, 28.46.8–11, 29.5.3–9, 30.33.5). It would be surprising if the Ligurians had not joined the Celts in aiding the Carthaginians, as, according to Livy, the Ligurians and Celts had traditionally come to each other's help, and wars against either group frequently involved the other (Liv. 36.39.6).

Unlike their Celtic neighbours, the Ligurians were apparently a slightly built people (Diod. 5.39.2). There were numerous Ligurian tribes – Livy alone mentions Ingauni, Celines, Ilvates, Celeiates, and Cerdiciates (Liv. 31.2.11, 10.2, 32.29.70). They almost always fought on foot, and were good at skirmishing and fighting at close quarters. Lightly armoured, if at all, they wore long-sleeved, round-necked, woollen tunics, possibly with cloaks, and leather shoes like those worn by the Celts. They carried shields of a similar design to Celtic ones, and swords of medium length (Diod. 5.39.7). Many Ligurians fought as skirmishers, in which case this sword would have been used as a secondary weapon, javelins being their basic offensive weapons (Diod. 5.39.7; Str. 4.6.2).

Skirmishers

Although it generally makes sense to study the Carthaginian forces by dividing them into national groupings rather than more conventional army groups such as infantry and cavalry, it is probably best to treat the light-armed infantry, or skirmishers, as a distinct group, as indeed Polybius himself does.[50] This is justifiable as the spearmen, who made up the greater part of the light troops, were almost certainly not a racially homogenous force – had they been a distinct national group Polybius would almost certainly have drawn attention to the fact. As has been pointed out already (pp. 31–2), the combined force of slingers and spearmen at Cannae came to about 8,000 men, based on the number of skirmishers at the Trebia (Polyb. 3.72.7), and assuming that casualties among the skirmishers were relatively low.[51]

Balearian slingers

Of these 8,000 the respective numbers of slingers and spearmen is uncertain. It is sometimes assumed that there were 2,000 Balearian slingers (Bagnall, 1990, p. 8; DeBeer, 1969, p. 98; Dodge, 1995 [1891], p. 21), but there is no real evidence for this, save perhaps a reference by Livy to 2,000 auxiliary troops sent from the Balearic islands to Carthage in 205 (Liv. 28.37.9). This is not to be taken as an indication that 2,000 was the standard size for a Balearian unit, and that there were, as a result, 2,000 such slingers in Hannibal's army. In fact, in 218 Hannibal sent 870 Balearian slingers to Africa and left 500 in Spain (Polyb. 3.33.11, 16; Liv. 21.21.12, 22.2), clear evidence that Balearians did not operate in bodies of 2,000. It has also been suggested that there were fewer than 1,000 slingers in his invasion force (Head, 1982, p. 35), but there is no evidence for this estimate, which seems too low in any case, considering that 870 slingers had accompanied 13,850 infantry and 1,200 cavalry to Africa in 218, whereas his own army had at least 20,000 infantry and 6,000 cavalry (Polyb. 3.56.4; Liv. 22.38.2). It would seem likely that there were substantially more than 1,000 Balearians with Hannibal in Italy, although the occasionally suggested 2,000 is probably too high an estimate.

The Balearians were clearly mercenaries; Polybius positively identifies them as such in his accounts of the Mercenaries' War following the First Punic War (Polyb. 1.67.7), and of the battle of Zama in 202, where the mercenaries made up the first of the three Carthaginian lines (Polyb. 15.11.1). It is unlikely that any other arrangement could have existed, as although Lancel describes their islands as being under the Punic protectorate, Carthaginian power does not seem to have penetrated further than the coast, and even there it is likely that their colonies were mere trading posts along the sea route from Sardinia to Spain, without any sovereignty over the natives.[52] How the Balearians were paid is unclear. It appears that when Carthage first began to employ Balearian mercenaries, whenever that was,[53] they were paid in wine and women, for they did not use money (Diod. 5.17.4), but this practice, if historical, may have been abandoned over time as is suggested by the presence of recruiting officers with large sums of money on the islands in the late fifth century (Griffith, 1935, pp. 208–9).

Although some Balearians were armed with fire-hardened javelins at the time when they first came in contact with the Carthaginians (Str. 3.5.1), the vast majority of Balearian soldiers were slingers. Livy does mention Balearians using javelins at the battle of the Trebia (Liv. 21.55.6), but here he seems to be merely using 'Balearians' as a generic term for the light-armed troops as a whole. Apparently, Balearian slings were made from black tufted rush, hair, or sinew, and slingers carried slings of different sizes, designed for long, medium, and short range respectively (Str. 3.5.1). They may have been carried wrapped around the head when not in use (Str. 3.5.1), or else one would be wrapped around the head, one around the waist, and one carried in the hand (Diod. 5.18.3). The Balearians, unlike their Rhodian counterparts (Xen., *Anab.* 3.3; Warry, 1980, p. 42), did not use lead bullets as slingshot, preferring instead to use stones, apparently much larger than those used by other slingers, each weighing about a *mina* (436 g) (Head, 1982, p. 150). Interestingly, stone shot from artillery, found near Numantia in Spain, has been classified as being of four weights, the smallest of which was a *mina* (Bishop and Coulston, 1993, p. 55). This might support the seemingly far-fetched claim of Diodorus that Balearian slingshot could have a force like that of a catapult, especially suited for use against defenders on battlements (Diod. 5.18.3). How such stones were carried is uncertain, as they were rather large as well as heavy. Perhaps they were stored in the folds of the slingers' cloaks, or carried in a bag of some sort.[54] Presumably not all the stones carried were as large and heavy as those mentioned by Diodorus, for large stones were difficult to aim (Xen., *Anab.* 3.3) and the Balearian slingers were famous for their accuracy (Str. 3.5.1; Diod. 5.18.4). Smaller stones would have been easier to carry, giving the slingers increased mobility and, perhaps, more ammunition. It is possible, though by no means certain, that Balearian slingers may have also carried small shields, which would have been strapped to the forearm in order to leave the hands free to load and use the sling (Head, 1982, pp. 150–1).

Spearmen

Nationality

What then of the spearmen, Polybius' *longchophoroi*, who made up by far the greater number of Hannibal's light-armed troops? As has been noted, they were almost certainly of mixed nationality, since Polybius never identifies them as a separate racial group;[55] presumably when they crossed the Arno swamps they were among 'the most serviceable portion' of Hannibal's army (Polyb. 3.79.1). There were certainly light-armed Spaniards and Africans employed by Carthage in 218, if Livy's claim that the troops transferred to Spain and Africa that year were mostly light-armed African spearmen and Spanish targeteers respectively is correct (Liv. 21.21.11–12). Livy does, admittedly, describe the Balearians at the Trebia as being armed with javelins rather than with slings (Liv. 21.55.6, 9), but as has been noted he is here merely using the term 'Balearians' as a synonym for 'skirmishers'. In fact, it would appear that most of the spearmen were Moors, since in 216, before the battle of Cannae, Hiero of Syracuse offered the Romans a force of light-armed troops:

> well adapted to cope with Moors and Balearians and any other tribes that fought with missiles.
>
> (Liv. 22.37.8)

It seems unlikely that all the light-armed spearmen were Moors, however, as the Spanish were apparently better skirmishers (Liv. 23.26.11), something Hannibal must have realised when he assembled his army, while the Libyans had traditionally fought as javelinmen (Gsell, 1928, p. 359; Lancel, 1998, p. 60). In addition, Livy's reference to Hannibal's Celtiberians and Lusitanians marauding on mountainous land in northern Italy suggests that they were light infantry (Liv. 21.57.5), and it is also possible that some of the skirmishers at Cannae were Celtic, in view of the fact that they made up such a large portion of Hannibal's army (Lazenby, 1978, p. 81).

Status

Any suggestions about the status of Hannibal's spearmen are highly speculative, but it seems quite likely that the greater number of them were mercenaries rather than allied troops. The Moors were certainly mercenaries, as were any Celtiberians and Lusitanians. Furthermore, the first Carthaginian line at Zama was composed of mercenaries, according to Polybius: Balearians, Moors, Celts, and Ligurians (Polyb. 15.11.1). While it is not certain that these troops acted as skirmishers at Zama (Walbank, 1967, p. 457), it is surely striking that they would all have supplied elements of Hannibal's light infantry at Cannae. If the vast majority of the spearmen were indeed mercenaries, their apparent absence from Hannibal's initial invasion force in 218 is easily understood, as the 6,000 cavalry, 12,000 Libyan infantry, and 8,000 Iberian infantry at the Po (Polyb. 3.56.4) would refer to subject or allied levies – in other words, to those troops who were formally committed to Hannibal, rather than simply serving for money and booty.

Equipment

Having established that the spearmen were of more than one nationality, their manner of armament must be examined. Polybius at one point describes the skirmishers as *psiloi*, suggesting that they were lightly clad troops such as javelinmen, archers, and slingers, armed only with missiles, and therefore unsuited for close combat (Polyb. 3.104.4; Head, 1982, p. 48). Livy supports this possibility when he describes Hasdrubal's light troops in Spain in 209 as:

> troops that are accustomed to skirmishing and, while avoiding the
> real battle by hurling long-range missiles, are protected by distance,
> but prove unsteady in the face of hand-to-hand combat.
>
> (Liv. 27.18.14)

However, it should be noted that Polybius' use of the term *psiloi* is exceptional, as he normally prefers the more general term *euzdonoi* when referring to light troops, and frequently distinguishes between the slingers, who could reasonably be described as *psiloi*, and the spearmen. The term *euzdonoi* is quite broad in meaning and can even refer to peltasts, the traditional skirmishers who were better suited to close combat than *psiloi*, being armed with a light shield and sword in addition to several javelins.[56]

Libyan infantry had traditionally been armed with javelins and a small round shield, with a dagger as a secondary weapon;[57] presumably any Libyan skirmishers in Hannibal's army were armed in this fashion. Moorish infantry were armed with javelins and a round, bossless leather shield (Head, 1982, pp. 145–7; Connolly, 1998, p. 149), and may also have carried swords for close combat once their javelins were spent.[58] Livy describes Spanish light troops as targeteers (Liv. 21.21.12, 23.26.11), that is, they carried small round shields, about 0.3 m – 0.6 m (1–2 feet) in diameter, made from hide, with a central boss. These troops were almost certainly javelinmen and probably carried a *falcata*-type sword as a sidearm, wearing caps made from sinew as helmets (Head, 1982, p. 148; Connolly, 1998, pp. 150–2; Samuels, 1990, p. 18). If Celts fought as skirmishers at Cannae, as they certainly had done at Telamon in 225 (Polyb. 2.27.6), they may have been armed with javelins, along with a dagger and a light shield, but this is far from certain (Head, 1982, p. 151). As noted above, Ligurians made excellent skirmishers and heavy infantry; Polybius' failure to refer specifically to Ligurian troops among the heavy infantry may indicate that Hannibal employed them as skirmishers.

It is not absolutely certain, however, that the spearmen used swords as sidearms when their javelins were spent. It has been suggested that Hannibal's spearmen were armed with a stabbing spear, rather than throwing spears alone, for Polybius never refers to the Roman skirmishers, who certainly were javelinmen, and Hannibal's spearmen by the same terms (Lazenby, 1978, pp. 14, 284). Plutarch's account of the death of the consul Marcellus in an ambush in 208 clearly distinguishes between javelinmen and spearmen in Hannibal's army, noting that not only were the Romans wounded with javelins, but they were also struck with spears:

> Marcellus was run through the side with a broad spear (the Latin name for which is *lancea*).
>
> (Plut., *Vit. Marc.* 29.8)

This broad-bladed stabbing spear may be the same as the short spear used by the Carthaginians in close combat at the siege of Nola, also according to Plutarch (Plut., *Vit. Marc.* 12.2). On the other hand, Polybius, in his account of the Mercenaries' War, refers to the Numidian Naravas as being armed with *longchai*, which indicates that the *longche* was a javelin of some sort (Polyb. 1.78.5). Considering the contradictory nature of the evidence, it is best not to be dogmatic; the term *longche* could refer to several types

Figure 8 Relief sculpture of Spanish *caetrati*, found at Osuna. Each man is carrying a *caetra*, and wearing a tunic and a sinew cap.

of light spear, which were usually intended for throwing, as in the case of the *lancea* used by Arrian's troops in Cappadocia (Head, 1982, p. 144; Goldsworthy, 1996, p. 229). There were numerous nationalities represented among the ranks of Hannibal's *longchophoroi*, and there must have been an equally diverse range of weapons, it being highly unlikely that Hannibal issued them with standardised equipment.

Conclusion

Hannibal's army was, on the surface, a diverse and unwieldy organisation. It consisted of many distinct national groupings with different laws, customs, languages, combat styles, and reasons for fighting for Carthage (Polyb. 11.19.4). Hardly any of its soldiers were ethnic Carthaginians, leading Polybius to contemptuously dismiss the Carthaginian army as being composed of uncommitted mercenaries and allied troops (Polyb. 6.52.4–5).[59]

Despite these apparent handicaps, the Carthaginian army seems to have been remarkably effective under the Barcids. The core of the army which Hannibal brought to Italy was made up of subject and allied levies of Libyan and Iberian infantry and Numidian and Iberian cavalry. These troops seem to have had a strong personal tie to Hannibal, having picked him as their commander following the death of Hasdrubal. This would have given the army a very high degree of *esprit de corps*, and a sense of having a common purpose, which would doubtless have spread to the various mercenary contingents in the army, as well as the new Celtic and Ligurian allies who joined the army when it arrived in Italy. Such a sense of purpose could well have assumed a greater importance than the individual motives of the respective national groups.

Not only did the army have an extremely high level of morale, it was also an exceptionally efficient fighting force. By allowing virtually all the national groupings to fight in their traditional styles the Barcids assembled an army composed of many specialised units, notably the Balearian slingers and Numidian light cavalry. This army, which could so easily have become impossible to co-ordinate, was welded into an effective machine through almost twenty years of warfare in Spain under Hamilcar, Hasdrubal, and Hannibal (Polyb. 3.35.8). By the time they faced the Romans at Cannae, it was the Hellenistic world's equivalent of Alexander's expeditionary force, a multinational army with a high proportion of cavalry to infantry, made up of experienced soldiers who were devoted to their general (Santosuosso, 1997, p. 170).

5

COMMAND AT CANNAE

Introduction

The nature of command

The battles of the Second Punic War were 'generals' battles', unlike the far simpler 'soldiers' battles' of classical Greece, for instance. The opposing commanders were thus clearly of central importance to the battle of Cannae. What exactly did command involve?

Command has been described as 'a function that has to be exercised, more or less continuously, if the army is to exist and to operate' (Van Crefeld, 1985, p. 5). The first responsibility, which can be termed 'function-related', is largely logistical and administrative in character, whereas the second responsibility, termed 'output-related', involves the army's basic purpose, which is to defeat the enemy in battle at minimum cost to itself (Van Crefeld, 1985, p. 6). Needless to say, these responsibilities frequently overlap. Nevertheless, the second responsibility is the primary focus of this chapter, which is concerned with how a commander could influence the outcome of a battle. The options available can be divided into two broad groups, again not mutually exclusive – generalship and leadership. The former involves such technical skills as intelligence gathering, tactical planning, and the communication of orders. Leadership is a more subtle concept, concerned less with co-ordination than with motivation and 'how a commander sought to inspire his men to fight harder or endure worse privations in order to beat the enemy' (Goldsworthy, 1996, p. 119).

Generalship before battle is largely to do with the acquisition of intelligence and the use of said information. This information can be gained through personal investigation or, more usually, through intermediaries such as spies, scouts, deserters, local inhabitants, etc. Information would normally be sought on a variety of subjects such as: the state of one's own forces; the enemy forces and their commander, if possible; terrain; and local weather conditions. This information having been received, it is necessary to analyse it in order to decide whether or not battle would be appropriate under the circumstances, and if so, what tactics should be adopted. Once this is done, orders must be given to high-ranking officers and then transmitted down through the ranks (Van Crefeld, 1985, p. 7). Finally, the army itself must be deployed for battle, in accordance with the commander's plans.

Once battle begins, generalship mainly involves monitoring the course of the battle to ensure the proper execution of orders. In this way the commander has as much influence over the course and outcome of the battle as possible; new orders can be issued based on changing circumstances. The necessity for generalship in battle is proportionate to the size and complexity of the army being commanded – the larger and more complex the army, the more difficult is the task of co-ordinating the various units. That said, a lack of sufficiently sophisticated equipment to help a commander in calculation and communication would effectively limit the size and complexity of his army. Alternatively, battlefield generalship could be virtually abandoned, as in hoplite warfare (Wheeler, 1991, pp. 121–70; Hanson, 1989, pp. 107 ff.), and in such cases the commander's role would be more that of a leader, sharing in his men's experiences, than that of a general, co-ordinating them from a distance.

Leadership, which essentially involves exploiting the moral and psychological factors affecting the troops' behaviour, is the other key technique of command (Adcock, 1957, p. 83). This is because the rational processes of generalship do not suffice to persuade men to march to possible death. Co-ordination and instruction must be augmented by motivation and inspiration, since when it is necessary to face death 'the incentives associated with the gainful pursuit of peace do not apply and must be replaced by an appeal to irrational motives' (Van Crefeld, 1985, p. 16). In theory, motivation is best carried out by a commander fighting alongside his men, whereas generalship is most efficient at some distance from the fighting. However, as has been stated, leadership and generalship are not mutually exclusive tasks, and leadership in particular is difficult to define rigidly. Troops could, for example, be highly motivated by the knowledge that their commander was a very capable and skilled general. In such circumstances, the commander would be an effective leader, while not 'leading' in any obvious fashion (Goldsworthy, 1996, p. 119).

The historiography of command

Leadership consists of more than a set of teachable skills, unlike generalship. The principles of strategy and tactics are 'absurdly simple' and because of this commanders have traditionally been examined and evaluated by historians with regard to these easy-to-grasp principles.[1] For instance, Hans Delbrück, one of the first modern military historians, although well aware of such intangible forces as motivation, nevertheless tended to emphasise those qualities which the great commanders throughout history have had

in common – essentially involving strategic and tactical ability – and consequently he attributed their successes to their generalship. Delbrück's analysis
of the battle of Cannae is a good example of this. Although he acknow-
ledges the effect of Hannibal's presence on the morale of the Celts around
him, he nevertheless concludes:

> At Cannae, the Carthaginians were victorious with their barbarian
> mercenaries because of their superiority in cavalry, because of their
> officer corps, the generals and staff officers, who had their troops
> well in hand and knew how to direct them tactically, and because
> of the commander, who with the unmistakable certainty of genius
> blended the forces at hand into an organically unified effectiveness.
>
> (Delbrück, 1990 [1920], p. 323)

Similarly, J.F.C. Fuller recognised the importance of leadership as one of the
two essential elements of command, but still saw it as far less significant
than the skills of generalship. For example, he accepted that Caesar's ability
as a commander was more commonly understood in the context of his being
rather 'a fighting than ... a thinking soldier', but he then proceeded to
examine his generalship in terms of tactics and to judge him accordingly
(Fuller, 1965, pp. 321–4). Analysing Alexander's generalship he quoted
Robert Johnson extensively to show that 'it is not the dry mechanical wisdom
of the plan of battle, so much as the animating spirit of the leader, which
may be considered as the pledge of success in war' (Fuller, 1960, p. 283).
Paradoxically, despite paying lip-service to Alexander's qualities as a leader
of men, Fuller proceeds to list the basic principles of strategy and tactics as
defined by Clausewitz, demonstrating Alexander's excellence as a commander
in accordance with these, claiming that 'their components flow into each
other and together constitute the art of war' (Fuller, 1960, pp. 293, 284–305).

In the last chapter of *Scipio Africanus: Greater than Napoleon*, B.H. Liddell
Hart explicitly sets about comparing the 'great captains' with regard to the
traditional concepts of generalship. Regarding tactics, he notes that:

> So general is the recognition of Hannibal's genius in this battle art
> that he is commonly termed the supreme tactician of history. Yet
> in ruse and stratagem the record of Scipio's battles is even richer.
>
> (Liddell Hart, 1994 [1926], p. 253)

As for strategy, he praises Scipio's manoeuvres as 'unequalled in the ancient
world' (p. 257), while in comparing Scipio with Napoleon himself, he
concludes:

> In the comparison of Scipio with Napoleon, if the latter's superi-
> ority in logistical strategy is recognised, we have to set against this

115

both his tactical and his grand strategical inferiority. As a grand strategist Napoleon's claims are marred not only by his failure to realise the aim of grand strategy – a prosperous and secure peace, – but by his several blunders over the psychology of his opponents, over the political and economic effects of his actions, and in the extravagant later use of his forces and resources.

(Liddell Hart, 1994 [1926], p. 271)

This approach, while useful, is of limited validity. As John Keegan points out:

the warfare of any one society may differ so much from that of another that commonality of trait and behaviour in those who direct it is overlaid altogether in importance by differences in the purposes they serve and the functions they perform.

(Keegan, 1987, p. 1)[2]

Generals can be not simply commanders of armies, but also kings, priests, diplomats, politicians, or professional soldiers. The source of a commander's power must be understood if the nature of that power is to be comprehended in its own right. By overemphasising such common features as strategy and tactics, the distinctive roles of commanders in different societies become obscured.

The particularity of leadership is best understood when the following is borne in mind:

An army is, to resort to cliché, an expression of the society from which it issues. The purposes for which it fights and the way it does so will therefore be determined in large measure by what a society wants from a war and how far it expects its army to go in delivering that outcome.

(Keegan, 1987, p. 2)

By the same token, the commander of the army is equally a man of his society and acts accordingly. Keegan (1987, pp. 315–38) divides the commander's duties, aside from those which are purely tactical and strategic in nature, into five basic categories, or imperatives:

1   Kinship – the creation of a bond between commander and men.
2   Prescriptions – the need for a commander to speak directly to his men.
3   Sanctions – the issuing of rewards and punishments.
4   Action – intelligence gathering and the formulation of plans.
5   Example – the most important imperative, the need for a commander to be seen to share dangers with his men.

Alexander's preference for personal combat was closely linked to the Macedonian warrior ethos, a tendency also evident in Celtic warfare (Keegan, 1987, pp. 13–91; Rawlings, 1996, pp. 81–95). Hoplite warfare has generally been regarded as essentially egalitarian in nature, with the commander at the front of the phalanx, until the rise of Macedon in the mid-fourth century. It appears, therefore, that the commander's position in Greek armies changed over time from being always in front to being in front only when absolutely necessary (Wheeler, 1991, pp. 124 ff.).

Polybius on command

A study of Polybius' *Histories,* written about fifty years after the Second Punic War, reveals much about what Polybius believed command to involve.[3] His views are probably not unrepresentative of conventional ideas about command during the second century, and although he was Greek, rather than Roman or Carthaginian, it is likely that his ideas can be used to reconstruct with a high degree of accuracy what was expected of generals during the Second Punic War.

To Polybius, command in war is 'the most honourable and serious of all employments', in which 'nature makes a single trivial error sufficient to cause failure in a design, but correctness in every detail barely enough for success' (Polyb. 9.20.9, 12.10). The most important characteristics of successful commanders come across as being shrewdness and courage – the qualities which apparently led to Hannibal's appointment (Polyb. 2.36.3). Shrewdness is more obviously linked to the skills of generalship than to those of leadership, and Polybius believes that the former can be learnt in three different ways: the study of military writings; instruction from experienced commanders; and personal experience of warfare (Polyb. 9.8.1–2). It is clearly imperative that the skills of generalship be learnt, Polybius points out, as 'most results in war are due to the skill or the reverse of the commanders' (Polyb. 11.14.2).

So what were these skills? One vital skill involved the use of intelligence, as Polybius makes clear when he points out that no general would march into a country about which he knew nothing (Polyb. 3.48.4). The importance of the acquisition and proper use of intelligence in a commander's repertoire of skills is expressed most clearly prior to his account of Hannibal's victory at Lake Trasimene in 217:

> For there is no denying that he who thinks that there is anything more essential to a general than the knowledge of his opponent's principles and character, is both ignorant and foolish . . . he who is in command must try to see in the enemy's general . . . what are the weak spots that can be discovered in his mind.
>
> (Polyb. 3.81.1–3)

He admits that it is best if a general observes such things at first hand, but that 'the next best thing is to make careful inquiries and not to rely on chance informants' (Polyb. 9.14.3). There were other skills involved in generalship, too, notably geometry and astronomy (Polyb. 9.14–20), along with horsemanship (Polyb. 36.8.1). The ability to deploy and manoeuvre troops was absolutely essential for a successful general. During the First Punic War, Xanthippus' skill in this regard made the Carthaginian generals he replaced seem incompetent (Polyb. 1.32.7).[4]

'Shrewdness' was, for Polybius, only one side of the coin of command; 'courage' was just as important. Hannibal's courage has already been mentioned, and Philopoemen displayed his at Mantineia, pursuing Machanidas and defeating him in single combat (Polyb. 11.18.4). It is important to note that this courage was appropriate under the circumstances of the battle and was not mere recklessness. Polybius praises Scipio's prudence in this regard:

> Having by this service gained a universally acknowledged reputation for bravery, he in subsequent times refrained from exposing his person without significant reason, when his country reposed her hopes of success on him – conduct characteristic not of a commander who relies on luck but on one gifted with intelligence.
>
> (Polyb. 10.3.7)

Marcellus, on the other hand, is criticised for having unnecessarily exposed himself to danger by personally taking part in a mere scouting mission, his subsequent death being attributed to 'ostentation and childish vanity or from inexperience or contempt of the enemy' (Polyb. 10.33.6). Such attitudes were believed to result from a lack of self-control in a general sense, along with other more specific flaws, such as laziness, drunkenness, licentiousness, and cowardice (Polyb. 3.81). The moral quality most prized by Polybius is rational self-control, courage balanced by prudence; discretion, he evidently believes, is often the better part of valour.[5]

While 'shrewdness' was essential for generalship, 'courage' was obviously linked with leadership. Polybius presents his generals as leading by example, frequently taking at least some part in the fighting in any given battle. Hannibal and Paullus are good examples of the type of generals Polybius most admires (Polyb. 3.116.1–5). It was his abilities as a leader that Polybius rated most significant about Hannibal as a commander. Hannibal is praised for his 'marches, tactics, and battles' and for his 'generalship, courage, and power in the field' (Polyb. 7.4.4), but his supreme achievement was that he kept:

> a large army free from sedition towards him or among themselves, and this although his regiments were not only of different nation-

alities but of different races ... the ability of their commander forced men so radically different to give ear to a single word of command and yield obedience to a single will.

(Polyb. 11.19.3–5)

If this is how Polybius saw Hannibal, as a leader at least as much as a general, then it is probable that this is the best yardstick by which to examine the commanders' roles at Cannae.

The consuls and their staff

Traditionally, the Roman forces at the Battle of Cannae were thought to have been commanded by Gaius Terentius Varro,[6] one of the two consuls elected for 216. Varro was a *novus homo* who had served as quaestor, plebeian and curule aedile, and praetor in 218 (Liv. 22.26.3). He has been unanimously condemned in the sources as a mere demagogue, Livy even describing him as the son of a butcher (Liv. 22.25.18–26.4; Plut., *Vit. Fab. Max.* 14; App., *Hann.* 17; Cass. Dio fr. 57.24). This is almost certainly incorrect and it rather seems that Varro, as a *novus homo*, was made a scapegoat by the aristocratic tradition for the debacle at Cannae. His supposedly 'populist' base seems highly unlikely, given the timocratic structure of the *comitia centuriata*, which elected the consuls, and the difficulty of being elected consul without some degree of senatorial support. Furthermore the only precise evidence for such demagogism is Livy's statement that he:

> with considerable shrewdness sought to capture the favour of the populace by exploiting their animosity against the dictator, with the result that he alone reaped all the popularity growing out of the populace.

(Liv. 22.26.4)

Who then was Lucius Aemilius Paullus, Varro's fellow consul? Like most of the other magistrates elected that year, Paullus' experience was note-worthy – he had served as consul in 219 and had campaigned successfully in Illyria against Demetrius of Pharos, returning to Rome:

> in triumph, acclaimed by all, for he seemed to have managed matters not only with ability but with very high courage.

(Polyb. 3.19.12–13)

In fact, he was the most recent recipient of a triumph, but despite his exper-ience he does not seem to have been popular and had recently been charged, along with his consular colleague of 219, Marcus Livius Salinator, with dishonesty.[7] Polybius does not comment on the mechanics of the elections of 216, but according to Livy there were initially six candidates, three patricians and three plebeians, of whom only Varro was elected. Although reluctant, Paullus was then persuaded to stand for the consulship, and his rivals withdrew. Apparently it was Varro himself who presided over his election (Liv. 22.35.1–4).[8]

The tendency to blame Varro rather than Paullus for the defeat at Cannae appears very odd when it is pointed out that Polybius does not mention any disagreements between the two consuls until they were in the vicinity of Cannae, and even then the disagreement was over the suitability of particular terrain for battle. Both consuls are presented as favouring battle but Aemilius Paullus is presented only as opposed to battle at that particular spot (Polyb. 3.110.2–3). Presumably, as the more experienced of the two in war, Paullus' views would generally have been deferred to by Varro. While there may have been genuine disagreements between the two, they have clearly been exaggerated out of all proportion by the sources. If this is, in fact, the case then it would seem that the aristocratic historiographical tradition developed to blame Varro, the *novus homo,* for the defeat at Cannae. Paullus' relations and descendants would have protected his reputation, absolving him of guilt, but Varro evidently lacked such powerful guardians of his reputation.[9] It is doubtless significant in this respect that Polybius' patron, Scipio Aemilianus, was the grandson of Aemilius Paullus.[10]

Who then was in charge on the day of the battle, bearing in mind that differences between the consuls have probably been greatly exaggerated? According to Polybius, when two consuls served with their forces combined they alternated the right to command and it was Varro who commanded on the day of the battle (Polyb. 3.110.4, 113.1). Livy and Plutarch support this, but Appian says that Varro, having decided on battle, allowed Paullus to command, and in his account of Hannibal's battle exhortation at Zama in 202, Polybius has Hannibal remind his men of the time they fought Paullus at Cannae. It has been argued that since Paullus commanded the right wing at Cannae (Polyb. 3.114.6), he must have been in command, since this position was traditionally reserved for the overall commander (Samuels, 1990, p. 23). This argument is far from persuasive, however, as the symmetrical grand-tactical manoeuvres which were the hallmark of battles in the Second Punic War did not require the overall commander to be stationed on the right wing and, unlike Greek armies, Roman armies tended to place their best troops, the legions, in the centre rather than on the right wing.[11] Furthermore, considering the size of the army at Cannae, it would have been difficult for a commander on the right wing to communicate with troops at the far end of the line.[12] Appian, who believed Paullus to be in command at Cannae, records that he was positioned in the centre (App., *Hann.* 19). On balance, it is probably impossible to ascertain who commanded the Roman forces on the day of the battle, and as the consuls seem to have been essentially of one mind in their desire to face Hannibal in battle, it is likely that the question of which one was nominally in charge is of very limited relevance.

The consuls had a wide range of functions both in peace and in war (Polyb. 6.12), but leadership in war was the core of the office for it was there that the consuls 'met their heaviest responsibilities and brightest opportunities' (Harris, 1979, p. 15). Leadership in war gave the consuls many powers. Polybius says that:

> they are empowered to make what demands they choose on the allies, to appoint military tribunes, to levy soldiers and select those who are fittest for service. They also have the right of inflicting, when on active service, punishment on anyone under their command and they are authorised to spend any sum they decide upon from the public funds.
>
> (Polyb. 6.12.6–8)

These powers are essentially administrative and 'function-related' in nature and leave out the basic role of the consul as a commander who must decide on the movements of the army and on whether to give battle, and on the time and place for battle. More important for the purpose of this study are the consul's tasks during battle itself, which involved directing the small details from close to the fighting and encouraging the troops (Goldsworthy, 1996, p. 165).

Rather than being monarchs or professional soldiers, the consuls were aristocratic magistrates who were elected on an annual basis by the *comitia centuriata*, an assembly of the people divided into 193 centuries, or voting blocks.[13] This system was blatantly weighted towards the wealthier elements in Roman society, elements which incidentally played a proportionately greater role in Rome's army (Rosenstein, 1990, p. 153). Eighteen centuries were given over to the *equites*, the wealthiest citizens, and the first *classis* under the old 'Servian' system were assigned seventy centuries. The other four *classes* would have had one hundred centuries between them, with five centuries reserved for those too poor to bear arms. A prospective consul would have been a member of the Roman élite, following a generally well-defined progression of positions, many of which would have been military in character (Goldsworthy, 1996, p. 121). To run for office, according to Polybius, ten years' military service was required (Polyb. 6.19.4), and apart from the military tribuneship no one is known to have held office without fulfilling this requirement until 76, with the exception of Scipio Africanus as aedile in 213.[14] Military experience was therefore normal for young Roman aristocrats and further experience could be acquired through serving as a quaestor and sometimes as a praetor or legate.[15] Presumably this experience would have made up for the prospective consul's lack of formal military training.

Roman society was extremely militaristic and the consulship gave the Roman élite an opportunity to justify their supremacy. Military success enabled such aristocrats to win prestige – *gloria* – among their fellows. This in turn benefited the state, as Sallust pointed out, even if he oversimplified considerably:

> Still the free state, once liberty was won, waxed incredibly strong and great in a remarkably short time, such was the thirst for glory that had filled men's minds.
>
> (Sall., *Cat.* 7.3)[16]

Nevertheless, as far as the aristocracy were concerned the consulship was mainly a chance to win *gloria,* and in doing so justify their position in society. The nobility which came from such fame was seen as hereditary, but aristocrats were expected to live up to the standards of their ancestors.[17] That said, a reputation for *virtus*, or courage, would not only enable a consul to acquire a sense of *gloria* but would also help prospective consuls in their bid to be elected (Harris, 1979, p. 33). It has been argued that military success was not absolutely necessary for a successful political career, since there seems to be no statistical correlation between military and subsequent electoral defeats (Rosenstein, 1990, p. 13), possibly because 'the shock of defeat gave rise to the belief that the support of the gods had vanished' (Rosenstein, 1990, p. 55). Military success must, however, have been extremely beneficial as a rule.

In order to assist him in carrying out his duties, each consul was assigned a quaestor, who was in practice under his orders, though the quaestors' original function was probably to act as a limit on the consul's financial powers while on campaign (Polyb. 6.12.8). The quaestor seems to have acted as some kind of quartermaster, with a depot in the camp (Polyb. 6.31.2). In addition each legion had six military tribunes, who were elected, in the case of the four legions of the standard levy, by the tribal assembly. The tribunes for any additional legions were chosen by the consuls themselves. The tribunes had important administrative roles, which have been already been discussed (p. 57–8) and would command the legion in pairs, serving for a month at a time while the remainder served the consul in a 'staff' function (Samuels, 1990, p. 13). It is admittedly anachronistic to refer to a 'general staff' in ancient armies, since the general staff proper was an invention of the nineteenth-century Prussian army, but it is hardly going too far to say that the Romans developed the nearest thing to it in the ancient world (Keegan, 1987, p. 40). In charge of the army at the lowest tactical level were the 'professional' centurions, who were probably the most experienced soldiers in the army. There were sixty of these per legion, thirty senior and thirty junior. Each maniple had two centuries, and hence two centurions, with the senior one, the *centurio prior*, in command overall. The first centurion chosen for the legion was part of the military council of the army. In addition, each centurion had an *optio*, a rearguard officer acting as a quartermaster for the century (Polyb. 6.24). The cavalry were divided into ten squadrons, each with three officers called decurions, and again an *optio* for each decurion (Polyb. 6.25.1–2). The command structure for the allies is less clear, but Roman officers, called *praefecti sociorum*, seem to have fulfilled similar roles to the military tribunes, while at lower levels the allies evidently provided their own officers.

So much for the theoretical structure of a consular army. The combined forces at Cannae must have been run on a rather different basis, however. There were two consuls, Paullus and Varro, each with a quaestor, whom Livy names as Lucius Atilius and Lucius Furius Bibaculus (Liv. 22.49.16). Polybius says that the two consuls of 217, Gnaeus Servilius Geminus and Flaminius' replacement Marcus Atilius Regulus, were present, commanding the centre (Polyb. 3.114.6), but Livy has Marcus Minucius Rufus, Fabius Maximus' Master of Horse, commanding instead of Atilius (Liv. 22.49.16), who had apparently been sent back to Rome because of his age (Liv. 22.40.6). Whether or not this was the reason, Atilius clearly did not die at Cannae, despite what Polybius says (Polyb. 3.116.11), for Livy records that he was elected censor for 214 (Liv. 24.11.6). Polybius is apparently wrong, presumably confusing Atilius Regulus and Minucius Rufus because they had the same *praenomen*, Marcus; Polybius refers to the previous year's consuls only as Marcus and Gnaeus (Polyb. 3.114.6). It is likely that Servilius commanded his soldiers of the previous year, while Minucius led Atilius' men (Lazenby, 1978, p. 80). If Polybius' claim that eight legions were raised for 216 is correct, then there must have been forty-eight military tribunes. This seems likely as Livy says that twenty-nine military tribunes were killed (Liv. 22.49.16) and at least seven survived, being Appius Claudius Pulcher, Gnaeus Cornelius Lentulus, Publius Cornelius Scipio, Quintus Fabius Maximus, Gnaeus Octavius, Lucius Publicius Bibulus, and Publius Sempronius Tuditanus.[18] Overall, among the dead at Cannae were:

> eighty distinguished men who were either members of the Senate, or had held offices which qualified for membership, and had, on this occasion, volunteered for service in the legions.
>
> (Liv. 22.49.17)

These men would clearly not have been ordinary soldiers and must have filled some position in the command system.

Hannibal and his staff

Hannibal was an extremely experienced general, apparently having been brought up in the arts of war in Spain by his father Hamilcar (Zon. 8.21) and serving under Hasdrubal as his 'lieutenant-general', with specific command over the cavalry (App., *Iber.* 6; Nep., *Hann.* 3.1), a position which earned him much respect, according to Livy:

> Never was the same nature more adaptable to things the more diverse – obedience and command. And so one could not readily have told whether he were dearer to the general or the army. When any bold or difficult deed was to be done, there was no one whom Hasdrubal liked better to entrust with it, nor did any other leader inspire his men with greater confidence or daring. To reckless courage in incurring dangers he united the greatest judgement when in the midst of them. . . . Both of horsemen and of foot-soldiers he was undoubtedly the first – foremost to enter battle, and last to leave it when the fighting had begun.
>
> (Liv. 21.4.3–5, 8)

This description, which continues in this vein, is probably highly conventional, describing what Livy expected Hannibal was like, but it is probably not too inaccurate, illustrating the blend of 'shrewdness' and 'courage' which Polybius expected in a general. That said, most Carthaginian advances in Spain during Hasdrubal's generalship, when Hannibal served under him, were diplomatic rather than military (Polyb. 2.36.2–3).

As a general in his own right, following the assassination of Hasdrubal in 221 (Polyb. 2.36.3), Hannibal gained wide experience in many types of warfare before the battle of Cannae. He fought against many tribes in Spain (Polyb. 3.13.5–14.8, 17, 35.2–4), on both sides of the Ebro, and in Gaul he fought local tribes crossing the Rhone and at the 'Island' (Polyb. 3.42–3, 49.5–10). Crossing the Alps he fought against the Allobroges and some treacherous natives (Polyb. 3.50–3). In general this type of warfare would have been irregular in nature, not quite guerrilla warfare but certainly not formal setpiece battles. Even the battles of the Ticinus and Lake Trasimene fit this irregular model of warfare. The former was essentially a skirmish involving solely cavalry on the Carthaginian side and cavalry and light troops on the Roman, while the battle at Lake Trasimene was basically a giant ambush rather than a formal head-to-head battle. However, the battle of the Trebia was a classic 'setpiece' engagement between Hannibal's army and the Roman forces. There are similarities between the battles, as discussed earlier (pp. 39–42), and his experience at the Trebia doubtless gave Hannibal a useful rehearsal for the much larger conflict at Cannae.

The Carthaginian office of general was very different from the Roman consular system. Carthaginian generals were not elected on an annual basis, but were instead appointed for a specific military task, something which was quite possibly unique in the ancient world (Lazenby, 1996a, p. 20). The chief executive officers of the state in civil matters were the two *suffetes*, who, like Rome's consuls, were elected annually (Warmington, 1960, p. 119). These had no military powers at all. This system of dividing civil and military powers, probably because of the mercenary nature of Carthage's army, had both advantages and disadvantages. Carthaginian generals could, in practice, become 'professionals' due to long experience of command since no time restriction was imposed on their office (Lazenby, 1996a, p. 20). It should, however, be borne in mind that their appointment was due not necessarily to ability but rather to wealth and social standing, as in Rome. Some families, such as the Magonids and the Barcids, developed a military tradition (Warmington, 1960, p. 121). On the other hand, though, the generals could be seen as mere employees to be left to their own devices who consequently could not rely on the support of the civil government (Lazenby, 1996a, p. 21), perhaps because the Carthaginian senate, unlike that of Rome, tended not to be made up of men with military experience (Lazenby, 1978, p. 7). Unsuccessful generals could be punished harshly too, for they were forced to account for their actions to the 'Hundred' – a body of 104 judges. Crucifixion could be the penalty for defeat (Rosenstein, 1990, p. 9).

In theory the generals were elected by the citizens in a popular assembly but in practice it seems that the people merely ratified the army's own choice (Lancel, 1995, p. 119). This may not always have been the case but the Xanthippus incident in the First Punic War may have marked the beginning of a change:

> But the troops, eager as they were for a battle, collecting in groups and calling on Xanthippus by name, clearly indicated their opinion that he should lead them forward at once. The generals when they saw the enthusiasm and keenness of the soldiers, Xanthippus at the same time imploring them not to let the opportunity slip, ordered the troops to get ready and gave Xanthippus authority to conduct operations as he himself thought most advantageous.
>
> (Polyb. 1.33.4–5)

Admittedly this refers only to battlefield command, rather than overall generalship. However, in the subsequent war with their mercenaries Hamilcar and Hanno shared command but quarrelled and the troops were asked to reject one of them (Polyb. 1.82.5, 12). Again, this situation is somewhat unusual as there would have been a larger citizen presence than customary in this particular army. Nevertheless, Diodorus says that on Hamilcar's death in Spain Hasdrubal was 'acclaimed as general by the army and by the Carthaginians alike' (Diod. 25.12.1), and Polybius records that on Hasdrubal's death the Carthaginians:

> at first waited for a pronouncement on the part of the troops, and when news reached them from their armies that the soldiers had

unanimously chosen Hannibal as their commander, they hastened
to summon a general assembly of the commons, which unanimously
ratified the choice of the soldiers.

(Polyb. 3.13.3–4)

It seems that a kind of surrogate patriotism had developed in Carthage's
army. The mercenary and allied soldiers were never motivated by love of
Carthage itself and simple greed was not enough to inspire them. Instead
an *esprit de corps* grew up focusing on the mystique of their leaders, who
virtually became a hereditary monarchy in Spain with political power in
Carthage based on and justified by their military authority and success
(Picard, 1964, pp. 137–8).

Furthermore, although they were in reality agents of the Carthaginian
state with limited powers (Walbank, 1957, p. 152), the Barcids seem to
have presented themselves to the Spanish tribes as something very different.
Diodorus claims that the Spanish tribes hailed Hasdrubal as *strategos
autokrator*, 'supreme commander', which is the same term he uses for the
title conferred upon Alexander by the League of Corinth (Diod. 25.12,
17.4.9). This is not to say that the Barcids were presenting themselves as
typical Hellenistic monarchs, as some modern writers argue (Scullard,
1989b, pp. 39–40; Picard and Picard, 1968, pp. 214–16; 1961, pp. 205
ff.), though the oversimplification of Hellenistic monarchs as 'little more
than *condottieri* who ruled over territory they had conquered' (Picard and
Picard, 1961, p. 206) is a valid enough description of the position of the
Barcids in Spain, in practice if not quite in theory.

Since, unlike Rome, Carthage was not a militaristic society, the question of what compelled members of the Carthaginian élite to risk the
punishment defeat would bring by entering a military rather than a commercial career must be considered. In the first place, it should be borne in
mind that economic gain normally goes hand in hand with successful warfare
so military and commercial careers are not inherently mutually exclusive
activities.[19] At the most basic level, for instance, plunder was a traditional
feature of ancient warfare, and Carthage's generals were evidently not slow
in acquiring booty if Hannibal's behaviour after taking Althea is represen-
tative (Polyb. 3.13.7). The fact that Hasdrubal was able to build a palatial
residence in Cartagena surely indicates that the Spanish project had tangible
financial benefits for the Barcids. However, there were doubtless other less
'rational' reasons, such as patriotism and desire for adventure and glory. The
Barcid military tradition, which seems to have begun with Hamilcar, is
sometimes seen as being driven by hatred of Rome, although this may
simply be part of the anti-Barcid tradition displayed by the sources (e.g.,
Polyb. 3.10.5–12.4; Zon. 8.21). Another possibility is that they desired the
political and commercial power that went with successful leadership in war,
for although Carthage was a primarily commercial society and was not

driven by a desire for glory, military success still had rewards,[20] as Appian records of Hasdrubal in Spain:

> Thus he made for himself an occasion for being away from home, and also for performing exploits and acquiring popularity. For whatever property he took he divided, giving one part to the soldiers, to stimulate their zeal for future plundering with him. Another part he sent to the treasury of Carthage, and a third he distributed to the chiefs of his own faction there.
>
> (App., *Iber.* 5)

Hannibal did not lead his army without assistance but, as one would expect, had help in planning and carrying out his decisions. Polybius refers to Hannibal consulting his 'council' on a number of occasions (Polyb. 3.71.5, 85.6, 9.24.4–8), and there are many instances of Hannibal delegating command of army sections, whether in battle or to conduct individual operations, to his officers (Gsell, 1928, p. 393). It is perhaps not surprising that there should have been a military council and a definite chain of command in the Barcid army – if Xanthippus had any long-term effects upon the Carthaginian army it is likely that the Carthaginian command structure was remodelled on something like Spartan lines.[21] The Spartan army had a clear chain of command, and Spartan commanders tended to be accompanied by their subordinate officers, who could offer advice and act upon orders (Anderson, 1970, pp. 69 ff.).

Family connections were clearly important among the top ranks of Hannibal's army. Hannibal's brother Mago, who had led the decisive ambush at the Trebia and who was positioned with Hannibal in the centre at Cannae, was certainly a member of the council. So too was Hanno, the son of Bomilcar, *suffete* and commander of the Numidian cavalry at Cannae; he may have been Hannibal's nephew. Unrelated to Hannibal was Hasdrubal, the head of the army service corps, who commanded the Celtic and Spanish cavalry at Cannae. Given their critical positions at Cannae, it is likely that these three were Hannibal's most senior lieutenants.[22]

Several other officers are known, all of whom, like the aforementioned trio, were Carthaginian aristocrats. Bagnall describes them as experienced veterans who may have served under Hamilcar and played a part in the election of Hannibal as general (Bagnall, 1990, p. 157). This is impossible to prove but very plausible. Maharbal, son of Himilco, is perhaps the most celebrated of these, and although Livy's claim that he commanded the Numidian cavalry at Cannae is contradicted by Polybius, he may well have served with the Numidians under the overall command of Hanno.[23] For what it is worth, in relaying the famous story of how Maharbal criticised Hannibal's failure to take advantage of his victory at Cannae, Plutarch refers to him as Barca, perhaps indicating that he too was related to Hannibal (Plut., *Vit. Fab. Max.*

17.1).[24] Another cavalry officer, Carthalo, captured the 2,000 Roman fugitives from the battlefield who reached the town of Cannae itself (Liv. 22.49.13, 58.7). He had apparently also led an impressive cavalry attack and pursuit the previous year (Liv. 22.15.8). Plutarch mentions one Gisgo, a Carthaginian of Hannibal's own rank, who accompanied him before the giving of battle at Cannae (Plut., *Vit. Fab. Max.* 15.2), and Livy later mentions a Himilco besieging the town of Petelia in Bruttium (Liv. 22.30.1); presumably they had important parts to play at Cannae.

Aside from Carthaginian officers, Hannibal was also accompanied in both Spain and Italy by *synedroi*, who were probably members of the Carthaginian senate, perhaps serving in a capacity not unlike that of Sparta's ephors.[25] Three of these – Mago, Myrcan, and Barmocar – were important enough to be mentioned along with Hannibal in the treaty of 215 with Philip of Macedon (Polyb. 7.9.1). Presumably they also took part in the deliberations of Hannibal's council. Some members of the council may not even have been Carthaginian. Muttines, for instance, the Liby-Phoenician who was sent to command the Numidian cavalry in Sicily in 212, had apparently been trained by Hannibal (Liv. 25.40.5), and if he had command experience he may have been a member of the council. Furthermore, the army's various national contingents may have been represented at deliberations. If this was the case there must also have been interpreters present.

There may have been an informal 'inner circle' among the army's leading Carthaginians. According to Polybius:

> After this [the victory at Lake Trasimene] he consulted with his brother and friends as to where and how it was best to deliver his attack, being now convinced of final success.
>
> (Polyb. 3.85.6)

The fact that Hannibal appears not to have discussed his overall strategy with his entire military council suggests that this body was somewhat unwieldy, perhaps having too many members. He apparently consulted only a few trusted friends when he had important decisions to make. Mago, Hanno, and Hasdrubal have already been mentioned, and Polybius specifically identifies two other officers – Hannibal Monomachus and Mago 'the Samnite' – as Hannibal's friends (Polyb. 9.24.5–6, 25). It seems that this small group of intimates formed the core of Hannibal's 'general staff'. Lancel may be correct when he describes a 'brotherhood of arms' existing between these officers, similar to that which later existed between the marshals of Napoleon's empire.[26]

Preparations for battle

Intelligent tactical decisions cannot be made without knowledge of such factors as the whereabouts and strength of the enemy forces, their abilities and limitations, the personality of their commander – if this can be discovered – local terrain and weather conditions, etc. (Engels, 1980, p. 327). The purpose of this section is to examine how such information was gathered by the Roman and Carthaginian commanders before the battle of Cannae. It will then be necessary to consider how this information was used to form military judgements. Did the commanders, having considered the known facts about their situation, make their decisions alone or in consultation with their officers? Following this, how were these decisions put into action? This would involve matters like issuing orders to subordinates and explaining what these orders involved.

Military intelligence can be defined as 'that which is accepted as fact, based on all available information about an actual or potential enemy or area of operations' (Austin and Rankov, 1995, p. 1). This can be divided into two broad categories: strategic and tactical intelligence. Strategic intelligence is long term in nature and tends to be needed for military campaigns. Polybius points out the importance of this in warfare:

> For in the first place can we imagine a more imprudent general or a more incompetent leader than Hannibal would have been, if with so large an army under his command and all his hopes of ultimate success resting on it, he did not know the roads and the country, as these writers say, and had absolutely no idea where he was marching or against whom, or in fact if his enterprise were feasible or not?
> (Polyb. 3.48.1–3)

Tactical intelligence is more immediately relevant to this book, as it is short term in nature. In an ancient context it would take over from strategic intelligence when the two opposing sides were virtually within sight of each other. It would involve factors influencing 'the choice of a battlefield, the positions taken up on that battlefield and the conduct of the fighting itself' (Austin and Rankov, 1995, p. 6). Vegetius discusses these factors at length, noting how a commander should understand the relative strengths and weaknesses of his own forces and those of the enemy, the nature of the terrain upon which a battle might be fought, the logistical situation of the enemy, the character of the opposing commander, and the level of morale in both armies (Veg. 3.9). What then were the means by which the commanders at Cannae acquired such information?

The immediate sequence of events leading up to the battle of Cannae can be seen to begin with the arrival of the new consuls at the Roman camp (Polyb. 3.108). On the second day the army marched towards 'the place where they heard that the enemy was' (Polyb. 3.110.1). This of course begs the question of how they heard this. In ancient warfare, the simple act of finding the enemy was vitally important, given the relatively small size of armies compared to possibly rather large areas of country within which campaigns could take place (Goldsworthy, 1996, p. 125). The battle of Cynoscephalae in 197, for instance, was a direct result of bad reconnaissance – first the Roman commander Flamininus was unable to discover the whereabouts of the Macedonian army (Polyb. 18.18.1), then the advanced sections of both armies encountered each other unexpectedly (Polyb. 18.19.6), and finally both armies withdrew and marched towards the same destination but:

> as there were high hills between the two armies in their march neither did the Romans perceive where the Macedonians were marching to nor the Macedonians the Romans.
>
> (Polyb. 18.20.4)

The upshot of this was that eventually the advance forces of each army met, again unexpectedly, and battle began on ground unsuitable for either cavalry or the rigid fighting style of the Macedonian phalanx (Polyb. 18.21; Hammond, 1988, pp. 60–82; Keppie, 1998, pp. 41–3; Connolly, 1998, pp. 205–7). The type of troops that would have fought in this action were *procursatores*, troops operating 'in a reconnaissance role immediately ahead of a force in the field' (Austin and Rankov, 1995, p. 9), who were, in practice, an advance guard of cavalry skirmishers.

On the other hand, the troops who had discovered the Carthaginian whereabouts were probably *exploratores*, scouts who would range further afield than the *procursatores*, specifically aiming to acquire advance intelligence (Austin and Rankov, 1995, p. 42). It is impossible to say whether there were formal units of *exploratores* in the army in 216, but it would be very bizarre if the Romans lacked scouts of any description. The precise terminology for such troops is not really relevant.

The third day after the consuls joined their army, the Romans 'coming in view of them [the Carthaginians] . . . encamped at a distance of about five miles from them' (Polyb. 3.110.1). This was within easy marching distance but, more importantly, it enabled the Romans to monitor the activity of the Carthaginians. This could be done both in a vague sense from a distance as a cloud of dust would betray any large-scale movements, but patrols could also be sent out to look for specific information about the enemy forces (Goldsworthy, 1996, p. 127). Of course, this meant that Hannibal had the same advantages and the next day he attacked the Roman advance guard with his own light-armed troops and cavalry (Polyb. 3.110.5). Polybius notes that the Carthaginians did not have the success they had hoped for (Polyb. 3.110.7) but the attack enabled Hannibal to see 'that it was imperative for him to give battle and attack the enemy' (Polyb. 3.111.1). Rather than a committed attack, the encounter seems more like a reconnaissance in force which turned into a skirmish, as at the battle of the Ticinus where both Scipio and Hannibal, having learnt from their scouts how close they were to each other, took the whole of their cavalry, and Publius his javelineers also, and advanced through the plain with the object of reconnoitring each other's forces. Upon their approaching each other and seeing the clouds of dust they at once got into order for action.

(Polyb. 3.65.3–4)

At Cannae, when the Romans encamped 5 miles from the Carthaginians, the consuls are presented as having disagreed over the suitability of the terrain for giving battle:

Aemilius, seeing that the district round was flat and treeless, was opposed to attacking the enemy there as they were superior in cavalry, his advice being to lure them on by advancing into a country where the battle would be decided by the infantry.

(Polyb. 3.110.2)

Varro, being less experienced in war, apparently disagreed. Of course if, as has been pointed out, the consuls were of like mind as to how to deal with Hannibal, Paullus did not even consider the fact that they were challenging Hannibal on terrain where he would have a significant tactical advantage, or else thought that the Roman superiority in numbers would nullify this advantage.

Hannibal, on the other hand, was seemingly well aware of the advantage of the terrain for his cavalry (Polyb. 3.111.4). Furthermore, he was also apparently well acquainted with the dry, dusty nature of the terrain and local weather conditions, as he supposedly positioned his army facing away from the prevailing wind so that dust would not be blown into their faces.[27] While it is important that the Romans chose the field of battle at Cannae by deploying first, Hannibal did have the option of declining their challenge. What certainly comes across in the evaluation of the terrain is the importance of personal observation or 'autopsy' by the commander, enabling him to make rapid and accurate assessments of the suitability of an area for battle (Austin and Rankov, 1995, p. 60). Polybius emphasised that this was the ideal situation for a commander though it was not always possible (Polyb. 9.14.1–3). This is supported by Napoleon's statement that:

A general who has to see things through other people's eyes will never be able to command an army as it should be commanded.[28]

Polybius claimed that the most important thing for a general to know about was the character of his opponent, since moral and psychological flaws lead to mistakes which an able commander can turn to his own advantage (Polyb. 3.81). It was knowledge of Flaminius' self-confidence that enabled Hannibal to lead him into the trap at Lake Trasimene (Polyb. 3.80.3), and similarly, when Fabius and Minucius shared command, Hannibal:

> partly from what he had heard from prisoners and partly from what he saw was going on, was aware of the rivalry of the two generals and of Marcus' impulsiveness and ambition. Considering then, that the present circumstances of the enemy were not against him but in his favour, he turned his attention to Minucius, being anxious to put a stop to his venturesomeness and anticipate his offensive.
> (Polyb. 3.104.1–2)

His subsequent tactics were based above all on the likelihood that Minucius would react rashly. Livy ascribes similar knowledge to Hannibal before the battle of Cannae, saying that:

> All the circumstances of his enemies were as familiar to him as his own: that their generals were unlike each other and were at logger-heads, and that nearly two-thirds of their army consisted of recruits.
> (Liv. 22.41.5–6)

As has been pointed out, this division between Paullus and Varro is probably an aristocratic fiction, but what is more important is the emphasis placed on knowing the state of the enemy forces and commander, remarkably similar to the famous injunction of Sun Tzu (1993, p. 106), the Chinese military thinker of the fifth century BC, to 'Know the enemy and know yourself; in a hundred battles you will never be defeated'. This was done through spying and through interrogation of prisoners (Polyb. 15.5.4, 3.104.1). Celts were doubtless used as spies, as Celtic allies served on both sides, making them relatively inconspicuous. Deserters would also have been questioned, and as Roman military and political careers overlapped, spies in Rome itself could have been used by the Carthaginians to gain information about the Roman generals' personalities. Indeed, one such spy was caught in 216 (Liv. 22.33.1). It is difficult to tell whether this information could have been brought to Hannibal in time to be of use.

Having obtained such information, the opposing commanders then had to act on it. On the day following the large-scale skirmish described above, Hannibal apparently addressed his troops (Polyb. 3.111), the next day ordering his men to prepare themselves for battle (Polyb. 3.112.1). The third day he drew up his army to offer battle but Paullus declined to fight (Polyb. 3.112.1–3). Varro led out his forces the next day (Polyb. 3.113.1). It is likely that Hannibal's plan of battle had been decided for the previous day so if Plutarch's anecdote about him riding to a nearby hill to watch the Romans deploy for battle is genuine (Plut., *Vit. Fab. Max.* 15.2), it must merely have been to check for himself whether his plan was feasible based on the Roman order of battle.

No evidence survives for how Hannibal made his decisions about fighting at Cannae, but his approach was probably very similar to that at the Trebia. There he first considered the terrain and its suitability for ambuscades (Polyb. 3.71.1–4) and evidently planned his tactics. He then discussed these proposed tactics with Mago and the rest of his staff and on their approval began issuing orders, to Mago first in this case (Polyb. 3.71.5–6). It is difficult to estimate the extent to which his staff would disagree with him – he seems to have anticipated no dissent, for some time before meeting his council he ordered the troops who were to lead in the planned ambush 'to come to his tent after supper' (Polyb. 3.71.7).[29] He then sent these out with more troops, who they had themselves picked, under Mago, who had been given detailed instructions (Polyb. 3.71.9). At daybreak he ordered his Numidian cavalry to draw out the Romans (Polyb. 3.71.10), after which he summoned his officers and exhorted them, presumably giving them instructions at the same time, and then told the troops to eat and prepare for battle (Polyb. 3.71.11). On seeing the Romans approaching, he sent out his light troops as a covering force and then led out his cavalry and heavy infantry, which he drew up in line of battle after marching for about 2 miles (Polyb. 3.72.7–10).

If similar procedures were followed at Cannae it is possible to reconstruct Hannibal's preparations for battle there. Having studied the local terrain and weather conditions, and what information he had about the enemy, Hannibal must have planned his tactics and then outlined them to his subordinates, expecting their approval, but perhaps being willing to listen to criticism. On securing their approval, the following morning or that evening he would have issued orders which would have been transmitted down through the ranks. Battle having been decided the first day, the same orders were probably issued the following day on seeing Varro lead out the army, although in this case the troops were required to cross the river rather than line up along it. The light troops were then sent out as a covering force to enable the troops of the line to deploy for battle. There was presumably a system for doing this if the account of Xanthippus' manoeuvring the Carthaginian forces in the First Punic War is accurate (Polyb. 1.32.7).

How then were decisions made in the Roman army? Polybius refers to the existence of military councils in Roman armies (Polyb. 6.35.4), and claims that the first centurion chosen from each legion, the *primus pilus*, had a place on this council (Polyb. 6.24.2; Walbank, 1957, p. 707). It might be countered that this was perhaps not standard practice in the early years of the Hannibalic War, but there is some evidence for the existence and composition of the army's council by 216. In 217, Fabius Maximus, the Roman dictator, quarrelled with his master of horse, Marcus Minucius. Polybius records that Minucius was supported by the tribunes and the centurions (Polyb. 3.92.4), and according to Appian, Varro was supported against Paullus in 216 by the various senators and *equites* who were officers in the army (App., *Hann.* 18). It would seem, then, that there was some sort of military council in the Roman army, which certainly included the consul, his quaestor, the military tribunes, and the *primus pilus* of each legion, giving a sixteen-man council. It is possible that the prefects of the allies were also present, and perhaps, although this is conjecture, the first decurion elected per legion. This would have enlarged the council to twenty-four or thirty men, depending on whether there were six prefects per consular army or per allied brigade. The army of Cannae would have had a much larger council, as it was effectively composed of two consular and two proconsular armies. If the four command systems were combined, the council could have been as large as 120 men, which must have been unwieldy and inefficient.

It is difficult to tell what function the council served. Certainly by the time of Julius Caesar, more than a century and a half after Cannae, the council was not, as a rule, a forum for general debate – rather, it was primarily an opportunity for the commander to outline his plan and give orders. Goldsworthy points out that the only known exception to this appears to have occurred because of a divided command between the two legates, Cotta and Sabinus, where the subordinate officers took sides and argued (Caes., *B Gall* 5.28; Goldsworthy, 1996, pp. 131–3). It is likely that a similar situation applied in the late third century. In 217, when Minucius was still Fabius' subordinate, Fabius' policy of avoiding battle with Hannibal was maintained despite its unpopularity (Polyb. 3.94.8). Assuming that criticism was voiced in the council, it is clear that decisions ultimately rested with the commander. This was probably the normal state of affairs, the council only becoming a forum for debate and even heated argument when there was a joint command, as between Fabius and Minucius after Minucius' powers were increased,[30] or, of course, between Paullus and Varro, although reports of their antagonism have doubtless been greatly exaggerated.

Although it is important to refrain from reading too much significance into the supposedly divided command at Cannae, especially since a defeat on that scale had to be explained somehow, it is clear that nothing could be properly planned in advance in a system of alternating commands, with the commanders at odds with each other. Anything decided upon by one commander could be countermanded the following morning by his colleague. In any case, Polybius provides a useful description of how orders were transmitted in the mornings, saying that at dawn the cavalry officers and centurions would meet with the tribunes who would in turn go to the consul for orders. On returning they would pass these on to the cavalry officers and centurions who would transmit them to their subordinates at the appropriate time (Polyb. 6.34.5–6).

The theatre of leadership

As has been pointed out already (p. 116), Keegan has identified five basic categories of duties for a commander apart from mere strategic and tactical functions (Keegan, 1987, pp. 315–38). The imperative of sanction – a commander's use of punishments and rewards – is discussed in the next chapter with regard to the morale of ordinary soldiers. The imperative of action, based on the commander's use of intelligence to plan operations, has already been dealt with in this chapter, and the imperative of example – the sharing of risk by a commander through his physical presence in battle – will be covered in the next section. The remaining two imperatives, those of kinship and of prescription, are more subtle, pertaining less to traditional outward signs of military activity and more to propaganda. They contribute nothing tangible to the army's administration or performance and are primarily concerned with the presentation of the commander. The imperative of kinship concerns the creation of a bond between the commander and his men, while that of prescription involves nothing more 'productive' than verbal contact between the two.

The imperative of kinship

Hellenistic armies apparently developed their *esprit de corps* based on the mystique of their leaders who could be seen as having almost 'supernatural' powers as they were granted triumphs by the gods (Picard, 1964, p. 137; Santosuosso, 1997, p. 146; Walbank, 1984, pp. 84 ff.). Alexander the Great, for instance, after seemingly being saluted as 'son of Zeus' at the shrine of Ammon at Siwah, was regarded as having a special relationship with Zeus.[31] Even in the Roman world, Scipio Africanus inculcated into his men the belief that his actions were divinely inspired (Polyb. 10.2.12).[32] Hannibal clearly had an extremely strange relationship with his troops and certainly would have appeared to some extent mysterious to them, being foreign, from a very different culture and with a different language.[33] In itself this would normally create a barrier between a commander and his men but the Carthaginian army was loyal not so much to Carthage, the city that technically employed it, but rather to its Barcid generals, who were in practice chosen by the army rather than by the citizens of Carthage. The fact that the army chose its own commander must have been a vital factor in creating a sense of kinship between the commander and the commanded in the Carthaginian army.

Even though the Roman consuls were not specifically appointed by the army, instead being elected officials at the highest step in the aristocratic *cursus*, with a year-long mandate to command, it should not be assumed that their position was regarded as either mundane or externally imposed. The Roman army of the Republic, despite its peculiar rituals, was not a separate society, unlike the essentially foreign army employed by the Carthaginians. Rather, it was composed of citizens, and it was the citizens of Rome who, in the *comitia centuriata*, elected the consuls (Nicolet, 1980, p. 109). This created a bond between the general and his men, but a sense of mystique was useful too, since it would mark the consul out as being in some way 'special'. For this to be facilitated, in 216 each soldier in the army of Cannae had to take a formal oath of loyalty to his commander, even though he had already taken a voluntary oath of allegiance to the commander on enrolment and other voluntary oaths of solidarity on being posted to his decury and century (Polyb. 6.21.2–3; Liv. 22.38.2–5).

This position may have been helped by the consuls' religious roles, which may have contributed towards a sense of distance between the leader and led. Onasander, writing in the first century AD, argued that a general should not enter into any action without first making a sacrifice and receiving favourable omens; consequently he should be accompanied by priests and should ideally be skilled in reading the omens himself (Onas. 10.25).[34] Onasander may have had Greek generals in mind when he wrote that, but his comments were equally applicable to Rome, where war and religion were inextricably linked. Under the terms of the *Ius Fetiale*, enemies could not be attacked without religious justification and without the proper rituals having taken place, culminating in a fetial priest declaring war and casting a spear into the enemy's territory. These procedures were initially quite complicated and became more difficult to perform as Rome's borders expanded, but they were simplified over time, and were apparently abandoned entirely after 171 (Rich, 1976, pp. 56–8; Harris, 1979, pp. 166–71). Consuls would take the auspices on their first day in office, then lead a procession to the temple of Jupiter on the Capitoline hill, where sacrifices would be given and vows made. Rituals of purification would be performed when the consuls joined their armies, and there would be frequent making of sacrifices and taking of auspices while on campaign, especially before giving battle (Rosenstein, 1990, pp. 59–60). A special part of the camp, called the *auguratorium*, was used for the taking of auspices, where the sacred chickens would be consulted. The auspices were valid only for the day on which they were taken (Linderski, 1986, pp. 2276, 2295). An example of such behaviour prior to the battle of Cannae is recorded by Livy, according to whom Paullus, taking the auspices, noted how the sacred chickens refused their food, and so stopped Varro from rushing into an ambush which Hannibal had laid (Liv. 22.42).[35]

Carthaginian generals apparently offered solemn sacrifices to the gods before any engagement.[36] Polybius may be referring to this sort of thing when he records that many barbarian tribes:

> when they are entering on a war or on the eve of a decisive battle sacrifice a horse, divining the issue from the way it falls.
>
> (Polyb. 12.4b.3)

Sacrifice before battle was certainly a regular feature of ancient warfare,[37] and sacrifices were an essential element in Carthaginian religion with, for instance, families pledging allegiance to the gods through the sacrifice of children (Lancel, 1995, pp. 193, 227–56). A wide variety of animals were also sacrificed, often by holocaust, or alternatively by the sacrificial carcass being either divided between giver and priest or retained by the priest (Warmington, 1960, p. 133).

Despite Livy's accusations of impiety (Liv. 21.4.9), Hannibal's leadership clearly had a religious aspect. The Barcids seem to have adopted Herakles-Melqart as their patron, in a manner reminiscent of Hellenistic monarchs. Hannibal himself visited the temple of Herakles-Melqart at Gades before his invasion of Italy in order to gain divine aid through making vows (Liv. 21.21.9),[38] and his passage through the Alps may have been publicised as an emulation of his patron, if Livy is to be believed (Liv. 21.41.7).[39] The Romans evidently did not dismiss this as empty propaganda, and appear to have taken steps to placate the Phoenician deity, albeit in the form of Hercules, his traditional Roman equivalent.[40]

In a more restrained religious role, Hannibal apparently 'understood divination by the inspection of entrails' (Cass. Dio fr. 54.3) and Polybius describes him publicly praying to the gods on behalf of his entire army before crossing the Rhone (Polyb. 3.44.13). According to Livy he sacrificed a lamb before the battle of the Ticinus, smashing its skull with a rock as an offering to 'Jupiter and the other gods' (Liv. 21.45.8–9).[41] Of course, Hannibal was not sacrificing to Roman gods, and it is likely that he was sacrificing to the same gods that are mentioned in his treaty with Philip V of Macedon (Lancel, 1998, p. 83), gods that unfortunately cannot be precisely identified since the text of the treaty as recorded by Polybius identifies them only by their Greek names (Polyb. 7.9.2–3).[42] Nevertheless, it is interesting to note that the treaty refers to 'all the gods of the army' (Polyb. 7.9.3), almost certainly not a reference to Carthaginian gods alone, but more likely to refer to the many deities worshipped by the various nationalities represented in the Barcid army.

The effect on the troops of religious ceremonies such as these is extremely difficult to determine – in one respect these traditions would have been reassuring to veteran soldiers, but new recruits could very well have found such behaviour both alien and unsettling (Goldsworthy, 1996, p. 149). According to Onasander at least, favourable omens were greatly beneficial to the men's morale:

> Soldiers are far more courageous when they believe they are facing dangers with the good will of the gods; for they themselves are on the alert, every man, and they watch closely for omens of sight and of sound, and an auspicious sacrifice for the whole army encourages even those who have private misgivings.
>
> (Onas. 10.26)

The imperative of prescription

Keegan's second imperative, that of prescription, insists that a commander must also know 'how to speak directly to his men at moments of crisis and thank them in victory' (Keegan, 1987, p. 318). Commanders would exhort their troops on the eve of battle, or perhaps just prior to the battle itself, in order to infuse courage into them. Keegan cites Raimondo Montecuccoli, a seventeenth-century general and military theorist, who identified four ways of doing this: first, 'arguments of use', essentially positive reasons based on stressing the need to fight, or the justness of the cause; second, 'exploiting the fear of infamy', which basically involved shaming the troops into fighting well; third, 'exciting the desire for riches and prestige', a barefaced appeal to the desires for loot and glory; and finally, 'developing confidence', particularly through cultivating an appearance of gaiety and nonchalance (Keegan, 1987, pp. 320–1).

An appropriate example of this last point is to be found in Plutarch's account of what happened at Cannae: Hannibal apparently flippantly remarked to Gisgo, a Carthaginian officer, that despite the size of the Roman army it lacked even one man called Gisgo; the subsequent laughter among the officers 'infused courage into the Carthaginians. They reasoned that their general must have a mighty contempt for the enemy if he laughed and jested so in the presence of danger' (Plut., *Vit. Fab. Max.* 15.2). Similarly, almost two hundred years later, Caesar's cheerfulness on his African campaign was to have a calming effect on his men (Caes., *B Afr* 10; Adcock, 1957, p. 83). Onasander discusses this aspect of leadership as follows:

> Whenever despondency or fear has fallen on an army because the enemy has received reinforcements or gained an advantage, then especially the general should show himself to his soldiers gay, cheerful, and undaunted. For the appearance of the leaders brings about a corresponding change in the minds of the subordinates, and if the general is cheerful and has a joyful look, the army also takes heart, believing that there is no danger.
>
> (Onas. 13.1–2)

He argues that it is more important for a general to look cheerful and confident than to be a gifted speaker, as many troops distrust speeches as being specially composed and, as a result, intentionally manipulative, whereas facial expressions could be seen as a natural and spontaneous, and therefore much more accurate, barometer of a general's expectations (Onas. 13.3).

If the substance of Paullus' battle exhortation at Cannae, as reported by Polybius, is correct, it was more important for Carthaginian and Hellenistic commanders to address their men explicitly than it was for Roman commanders:

For those who in some countries serve for hire or for those who are about to fight for their neighbours by the terms of an alliance, the moment of greatest peril is during the battle itself, but the result makes little difference to them, and in such a case exhortation is necessary.

(Polyb. 3.109.6)

Roman soldiers, on the other hand, were fighting for their families and country and consequently required 'not to be exhorted to do their duty but only to be reminded of it' (Polyb. 3.109.7). It is impossible to ascertain if Paullus ever really said such a thing, or whether Polybius believed this himself and deemed it likely that Paullus expressed such a sentiment on this occasion, but it is striking that an examination of Polybius' history up to this point seems to support this claim. Paullus' speech at Cannae is only the second recorded exhortation by a Roman, the other occasion being by Publius Scipio before the battle of the Ticinus (Polyb. 3.64). However, Polybius records that Hannibal exhorted his army, or sometimes just its officers, on numerous occasions (e.g., Polyb. 3.34.7–9, 43.11, 44.4–13, 54.1–3, 63, 71.8, 10, 11, 111), and whereas he mentions no Roman exhortations in the First Punic War there are several references to Carthaginian ones (Polyb. 1.27.1, 32.8, 44.1, 45.2–4, 49.10). It is possible that these statistics may be merely due to the nature of Polybius' evidence, or that he is inserting unhistorical references to exhortations into his narrative in accordance with his own theories about the unreliability of foreign or mercenary armies, but it must be admitted that the evidence as it stands indicates that Paullus, or at least Polybius, was right in this respect. Exhortation, therefore, seems to have been one of the most important duties of Carthaginian commanders, and its frequency was a hallmark of their style of leadership.

This begs the question of whether or not it was genuinely possible to address the entire army at once, as both Paullus and Hannibal are presented as doing on this occasion (Polyb. 3.109, 111). Bearing in mind that the Roman and Carthaginian armies may have been over 80,000 and 40,000 men respectively, this would seem unlikely, considering that Lincoln, though audible, was badly heard at Gettysburg when he addressed 15,000 men (Keegan, 1987, p. 55). It may, however, have in fact been possible to address numbers larger than this – Benjamin Franklin, through carrying out a rather rudimentary experiment, became convinced that a certain travelling preacher, reputed to have preached to audiences of over 25,000, could probably be heard by a crowd of over 30,000 listeners (Clark, 1995, p. 376); Keegan (1987, p. 55), discussing the oratory of Alexander the Great, admits that it may have been possible to address very large bodies of men if they were in a natural amphitheatre, or maybe even paraded against a steep hillside; Philip V of Macedon is known to have summoned his army in Corinth to a theatre to address them (Polyb. 5.25.4–5), but the fact that he did so probably implies that this was necessary, or at least desirable, in order to address a very large army effectively.

Hansen argues that the battle speeches recorded by ancient historians were rhetorical inventions, and that in reality the commander probably rode amongst the army or along the line of battle addressing the army in small sections, probably of at most 5,000 men (Hansen, 1993, p. 169; Goldsworthy, 1996, p. 146). That this sort of thing did happen is well attested by Polybius. At the battle of Raphia in 217, when the Egyptian and Syrian armies were drawn up facing each other, Ptolemy and Antiochus rode along their respective lines addressing their men as they passed; different speeches were evidently made to different parts of the armies as the opposing monarchs appealed most earnestly to the phalanxes on which they relied most heavily (Polyb. 5.83.1). At Mantineia, Philopoemen also tried to address his men in this manner, as 'he rode along the divisions of the phalanx and addressed them in a few brief words' (Polyb. 11.12.1). Interestingly, even then his men had difficulty hearing him, as:

> such was their ardour and zeal that they responded to his address by what was almost a transport of enthusiasm, exhorting him to lead them on and be of good heart.
>
> (Polyb. 11.12.2)

Moreover, Hansen points out (1993, p. 169) that rattling armour and weapons could easily drown out a commander's speech, making it even less likely that a general could address his entire army *en masse*. At Zama, Scipio exhorted his men by addressing various contingents while travelling along the line (Polyb. 15.10.1), whereas Hannibal, having told the mercenary and Carthaginian officers to address their own men, 'went the round of his own troops' (Polyb. 15.11.6).[43]

Hansen goes so far as to cast doubt on the existence of battle exhortations in any form in ancient warfare. He argues that it was far more probable that a general, rather than making one coherent speech to be delivered at various points along the line, would 'invent a few encouraging apophthegms that, with variations, could be shouted to the soldiers as he walked along the front line of the phalanx' (1993, p. 169). However, Ehrhardt notes (1995, p. 121) that a passage in Caesar's account of his Gallic Wars (*B Gall* 2.20.1–2) implies that it was normal, indeed almost obligatory, for a commander to exhort his men properly before battle. Onasander also seems to support the argument that full-scale speeches did take place by claiming that the ideal general should be a skilful speaker:

> For if a general is drawing up his men before battle, the encouragement of his words makes them despise the danger and covet

the honour; and a trumpet-call resounding in the ears does not so effectively awaken the soul to the conflict of battle as a speech that urges to strenuous valour rouses the martial spirit to confront danger.

(Onas. 1.13)

Hansen (1993, p. 166), while acknowledging that the commander certainly said something to his men, argues that Onasander fails to indicate the style or duration of such addresses, but this is to disregard Onasander's later comments on the importance of the commander appearing confident, when he states that:

the general must inspire cheerfulness in the army, more by the strategy of his facial expressions than by his words; for many distrust speeches on the ground that they have been concocted especially for the occasion.

(Onas. 13.3)

This seems to imply that pre-battle harangues were genuine, since the 'few encouraging apophthegms' of Hansen's hypothesis could hardly be described as artificially contrived speeches.

Ehrhardt notes that the speeches recorded by Polybius as having been made at Cannae were given, at least according to Polybius, a few days before the battle.[44] This would seem to indicate that they were not subject to the same time constraints as the type of harangues given immediately before battle, and as the troops would have been unarmed, the commander's speech would not have been drowned out by rattling weaponry. However, the basic problem must have remained: how could armies of such a gigantic scale as fought at Cannae have been addressed by their generals? It seems unlikely that they could have been, but before suggesting possible solutions to this problem, one further issue must be examined.

Hannibal's army was a multinational force, which could be essentially described as being composed of:

Africans, Spaniards, Ligurians, Celts, Phoenicians, Italians, and Greeks, people who neither in their laws, customs or language, nor in any other respect had anything naturally in common.

(Polyb. 11.19.4)

With such an ethnic range, the linguistic diversity of the Barcid host would have made it impossible for Hannibal to address his entire army at once. Polybius largely attributes the unrest which developed among Carthage's mercenaries after the First Punic War to mutual incomprehension, pointing out that as the army was a polyglot force:

It was therefore impossible to assemble them and address them as a body, or indeed by any other means; for how could the general be expected to know all the languages?

(Polyb. 1.67.8–9)

This problem may have also arisen, albeit to a lesser extent, in Rome's army under Paullus for, apart from the Latins, the Italian allies spoke a range of languages (Salmon, 1982, p. 66). On the other hand, Latin was not unknown to the Italians and long-serving allied troops had doubtless acquired some knowledge of the language (Rochette, 1997, p. 157). Zonaras' claim that Hannibal knew a number of languages, including Latin (Zon. 8.24), is unconvincing, although he does appear to have known Greek, the *lingua franca* of the third-century Mediterranean.[45] Still, it was surely not unheard of for a member of a Carthaginian family with a military tradition to have at least some knowledge of the languages of his future subordinates, and Plautus' *Poenulus* (112–13) implies that Carthaginians in general were believed to know all languages (Rochette, 1997, p. 157; Palmer, 1997, p. 29), an understandable belief considering their mercantile expertise.

An obvious way to overcome this linguistic difficulty was to employ interpreters, who were not uncommon in the ancient world – Herodotus records that they made up one of the seven classes of Egyptian society (Hdt. 2.164), and they must have been absolutely essential to the great multiracial armies of antiquity. Onasander, writing in the first century AD, clearly envisages the possible delays that could be caused by mutual incomprehension in a multinational army (Onas. 26.2). The armies at Raphia were multiracial organisations and in addressing them the two kings sometimes had to use interpreters (Polyb. 5.83.7). Interpreters certainly seem to have been an important feature of Carthaginian armies, and there are occasional scattered references to them in the sources (Diod. 23.16.1; Polyb. 1.67.9, 3.44.5, 15.6.3; Liv. 30.30.1, 33.12).

Given that the armies of Cannae were vast, polyglot forces, the basic problem, concerning the speeches Polybius ascribes to the commanders, is how such sentiments could have been communicated. Once this has been considered, the historicity of the sentiments can be examined.

Although both Polybius and Livy tend to ignore the mechanics of speaking to such large and linguistically diverse forces (Bagnall, 1990, p. 172), their accounts of the battle of Zama are notable for attempting to address this very issue. According to Polybius, Hannibal told his officers what to say to their men on his behalf; the Ligurians, Celts, Balearic Islanders, and Moors were then addressed by their own officers, as were the Carthaginians themselves (Polyb. 15.11.4–5). Livy elaborates slightly on this, noting that the various national leaders addressed their own units with the aid of interpreters owing to the admixture of foreign troops (Liv. 30.33.12). Hannibal himself apparently addressed his own veterans, many of whom were presumably Spanish and African since according to Polybius he implored them to remember the seventeen years they had served together (Polyb. 15.11.6).[46] He may have addressed these troops in Punic, rather than their own languages, for it appears that Punic became something of a *lingua franca* for the army of the First Punic War, as discussed in Chapter 3. Considering that the troops at Zama were veterans of the Carthaginian army, it is likely that a certain amount of Punic had been learnt.

Having briefly examined the manner in which Hannibal communicated with his men at Zama, it is possible to attempt to reconstruct the manner in which the troops at Cannae were addressed. Like Alexander at Gaugamela (Arr., *Anab.* 3.9.5–8), Hannibal would first have assembled his officers in order to encourage them and tell them what to tell their men.[47] This assembly must have included not only officers but also interpreters, since it is highly unlikely that Hannibal could have personally exhorted the leaders of all the various national contingents in their own tongues. After being addressed by Hannibal the officers would themselves have exhorted their own men, passing on the commander's sentiments. Polybius, discussing the linguistic problems in the Carthaginian army after the First Punic War, notes that the only practical way for Carthaginian commanders to communicate with their troops was indeed to do so through their officers (Polyb. 1.67.10). It is probable that in the case of the Roman army a similar procedure was followed, although it is far less likely that interpreters would have been necessary, as the junior officers who would have passed on Paullus' words, military tribunes and Prefects of the Allies, were all Roman citizens.

As it seems probable that the commanders at Cannae did indeed exhort their troops in some way, even indirectly, the substance of their purported speeches should be considered. These almost certainly fail to replicate what was genuinely said by Paullus and Hannibal but do reflect at least what Polybius believed appropriate to have been said under the circumstances;[48] Walbank (1957, p. 442) points out that the speeches are 'full of commonplaces' and suspects that they do not derive from a genuine record, suggesting that Polybius may have adopted them from Fabius Pictor's account. Even if this was the case, however, it is unlikely that Polybius would have used them in his account unless they seemed plausible.[49] It is important to remember that these speeches, if they are in any respect genuine, represent what Hannibal and Paullus said to their officers only, not to their armies, despite what Polybius may say.

Most of Paullus' speech was apparently devoted to explaining away the previous defeats at Hannibal's hands (Polyb. 3.108.3), and then to indicating why the current army should win: both consuls were present with the previous year's consuls to support them, the army was familiar with the enemy and was experienced in battle itself (Polyb. 3.109.1–2).[50] This was clearly a way of 'developing confidence' in his men, before resorting to 'arguments of use' by pointing out who they were fighting for – themselves, their country, and their families (Polyb. 3.109.7). Finally, Paullus' speech involved exploiting his men's 'fear of infamy' when he said that the troops at Cannae were all Rome had left to defend it:

> For if the issue of the day be adverse, she has no further resources to overcome her foes; but she has centred all her power and spirit in you, and in you lies her sole hope of safety.
>
> (Polyb. 3.109.10–11)

Hannibal's speech, if Polybius is in any way accurate, seems to have been more positive in tone, based on 'developing confidence' through pointing out the suitability of the terrain for his army to manoeuvre on and then praising the skill and courage of his soldiers (Polyb. 3.111.2–7). Following that he made a more base appeal, 'exciting the desire for riches and prestige', by saying that previous success in battle had won them the wealth of the countryside and the coming battle would be for the wealth of the cities which would give his men power over everything (Polyb. 3.111.8–10). After this speech the army apparently applauded him, leading him to thank them before dismissing them to rest and prepare for the coming battle (Polyb. 3.111.11). This applause seems to have been an element of some significance in the relationship between the commander and his men, and it seems to have been normal.[51] Interestingly, Polybius does not mention this traditional applause and thanks following Paullus' speech, instead simply noting that the troops were dismissed (Polyb. 3.109.13).

Even if these speeches do in any respect represent the reality of what Hannibal and Paullus said to their officers before the battle of Cannae, it is important to emphasise that this is not what the men would have heard. Their officers would have passed on the commanders' message to them, altering it as they did so, whether intentionally or otherwise. Discussing the speeches at Zama, Livy notes that different appeals had to be made to the various national contingents:

> In an army made up of so many men who had no language, no customs, no law, no arms, no clothing and general appearance in common, nor the same reason for serving, exhortation took various forms.
>
> (Liv. 30.33.8)

It is questionable whether it would have been as necessary to appeal to the different units in different ways at Cannae as it was at Zama. At Zama some national units were basically fighting for financial gain, some were traditional enemies of Rome, whereas others were fighting for their freedom or even survival. At Cannae, however, the Carthaginian army had the upper hand, being a proven army successfully fighting a war on enemy territory, and it is very likely that the speeches given to the troops had as common factors the army's record of success and the booty which could be acquired following a victory. Against this, the Celts may indeed have been fighting for revenge on Rome, following their defeats the previous decade, and Hannibal's veterans whom he had brought from Spain may have been inspired by their link with their leader. References to these factors may have been the only significant differences between the speeches passed on to the men.

To conclude, it was vital for purposes of morale that commanders be willing and able to communicate with their men. This was especially important in the Carthaginian army, as it was composed almost entirely of troops who had no direct link with Carthage, unlike the Roman citizen militia. Owing to problems of scale and linguistic diversity it was extremely difficult for the commanders at Cannae to address their armies. To compensate for this, commanders would address their officers who would in turn exhort their own troops. Interpreters may have been used at some point in this arrangement. The speeches as recorded by Polybius may reflect the reality of the commanders' exhortations to their officers, but this is impossible to prove. In any case, they certainly appear to reflect the sort of things which the generals would have been expected to say under such circumstances.

The commanders' battle

As the existing accounts of the battle of Cannae are relatively short, the sources offer few positive statements about what the commanders did in the battle. Any attempt to understand the commanders' experience and behaviour at Cannae must therefore rely quite heavily upon accounts of the actions of commanders in other ancient battles, and upon ancient manuals on generalship. This is the only practical approach to this issue, but it is a highly problematic one, as representations of commanders' behaviour in these sources are subject to a high degree of distortion. Historians often glorify or denigrate individuals for personal, dramatic, patriotic, or ideological reasons, while manuals such as Onasander's describe how the ideal commander ought to act, rather than explaining how real commanders behaved in practice.

The signal for battle on the Roman side would usually be given by raising the red *vexillum* outside the consul's tent (Goldsworthy, 1996, p. 148). Livy and Plutarch record that this was done outside Varro's tent on the morning of the battle, as it was Varro's turn to command the combined Roman forces (Liv. 22.45.5; Plut., *Vit. Fab. Max.* 15.1). However, as discussed already, it is possible that Paullus, rather than Varro, commanded the Roman forces at Cannae, in which case the signal would have been given from his tent. In any case, the signal must have been given at first light,[52] allowing the troops time to eat and prepare for battle, since Polybius claims that the troops began to move out of camp just after dawn (Polyb. 3.113.1), but he does not refer to their being hungry or tired, unlike his account of the fighting at the Trebia (Polyb. 3.72.3, 5). According to Polybius, the tribunes would normally attend upon the consuls at dawn to receive their orders, which would then be passed on to the decurions and centurions, and in turn to the men (Polyb. 6.34.5). The consuls would then emerge from their headquarters, wearing the traditional scarlet battle cloak, which made them quite conspicuous to their men (Plin., *Nat. Hist.* 22.3; Caes., *B Gall* 7.88; Goldsworthy, 1996, p. 148). The mechanics of leading out and deploying the troops in the line of battle are discussed in the next chapter.

Polybius, Livy, and Appian all simply say that the Carthaginian army deployed for battle, but Plutarch paints a fuller picture, emphasising the fact that Hannibal was reacting to the Romans taking the initiative (Polyb. 3.113.6; Liv. 22.46.1; App., *Hann.* 19; Plut., *Vit. Fab. Max.* 15.1–3). Although the regular troops are described as being surprised by the Romans being led out, Plutarch attributes no such surprise to Hannibal, who calmly ordered his men to prepare for battle and then rode with some companions to a nearby vantage point to study the Roman dispositions, presumably in an attempt to ascertain their intended tactics. He then rode back to his camp, where he would have issued any new orders and performed his religious duties.

When the two armies were lined out against each other, the commanders may have taken the time to ride amongst their men, briefly exhorting individual units (App., *Hann.* 21), through interpreters if need be. This would have ensured that the commanders obeyed the 'imperative of prescription' by directly addressing at least some of their men. Eventually, battle began. Polybius and Livy seem to present this as happening spontaneously, with the light troops rushing at each other (Polyb. 3.115.1; Liv. 22.47.1), but this seems highly unlikely, as the commanders must surely have signalled for them to advance (Goldsworthy, 1996, pp. 149–50). Trumpets and horns of various kinds seem to have been in use in both Roman and Carthaginian armies.[53] Horn signals were particularly useful in ancient warfare, because their high-pitched sound carried particularly well and could be heard even through the din of battle.[54] Oddly, Greek armies did not use them extensively in battle, where their main function was to sound the charge and the retreat. This was perhaps due to the straightforward nature of traditional hoplite tactics and the relatively small size of the armies of the city-states. Roman armies, in contrast, used them much more imaginatively – a wide range of horn signals were used to manoeuvre the troops (Krentz, 1991, pp. 114–18).[55] It is likely that horn signals were particularly important in Carthaginian armies, for considering the wide range of languages spoken by the men, a universal, non-linguistic code would have been extremely useful.

The commanders had important roles during the fighting, as they attempted to influence the course of the battle in whatever way they could. It is also worth bearing in mind that the commanders had a large number of subordinate officers, who would in turn have been commanding groups of men, and their command methods should also be considered.

Bravery appears to be the quality troops most value in their leaders, and in order to demonstrate this bravery, commanders must be seen to participate actively in battle. Keegan identifies this 'imperative of example' as the most important of the commander's duties, succinctly making the point that 'those who impose risk must be seen to share it'. Whereas failure to share risks can result in alienation, desertion, and even mutiny,[56] personal involvement can dramatically boost morale – Keegan (1987, p. 90) claims of Alexander that 'the knowledge that he was risking his skin with theirs was enough to ensure that the whole army, from that moment onwards, fought with an energy equal to his'. Practical leadership therefore virtually demands that commanders be seen to involve themselves in the fighting in some way, leading their men in a literal sense.

However, for the commanders in ancient battles to have personally engaged in the fighting would have posed an equally significant risk. By being actively involved in combat, commanders not only shared their men's risks, but also shared their men's perceptions of the battle. As has been mentioned earlier and will be discussed fully in the next chapter, these perceptions would have been extremely limited – after all, during combat, most participants have very little idea of what goes on beyond their immediate surroundings. Taking part in the fighting would therefore have denied commanders the ability to observe the battle from a distance, preventing them from studying the overall progress of the battle and ensuring that they had no means of controlling it (Goldsworthy, 1996, pp. 154–6). It was also, needless to say, extremely dangerous, and many hoplite commanders died in battle while leading their men from the front.[57]

Neither of these options would have been particularly desirable for the commanders at Cannae. Directing their men from behind would almost certainly demoralise the troops, but throwing themselves into the thick of things would deprive the commanders of the ability to influence the battle beyond their immediate vicinity. Luckily, there was another option, a third command model, which attempted to compromise between the two extremities discussed above. Onasander discusses this style of command:

> Hence the general must show himself brave before the army, that he may call forth the zeal of his soldiers, but he must fight cautiously; he should not despise death if his army is defeated and not desire to live, but if his army is preserved he should guard his personal safety. . . . The duty of the general is to ride by the ranks on horseback, show himself to those in danger, praise the brave,

threaten the cowardly, encourage the lazy, fill up gaps, transpose a company if necessary, bring aid to the weary, anticipate the crisis, the hour, and the outcome.

(Onas. 33.5–6)

Sabin points out that although the commanders in the Second Punic War did indeed get involved in the fighting, they did so prudently, and tended not to risk their own lives unless their army was clearly defeated. Instead they tended to move around behind the lines, close to the front, encouraging those in front of them and directing what reserves there were (Sabin, 1996, p. 68).

This command technique was useful in terms both of leadership, as the commanders' presence would inspire the men around them, and of generalship. Although moving about close to the front line deprived commanders of an overall view of the battle, it did enable them to evaluate their men's morale and to observe the situation at given points along the line from close quarters, giving them the chance to change things if necessary (Goldsworthy, 1996, pp. 161–2). Scipio apparently commanded this way to remarkable effect while taking Cartagena:

All this time Scipio himself had by no means remained aloof from the fighting, but had also taken all possible precautions for his safety. He had with him three men carrying large shields, which they held so as to cover him completely on the side which was exposed to the wall, and thus protected him from missiles. In this way he could pass along the lines, or survey the battle from higher ground, and so contributed a great deal to the needs of the moment, for not only could he see how the battle was developing, but the fact that he was in full view of his men inspired them to fight with redoubled spirit. The result was that nothing which could contribute to the success of Roman arms was left undone, and as soon as the situation suggested that some fresh measure was required, the need was quickly and effectively supplied.

(Polyb. 10.13.1–5)

At Cannae, Paullus was stationed on the right wing, the traditional position of honour, commanding the citizen cavalry, with Varro commanding the allied horse over on the left, Minucius and Servilius being stationed with the legions. Hannibal and his brother Mago were with the Celts and Spaniards in the Carthaginian centre, with Hasdrubal and Hanno commanding the cavalry on the left and right wings respectively (Polyb. 3.114.6–7). The most important direct piece of evidence for the commanders' actions is the following passage from Polybius:

Aemilius, though he had been on the right wing from the outset and had taken part in the cavalry action, was still safe and sound; but wishing to act up to what he had said in his address to the troops, and to be present himself at the fighting, and seeing that the decision of the battle lay mainly with the legions, he rode along to the centre of the whole line, where he not only threw himself personally into the combat and exchanged blows with the enemy but kept cheering on and exhorting his men. Hannibal, who had been in this part of the field since the commencement of the battle, did likewise.

(Polyb. 3.116.1–4)

Polybius also states that Hasdrubal, having defeated the Roman citizen cavalry and scared away the Italian allied cavalry, decided to leave the pursuit of the fugitives up to the Numidians and led his own cavalry against the Roman rear (Polyb. 3.116.6–8). Paullus was apparently killed at this point, having already suffered several wounds, and Minucius and Servilius were also killed in the fighting (Polyb. 3.116.9–12). Of the Roman commanders only Varro escaped, disgracing himself, according to Polybius, by fleeing to Venusia with about seventy cavalry (Polyb. 3.116.3, 117.2).

The Roman commanders were both mounted, this being normal practice during the Hellenistic era, primarily because of the mobility and enhanced visibility it brought (Wheeler, 1991, p. 152). The fact that Varro appears to have escaped injury, and certainly managed to evade the pursuing Numidians, suggests that he was stationed some distance back from the front ranks of the cavalry. Against this, it should be borne in mind that his escape was not as ignominious as Polybius makes out. It appears that the allied cavalry had been inconclusively pinned down by the Numidians until Hasdrubal arrived with his Celtic and Spanish cavalry, and on seeing this fresh force bearing down upon them the allies fled *en masse* – it is almost certain that Varro was merely swept up in the rush (Polyb. 3.116.6).

According to Polybius, Paullus was not injured in the opening stages of the battle, despite having taken part in the cavalry combat from the start (Polyb. 3.116.1). This seems peculiar, considering the reported ferocity of the combat on the Roman right wing (Polyb. 3.115.2–4; Liv. 22.47.1–3), and indeed Livy records that he had been wounded by a slingshot at the very beginning of the battle, and had heroically fought on (Liv. 22.49.1–12). However, Livy is not to be trusted on this, for although his account of Paullus' actions and death at Cannae does contain certain convincing details, it clearly relies very heavily upon the writer's imagination. Polybius, given his connections with the Aemilii, would have been in a position to know whether Paullus really had been wounded so early in the battle, and would have had no reason to state that he was unharmed in the cavalry action if that was not the case. If he was not wounded in the initial cavalry clash, despite the fact that that incident was notable for its ferocity, this surely indicates that he was not stationed in the front ranks.

So where were the two consuls stationed, and what were they doing, if they were not in the thick of the fighting? Presumably their behaviour was similar to the third command style discussed above. Paullus certainly commanded in this fashion when he joined the infantry – there he rode to the centre of the line, the point where he thought his troops would benefit most from his presence, and got involved, exchanging blows with the enemy and encouraging his men (Polyb. 3.116.2–3). It is likely that when with the cavalry, Paullus and Varro moved about, watching out for weak points and, on spotting any, riding there to encourage the beleaguered combatants and direct whatever reserves were available to support them (Goldsworthy, 1996, p. 156).

It made sense for Paullus to head for the centre of the line, as Hannibal was also stationed 'close to the front' in the centre of his own line. Livy states that he:

> repeatedly opposed himself to Hannibal, with his men in close formation, and at several points restored the fight.
>
> (Liv. 22.49.2)

This may have been a simple attempt to compensate for the fact that the Carthaginian forces at that point in the line, inspired by the presence of their general, were gaining ground, or to replace Servilius or Minucius, either of whom could have been struck down by this point. However, as presented by Livy, it certainly appears that his specific aim was to pierce the Carthaginian line, with the intention of eliminating Hannibal himself (Liv. 22.49.1–2). Whatever his intentions, they clearly came to nothing for, weakened by wounds, Paullus was forced to dismount in order to fight on, apparently much to Hannibal's delight (Liv. 22.49.2–3). Dismounting meant that the commander had surrendered his mobility and would fight where he stood, a powerful symbolic statement that even if victory was no longer possible, surrender was unthinkable. If Livy's account is to be trusted, Paullus' men clearly understood this, and fought accordingly (Liv. 22.49.4). At some stage he seems to have made his way towards the fighting at the Roman rear, since Polybius states that Paullus finally died fighting there, then under attack from Hasdrubal's cavalry (Polyb. 3.116.8–9).[58]

Hannibal also seemed to favour such a command style, which Keegan (1987, p. 119) describes as being 'in front sometimes'. At the start of the battle he placed himself, with his brother Mago, at the centre of the Carthaginian line, a sensible position which would have facilitated communications with the extremities of his line.[59] According to Polybius, he took part in the fighting as well as exhorting the men around him (Polyb. 3.114.7, 116.3–4).[60] It was important that he do this, as the centre of his line was made up of his least reliable troops and his presence there couldinspire them to fulfil their difficult task – to withdraw steadily in the face of the Roman onslaught without losing their nerve, which could have caused them to break and run. The fact that the Celts and Spaniards managed this so successfully is testament to the moral effect of having their commander in their midst. Delbrück (1990 [1920], p. 322) described Hannibal at Cannae as being the spiritual and physical 'midpoint of the battle', whose personal presence had a decisive effect on the battle.

Hannibal's physical presence with the Celts and Spaniards in the centre may have been decisive there, but it is difficult to fathom the extent to which commanders leading in this way were able to influence events elsewhere on the battlefield. Roman commanders were normally accompanied by bodyguards, and the Carthaginians were probably no different.[61] Such escorts would doubtless have included messengers, giving the commander a certain measure of control over his forces in general, rather than just those in his immediate vicinity. Did the opposing commanders try to affect the course of the battle as a whole, or did they simply restrict themselves to co-ordinating matters at crucial points?

There is no record of either Hannibal or the Roman commanders issuing orders to their subordinates during the battle. Polybius, Livy, and other sources present the battle as happening, in the main, as if by clockwork, although this was surely not the case. There were clearly a number of points in the battle when orders must have been given from the overall commander: the advance of light-armed skirmishers; the advance of cavalry on both wings; the withdrawal of the skirmishers into the ranks of the line infantry; and the advance of the line infantry (Polyb. 3.115.1–4). The fact that these straightforward orders are unmentioned in the sources is not surprising, since their audiences could simply have assumed that such orders were given, received, and carried out without any complications. Horn signals, as discussed above, would perhaps have been the easiest and most direct way of issuing such orders; at Zama, Scipio used bugles to recall those *hastati* who were pursuing the Carthaginians (Polyb. 15.14.3).

Matters would have become far more complicated once the line infantry advanced. Hannibal, as reported above, placed himself at the centre of the Carthaginian line, so that he could display his worth as a leader to the Celts and Spaniards by fighting alongside them and exhorting them. Paullus soon followed his example by joining his legionaries in the centre. The problem with getting so actively involved in the fighting is that it must have immensely limited the commanders' ability to transmit orders. It appears that the Romans did not even attempt any new manoeuvres once Paullus became actively involved in the infantry combat, if the silence of the sources means anything at all. This may reflect his ignorance of the battle in general, or an inability to transmit or carry out what orders he gave.

The Carthaginians, on the other hand, were far from finished, and even though their overall commander was actively involved in the battle they managed two significant large-scale manoeuvres: the columns of Libyan infantry, at either end on the line of Celts and Spaniards, turned inwards to attack the advancing Roman infantry on their flanks (Polyb. 3.115.8–12), and having driven off the cavalry of the Italian allies, Hasdrubal, reportedly on his own initiative, left the pursuit of the fugitives in the capable hands of the Numidians, while he returned to the battle, leading his cavalry squadrons to harass the Roman rear (Polyb. 3.116.6–8).

How were such manoeuvres carried out, when the commander was involved elsewhere? Sabin (1996, p. 68) argues that the secret behind the elaborate grand-tactical manoeuvres which marked the battles of the Second Punic War lay in careful planning along with delegation to trusted subordinates. Walbank (1957, p. 447) suggests that Hasdrubal's cavalry action was planned in advance by Hannibal, rather than being an improvisation of Hasdrubal's. While this is plausible, it seems odd that the manoeuvre was credited to Hasdrubal if he had not in fact initiated it. It is perhaps more likely that, in planning the battle, this scenario was discussed, and Hannibal may have allowed Hasdrubal the freedom to do as he thought appropriate, based on the circumstances in which he found himself at the time.

What then of the Libyans' assault on the Roman flanks? Delbrück (1990 [1920], p. 322) notes that this is the only command that Hannibal would have had to give after the infantry had advanced, but again it is difficult to tell what happened here. Sabin (1996, p. 68) notes that symmetrical actions such as this were common in this war, and suggests that delegation to reliable subordinates may have been a factor here. An example can be seen in Livy's account of the battle of Ilipa in 205:

> Then, when it was time to begin the battle, he ordered the Spaniards – they formed the centre of the line – to advance at a slow pace. From the right wing – for he was himself in command there – he sent a message to Silanus and Marcius that they should prolong their wing towards the left, just as they had seen him pressing to the right, and with the light infantry and cavalry should engage the enemy before the centres could come together.
>
> (Liv. 28.14.16)

It is possible that at Cannae, Hannibal and another officer, probably Mago, on judging the time to be right, rode from their positions in the centre to the Libyan units, on either side of them, in order to co-ordinate their assault on the Roman flanks. Such a direct method of command would have had the advantage of minimising the chances of instructions being misunderstood (Goldsworthy, 1996, p. 161).

If this was not the case, both columns of Libyan line infantry must have been under the immediate command of trusted senior officers, presumably members of Hannibal's council. These officers would then have acted upon orders from Hannibal, commanding their men to move forward and then turn in against the flanks of the Roman infantry. How these orders were transmitted from Hannibal to the officers is unclear, but a number of options spring to mind. In the first place, the officers could have been informed of their task in advance and instructed to carry out their manoeuvre once certain circumstances had been achieved, most probably the exposure of the Roman infantry's flanks after the effective removal of their cavalry from the field. Alternatively, Hannibal may have observed the fact that the Roman infantry had been sucked into the Carthaginian centre and that the wings were now clear of cavalry, which would permit the Libyan infantry to manoeuvre and attack the Roman flanks. He could then have instructed the officers to carry out their prearranged orders either by horn signals or by sending messengers to them. This latter possibility is perhaps to be favoured, but it presupposes that Hannibal was in a position to observe the general course of the battle.

An issue worth considering is how much danger the commanders were in when they led their men in this fashion. According to Polybius, both Hannibal and Paullus were exchanging blows with the enemy (Polyb. 3.116.2–4), and this certainly seems to have been the case with Paullus, who apparently suffered many wounds in the fighting (Polyb. 3.116.9). Hannibal, however, does not appear to have been injured at all, which might at first glance suggest that his involvement was not so enthusiastic as Polybius' account suggests. On the other hand, he does not appear to have been the sort to avoid risks. In fact, Livy describes him as follows:

> When any bold or difficult deed was to be done, there was no one to whom Hasdrubal liked better to entrust with it, nor did any other leader inspire his men with greater confidence or daring. To reckless courage in incurring dangers he united the greatest judgement when in the midst of them. ... Both of horsemen and foot-soldiers he was undoubtedly the first – foremost to enter battle and last to leave it when the fighting had begun.
>
> (Liv. 21.4.4–8)

This passage, while almost certainly full of commonplaces, nevertheless seems to be borne out by the fact that at the siege of Saguntum he recklessly got too close to the enemy and was seriously wounded when struck in the thigh by a javelin (Liv. 21.7.10). He is also known to have been wounded shortly after the battle of the Trebia, while attempting to take a magazine near Placentia (Liv. 21.57.8–9), and the loss of his eye through infection while crossing the Arno swamps testifies to the risks that he was willing to take with himself and his army (Polyb. 3.79.12).

Why then was Hannibal apparently unharmed, when Paullus appears to have suffered several wounds here? Livy's account of Flaminius' behaviour at Trasimene may provide the answer:

The conflict lasted for about three hours and was bitterly contested at every point; but nowhere did it rage so fiercely as about the consul. He was attended by the bravest of his soldiers and stoutly lent a hand himself, whenever he saw the Romans hard pressed and in dire straits. His arms made him conspicuous, and the enemy attacked and his own people defended him with the greatest fury, until an Insubrian horseman, named Ducarius, who recognised the consul also by his face ... clapping spurs to his horse, he dashed through the very thick of his enemies, and first cutting down the armour-bearer, who had thrown himself in the way ... , transfixed the consul with his spear.

(Liv. 22.6.1–4)

In other words, the consul, Flaminius in this case, but equally Paullus, tended to be highly conspicuous, dressed as he was in his distinctive scarlet battle cloak, the main function of which was to make him easily visible to his men. Such visibility was a two-edged sword, for it also made him a clear target for the enemy, ensuring that wherever the consul based himself, not only would his men fight harder, inspired by his presence, but so too would the enemy, in an attempt to reach him.[62] Even with a bodyguard of élite troops surrounding him, Paullus was not invulnerable.

Describing Hannibal, Livy notes that:

His dress was in no way superior to that of his fellows, but his arms and horses were conspicuous.

(Liv. 21.4.8)

It is difficult to ascertain the intended meaning of this somewhat paradoxical statement, but it may mean that while Hannibal's equipment was of obviously high quality, he did not advertise his identity through wearing unnecessarily ostentatious clothing. Although Hannibal's Carthaginian officer dress was surely distinctive, at least compared to the Celts and Spaniards nearby, he does not appear to have advertised his identity in any way, unlike the Roman commanders. His men, familiar with his appearance, would still have been inspired by his presence, but to any Romans in the vicinity he may simply have appeared as one of several Carthaginian officers – Mago, for instance, was also nearby – and not, therefore, an obvious target for their assaults. In any case, he too had his bodyguards, and being an accomplished soldier would probably have been capable of taking care of himself should his situation become too dangerous.

Finally, it should be remembered that leadership was not the exclusive responsibility of the opposing commanders. In both armies there were many subordinate officers who would have been stationed along the lines with the responsibility of leading individual units. Command techniques would have varied according to the individual,[63] but if a general trend could be detected, it would probably be towards the more 'leadership'-oriented style of command, based on personal example, and sharing in the danger of the men. One reason for this is that as subordinate officers they simply did not need an overall view of the battle, so it would have made sense to concentrate on leading their men in the fighting. In addition, military tribunes, Rome's junior officers, were generally young aristocrats out to gain a reputation, and the most effective way of doing this would have been through displaying personal courage, or *virtus*, in battle (Harris, 1979, p. 20). Furthermore, young Carthaginian officers may well have sought to emulate their commander's leadership style as described by Livy (Liv. 21.4.4–8), while among Hannibal's Celtic allies, the heroic ethos of Celtic society would also have done much to foster a style of leadership heavily reliant upon personal displays of courage.[64]

6

CANNAE: 'THE FACE OF BATTLE'

Introduction

In Chapter 2 we dealt with the battle in terms of such general issues as strategy, tactics, manpower, and topography, while in Chapter 5 we concentrated on the duties and experiences of the opposing commanders at Cannae. This chapter aims to complement this by studying the battle on a more 'intimate' scale, considering the mechanics of battle and the physical and psychological realities of the battlefield. The 'Keegan Model', pioneered in *The Face of Battle*, is particularly useful for this, as in a manner conducive to systematic analysis, it divides the fighting up into several different stages, each characterised by specific types of combat. Since the Roman and Carthaginian armies were composed of a variety of troops, many of whom had distinctive styles of fighting, Chapters 3 and 4 analysed them in detail, with the intention of facilitating the application of the 'Keegan Model' to the study of Cannae.

In taking a more 'intimate' approach to the study of the battle, this chapter seeks to recover the experience of Cannae as undergone by the individual soldiers who fought there. Conventional studies of Cannae, as briefly discussed in the Preface, have mainly tended to concentrate on such broad issues as tactics and strategy. However, the vast majority of the participants in the battle would have been largely ignorant of these general aspects of the battle, their interest instead being focused almost solely on their immediate surroundings. In combat situations it appears that soldiers do not think of themselves as members of a single enormous military organisation, but rather as approximate equals within a small group of their peers (Keegan, 1976, p. 53). The basic concern of individual soldiers within these groups is survival; the fate of the army as a whole is generally secondary to this.

Prelude to battle: formations and deployment

The deployment of Roman and Carthaginian troops at Cannae has already been discussed, with regard to analysing the tactical aims of the opposing generals. The purpose of this section is to examine the practicalities of deployment in armies as large and diverse as those which fought at Cannae. This has significance for understanding the mechanics of the various types of fighting which took place there, as well as aiding any attempts to understand the part that morale played in the battle.

Roman forces

The Roman formation followed the standard pattern of line infantry in the centre, with cavalry on the wings and a screen of light infantry in front. According to Livy, the deployment was as follows:

> on the right wing – the one nearer the river – they placed the Roman cavalry, and next to them the Roman foot; the left wing had on the outside the cavalry of the allies; and nearer the centre, in contact with the Roman legions, the infantry of the allies. The javelins and other light-armed auxiliaries were formed up in front.
>
> (Liv. 22.45.6–7)

Although Livy is quite clear on this deployment, the crude right–left division of citizen and allied infantry seems extremely unlikely. The Latin term for an allied brigade was *ala sociorum*, and *ala* means 'wing', reflecting the position of the allied infantry on the flanks of the citizen legions. Polybius even states that the allied brigades were called the 'left wing' and 'right wing' (Polyb. 6.26.9; Keppie, 1998, p. 22).

In a standard, two-legion consular army, these brigades would therefore deploy on either side of the legions. At Cannae, however, there were effectively four consular armies, and it is likely that the infantry deployed as one line composed of four distinct armies: Paullus' troops would have been at the right end of the line,[1] beyond which he was positioned with the citizen cavalry, while Varro's would have been at the left end, near his allied cavalry. Minucius' and Servilius' armies would have formed the centre (Lazenby, 1978, p. 80; Samuels, 1990, p. 23). Such a system would have been good for morale, in that each commander was in the general vicinity of his own troops, giving him an opportunity to spur his men into action. Against this, the system had a serious tactical flaw: the least experienced troops, Paullus' and Varro's new recruits, were stationed on the wings. This was surely a factor in the devastation caused by Hannibal's Libyans when they turned on the Roman flanks.

A less likely possibility is that the entire infantry centre would have been composed of legions, with the allied brigades on their flanks (Connolly, 1998, p. 186; Healy, 1994, p. 76). This seems improbable for a number of reasons. The Roman army which fought at Cannae was not really one unified army, to be reorganised on a whim, but was rather a composite force made up of four separate consular armies, each consisting of two legions and two *alae*, and each with its own commander. These consular armies were traditional entities, which would surely not have been split up without very good reason, and it is difficult to see what would have been gained by dividing them. A division of the consular armies would have necessitated a command reorganisation, since under normal circumstances the tribunes and prefects would have reported to their consul. If the armies were split, Paullus' prefects would have been with his *alae* on the far side of the field, while Varro's tribunes would have been with his legions, out on the right wing. While this may seem a trifling point, such a reorganisation could have caused serious confusion in the ranks. Furthermore, each army, as discussed in Chapter 3, tended to see itself as being in some sense a separate society, the oath of loyalty being a major factor in this. It could have been very damaging to the morale of the armies to divide them up, and it might have been difficult to persuade the older legions and *alae* to serve alongside the new recruits. Alcibiades had a similar problem at Lampsacus in 409 when he wanted the old soldiers there to serve with other, recently beaten, units as one army (Xen., *Hell.* 1.2.15).[2] Finally, it is hard to imagine Hannibal focusing his attack on the infantry flanks if all the troops stationed there were allied rather than citizen troops. Considering Hannibal's general aim of winning over the allies, it seems unlikely that he would have wished to appear to be concentrating his attack on them.

So much for the order in which these units were deployed. A more pertinent question might be to ask how these units were organised in terms of ranks and files. Polybius states clearly that the maniples were stationed close together and were several times deeper than they were wide (Polyb. 3.113.3). It is extremely difficult to estimate the dimensions of these formations, but it is desirable to make the attempt.

The theoretical strength of each maniple of *hastati* or *principes* at Cannae has already been proposed as 144, the maniples in turn being subdivided into two centuries of seventy-two men each. The *triarii* were of course divided into the regulation-sized maniples of sixty men. The century of seventy-two men would have been very flexible, capable of being easily deployed in a range of depths. Given that the maniples of Cannae were reportedly deployed in such a way that their depth was several times greater than their width, their most likely deployment would have been six men wide, giving the *hastati* and *principes* maniples a depth of twenty-four, and the *triarii* a depth of ten. To facilitate this exceptionally deep formation, the maniples would have been deployed with the *prior* centuries placed in front of the *posterior*, rather than beside them. The total depth of the heavy infantry would therefore have been fifty-eight man-spaces, with gaps between each of the three lines, and presumably some sort of gaps between the centuries.[3]

Onasander, writing in the first century AD, indicates that it was normal for troops to have regular positions within the rank and file of their formations, and that well-trained troops could easily fall into these positions (Onas. 10.2–3). This was presumably as true for the Roman army of the middle Republic as it was in Onasander's day. The position of individual soldiers within such formations largely depended upon a basic tactical principle recognised even by Homer, who has Nestor deploy his infantry as follows:

> and behind them the footsoldiers, many and brave, to be a bulwark
> of battle; but the cowards he drove to the middle, so that, even
> unwilling, a man would fight out of necessity.
>
> (Homer, *Iliad* 4.298–300)

Greek military theorists believed that the best troops ought to be deployed in the first and last ranks, as the ones in front would be the most effective fighters – Asclepiodotus compares them to 'the cutting edge of the sword' – while the ones at the rear would prevent the less reliable troops in the middle from shirking their duty, or even fleeing (Xen., *Mem.* 3.1.8, *Cyr.* 7.5.5; Asclep. 3.5–6). The front rank, composed of what Greek writers termed *lochagoi* or 'file-leaders', was a position of honour, and Connolly thinks that this position was almost certainly reserved for the senior soldiers in the *contubernia*, because, he argues, the individual files were almost certainly organised along the same lines as the tent-units, to ensure that each man knew and trusted the troops placed closest to him (Connolly, 1998, p. 142; see Holmes, 1985, pp. 293–4). The centurions evidently led by example from the front, Goldsworthy (1996, p. 182) noting that they appear to have had an extremely high casualty rate. They were probably positioned in the front rank itself, or possibly slightly to the right of the unit's front rank. Each centurion was assisted by an *optio*, a rear-rank officer who maintained unit cohesion from the rear. He would have been positioned either in the rear rank, or else behind it, which would have given him a clearer view of the state of affairs in the unit as a whole (Goldsworthy, 1996, p. 182).

As it is impossible to tell how big were the gaps between various units, whether legions, maniples, or centuries, the total area covered by the infantry cannot be ascertained. It is useful, however, to consider how much space, on average, the individual Roman soldier occupied. According to Polybius, each Roman had a frontage of six Roman feet (1.75 m) and an equivalent depth (Polyb. 18.30.6–8). Such a broad frontage was necessary, he argues, because:

> Now in the case of the Romans also each soldier with his arms
> occupies a space of three feet in breadth, but as in their mode of
> fighting each man must move separately, as he has to cover his
> person with his long shield, turning to meet each expected blow,

and as he uses his sword both for cutting and thrusting it is obvious that a looser order is required . . . if they are to be of proper use.

(Polyb. 18.30.6–7)[4]

This order of battle would give each man at least three Roman feet (0.9 m) on either side of him, and a further three feet both in front and behind, allowing him room to throw his *pilum*. This analysis may be overly dogmatic, however, as Vegetius, admittedly writing several centuries later but clearly referring to the Roman army of a much earlier day, records that Roman troops had a frontage of three feet, rather than six, and that there was a space of six feet between each line of men (Veg. 3.14–15). Vegetius' figures regarding frontage correspond to Asclepiodotus' 'compact spacing', the formation commonly used by Greek troops when advancing against the enemy (Asclep. 4.1.3; Polyb. 18.29.2).[5] Sabin regards the wide frontage described by Polybius as 'dubious', and Goldsworthy argues that it was almost certainly unnecessarily wide, Vegetius' figures giving the Roman swordsmen ample room in which to fight, as soldiers would not have occupied a full three-foot width (Sabin, 1996, p. 71; Goldsworthy, 1996, p. 179).

It is significant that Polybius describes the Romans fighting in a very open formation in the context of explaining how they defeated the rigid phalanxes of the Macedonians. In his analysis, the Romans, by using a loose formation, were able to operate on all sorts of terrain, ensuring their tactical and individual superiority over the Macedonian phalangites. It certainly appears that the Romans did not always fight in the loose formation allowed them by Polybius' reckoning. In a battle against Celts in the late 220s, Polybius records that:

> The Romans, on the contrary, instead of slashing, continued to thrust with their swords which did not bend, the points being very effective. Thus, striking one blow after another on the breast or face, they slew the greater part of their adversaries.
>
> (Polyb. 2.33.6)

The fact that the Romans opted only to thrust, rather than slash, with their swords seems to suggest that they were fighting in a formation which did not allow them room to slash. After all, their swords were suitable for both, as has already been discussed. It would not be surprising if the Romans had adopted a close formation on this occasion, as, according to Polybius, the front ranks of the Romans in this encounter had begun the fighting with the long spears of the *triarii* (Polyb. 2.33.4–5). As mentioned above, the 'compact formation' of a three-feet frontage per man seems to have been normal for spearmen, so the Romans were probably deployed initially in this manner and continued to fight so.

Polybius states that at Cannae the maniples were placed closer together than usual and that the Romans adopted a peculiarly deep formation. This suggests that the Romans had tried to emulate phalanx tactics, which would surely have demanded that the men deploy in the close formation standard for phalangites. Furthermore, the majority of Hannibal's infantry at Cannae were Celtic, and it is likely that if the Romans were deployed primarily to face Celtic troops they would indeed have favoured a close formation, as it had proved so effective against Celts some years earlier. Livy supports this, describing the Roman troops making impressive gains against Hannibal's Celts by fighting in 'an even front and a dense line' (Liv. 22.47.5). Such a close formation would also have had the advantage of maximising the number of men who could be deployed in the front line, giving the front line twice the 'firepower' of a line deployed in an open formation. *hopelessly unscientific.*

If this were the case, each maniple would have been approximately eighteen Roman feet (5.4 m) wide, but owing to the fact that the exact dimensions of the gaps between maniples and between legions are unknown, it is impossible to calculate the width of a legion or the length of the entire infantry line. All that can be said with any degree of certainty is that each legion was sixty men wide – assuming each maniple was deployed six across – meaning that the total length of the Roman infantry line was about 840 men,[6] not allowing for gaps between units.

What then of the cavalry? There were slightly over 6,000 cavalry in the Roman forces at Cannae, according to Polybius (Polyb. 3.113.5). Assuming that each legion had its full complement of 300 horse, there would have been about 2,400 citizen cavalry at Cannae, the remaining 3,600 being supplied by Rome's allies. The citizen cavalry were deployed to the right of the infantry, next to the river, while the allies were stationed on the left wing, where there was more room to manoeuvre. There is no evidence to indicate that either cavalry section was deployed in any formation other than a simple line.

According to Polybius, cavalry would ideally be deployed eight horses deep, with individual squadrons separated by intervals equal in size to the space occupied by the squadrons themselves (Polyb. 12.18.3–4). Eight hundred cavalry deployed in this fashion would occupy one *stade* (approximately 600 feet, or 180 m). Given that half the available space was left free, each of the 100 horses which made up the front line would have occupied a frontage of about three feet (0.9 m) (Walbank, 1967, p. 370) – such a deployment would have been virtually knee-to-knee. Goldsworthy (1996, pp. 182–3) suggests that the maximum frontage per horse, even if deployed knee-to-knee, was 1 metre, and that a possible depth per horse was about 4 metres.

The citizen cavalry at Cannae almost certainly fought in such a close formation, if Livy's analysis of their behaviour at Cannae is accurate:

For they had to charge front to front, there being no room to move out round the flank, for the river shut them in on one side and the ranks of the infantry on the other. Both parties pushed straight ahead, and as the horses came to a standstill, packed together in a throng, the riders began to grapple with their enemies and drag them from their seats.

(Liv. 22.47.2–3)

Rome's citizen cavalry, as already discussed, were organised into squadrons of thirty, called *turmae*, each commanded by three decurions, one with overall responsibility for the squadron as a whole, and three *optiones*, rear-rank officers, who assisted the decurions. The cavalry seems designed to have operated as either three files of ten or six files of five. The space restrictions Livy describes at Cannae probably led to their being deployed ten deep with the squadrons, at least initially, being deployed knee-to-knee, as Polybius seems to suggest. In the seventeenth century theorists argued that cavalry should deploy knee-to-knee, but in practice individual horses needed more room to manoeuvre (Carlton, 1992, p. 135).

The approximately 3,600 allied cavalry were stationed to the left of the infantry, but unlike the citizen cavalry their own left flank was exposed, which clearly gave them room to manoeuvre, as their role in the battle was largely confined to skirmishing with Hannibal's Numidians (Polyb. 3.116.5). It is quite possible that their formation was somewhat looser than that of the citizen cavalry. However, Polybius evidently believed that formations such as that described above did give cavalry plenty of room in which to manoeuvre (Polyb. 12.18.2–3), so it is equally possible, and perhaps more likely, that the allied cavalry were deployed in the same fashion as their Roman counterparts: ten deep, 1-metre frontage per horse, and spaces between squadrons equal in width to the squadrons themselves.

With virtually no evidence for how the skirmishers were deployed, any discussion of this is unavoidably speculative. They were clearly positioned some distance ahead of the main body of the army (Polyb. 3.113.4; Liv. 22.45.7), and perhaps only in front of the infantry, as they seem not to have become involved in the cavalry action on either flank, despite being still on the field when the cavalry advanced (Polyb. 3.115.1–4; Liv. 22.47.1–4). Onasander notes that light troops would normally be positioned in front of the main army since their weapons would be ineffective behind large bodies of men and, if used, would cause more harm to their own troops than those of the enemy (Onas. 17.1). The *velites* were divided up amongst the heavy infantry maniples, so that a normal legion would have had, in theory, thirty companies of forty *velites*. The larger legions at Cannae may have had over fifty *velites* per company. Whether these companies were tactical or merely administrative units is uncertain, but it seems likely that they were stationed in front of their respective maniples, when deployed for battle.

It is generally thought that Viking armies normally began battle in a loose formation to facilitate missile action (Griffith, 1995, p. 194), and it is almost certain that Rome's light-armed troops were similarly deployed in a dispersed manner. Onasander specifically notes that a loose formation is appropriate for light-armed troops in order to enable them to cast their javelins and use their slings (Onas. 17.1). The *velites*, which were divided into large companies of over forty men each, in practice probably operated as several smaller teams, possibly organised around *contubernia*, with the most experienced soldiers in each group acting as unofficial leaders. How these teams were deployed is not susceptible to proof, but it is worth bearing in mind that the maniples, as discussed above, seem to have had a frontage of about 18 feet (5.4 m); with about 1,520 *velites* per legion, there would have been approximately 152 *velites* in front of each such maniple. Although this rough calculation does not allow for gaps between maniples, it seems clear that the *velites* must have been deployed in great depth in order to allow each man enough space to use his weapons.

It is impossible to ascertain where the Syracusan auxiliaries, many of whom appear to have been Cretan archers, were stationed. Livy says that such archers would normally fire volleys of arrows against an advancing force (Liv. 31.35.3), apparently implying that they fought as units rather than as individuals. Gabriel and Metz argue that ancient armies usually placed their archers behind their main body of infantry, from where they could have fired over the heads of their own men against the enemy troops,[7] but here the exceptionally deep deployment of the infantry would have almost certainly rendered this impossible. The archers must therefore have been deployed with the skirmishers in front of the infantry. Large units would obviously have obstructed the movement of the skirmishing *velites*, so they were probably positioned at either or both ends of the *velites'* line. They would thus have been able to concentrate their fire, at least for a time, against the Carthaginian cavalry who were stationed on the wings, for the horses' unprotected bodies would have made particularly inviting targets.

Carthaginian forces

Onasander points out that it was normal practice for commanders to position their cavalry in opposition to that of the enemy (Onas. 16.1), and Hannibal, who was responding to the Roman challenge, appears to have done just this, placing his Numidian cavalry opposite Rome's allied horse while his Celtic and Spanish horse faced the Roman citizen cavalry (Polyb. 3.113.7, 115.2–4, 116.5). There is no evidence that cavalry and line infantry were required to fight one another in the early stages of the battle. The opposing cavalry and line infantry forces must have occupied approximately the same frontage as each other.

Hannibal's Celtic and Spanish cavalry, positioned on his left wing beside the river, were significantly more numerous than the Roman cavalry opposite them. Although there is no evidence for how the cavalry were organised, it would be extremely surprising if they were not divided, like the infantry, along national lines. It is generally thought that between 6,000 and 8,000 Carthaginian cavalry were on the left wing, whereas it is likely that only about 2,400 horse opposed them. As there is no evidence that Hannibal's cavalry were deployed in anything other than a basic oblong formation, they must have been deployed at least twenty-five deep, assuming an approximate frontage of 240 horses.[8] The majority of these cavalry were almost certainly noblemen and their retainers, and, considering the warrior ethos which seems to have been prevalent in Celtic and Spanish societies, the front rank were probably noblemen eager to demonstrate their prowess and courage by leading their followers into battle.

There were perhaps about 4,000 Numidian cavalry on the Carthaginian right wing, opposite Rome's allied cavalry. If so, the Numidians were probably deployed in only slightly greater depth than the Italians, as they did not outnumber them by much. They were probably deployed in a roughly oblong formation, but bearing in mind that the Numidian squadrons skirmished in an exceptionally fluid manner, which will be described later, it is almost inconceivable that they were deployed along a rigid system of ranks and files – a far looser structure was probably preferred (Lazenby, 1978, p. 15).

Hannibal's infantry skirmishers must have been deployed along virtually identical principles to their Roman and Italian counterparts. However, as they initially formed a covering force to allow the main body of the army to deploy safely (Polyb. 3.113.6; Liv. 22.46.1), they probably began the battle stretched along the entire length of the line, before contracting to allow the cavalry advance on the wings. In addition, they would have been deployed in a significantly shallower formation than the Romans, as there were only about 8,000 of them, compared to 15,000 or more *velites*.[9]

In analysing the deployment of Hannibal's line infantry, it is essential to bear in mind their peculiar formation, as discussed earlier: two units of Libyan troops, each probably about 5,000 strong, positioned at either end of a long curved line, tapering towards the ends, composed of alternating units of Celtic and Spanish troops, about 16,000 of the former and 6,000 of the latter.

The Libyans were almost certainly deployed in column with a rather narrow front, rather than in line with the other troops, as their role in the battle required each man to turn individually to attack the Roman flanks. In other words, a deep formation would have maximised the number of men who could have actively attacked the Roman flanks.[10] A column which was forty men wide and 125 men deep would have been suitable for this purpose, enabling the Libyans to strike along the entire length of each

Roman flank, even allowing for gaps between Roman lines.[11] Furthermore, although nothing is known of how the Libyans were organised, it is possible that with a depth of forty men, tactical sub-units may have been positioned behind each other, facilitating the extension of the line if necessary by moving the rear units to the ends of the column and then bringing them forward. It is impossible to tell where the officers stood in the sub-units, or under what principles troops were positioned next to each other. All that can be said for certain is that being armed with Roman equipment, these Libyan infantry must have occupied the same amount of space, man for man, as the Romans.

The Celts and Spaniards were originally deployed in a simple line of approximately the same length as that of the Roman infantry. This formation was not retained, however, as Hannibal led the central companies of this line forward in such a way that the line became a crescent-shaped formation, thinner at the ends than the centre (Polyb. 3.113.8–9). The width of the Roman line has already been estimated at 840 men, not allowing for gaps between units. If the approximately 22,000 Celts and Spaniards were also deployed 840 men across, the average depth of their line would have been slightly over twenty-six men.[12] This would have been much shallower than the Roman formation, and approximately as deep as the *hastati* alone. In practice, however, it is likely that the depth of the line was not uniform. Both Celts and Spaniards were divided at Cannae into units which Polybius calls *speirai*, the same term he uses for maniples (Polyb. 3.114.4, 6.24.5). These were probably tribal groups, either levies recruited from individual settlements in the case of the Spaniards, or the retinues of individual noblemen in the case of the Celts. Such units must have been of irregular size, and were quite possibly deployed in varying depths.[13] In any case, following the transformation of the line into a long narrow crescent, only the central companies would have retained their original depth, with the flanking companies growing progressively shallower.

It is likely that in tribal groups such as these the men tended to be stationed next to close friends or family members, contributing to a very high level of *esprit de corps*. Considering the warrior culture which seems to have prevailed in the Celtic and Spanish societies, it is likely that the bravest and best-equipped troops tended to fight in the front ranks (Rawlings, 1996, p. 90; Goldsworthy, 1996, p. 59). It therefore seems certain that unit commanders, whether Celtic, Spanish, or Carthaginian, must have also been stationed in the front rank, in order to lead their men effectively. That said, the term 'front rank' may be something of a misnomer in this context. Since Carthaginian armies tended not to standardise their troops – allowing them instead to fight in their traditional style – and since these were probably tribal groups rather than regular military units, it is perhaps more likely that rather than being divided into formalised ranks and files, the Celts and Spaniards would have fought as informal but compact groups, with the best troops in the front.[14] The Spanish troops may have fought in a close formation like the Romans, owing to the similarity of their weapons, but individual Celts would probably have required more space, since they needed room to swing their long slashing swords (Polyb. 2.30.8, 3.114.3). They must therefore have deployed in a somewhat looser formation – though still a rather dense one – than the Spaniards (Goldsworthy, 1996, p. 59).

The physical circumstances of battle

Du Picq[15] argued that in ancient battles, assuming similar levels of morale, the least fatigued side always won, something which the evidence appears to bear out.[16] The armies of Cannae seem to have been fairly evenly matched in this respect, since the Carthaginians had left Geronium for Cannae about a month before the battle, while the Romans had encamped near Cannae only a few days beforehand (Polyb. 3.110–13), meaning that neither army would have suffered from tiredness brought on by any recent arduous marching.[17] Furthermore, there is no evidence that the armies at Cannae lacked supplies, at least in the short term, Hannibal's forces having even captured the grain magazine there (Polyb. 3.107.3–5). Nor do the sources give any indication that either army lacked opportunity for sleep or food immediately before the battle, as had been the case with the Roman forces – unlike their Carthaginian enemies – at the Trebia (Polyb. 3.72.3–6; Liv. 21.54.8–55.1). It is therefore likely that the Roman and Carthaginian armies entered battle at least with neither side appearing more prone than the other to physical exhaustion.

Against this, the troops were almost certainly on edge,[18] and as a result may not have slept well the previous night or eaten properly that morning (see Xen., *Hiero* 6.7), which would have had a significant impact on their powers of endurance and concentration during the battle. The day before the battle Hannibal led his army out, challenging the Romans to face them, but the Roman commanders declined the offer, for reasons which have already been discussed. Their failure to accept the challenge evidently embarrassed the Romans, who clearly wanted a chance to redeem themselves and, perhaps more importantly, to get the seemingly inevitable battle over with (Polyb. 3.112.4–5; Liv. 22.45.4). This sense of apprehension must have been shared, to some degree, by the Carthaginian troops, although they were, as a rule, considerably more experienced than their Roman counterparts. Although Hannibal had led them to victory more than once before, he had never done so when facing a Roman army so much larger than his own.

Both armies therefore had the potential to become exhausted if the battle was to last for a long time, and there are good grounds for believing that this was the case. Vegetius declares that pitched battles tended to be characterised by a struggle of two or three hours' duration, after which one side would be clearly beaten (Veg. 3.9). In practice, battles frequently appear to have lasted for longer than this,[19] although probably only if the prelude and aftermath of the central struggle of phalanxes are included. Livy describes some Second Punic War battles as lasting for two, three, or four Roman hours,[20] and it seems certain that the battle of Cannae was a much more protracted affair. Appian claims that the fighting began after the second hour of the day and continued until there were fewer than two hours to nightfall. Roman hours varied in length, depending on the time of year, because the Roman day consisted of twelve hours of daylight, the amount of which was obviously variable (Milner, 1996, p. 10, n.6). At Rome's latitude, a summer day would have lasted for an average of 14.5 modern hours, and Cannae, being further south, would have had a slightly shorter day. Appian indicates that the fighting at Cannae continued for over eight Roman hours (App., *Hann.* 25), so that, if this is accurate, it lasted for more than nine modern hours. Although Appian is not the most reliable source for the battle of Cannae, this detail certainly seems plausible, considering the number of men who died there. If Hanson's somewhat rhetorical estimate of 'over 100 men killed each minute' is accurate then no fewer than eight modern hours would have been needed to account for 50,000 dead.[21]

It is important to remember that the troops were up some hours before the fighting began, crossing the river, presumably after breakfast, at first light according to Livy (Liv. 22.46.1), at dawn according to Polybius (Polyb. 3.113.1), and then waiting in the ranks for a couple of hours if Appian is to be believed (App., *Hann.* 20). They would have grown progressively more exhausted over the course of the day, a condition which would have been exacerbated by the heat of the southern Italian sun. It appears that the Carthaginian troops suffered from the heat of the midday sun at the battles of the Metaurus and Ilipa (Polyb. 11.24.5; Liv. 27.48.17, 28.15.2–4). The sources single out the Celts in particular as lacking in stamina, but this is probably no more than the typical anti-Celtic prejudice of classical authors (Liv. 48.16–17). In any case, the fact remains that the heat of the sun at Cannae must have contributed immensely to the growing exhaustion of the Roman and Carthaginian forces as the day wore on. Another factor to be considered in this context is the weight of the weapons and armour carried by the various troops. Admittedly, many troops would not have been particularly hampered in this respect, but large numbers of the Roman and Libyan infantry were wearing full coats of mail along with bronze helmets and greaves, and were carrying large shields, short swords, and throwing spears. The sheer weight of this equipment must have begun to take its toll sooner rather than later.[22]

The men at Cannae were not merely victims of tiredness, but must also have been afraid, and as a result would surely have exhibited many of the classic symptoms of battlefield stress and fear. The psychological aspects of this are considered later; for now it is significant only to note their physical

effects. According to research on modern soldiers, the most common physical manifestation of fear is 'a violent pounding of the heart', but other
common symptoms include 'a sinking feeling in the stomach, uncontrollable
trembling, a cold sweat, a feeling of weakness or stiffness and vomiting' and,
most unwelcome of all, involuntary urination or defecation (Holmes, 1985,
p. 205). Ancient soldiers would have been no less susceptible to these symptoms than their modern counterparts, and may even have been more so.[23]

Once battle began, each soldier's perceptions of his surroundings would
have been severely hampered. In an account of night-fighting outside
Syracuse in 413, Thucydides pertinently observed that even in broad daylight nobody has any real idea of what is happening beyond his immediate
vicinity (Thuc. 7.44.1). Various factors would have contributed to this, most
famously – in the case of Cannae – the dust which was reportedly blown into
the Roman faces by the local wind, the Volturnus. The authenticity of this
detail, absent from Polybius' account, has already been discussed (p. 43), and
it seems likely to be genuine, if somewhat exaggerated by the sources which
refer to it. Armies tended to kick up large quantities of dust, especially in
battles, as many sources testify,[24] and this must have affected visibility to
some degree. Livy claims that the fog at Trasimene was so thick that the
Romans were forced to rely on hearing rather than on sight (Liv. 22.5.3–4).
Similar conditions must have applied at Cannae, save that, as Hanson points
out, wind-blown dust would have had an even worse effect, as it would not
simply have reduced visibility, but would actively have irritated the eyes of
many troops, causing the men to rub their eyes and possibly even drop their
weapons (Hanson, 1992, p. 46). Thucydides describes the fighting at Pylos
as follows:

> The shouting with which the Athenians accompanied their charge
> caused consternation among the Lacedaemonians, who were unac-
> customed to this manner of fighting; and the dust from the
> newly-burned forest rose in clouds to the sky, so that a man could
> not see what was in front of him by reason of the arrows and stones,
> hurled, in the midst of the dust, by so many hands.
>
> (Thuc. 4.34.2)

It is significant that Thucydides, an experienced soldier, should comment
in this fashion on how airborne dust and missiles could impair visibility
to such a degree.[25] He lends an air of credibility to Appian's claim that
the Romans at Cannae were unable to see their foes (App., *Hann.* 22).
Hanson also sensibly adds that the sheer size and density of the Roman
army would have made this even worse, as thousands of plumed helmets
and raised shields would have further reduced visibility.[26]

If then, as at Trasimene, the Romans were forced to rely on their hearing
rather than their sight, the obvious question is 'What did they hear?' Carlton

(1992, p. 132), in his analysis of the British Civil Wars, makes the point that the inhabitants of pre-industrial societies lived in a quiet world, so the din of battle would have been particularly distressing for the combatants. The firing of small arms and artillery may have become the dominant noises on the modern battlefield (Keegan, 1976, pp. 141–2; Holmes, 1985, pp. 161–3), but even without these, ancient battle was a deafening affair. Livy's description of the chaos at Trasimene attempts to recreate this:

> But the din and confusion were so great that neither advice nor orders could be heard. . . . Indeed the fog was so thick that ears were of more use than eyes, and the groans of the wounded, the sound of blows on body or armour and the mingled shouts and screams of assailants made them turn and gaze, now this way and now that.
>
> (Liv. 22.5.3–4)

This passage could all too easily be dismissed as a typical example of Livy's tendency to enliven his narrative through vivid descriptive passages owing more to his dramatic talent and vivid imagination than to historical rigour. However, such a judgement would be unduly critical, as the battle narratives of Ammianus Marcellinus, a fourth-century AD soldier and historian, and a more reliable authority on such matters, make clear. Describing the battle of Strasbourg in 357 AD, he commented on the sheer noise raised by the war-cry of the Cornuti and Bracchiati, and on the hissing sound produced by volleys of javelins (Amm. 16.12.43), arrows apparently also making a similar noise (Amm. 25.3.13). The noise produced by the battle in 363 AD in which the Emperor Julian was mortally wounded is concisely, but effectively, described:

> Further off, the trampling of the combatants, the groans of the falling, the panting of the horses, and the ring of arms were heard.
>
> (Amm. 25.3.11)

It seems, therefore, that there were many discordant types of sound on the battlefield, producing a dreadful din. Many of these sounds would have been unavoidable: the snorting of horses could not have been controlled, while thousands of men arrayed in close proximity to each other could not possibly avoid making a noise through accidentally bumping into each other, causing their weapons and armour to rattle.[27] Weapons would also unavoidably have made a great deal of noise, whether through the aforementioned hiss of javelin and arrow volleys through the air, or the constant clatter of the mêlée as swords and spears clashed and struck shields, armour, and flesh. It is difficult to conceive of the noise that this made, but some indication may be given by the fact that British sabres striking French

169

cuirasses at Waterloo allegedly sounded like 'a thousand coppersmiths at work' (Holmes, 1985, p. 163). This metallic sound may well have been similar to the clash of sword against sword at Cannae, but weapons striking shields must have created a somewhat duller sound, for these shields were primarily composed of wood, albeit frequently with metal edging. Bullets hitting swords or bayonets at Waterloo produced a strange harmonic vibration, or else resulted in a sound like a stick being drawn along railings (Keegan, 1976, p. 41), and a similar effect may have been caused by the stones fired by Hannibal's Balearian slingers, hitting weapons and armour.[28] Just as inevitable would have been the 'grunts and groans of men engaged in harsh exertion' (Holmes, 1985, p. 165), and the screams and moans of wounded men and beasts.[29]

Various intentional sounds would have added to this nightmarish symphony, as both sides attempted to raise their own spirits while simultaneously intimidating the enemy. According to Polybius, it was normal for the Roman troops to raise their war-cry and clash their weapons together as they advanced (Polyb. 1.34.2, 15.12.8).[30] The nature of this war-cry is unclear, as war-cries can differ widely (Hanson, 1989, p. 149; Goldsworthy, 1996, pp. 195–7), but it must have been a standard cry of some sort, presumably in Latin, if Polybius' juxtaposition of it with the discordant polyglot roar of Hannibal's multinational army is appropriate (Polyb. 15.12.8–9). It is curious that Polybius implies that the uniformity of the Roman battle-cry would have been beneficial for morale, in contrast to the diverse cries of Hannibal's army. This may have some truth, in that a single war-cry in a common language could well have aided Roman *esprit de corps*, but it is perhaps just as likely that the 'arrogant, discordant cries of Hannibal's men in a dozen languages' (Hanson, 1992, p. 45) would have had an especially shocking effect. In 225 the Romans had been terrified by the Celts at Telamon, and considering that many of Hannibal's troops were Celts from Cisalpine Gaul it is likely that the Romans' impressions of the Celts at Cannae were similar:

> [The Romans] were terrified by the fine order of the Celtic host and the dreadful din, for there were innumerable horn-blowers and trumpeters, and, as the whole army were shouting their war-cries at the same time, there was such a tumult of sound that it seemed that not only the trumpets and the soldiers but all the country round had got a voice and caught up the cry.
>
> (Polyb. 2.29.5–6)

Goldsworthy (1996, p. 195) notes that the Celtic battle horn, the carnyx, was used in battle by many European tribes. Horns and trumpets of various kinds, which would be used for signalling, were probably common in the Carthaginian army as a whole, as they certainly were in the Roman forces, due to the fact that their loud, piercing sounds could be heard over the din of battle (Krentz, 1991, pp. 110, 112–13). It is not surprising that, as Arrian notes, verbal commands were frequently inaudible in such circumstances (Arr., *Tact.* 27).[31]

As the battle progressed, the number of casualties would have increased, in turn affecting the battlefield environment in ways far more extensive than simply adding to the noise of battle with agonised moans and screams.[32] Corpses stink, and even freshly spilled blood and entrails 'reek of the slaughter-house'. This stench of death would have combined with other smells, including vomit, sweat, and the involuntary urination and defecation of frightened and dying men, to give the battlefield a distinctively unpleasant odour (Holmes, 1985, pp. 177–8). The dust at Cannae may have impeded soldiers' visibility, but not to the extent that they could not perceive their immediate surroundings, and since the killing in ancient warfare took place at close quarters, the sheer carnage of the battle would have been fully visible, as one's friends were stabbed, or cut down, or hit by missiles right in front of one's very eyes (Carlton, 1992, pp. 132–3). Adding to this horror would have been the fact that countless soldiers must have been literally coated with blood (Hanson, 1989, p. 191), often that of their friends and relatives.

Dead and seriously wounded soldiers would have fallen where they were hit, and could not have been moved to safety, so that the battlefield would have been strewn with corpses and injured men, sometimes piled two or even three deep.[33] Gaping wounds from sword and spear would have drained these bodies of much of their blood, so that the field itself would have been drenched (Hanson, 1989, p. 203). In such circumstances it would have been something of an achievement even to remain on one's feet, as Scipio evidently realised at Zama:

> The space which separated the two armies still on the field was now covered with blood, slaughter, and dead bodies, and the Roman general was placed in great difficulty by this obstacle to his completing the rout of the enemy. For he saw that it would be very difficult to pass over the ground without breaking his ranks owing to the quantity of slippery corpses which were still soaked in blood and had fallen in heaps and the number of arms thrown away at haphazard.
>
> (Polyb. 15.14.1–2)

Scipio's fears were fully justifiable, as at Adrianople in 378 AD many troops slipped and fell on a battlefield that Ammianus describes as 'discoloured with the hue of dark blood' (Amm. 31.13.6).

Under these conditions it would be surprising if some soldiers did not suffer psychiatric breakdown, of the type which is commonly known as 'battleshock' or 'battle fatigue'.[34] Hanson argues that symptoms of 'battleshock' in ancient warfare may have included hallucinations, which explains some of the apparitions allegedly witnessed during ancient battles, and soldiers irrationally risking their lives or even choosing to die.[35] Hanson's evidence is more plausible than compelling on this issue, but his point still stands – the experience of ancient battle must have been hellishly traumatic, making psychiatric casualties inevitable. According to Livy, the Roman dead at Cannae included some soldiers who were found with their heads buried in holes in the ground. They had apparently dug these holes and then heaped the dirt over their faces (Liv. 22.51.8), attempting either to commit suicide, or perhaps to 'hide' from the battle, ostrich-fashion. If there is any truth to this bizarre story, it must be regarded as evidence that soldiers at Cannae suffered from 'battleshock', and considering that Cannae was probably the bloodiest battle in antiquity, this is hardly surprising.

[handwritten margin note: MAYBE THEY FORGOT WHICH END TO SHIT FROM.]

Infantry skirmishing

At Cannae both commanders, as described earlier, had positioned their light-armed skirmishers some distance ahead of their cavalry and line infantry, in order to act as a covering force enabling the troops behind to deploy without disruption. The skirmishers then began the fighting, and were evenly matched, before being recalled and replaced by the line infantry (Polyb. 3.113.4–6, 115.1, 4; Liv. 22.45.7, 46.1, 47.1, 4; App., *Hann.* 21).

Although the initial use of skirmishers as covering forces is understandable, it is difficult to ascertain why they were used to open the fighting proper, with the main forces standing by looking on (Pritchett, 1985, p. 51). One function of light-armed skirmishers, according to Arrian, was to test the armament of the enemy (Arr., *Tact.* 13.1), and it is indeed possible that the basic reason for commencing battle with missile troops was to 'soften up' the main body of the enemy through aerial bombardment.[36] This would not have happened at Cannae, as both armies deployed skirmishers to open the fighting, but had either side failed to indulge in this preliminary bout of missile exchange and skirmishing it would have given the initiative to its opponent. In can therefore be argued that the basic function of the skirmishers' advance was to absorb the attack of the other skirmishers.

It is perhaps unfair to deduce from this that the preliminary bouts of skirmishing were entirely insignificant. Certainly, they were frequently inconclusive, as Thucydides notes of the skirmishing prior to the first battle at Syracuse in 415:

> And at first the stone-throwers and slingers and bowmen skirmished, driving each other back, first one side and then the other, as light-armed troops would be likely to do.
>
> (Thuc. 6.69.2)

This does not mean that they were irrelevant. The sources, perhaps inspired by a traditional Greek belief that missile warfare was somehow cowardly,[37] may be underrating the importance of the initial period of skirmishing.[38]

Goldsworthy (1996, ch. 4) has argued that the use of Grand Tactics was by no means the most crucial skill for Roman generals, leadership and mastery of small-unit tactics being far more important. Similarly, although preliminary skirmishing before battles such as Cannae indeed had very little Grand Tactical significance, such behaviour may have had other benefits. The main bodies of line infantry and cavalry, stationed some distance behind their skirmishers, waited in position and observed the ebb and flow of this peculiarly ritualistic and tactically insignificant martial overture.[39] It is very possible that the importance of this phase of battle was primarily moral or psychological rather than tactical; it may perhaps have served as a crude and highly informal augury, foreshadowing how the ensuing battle would develop. Such auguries could well have been, to some extent, self-fulfilling prophecies. In such circumstances one of the most important duties of the lightly armed skirmishers would have been to display their courage.[40] Preceded in this way by such exhibitions of bravado by troops worse-equipped and either younger or poorer than themselves,[41] any line infantry and cavalry who shirked their duty and were reluctant to fight would have been exposed to ridicule.[42] An enthusiastic performance by the skirmishers would in this way have inspired the main forces to fight harder when the 'real' fighting started.

Before considering what exactly the mechanics of infantry skirmishing may have been like, it is important to remember that the skirmishers at Cannae fell into two broad categories: 'light-armed' troops and what may be somewhat imprecisely termed peltasts.[43] Hannibal's Balearian slingers would have been 'light-armed' troops in the strict sense of the term, as also were the Cretan archers serving with the Roman forces for Syracusan pay and those skirmishers on either side who lacked shields or armour of any sort, being equipped only with javelins. On the other hand, the majority of Rome's *velites* and Hannibal's 'spearmen' could have been roughly classed as peltasts, in that although they lacked body armour, they were equipped with shields and some sort of side-arm, whether a sword or thrusting spear, in addition to their javelins.

From modern experiments, it is possible to estimate the theoretical capabilities of these weapons. The majority of skirmishers in both armies used javelins or throwing spears of some kind. Trials carried out under Napoleon III in the second half of the nineteenth century suggest that the *pilum*, essentially a heavy throwing spear designed to pierce enemy shields or armour, had a maximum range of about 30 m. Most javelins were substantially lighter than this, and may have compensated for reduced penetration potential with greater range – possibly capable of being thrown twice as far as a *pilum* (Goldsworthy, 1996, p. 183). Accuracy and range could have been improved through the use of a throwing-loop at the centre of the javelin (Snodgrass, 1999, pp. 79–80). The Cretans seem to have used the 'composite bow',[44] a skilfully designed weapon composed of wood, horn, and oxen tendons, laminated together into a weapon of remarkable power. In theory archers could hit targets 270 m away, although in practice they could shoot with accuracy only over distances of at most 135 m (Hanson, 1999, p. 154; Gabriel and Metz, 1991, p. 71). The range of Cretan archers may have been somewhat lessened again by their penchant for arrows with large, heavy tanged heads, unlike the tiny arrowheads more suited to the composite bow.[45] Slingers may have had the greatest range of all the skirmishers,[46] although much must have depended on the proficiency of individual slingers and on general battlefield conditions (Goldsworthy, 1996, p. 186; Gabriel and Metz, 1991, p. 76), which are discussed below.

As explained already, with such a large number of light troops engaged, particularly on the Roman side, it would have been necessary to deploy them in great depth. Two key factors would have dictated how the skirmishers operated: ammunition supply and room in which to manoeuvre. Du Picq argued (1987, p. 189), albeit in the context of nineteenth-century armies, that the need to replenish the ammunition supply made it foolish to deploy all skirmishing units simultaneously, it being better to keep some units in reserve in order to replace others when they ran out of ammunition. He also argued (p. 190) that in his day there was no need to deploy skirmishers in a continuous line, since there was no danger of enemy units being able to advance into intervals in the line – the range of nineteenth-century firepower, significantly greater than that of javelins, bows, and slings, ensured that opposing lines kept their distance from each other.

Du Picq's theories are extremely useful in considering how ancient skirmishers fought. As he has made clear, ancient skirmishers must have deployed, at least initially, as unbroken lines. They must have been deployed in great depth, as it appears that groups of 150 or more *velites* operated in narrow 'corridors', each perhaps no more than 5.4 m wide. The *velites* were organised into units which accompanied the legion's thirty maniples, so three units of *velites* would have been positioned in each of these 'corridors'. These units would probably have been stationed in accordance with their maniples' positions. In other words, *velites* who were brigaded with *hastati* would be at the front, those with *principes* would be in the middle, and those with *triarii* would bring up the rear. It is likely that these units operated along the lines suggested by du Picq above, each unit withdrawing when it had spent most or all of its ammunition and being replaced by the fresh troops behind; after all, Rome's heavy infantry operated in accordance with a similar practice of line replacement.

Rome's skirmishers would therefore have attacked in a series of waves, and although they were surely not organised in the same way, it would seem probable that Hannibal's skirmishers would have fought in a similar fashion, as du Picq's principles seem to be universally applicable. There were at least 15,000 Roman skirmishers at Cannae, but Hannibal had only about 8,000 skirmishers at the Trebia (Polyb. 3.72.7), and it is likely that a similar number fought at Cannae.[47] Outnumbered in this way, the Carthaginian skirmishers would probably have run out of ammunition long before their Roman opponents,[48] but this does not appear to have been a problem. Evidently the skirmishers were withdrawn to be replaced by the line infantry while they still had a substantial supply of missiles.

The skirmishers seem to have fought as waves, but a uniformly dispersed formation was probably not used, although they may have begun battle in this manner. It has already been suggested that the Roman skirmishers were divided into small teams, perhaps based upon their *contubernia*, each unit of *velites* being composed of several such teams. It would be strange if Hannibal's skirmishers were not similarly organised, for small groups can be highly cohesive, and armies tend to foster their development, recognising the benefits of this for *esprit de corps* and overall effectiveness (Holmes, 1985, pp. 293 ff.). Marshall points out that soldiers acting in isolation, without feeling themselves to be part of a group, are ineffective:

> The thing which enables an infantry soldier to keep going with his weapons is the near presence or the presumed presence of a comrade . . . He must have at least some feeling of spiritual unity with them if he is to do an efficient job of moving and fighting. Should he lack this feeling for any reason, whether it is because he is congenitally a social misfit or because he has lost physical contact or because he has been denied a chance to establish himself with them, he will become a castaway in the middle of a battle and as incapable of effective offensive action as if he were stranded somewhere without weapons.
>
> (Marshall, 1947, p. 42)

Such desire for the physical proximity of one's colleagues can go too far, leading to the phenomenon known as 'bunching', where soldiers under fire gather into clusters. This is psychologically useful in that, by providing a feeling of collective security it enables soldiers to stand firm in the face of danger and even perform feats of exceptional bravery (Holmes, 1985, pp. 158–9). Behaviour like this, especially common among inexperienced troops, is perfectly normal when facing enemy fire, so the furthest advanced skirmishers at any given point should be conceived of as small clusters of men rather than an 'ideal' loose formation. Most of these clusters of advanced skirmishers would have been armed with javelins, which had a shorter range than either bows or slings, so that those using them needed to be quite close to the enemy in order to wield them effectively. These clusters would not have included more than ten men each as a rule, since they would almost inevitably have been based upon the small groups or teams discussed above, and ten was the maximum size for such 'primary groups' (Holmes, 1985, p. 293).

The problem with this phenomenon, however, is that it would in some ways have reduced the effectiveness of the team. On the most obvious level, clusters of soldiers must have provided easier targets for enemy fire than did individuals acting in isolation (Holmes, 1985, p. 159). Perhaps more importantly, it would have been impossible for missile troops to use their weapons while in such clusters. Onasander makes it clear that it was essential for skirmishers to have room to use their weapons, as slingers needed to whirl their slings in the air in order to release their shot, while javelins would normally be thrown after either a backwards step or a forward charge (Onas. 17).

Troops in the van of both skirmishing forces would therefore have been primarily javelin-throwers, gathered into small clumps in order to feel secure. This was inevitable, as getting close enough to hit the enemy necessitated coming within reach of enemy fire, entering the 'killing zone' of enemy missiles. It was futile, if not impossible, to fire from within the cluster, making it necessary to step away from one's fellows in order to use one's weapons.[49] A high degree of courage would have been required for this, since it meant exposing oneself as an individual to enemy fire. In reality, isolated soldiers would probably have been marginally safer than their clustered friends, for they were smaller targets, but appearance may well have been more important than reality in this case. It is highly likely that there was a distinct culture of display among the skirmishers, with dominant individuals gaining prestige through exhibitions of courage. This argument is admittedly largely based on inference, but Polybius does provide some direct evidence for it, when he notes that some *velites* covered their helmets with wolfskin so that they would be easily identifiable to their officers, who could then judge whether they fought courageously or not (Polyb. 6.22.3).

The fact that the emphasis here is on the courage rather than the skill of the skirmishers is telling. As suggested earlier, the main importance of preliminary skirmishing was probably moral or psychological, and ancient writers were almost certainly right to regard this initial phase of battle as inconclusive and tactically insignificant, since it is quite likely that very few troops were killed or even wounded in it. It is useful, for comparative purposes, to consider the arguments of S.L.A. Marshall (1947, pp. 50–63), who studied the performance of American infantry during the Second World War, and observed that on average no more than 15 per cent of men ever used their weapons in any given engagement. This figure rose to 25 per cent in the most aggressive companies when under extreme pressure. The basic reason for such a low rate of fire, according to Marshall (p. 78), was the soldiers' upbringing: there was such a great taboo on killing and violence in general in twentieth-century America that a mental block was created, preventing the taking of life in war.

This would not have been such a big problem for the armies at Cannae: Roman society was highly militarised and martial virtues were universally admired, while Hannibal's troops tended to be hardened mercenaries, frequently coming from warrior societies. Furthermore, it is probable, given the nature of skirmishing described above, that virtually all skirmishers in advanced units were obliged to use their weapons, being in such close proximity to their colleagues that failure to fire would have been quite obvious.[50] Many frightened troops would have used their weapons in these circumstances out of a desire not to appear weak in front of their friends.[51] However, it is equally certain that a large proportion of these would have fired blindly, without even attempting to aim.[52] Being a distinct target within range of enemy missiles would not have been conducive to concentration, and many of those firing would simply have wished to return to the 'security' of the group.

Furthermore, it was surely the case that the majority of missiles which were aimed properly missed their mark. The Balearian slingers were notorious for their accuracy (Str. 3.5.1; Diod. 5.18.3–4; Veg. 1.16), and in theory archers ought to have been able to hit bundles of straw at a distance of about 580 feet (177 m) (Veg. 2.23). However, battlefield conditions can have a detrimental effect on accuracy and general performance. For instance, it required immense strength to draw the composite bow, and after ten shots at most, distance, accuracy, and rate of fire would begin to deteriorate (Hanson, 1999, p. 157; Gabriel and Metz, 1991, p. 69). It appears that in the eighteenth and nineteenth centuries it was rare for even 5 per cent of musket balls to hit their target, which would normally be a large group of men deployed in close order. This estimate includes those troops who fired without aiming at all, and other factors were at work too, but it does serve to demonstrate how easy it was to miss one's target (Goldsworthy, 1996, pp. 187–8; Gabriel and Metz, 1991, pp. 71–2). When that target was an isolated individual or a small group of men, the chances of hitting one's mark must have been extremely slim, especially given the fact that the firer was himself a potential target, so that strong nerves would have been at least as desirable as good aim. Furthermore, the fact that the target was frequently equipped with a shield of some sort would have reduced still further the danger of being hit. The effects of such wounds will be described later on.

Finally, it should be remembered that these troops were sometimes required to skirmish at close quarters. It was for this reason that many of them were equipped with side-arms of some sort, usually a sword, but possibly a stabbing spear. On a couple of occasions Livy describes Roman *velites* who, having hurled their javelins, fought enemy troops with their swords (Liv. 31.35.4–6, 38.21.12–13). Given the sheer number of troops at Cannae, and the quantity of ammunition that was available, close-quarter fighting between skirmishers was probably a rarity. Whenever troops ran out of equipment they could simply have been withdrawn and replaced with fresh, fully equipped troops. When it did happen, it probably occurred because the 'bunching' tendency would have caused small gaps to appear in the opposing lines, and as du Picq pointed out (1987, p. 190), over short distances gaps in the line could well be invaded by enemy skirmishers. In such circumstances, it would be surprising if fighting did not remain purely at the level of missile exchange.[53]

Cavalry against cavalry

In evaluating the Carthaginian victory at Cannae, Polybius noted that:

> it demonstrated to posterity that in times of war it is better to give battle with half as many infantry as the enemy and an over-whelming force of cavalry than to be in all respects his equal.
>
> (Polyb. 3.117.5)

Combat between cavalry at Cannae took place on the edges of the battlefield, flanking the central infantry contest. These two separate encounters were not merely spatially independent but also quite distinct in character. On the Carthaginian left, the Roman right, the Roman citizen cavalry faced Hannibal's 'steady and bridled' cavalry, primarily composed of Celts and Spaniards. On the far side of the battlefield, the Carthaginian right and Roman left, the cavalry of Rome's Italian and Latin allies faced the Numidian cavalry.

Roman citizens against Celts and Spaniards

Polybius describes the riverside encounter between the Roman citizen cavalry, led by Paullus, and the Celtic and Spanish cavalry, led by Hasdrubal, in vivid yet problematic terms:

> when the Spanish and Celtic horse on the left wing came into colli-sion with the Roman cavalry, the struggle that ensued was truly barbaric; for there were none of the normal wheeling evolutions, but having once met they dismounted and fought man to man. The Carthaginians finally got the upper hand, killed most of the enemy in the mellay, all the Romans fighting with desperate bravery, and began to drive the rest along the river, cutting them down mercilessly.
>
> (Polyb. 3.115.2–4)

Livy supports this account of the encounter, sensibly attributing the pecu-liar nature of the contest to lack of space, with the two forces being hemmed in by the river on one side and the main bodies of infantry on the other (Liv. 22.47.1–2).

The first major problem with this account lies in Polybius' claim that the opposing cavalry forces 'came into collision' with each other. This almost automatically conjures up images of two solid masses of cavalry crashing into each other at full tilt. It seems most improbable that this could have been the case for the results of such a collision would have been mutually catastrophic. Keegan points out (1976, p. 147) that such an encounter would clearly lead to 'a collapsed scrummage of horses and men, growing bigger as succeeding ranks are carried on to the leading ones by their own impetus'. It is easy to imagine the consequences of such a 'collapsed scrummage', each side suffering numerous casualties through 'friendly fire', being crushed or trampled by their own horses, in addition to being accidentally pierced by or even impaled upon the spears and javelins of their fellow soldiers.

It has already been proposed that the Roman cavalry were deployed ten deep along a frontage of 240 horses, with the opposing Carthaginians sharing approximately the same frontage while being deployed at least twenty-five deep. The 240-horse frontage would have been perhaps 480 m wide, allowing 1 metre per horse and gaps between units equal to the units themselves. The benefits of such a close formation would have been moral rather than physical: the rear ranks could not have physically pressed the horses in front of them forward, but their very presence would have prevented the more reluctant ones from shirking their duty by hanging back or even fleeing (Goldsworthy, 1996, pp. 235–6). Speed tends to excite horses, so if the cavalry actually charged at high speed, the horses would have spread out because of differences in their speed, strength, and temperament. While nervous mares and dominant horses of either sex would have forced their way through to the front,[54] more reluctant horsemen could have held their mounts back or possibly fled, either way avoiding combat (Goldsworthy, 1996, p. 236). To prevent this happening, it would have been necessary for the cavalry to advance at a slower pace, a walk or trot,[55] charging only when close to the enemy, minimising the danger of formations disintegrating. Goldsworthy cites a nineteenth-century British manual which suggested that the gallop should begin about 137 m from advancing enemy cavalry (Goldsworthy, 1996, p. 236).

At this stage, nearing the enemy, riders armed with missile weapons would have used them. Such missiles were surely lacking in accuracy. Goldsworthy points out (1996, p. 232), using an admittedly anachronistic term, that a horse's irregular motion would have made it an 'unstable gun platform'. However, the gallop is a more 'compliant' or 'smooth' gait than the trot, owing to the fact that the legs touch the ground sequentially, and the peak up-and-down accelerations of the body are lower, reducing the force of impact and the subsequent danger of injury to the horse.[56] One important advantage of changing from a trot to a gallop would have been that this new 'smoothness' could to some degree have improved the accuracy of riders attempting to hurl javelins at the enemy. It might at any rate have compensated for any loss in accuracy brought about by enhanced speed. Arrian describes cavalry hurling many javelins while charging, in exhibitions of this skill (Arr., *Tact.* 40), and Saracen horse-archers were recommended to fire mid-stride when on a galloping horse (Goldsworthy, 1996, pp. 232–3).

Spanish cavalry were almost certainly armed with javelins, but it appears that both Celtic and Roman cavalry lacked missile weapons. As a result, before coming to close quarters, the Roman cavalry would have been subject to a short-lived hail of Spanish javelins, while being unable to respond aggressively. How great a threat such a brief missile assault could pose is uncertain. It appears that Spanish cavalry carried only two javelins each, and it indeed seems unlikely that individual riders would have had time to hurl more than two, considering that javelins probably had a maximum range of 60 m, a distance which the advancing cavalry forces would have swiftly covered. If there were 2,000 Spanish cavalry at Cannae, there could not have been more than 4,000 javelins while charging, and a far lower number would seem more likely. These javelins were surely hurled at the enemy as a unit, rather than at individual moving targets, but even then the vast majority of these missiles would have missed, for the same reasons discussed with reference to infantry skirmishing. Assuming a highly optimistic hit rate of 5 per cent, no more than 200 Roman cavalry would have been hit, and probably far fewer.[57] However, any 'hits' could have been highly effective, especially since the Roman horses lacked armour – falling horses would have led to chaos in the Roman ranks, causing other horses to panic, stumble, and fall.

What actually happened when the opposing cavalry forces met each other? Under normal circumstances, one side would apparently have been intimidated by the other and given way before colliding with them.[58] This is reasonable, for horses will not charge into solid objects, and a 'wall' of enemy cavalry could well have been perceived as just such an impenetrable object (Keegan, 1976, pp. 95–6; Spence, 1993, pp. 103 ff.) Moreover, the horses' riders would themselves have been all too aware of the potential catastrophe that could occur if the opposing forces crashed into each other. Under normal circumstances the riders' nerve would fail (Goldsworthy, 1996, p. 236; du Picq, 1987, p. 211). 'Shock' cavalry nearly always relied upon moral rather than physical shock to cause the enemy to break and run.

However, if Livy's analysis is correct, and in this respect there is no reason to doubt it, space restrictions prevented either cavalry force from withdrawing or manoeuvring, so that there was no option but to engage at close quarters with the enemy (du Picq, 1987, p. 88). Polybius' bald description of the two forces meeting, dismounting, and fighting on foot seems too neat, surely not reflecting the reality of the mêlée (Polyb. 3.115.3). Livy is more detailed and plausible:

Both parties pushed straight ahead, and as the horses came to a standstill, packed together in the throng, the riders began to grapple with their enemies and drag them from their seats.

(Liv. 22.47.3)

This is more convincing, especially in the light of more recent cavalry encounters. Keegan's descriptions of cavalry combat at Waterloo (1976, pp. 148–9) are particularly enlightening – the opposing forces allowed gaps to appear in their ranks, enabling groups of the enemy to penetrate their lines, and a mêlée to take place without the two lines of cavalry actually colliding. Fighting under such circumstances was between small groups or even individuals, not between formations, as the opposing forces mingled with each other; Livy's reference to horses 'packed together in the throng' seems to describe such a situation.

The closeness of horses and riders would have made such grappling as Livy mentions almost inevitable. Spears required a certain amount of room to be wielded effectively, room which was probably not readily available in such a tight mêlée as developed at Cannae.[59] It is not surprising that grappling riders would have fallen from their mounts, seeing that they lacked the added security offered by stirrups.[60] Broken bones, a type of injury common to cavalrymen throughout history,[61] would have been a frequent consequence of this. Once on the ground, those soldiers who were unharmed after being unseated would have had a solid base from which to fight, allowing them to wield their swords somewhat more effectively (Xen., *Anab.* 3.2.19), but this gain would have been heavily outweighed by the added dangers posed by their being exposed to spear-thrusts and sword-strokes from above. Xenophon notes that the *kopis*, effectively the same weapon as the Spanish *falcata*, was most effective when used from a height (Xen., *Eq.* 12.11); an overarm stroke would probably be used. A mounted soldier armed with a *falcata* would probably have concentrated his attack on the neck of a dismounted enemy, since the neck was invariably exposed, unlike the head and shoulders which were frequently protected by a helmet and cuirass. Whenever a head was exposed it would have made an obvious target, for head wounds were particularly dangerous when received from above (Spence, 1993, p. 54). In addition to facing threats from mounted warriors, troops on the ground in the midst of a cavalry mêlée must have been in constant danger of being kicked or trampled upon by horses from either side. Should any horses have been killed, their falling corpses would probably have crushed dismounted cavalrymen.[62] Roman cavalrymen would have attempted to defend themselves with their *gladii*, which were capable of severing limbs, but it is likely that few such wounds were inflicted, owing to the mounted Romans trying simultaneously to control their horses and protect themselves.[63]

This confusion probably did not extend beyond the first few ranks on either side, as it is highly unlikely that the Roman resistance was nearly as staunch as Polybius presents it, describing them as having fought with 'desperate bravery' (Polyb. 3.115.4). According to Polybius, only 200 Carthaginian cavalry fell at Cannae (Polyb. 3.117.6), whereas the entire force of 2,400 Roman citizen cavalry was apparently wiped out; 300 allied cavalry escaped to various towns in the area, and the cavalry who escaped to Venusia with Varro were surely allied cavalry also, in view of the fact that Varro was stationed with them during the battle (Polyb. 3.117.2). Livy allows for approximately 1,350 deaths among the citizen cavalry, saying that 2,700 cavalry were killed, in approximately equal numbers of citizens and allies (Liv. 22.49.15). This is a significantly lower figure than that given by Polybius, but nevertheless the Romans certainly appear to have suffered far more casualties than the Carthaginians. Du Picq points out (1987, p. 89) that the difference in losses would not have been so dispro-portionate if the Romans had actively resisted, and argues that while the foremost troops were engaged with the Carthaginian cavalry, those troops behind them panicked, wheeled their horses about, and fled. Such cowardice seems to have done them no good. The Romans who were actually fighting the Carthaginians did not form an unbroken line but, as described above, fought in small groups rather than as a single formation, so Celtic and Spanish cavalry could have poured through the Roman 'line' in pursuit of the fleeing Roman cavalry.

Such a pursuit would have been extremely short lived, as the cavalry were needed elsewhere on the battlefield. Hasdrubal must have signalled for them to regroup in order to lead them to the far side of the field, where the Numidians were still skirmishing with Rome's allied cavalry forces.[64]

Numidian skirmishers against Rome's allied cavalry

Since most of the factors affecting cavalry skirmishing have been discussed above, this section will be brief.

There were perhaps as many as 4,000 Numidian cavalry under Hanno's command on the Carthaginian right wing, facing about 3,600 Italian and Latin cavalry led by Varro. Although the infantry forces were stationed to one side of the cavalry forces, their other side was exposed, allowing them room to skirmish. This was a style of combat in which the Numidians excelled, as is made clear by Appian's account of how Masinissa assembled a force of cavalry some decades later:

> a body of cavalry who were trained day and night to hurl showers of javelins, advancing and retreating and again advancing. These, in fact, are the tactics which they always employ, alternate flight and pursuit.
>
> (App., *Pun.* 11)

Hannibal clearly took advantage of this, relying on the Numidians not to defeat the allied cavalry, but simply to neutralise them:

> The Numidians meanwhile on the right wing, attacking the cavalry opposite them on the Roman left, neither gained any great advantage nor suffered any particular loss owing to their particular mode of fighting, but they kept the enemy's cavalry out of action by drawing them off and attacking them from all sides at once.
>
> (Polyb. 3.116.5)

Although they may well have carried a javelin for the initial assault, there is no evidence to indicate that Rome's allied cavalry were armed in a significantly different fashion from the citizen cavalry, so it should not be assumed that they were 'light' cavalry like the Numidians. However, as Goldsworthy says (1996, p. 235), even 'shock' cavalry fought in such a way that 'a successful assault could very quickly be followed by an enforced retreat'. It is significant that wheeling manoeuvres and attempts to outflank the enemy were regarded as normal tactics for the 'shock' cavalry supplied by Rome's citizens.[65]

As noted above, skirmishing between groups of light-armed infantry tended to be indecisive, largely owing to the fact that troops were at least as keen to avoid being hit as they were to cause actual harm to the enemy; the same principle must have been in play here, except that cavalry moved much faster than infantry. It would have been hard for troops to aim properly since, as discussed above, horses were unstable 'gun platforms', and, although large, the enemy horses were moving targets, liable to change direction at any moment, unlike the cavalry on the far side of the field, who lacked the space for such manoeuvres. Lack of accuracy must have led to a correspondingly low casualty rate (Goldsworthy, 1996, p. 242).

This pattern of combat was therefore highly inconclusive, presumably marked by constant advances and withdrawals on either side. However, Hasdrubal eventually led his Celtic and Spanish cavalry over from the far side of the field. In a perfect illustration of du Picq's argument that 'shock' in battle is moral rather than physical in nature, the allied cavalry panicked and fled when they saw these fresh troops approaching from their right (Polyb. 3.116.6).[66] The panic would have started from the rear, as was normal, but it clearly engulfed the entire cavalry force. Hasdrubal's cavalry never even got close to the fleeing allies, instead turning to attack the Roman rear:

> for in view of the fact that the Numidians were very numerous and most efficient and formidable when in pursuit of a flying foe he left them to deal with the Roman cavalry and led his squadrons on with the object of supporting the Africans.
>
> (Polyb. 3.116.7)[67]

The Numidians' pursuit was devastating, as the fleeing troops were virtually unable to defend themselves because their backs were turned. Du Picq pointed out that attempts to flee when the enemy were close almost inevitably led to butchery (Du Picq, 1987, p. 114; Keegan, 1976, p. 71). The destructive power of cavalry in pursuit is powerfully illustrated by Oliver Cromwell's comment that his cavalry had 'chase and execution [for] about five or six miles' after the battle of Gainsborough.[68] In such circumstances, the defenceless fugitives could only hope that their steeds were fast enough to get them to safety, or that the enemy would discontinue the pursuit, either through exhaustion (e.g., Caes., *B Gall* 8.29) or for tactical reasons. The Numidians' pursuit was very effective, as their small, swift mounts galloped after the fugitives, javelins being used to strike down horses and men from behind. Any experience they would have had at hunting would have been particularly useful for this task (Xen., *Cyn.* 12.1–9).[69] An unseated cavalryman had very little chance of survival, even if he was not wounded at the time of losing his mount, for the Numidian horses could easily outpace him, especially since many Roman cavalrymen would have been encumbered with heavy cuirasses.

The efficiency of the Numidian pursuit can be gauged by the casualty figures reported by Polybius and Livy. Polybius records that of the Roman force's 6,000 cavalry, seventy escaped to Venusia with Varro, and 300 of the allied cavalry reached other cities in the region (Polyb. 3.117.2). If this is correct, over 5,630 cavalry were either killed or captured at Cannae. Livy's figures seem more likely in view of the fact that most of the citizen cavalry, if not the allies, had a sizeable lead on their Numidian pursuers. He claims that about 2,700 cavalry were killed, in approximately equal numbers of citizens and allies, and a further 1,500 were captured in the battle itself (Liv. 22.49.15, 18). Not all of those who were killed in the battle would have died immediately – seriously wounded men would have been incapable of escape so the Numidians would have been content to immobilise them by slashing at their backs and hamstrings[70] before moving on to fresh prey.

Line infantry against line infantry

After the light-armed skirmishers had been withdrawn, the 'real' battle began, when the opposing forces of line infantry met. It was normal in ancient battles for the opposing forces to advance over a distance of several hundred metres before charging at the enemy (Hanson, 1989, pp. 135 ff.; Goldsworthy, 1996, pp. 192–3), but it is likely that Hannibal's Celts and Spaniards stayed in position until the Romans were very close, perhaps within missile range. When advancing in formation, each man judges his position by reference to those on either side, and it is thus extremely difficult for soldiers to advance in a straight line even under ideal conditions, for a mistake by just one man can be passed on through the entire formation, often making it necessary to stop and dress ranks.[71] Ancient armies did not march in step, and on ground which was even slightly irregular and with nervous troops this problem would have been much more significant: gaps would have developed between individual soldiers, the overall direction of march could shift, and as a result armies which had begun their advance as cohesive units could reach the enemy as a scattered mob. If this was a problem for troops deployed in line, as the Romans were, it would have been an infinitely greater one for Hannibal's men. It was absolutely necessary for the peculiar 'crescent' formation to be maintained, so that the thin 'horns' of the crescent would be kept out of the fighting for as long as possible, because if the troops there broke early in the battle, the entire Carthaginian plan would collapse.

The Romans then would have advanced to meet the Celts and Spaniards. Polybius describes the Romans at Zama as advancing slowly and impressively (Polyb. 15.12.7). Such a steady advance would have appeared intimidating, indicative of an army's confidence and discipline, as a nervous desire to get the battle over with would often incite troops to advance as quickly as possible (Goldsworthy, 1996, pp. 194, 197). The behaviour of the opposing armies at Cannae must have been similar to that of those at Zama fourteen years later:

> When the phalanxes were close to each other, the Romans fell upon their foes, raising their war-cry and clashing their shields with their weapons, as is their practice, while there was a strange confusion of shouts raised by the Carthaginian mercenaries.
>
> (Polyb. 15.12.8–9)[72]

At this point the two armies would normally throw their *pila* or other missiles and then charge. However, at Cannae things must have been different.

If the Romans maintained formation, their line would effectively have formed a tangent to the Carthaginian crescent, ensuring that the early fighting would take place along a very narrow front (Polyb. 3.115.7). As the Carthaginian centre was pushed back the curve would flatten out, giving the 'killing zone' extra width, as was illustrated in a simplified fashion in Figure 1(d).

The Roman *hastati* would normally commence fighting by throwing their *pila* at the enemy. An order would be given to prepare to cast *pila*, and each soldier would draw back his weapon with his right hand, before launching it on a second order.[73] The *pilum* had a maximum range of 30 metres but was more effective at shorter distances, so it may have been thrown from much closer to the enemy. It was a particularly powerful missile, as its pyramidal head could penetrate an enemy's shield and possibly even strike the person holding it. At the very least the protruding spear would render the shield useless.

The *pilum* assault, which could be devastating, would have been considerably less so at Cannae. Its main function was to 'soften up' the enemy line, before the close fighting began. However, only the central units of Celts and Spaniards, those at the most advanced part of the crescent, would have been exposed to the initial shock of this. While it would be foolish to assume that all *pila* were cast at once, it is likely that many were cast in vain at enemy troops who were well out of range. In addition, the Romans' deep formation would have prevented most troops from using their *pila*. Goldsworthy points out (1996, pp. 198–9) that only the troops in the first six ranks could have used their *pila* safely, without risking injury to their own men through 'friendly fire'. Yet the Roman *hastati* were drawn up extremely deep, perhaps as many as twenty-four men. If this was the case, only the front 25 per cent of *hastati* would have been able to fire at the enemy.

This *pila* volley was not unopposed. Both the Celts and Spaniards carried javelins of various sorts, many of which were just as lethal as the *pilum*. Diodorus mentions Celtic throwing spears that had ornately forged heads designed to mangle flesh (Diod. 5.30.4),[74] while Spanish missiles included *pilum*-type spears, the incendiary *falarica*, and the *saunion*, which was made entirely of iron. However, the same factors apply to these volleys as to missile exchange between skirmishers, as discussed above. Many soldiers probably failed to aim properly, reducing the number of casualties, and rendering this phase of battle rather inconclusive (e.g., Liv., 34.14.9–11). Nevertheless, those men who were hit would have suffered hideous injuries – Caesar describes one soldier in Gaul, for example, having both his thighs pierced by a single javelin (Caes., *B Gall* 5.35.6).

Having thrown their missiles, the opposing forces would have advanced in a fashion similar to the seventeenth-century 'Highland Charge' (Carlton, 1992, pp. 134–5). Both sides rushed at each other, yelling as they did so. As with the cavalry, the two forces were not going to collide, but instead this wild rush was designed to terrify the enemy, causing them to break and run.[75] This was the same principle which made nineteenth-century bayonet charges so frequently effective; there are virtually no known cases of troops actually fighting each other with bayonets (Griffith, 1989, p. 141; Muir, 1998, pp. 86–8). At Cannae neither army broke. The Celts and Iberians were seasoned soldiers who had already been victorious over Roman troops, and were reassured by the presence of Hannibal himself alongside them, while the Romans were deployed in an exceptionally deep formation, preventing the troops in the van from panicking and trying to flee, should they be inclined to do so.

The central portions of the lines would therefore have come within striking distance of each other before slowing down and fighting at close quarters. Armed now with swords, their 'killing zone' can only have been about a metre in depth. This phase in the fighting is best characterised as an enormous series of duels between individual soldiers.[76] The Celtic sword was a long double-edged weapon better suited for slashing than thrusting, although it did have a point; on the other hand, the Roman *gladius*, while perfectly capable of cutting, was primarily a thrusting weapon. In addition, the curved, oblong *scutum* was a weapon of offence as well as defence in that its central boss could be used to push and punch at the enemy, although its great weight meant that it could not be manoeuvred easily. The Spaniards would have fought along similar lines to the Romans if armed with a *gladius*-type sword, but those armed with a *falcata* may have fought in a fashion not unlike that of the Celts, to take advantage of the weapon's curved blade, particularly suited to slashing.

Close combat between Romans and Celts was a clash of two very different techniques. The Celts would have required plenty of room in which to swing their long swords while simultaneously manoeuvring their flat oblong shields to block any Roman strokes (Polyb. 2.30.3, 8, 3.114.3). They probably fought fully upright, and could therefore slash at the Romans from a height, focusing their attack on the exposed neck and shoulders of the *hastati*.[77] The Romans would have attempted to use the metal rim of the *scutum* to ward off such attacks, but should they fail in this they were not entirely vulnerable. The narrow peak at the back of the Roman helmet would have given some protection against this type of assault (Connolly, 1989, pp. 358; 1998, p. 120; Gabriel and Metz, 1991, p. 52), and any Romans who were wearing the *lorica* would have been well protected since chain mail is vulnerable to thrusts rather than slashes (Gabriel and Metz, 1991, p. 52). Cuirasses with shoulder-doubling would have given even better protection, possibly absorbing much of a stroke's impact and reducing the risk of the underlying bones being broken.[78] The typical Roman, on the other hand, probably stood in a very slight crouch, with left foot forward, holding the *scutum* in front with the left hand and using it to protect the upper legs, the torso, and the lower face. The sword would then probably be used primarily in an upward thrust, although slashes and downward stokes were also possible.[79] A relief sculpture at the base of a column in Mainz depicts a soldier from the early Imperial period in this position (Figure 9). Upward thrusts would have attempted to get under the enemy's shield, striking at his abdomen and groin. Wounds to these unprotected areas were almost invariably fatal, due to loss of blood, shock, and the likelihood of peritonitis or other infections (Hanson, 1989, pp. 162, 212–13). Polybius, in an account of a battle between Romans and Celts in 223, describes the two sides getting so close that the Celts could not effectively use their swords, while the Romans stabbed at their chests and faces. Such wounds could have caused death in minutes, if not instantly (Polyb. 2.33.6),[80] and consequently must have been comparatively rare among otherwise fresh troops, who would have used their shields to guard carefully against them.

Although the Celts and Romans probably concentrated their attacks on the enemy shoulders and abdomens respectively, it is likely that, as was

Figure 9 Relief sculpture of Roman infantrymen, found at Mainz. The soldier in front is equipped with a *scutum* and *gladius*, and is in the classic fighting stance of a Roman infantryman. The soldier behind him is holding a *pilum*.

usual in ancient battle, most wounds were to areas normally not protected by a shield: head, legs, and right arm (Goldsworthy, 1996, p. 220). Wounds to limbs were rarely as dangerous as head wounds (Hanson, 1989, p. 216), but they could frequently weaken or unbalance a soldier, eventually causing him to drop his guard, lose the ability to strike at the enemy, or even fall to the ground. Once any of these things happened his fate was effectively sealed (Gabriel and Metz, 1991, p. 60), as far more serious wounds would be received. A deep wound in the leg could cripple any soldier,[81] but the Celts did not wear greaves and must have been much more at risk than the Romans. The Roman *gladius*, although without the reach of the longer Celtic sword, could still slash very effectively – Livy records the horror felt by Greeks on seeing the mutilated corpses of troops who had been killed by Roman cavalry armed with *gladii*, some with their arms cut off, others decapitated (Liv. 31.34).

It seems unsafe to apply Marshall's statistical findings to this type of battle, as Goldsworthy does (1996, p. 219), in order to speculate on how 'typical' this style of fighting really was. As discussed already, Marshall found that no more than 25 per cent of a unit's soldiers used their weapons in any given situation, and that it was almost always the same soldiers who used their weapons in different encounters (1947, pp. 50–65). From this basis, Goldsworthy hypothesises (1996, p. 219) that most of the troops in the front ranks fought mainly with the intention of staying alive rather than of killing the enemy. However, as discussed above, it is likely that the best soldiers in the Roman maniples were generally stationed in the front ranks while the bravest warriors in the Celtic and Spanish lines would have naturally gravitated to the front. These were exactly the type of troops most likely to attack the enemy actively. In other words, many of Marshall's 25 per cent, if his findings are in any way applicable, were actually in the front ranks, at least in the early stages of the fighting, before they were replaced by rear rankers because of death, injuries, or simple exhaustion (Adcock, 1957, p. 10).

Troops would have begun to stumble as the ground became littered with corpses, making it ever more difficult to manoeuvre or even to stand one's ground and fight. In addition to wounds and difficulty in moving about, troops fighting in this fashion must simply have become exhausted very quickly. Fuller (1965, p. 91) estimated a period of fifteen minutes' fighting before men became exhausted, and Kromayer (in Kromayer and Veith, 1912, p. 354) and Goldsworthy (1996, p. 224) estimate even less. After a certain period of fighting it would have been necessary for the lines to draw apart, perhaps by only a few metres, in order to allow both sides to rest. Meanwhile, wounded troops might be brought to safety and line replacement could occur. Sabin argues that these rests were the natural state of the fighting, with the troops standing a distance apart, hurling insults at each other or simply catching their breath, before advancing once more.[82] Any single combat which may have taken place would have happened during such lulls. While rare at this period, single combat was not unheard of, and there appears to have been something of a tradition of Roman aristocrats facing Celtic nobles in this way (Oakley, 1985, pp. 392–410). Successive advances would have lacked the power of the initial charge, primarily because troops would have been tired, and the pauses would have begun to last for longer than the fighting itself (Goldsworthy, 1996, p. 224; 1997, p. 21). It was under such circumstances that battles could go on for hours.

The Romans clearly had the upper hand in this early phase of the battle, Polybius noting that:

> For a time the Spaniards and Celts kept their ranks and struggled bravely with the Romans, but soon, borne down by the weight of the legions, they gave way and fell back, breaking up the crescent.
>
> (Polyb. 3.114.5)

That the Romans were so successful in this part of the field is perhaps not surprising – not only were the troops at the front of each maniple the best soldiers in the unit, but the central legions, the ones which came in contact with the Celts and Spaniards at the start, were those commanded by Minucius and Servilius, the more experienced legions. The sheer depth of their units might have given the leading ranks a significant boost in morale, and would certainly have prevented them from attempting to flee, should they foolishly try to do so (Goldsworthy, 1996, p. 178). The Celts, on the other hand, had a reputation – possibly unjustified – for tiring easily, and did not have the beneficial moral pressure of having fifty men behind every front ranker. Romans tended to be better protected than either Celts or Spaniards, since some Romans had cuirasses in addition to their regular helmets and greaves, whereas most Celts were apparently bare-chested and the Spaniards wore linen tunics. These troops would have been virtually helpless if their shields were rendered ineffective by *pila*.

Livy claims that the Romans pushed the Celts and Spaniards back with 'an even front and a dense line' (Liv. 22.47.5), but this seems unlikely. As the troops tired they would have relied to some extent on individuals taking the initiative and renewing the assault, hoping that other troops would join them (Goldsworthy, 1997, p. 21). Such advances would naturally have been localised in nature, meaning that the Roman line would have been ragged, with many forward projections, rather than being straight and even. Such situations were normal in ancient battle: Plutarch describes how the Macedonian army at Pydna developed a ragged line, full of breaches, 'as it normally happens in all great armies, according to the different efforts of the combatants, who in part press forward in eagerness, in another are forced to fall back' (Plut., *Vit. Aem.* 20.4–5). Polybius states that the Roman maniples penetrated the Carthaginian front (Polyb. 3.115.6), but it is probable that this refers to several minor incursions, rather than a major breakthrough. Individual soldiers leading groups could have resulted in wedge-like formations which might well have been capable of piercing the enemy line.[83] That there was not a major breakthrough is clear from a comparison of Polybius' and Livy's accounts. Livy claims that when the line was breached the Celts and Spaniards panicked and fled (Liv. 22.47.5–6), which would have been the natural response. Given that Hannibal was stationed alongside them, he would almost certainly have been swept up in such a stampede, which would in turn have surely led to the remaining Carthaginian forces breaking and running. Polybius does say that the Romans penetrated the Carthaginian front, but he qualifies that statement by saying that they were following the Celts and pressing on the centre and that part of the line which was giving way (Polyb. 3.115.6, 8). This suggests primarily that the Carthaginian crescent was buckling; there may have been breaches of the line, but they were probably minor incursions.[84] The Celts and Spaniards should be regarded as giving way slowly and steadily, like the Celts at Telamon in 225 (Polyb. 2.30.4). It is perhaps likely that each time the opposing lines engaged the Celts were the first to disengage, gradually pulling further and further away. Such a controlled withdrawal must have been slow enough to maintain cohesion, while simultaneously being fast enough to convince the Romans that victory was theirs.

The effects of this on the battle as a whole were dramatic and devastating. As the Celtic and Spanish crescent was gradually pushed back it levelled out, lengthening the line along which fighting took place. It then began to buckle further, and to be pushed back. This weakening was most acute at the centre, the area which had been longest exposed to fighting, and the Romans there began excitedly to push ahead, scenting victory. As they pushed on in an ever more compact formation, a 'vacuum' developed behind them, and the troops on either side began to edge towards the centre, narrowing the Roman front as they did.

Encirclement

The final stage of the battle as described by Polybius and Livy involved the encirclement and annihilation of the Roman and allied infantry. Polybius mentions three stages in this. First, the advancing Romans pushed back the Carthaginian crescent so far that the Libyan columns, still facing forward, were on either side of the Romans. The Libyans then man by man turned inwards to face the Romans (Polyb. 3.115.8–10), who in response:

> no longer kept their compact formation but turned singly or in companies to deal with the enemy who was falling on their flanks.
> (Polyb. 3.115.12)

Soon after this assault on the Roman flanks Hasdrubal led his cavalry against the Roman rear, where:

> delivering repeated charges at various points all at once, he raised the spirits of the Africans and cowed and dismayed the Romans.
> (Polyb. 3.116.8)

With the Romans surrounded in this fashion, Polybius implies, it was only a matter of time before they were entirely defeated:

> The Romans, as long as they could turn and present a face on every side to the enemy, held out, but as the outer ranks continued to fall, and the rest were gradually huddled in and surrounded, they finally were all killed where they stood.
> (Polyb. 3.116.10–11)

It is hard to imagine what happened at Cannae on the mere evidence of such bald statements as these. The main difficulty lies in establishing why attacks on the flanks and rear were so decisive. After all, in his analysis of the Roman forces at Zama, Polybius notes that the great advantage of the Roman tactical system was that it allowed soldiers to turn individually or as part of a group to face any threat (Polyb. 15.15.7). In order to recover the experience of the final stages of Cannae, it is useful to break the battle down artificially into a number of separate phases. Analysis of these phases must inevitably be speculative, owing to lack of positive evidence. However, application of Whatley's 'five aids'; in particular general-tactical principles, common sense, and knowledge of the opposing forces make it possible to reach conclusions which fall, in Keegan's words, 'within a fairly narrow bracket of probability' (Keegan, 1976, p. 87; Whatley, 1964, pp. 123 ff.).

Libyans on the flanks

As mentioned above, Polybius says that the Romans had advanced so far ahead in pushing back the Celts that the Libyans were on their flanks. It is improbable that the Romans would have advanced in this manner if they knew that they were allowing themselves to be outflanked, so perhaps there was some distance between the Roman flanks and the Libyans, and possibly a screen of skirmishers between the two, blocking the Romans' view and preventing them from realising that they were about to be outflanked.[85] This theory has the advantage of explaining why the thin horns of the Carthaginian crescent appear to have held, for the light-armed troops on the wings could have acted as support troops, using volleys of stones and javelins to keep the Roman wings away from the extremities of the crescent. Alternatively, the Libyan columns may have moved forward once the Carthaginian cavalry had cleared the Roman flanks. This would have been possible because the Libyans were deployed in very deep columns, a formation highly conducive to rapid movement.[86] The Libyans may not have attacked the Roman flanks alone – Livy states that they extended their wings to attack the Roman rear (Liv. 22.47.8). Polybius makes no mention of this, but such a move seems plausible, and if authentic, was presumably achieved after the Libyans had turned towards the Roman flanks, through bringing the rear ranks in line with the front ones and then wheeling them inwards.

The Libyans would surely have begun their assault on the Roman flanks with an initial missile bombardment. Onasander notes that missiles are most effective against an army's flanks (Onas. 19.2). The Roman equipment with which the Libyans were armed may have included *pila*, but even if this was not the case it is likely that the Libyans had adopted some of the Spanish throwing spears described above. Weapons like the *pilum* or *falarica* would have had a devastating effect on an enemy's flank. The *pilum* was an armour-piercing missile, the prime function of which was either to strike an enemy through his shield, or, failing that, to disable the shield by transfixing it. It is likely that the Libyans got quite close to the Romans before hurling their missiles, as the Romans were probably not returning fire, terrified by this sudden, unexpected attack from a new direction. Throwing *pila* at close range would have improved both accuracy and armour penetration (Goldsworthy, 1996, pp. 198–9).

After the *pilum* volley the Libyans would have advanced with their swords against the Roman flanks. Many of those left standing facing the Libyans were wounded or shieldless after the missile attack, so they would have been extremely vulnerable. Those Romans who fell, injured or dead, would have obstructed those behind them, making it hard for them to strike at the advancing Libyans without stepping on or over the bodies on the ground. This in turn could lead more troops to stumble and fall, creating a cumulative 'tumbling effect' all along the Roman flanks.[87]

As discussed in the previous section, lulls in fighting are natural, and the Libyans may have taken advantage of them to replace tired troops with fresh ones from the rear ranks. They would thus be able to repeat the pattern of volleys and charges until they ran out of missiles.

These flank attacks were effective largely because they focused on the newest recruits, Varro's and Paullus' legions, or, more probably, their allied brigades, while the more experienced troops were otherwise occupied making progress in the centre of the field against Hannibal's Celts and Spaniards. More importantly, flank attacks would in any circumstances have struck primarily at the weakest troops. The best troops in each century were deployed at the very front and the very back, while the more ordinary and reluctant troops would be stationed in the middle. These troops may never have expected to have to do any actual fighting in the battle. As Sabin points out (1996, p. 76), they were certainly not mentally prepared for this new and highly dangerous situation. If, as seems probable, their main concern was self-preservation rather than a desire to kill the enemy (Goldsworthy, 1996, p. 219), they would have been unlikely to initiate retaliatory assaults on the Libyans.

Polybius says that the Romans turned 'singly or in companies' to deal with the threat (Polyb. 3.115.12). Although *speirai*, 'companies', is the term Polybius normally uses for maniples, in this context it probably refers to informal groups. Given their abnormally close deployment, the extremely deep maniples could hardly have wheeled about to face the Libyan threat. Unit cohesion would have evaporated in such circumstances, as the maniples ceased to function as tactical units. Even if they could have turned, they could not have been very effective, since there would have been enormous gaps between them (see Fig. 10). Units 'behind' these turned maniples would have been facing forward and could not have covered the gaps, unless they too turned. This would have been difficult in any circumstances, but would have been especially so if, as proposed above, the units at the ends of the Roman line were composed of relatively new recruits whose standard of drill may not have been particularly high.

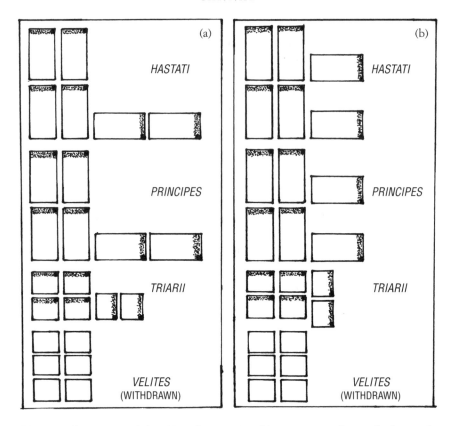

Figure 10 Roman maniples (a) and centuries (b) turning to face a flank attack. Note the size of the gaps between the turned maniples.

With units being unable to turn, their command system would have become completely ineffective, relying heavily as it did on the personal example of the centurions. As discussed elsewhere, they probably fought on the right of the century, either in the front rank or just to the side of it – very useful for the army facing enemies in front. At Cannae in a line of 840 men there were 140 centurions, on the assumption that maniples were deployed six wide, every sixth man being a centurion, and also of course that the allies too were divided into maniples, with a similar command structure to the Roman system. However, on the right flank there would have been at best six centurions out of fifty-eight line infantry,[88] while on the left flank there would have been no centurions at all. Furthermore, there is a good chance that most of the centurions on the right flank were killed or seriously wounded either in the initial *pilum* volley or in the subsequent collision, meaning that the nearest officers on either flank were perhaps 5 metres away. If the crush was too tight they may have had difficulty moving over to the flank, the new front, to lead their men.

Morale would have disintegrated under such circumstances, with no centurions leading by example and weak troops under pressure from an entirely unexpected source. Moreover, the fact that the Libyans were dressed in Roman armour would have added to the Romans' dismay; Appian describes how Carthaginian soldiers, Celtiberians in his muddled account, created confusion in the Roman ranks by using Roman shields, making it difficult to tell friend from foe (App., *Hann.* 23). Hanson (1992, p. 47) points out that a moment's hesitation when faced with an enemy in Roman equipment could prove fatal. Furthermore, some Romans may have panicked and struck at their own men in the confusion of the mêlée, momentarily mistaking them for Libyans.

Sabin (1996, p. 76) sensibly argues that this need to respond to attacks on the flanks would have prevented the Romans from continuing their concerted forward drive against the retreating Celts and Spaniards (see also Kromayer and Veith, 1912, p. 321). Fear, panic, and confusion, spreading inwards from the flanks and rear, may have been even more important in slowing and even stopping the Roman advance.[89] No longer being forced back by Roman pressure, the Celts and Spaniards would have been encouraged and would have got a 'second wind', enabling them to fight with the object of actually killing Romans rather than simply staying alive, which must have been their priority when retreating.

Cavalry at the rear

Polybius and Livy both present the Celtic and Spanish cavalry turning to attack the Roman rear, Polybius saying that they delivered repeated charges at various points (Polyb. 3.116.8; Liv. 22.48.5). It is difficult to understand how this could have been as effective as it apparently was, for ancient cavalry were almost certainly incapable of charging into intact formations of line infantry (Spence, 1993, pp. 103 ff.; Goldsworthy, 1996, p. 230; Adcock, 1957, pp. 49–51). (The main causes of this have already been discussed, namely, the lack of stirrups, and the fact that horses will not charge into solid objects, the impression a wall of shield-bearing men in close formation would certainly have given.) Furthermore, the Roman *triarii*, the last line of infantry, would appear to have been ideally equipped to ward off cavalry assaults, since in addition to his large *scutum*, each man carried a long spear, a *hasta*, instead of the usual *pilum*. If the *triarii* simply went down on one knee, with their spears protruding and their shields resting against their left shoulder, they would have presented an impenetrable obstacle,[90] provided that they did not lose their nerve, because any horses which did manage to charge would find themselves impaled upon the advanced *hastae* (Goldsworthy, 1996, p. 230).

Most of these problems disappear when it is remembered that the *velites* had been withdrawn through the Roman ranks (Polyb. 3.115.4; see also

3.73.6). They must have been placed at the back, behind the *triarii*, there being no evidence for them having attempted to assist the cavalry on the flanks.[91] The effects of this can be easily imagined. Rather than being a solid wall of heavily armed and experienced spearmen, the Roman rear was cluttered with over 15,000 lightly armed troops in loose formation, many of whom would have been very young. Such troops would have been particularly vulnerable to a cavalry assault, as they were not trained to fight in formation and lacked protection aside from their shields (Spence, 1993, pp. 109, 116–17). Terrified by the enemy horses, they would almost certainly have been unable to cast what remaining javelins they had. Marshall's research (1947, pp. 48–9) indicated that many troops will simply not use their weapons unless told to do so, and it is unlikely that there were any tribunes at the rear to co-ordinate resistance – they were probably up at the front attempting to earn a reputation. Trying to flee, the *velites* would have turned inwards towards the heavy infantry, exposing their heads, necks, backs, and hamstrings to the thrusting spears and slashing swords of the Celtic and Spanish cavalry, and any troops who were wounded or simply fell stood a high chance of being trampled upon by men or horses.[92]

'Aerial bombardment'

Appian refers to missiles being exchanged throughout the battle (App., *Hann.* 22). Polybius and Livy make no mention of this, but it nevertheless seems very likely. Given the fact that the Carthaginians were heavily outnumbered, Hannibal would surely have had his skirmishers return to the fray, as they had done at the Trebia (Polyb. 3.73.7). Circumstances were ideal for such a return. Pinned in place by the surrounding cavalry and line infantry, the trapped Romans shrank back from the enemy, pushing closer into the Roman centre, transforming a recognisable military formation into a densely packed crowd. Similar situations developed in 55 at Carrhae and at Adrianople in 378 AD, on both occasions making the Romans an easy target for lightly armed missile troops. Brief descriptions of the experiences of the trapped Roman forces at Carrhae and Adrianople can help explain the fate of the army at Cannae.

Plutarch records that the Parthian heavy cavalry at Carrhae used their long spears to drive the Romans closer and closer together, while the light cavalry shot at them with arrows (Plut., *Vit. Crass.* 27). Through what Luttwak calls a 'classic combination of fire and shock' (1999 [1976], p. 43), the compressed legions became a single target to be destroyed by a constant hail of arrows:

> But the Parthians now stood at long intervals from one another and began to shoot their arrows from all sides at once, not with any accurate aim (for the dense formation of the Romans would

not suffer an archer to miss it even if he had wished it). . . . At
once then, the plight of the Romans was a grievous one; for if they
kept their ranks, they were wounded in great numbers, and if they
tried to come to close quarters with the enemy, they were just as
far from effecting anything and suffered just as much.

(Plut., *Vit. Crass.* 24.5–6)

At Adrianople the Roman infantry were deprived of cavalry support and
were surrounded by Goths, whose attacks forced the Romans to press
together, with deadly results:

The foot-soldiers thus stood unprotected, and their companies were
so crowded together that hardly anyone could pull out his sword
or draw back his arm. Because of clouds of dust the heavens could
no longer be seen, and echoed with frightful cries. Hence the arrows,
whirling death from every side, always found their mark with fatal
effect, since they could not be seen beforehand nor guarded against.

(Amm. 31.13.2)

If Hannibal's slingers and spearmen had returned to the battle, their
subsequent hail of stones and javelins would have had a similar effect.
Hanson envisages the Romans being struck down without warning by
missiles, even minor wounds resulting in havoc as men fell to the ground,
causing their fellows to stumble over them.[93] Such minor wounds may well
have been far more common than direct fatalities (Goldsworthy, 1996, p.
185), but those who fell stood a high chance of being trampled to death.
Some modern experiments suggest that slingshot would have been
completely ineffective (Gabriel and Metz, 1991, pp. 74–5), but this is difficult to believe – Balearian slingers would surely not have been employed
by the Carthaginians if this were so. In fact, the opposite seems to have
been the case, and slingshot was apparently particularly effective against
armour (Arr., *Tact.* 15). The Balearians were famed for their accuracy, even
over long distances, and tended to use larger stones than other slingers,
enabling them to damage shields and helmets (Str. 3.5.1; Diod. 5.18.3–4;
see Pritchett, 1991, pp. 24–5). If such stones hit a helmeted Roman at
high speed, he would be quite likely to suffer concussion, if not more serious
injury (Goldsworthy, 1996, p. 186).

Onasander describes the sling as being particularly dangerous, its shot
being so small that it was virtually invisible, and therefore impossible to
defend against (Onas. 19.3).[94] The dust at Cannae would have contributed
to this problem, rendering troops unable to see either stones or javelins
until it was too late (App., *Hann.* 22). It is quite possible that one of the
most significant effects of this hail of missiles was to shatter Roman morale.
As Holmes points out (1985, p. 211), 'Central to the question of fear is

the soldier's perception of his ability to do something about it.' Terrified Romans must have attempted to flee from this deadly barrage, those at the edges of the seething Roman mass trying in vain to break through the ring of line infantry and cavalry, only to be cut down, while those trapped within the crowd may even have tried to force their way further into the centre, perhaps imagining that safety lay that way. Some may even have cut down their fellow Romans in a desperate quest to save themselves.

Annihilation

As Hanson rightly says (1992, p. 47), the Romans were 'not to be executed sterilely through aerial bombardment alone . . . many had to be dispatched with hand weapons'. Pressure from within would have pushed many Romans directly against the enemy infantry. Terrified, they may have been completely unable to defend themselves, and many must have begged, futilely, for mercy (Sabin, 1996, p. 77). Huge numbers of *velites* would have fallen to the repeated charges of the cavalry, while the reinvigorated Celts and Spaniards excitedly got revenge for their earlier humiliating retreat by savagely attacking the *hastati*, who would have been paralysed by terror and disbelief – how could they be losing a battle which so recently appeared to have been won? Some troops would have turned to face inwards, in a foolish attempt to reach safety among the central ranks, but this would merely render them entirely defenceless against the inevitable thrusts and slashes at their exposed backs. On the flanks, meanwhile, the weaker troops would have suffered the brunt of the Libyan attack, doubtless being cut down in similar fashion, while small pockets of the better troops, those who were normally stationed at front and rear, remained on their feet.

Polybius claims that all the Romans held their position until they were cut down (Polyb. 3.116.10–11), but this was surely not the case. The fact that two legions were later formed from the fugitives from Cannae indicates that many Romans and allies must have escaped. Livy and Appian both record that the death of the commanders was followed by a rout (Liv. 22.49.9, 12; App., *Hann.* 24), as all pretence at cohesion was abandoned, and the remaining troops attempted to flee.[95] Most such efforts would have met with failure, the fugitives being slain as they tried to break through the Carthaginian lines. Some groups of allied troops would have thrown themselves on the mercy of the enemy, hoping to receive the clemency offered to allied prisoners after the battle at Lake Trasimene the previous year (Polyb. 3.85.3–4). Livy records that some 3,000 infantry and 1,500 cavalry were captured in the battle itself (Liv. 22.49.18). Others would have forced their way, perhaps in wedge-like formations, through gaps in the thin Carthaginian lines. Such attempts at escape may not have met with much resistance, if they were made late enough in the day, as various Carthaginian soldiers, exhausted with the butchery that day, may simply no longer have cared what happened to the Romans. With the battle clearly won, why should they risk their own lives to stop an insignificant band of fugitives?[96] Finally, many small pockets of troops doubtless did fight on, and their protracted resistance must have infuriated their enemies, who concentrated their efforts and savagely cut them down where they stood (Liv. 22.49.4).[97]

The will to fight

It is impossible to be certain why the combatants at Cannae actually fought, rather than fleeing, considering that the natural instinct towards self-preservation is almost always stronger than that towards aggression. Nevertheless, some attempt should be made to answer this perplexing question.[98]

The commanders' roles at Cannae have already been discussed, and it is likely that their attempts to propitiate the gods, their exhortations, and most importantly their physical presence on the battlefield served to inspire their men to fight, and to keep fighting. Leadership would not simply have been a matter for the overall commanders, however, as tribunes, centurions, and their equivalents among the Carthaginian forces, would have had a similarly inspirational role.[99] Livy states that many illustrious Romans fought and died at Cannae (Liv. 22.49.16–17); their presence in the ranks must have encouraged the ordinary soldiers to fight, at least at first.[100]

Cowardice in battle was unacceptable in the Roman army, individuals who threw away their arms being punished by being beaten to death by their fellows (Polyb. 6.37.13). Furthermore, if entire maniples deserted their posts under pressure they would be subject to 'decimation', where approximately 10 per cent of the offenders would be chosen by lot to be beaten to death, the remaining troops being given barley instead of wheat as rations and having to camp in an exposed spot outside the main camp (Polyb. 6.38). It is significant that these punishments were inflicted by the army as a whole, as the offenders' cowardice had endangered the other soldiers; crimes against the unit were punished by the unit.[101] Compulsion must have played a similar role in driving the various elements of the Carthaginian army to fight, although nothing is known about their system of punishments.

The desire for plunder may have been at least as strong. Polybius refers to the Romans at Telamon in 225 being terrified by the appearance of the Celts, while simultaneously keen to fight them in order to win as loot their gold torques and armlets (Polyb. 2.29.9). Keegan argues that the opportunity to enrich oneself was the most powerful incentive to fight for participants in medieval battles,[102] and there is no reason to believe it was any less strong in ancient warfare. It is probable that the desire for loot was more significant in the Carthaginian than the Roman army; the prospect of booty may have been enough to persuade mercenaries from many nations to volunteer for Hannibal's expedition into Italy.

Social values could have encouraged individual troops to stand their ground, and endorsed their killing of others. Roman society was highly militarised, and active service was considered an honour – citizens were expected to fight. Similarly, in Celtic and Spanish societies a heroic ethos seems to have prevailed, whereby warriors were expected to display their courage in battle (Rawlings, 1996, p. 90). In other words, Romans, Celts, Spaniards, and quite probably others at Cannae, would have fought out of a sense of social obligation, and for personal glory.

Esprit de corps is a very important factor in persuading troops to fight, and the cultivation of unit-identity has already been discussed with reference to the Roman army. Holmes argues (1985, pp. 293 ff.) that the roots of group identity lie in the very smallest groups, such as the Roman *contubernia* (see also Griffith, 1989, pp. 109–10). Essentially, groups of friends or even relatives, if stationed next to each other in battle, will fight to protect themselves and each other, but perhaps more importantly, will take a more aggressive role in order to prove their own worth. Jim Jones, in attempting to explain why so many Americans had fought and died at Antietam in September 1862 AD, said that they did so 'because they didn't want to appear unmanly in front of their friends'.[103] It is instructive to quote Marshall at length on this point:

> During combat the soldier may become so gripped by fear that most of his thought is directed toward escape. But if he is serving among men whom he has known for a long period or whose judgment of him counts for any reason, he still will strive to hide his terror from them.
>
> Wherever one surveys the forces of the battlefield, it is to see that fear is general among men, but to observe further that men commonly are loath that their fear will be expressed in specific acts which their comrades will recognize as cowardice. The majority are unwilling to take extraordinary risks and do not aspire to a hero's role, but they are equally unwilling that they should be considered the least worthy among those present.
>
> (Marshall, 1947, p. 149)

This is almost certainly the most important reason why troops fought, and continue to do so. Even so, it may still be something of an oversimplification. Many of those men who fought at Antietam did so under the influence of what can really only be described as a strange fighting madness. One of them has described what McPherson calls 'as good an example of behavior in battle as one is likely to find anywhere':

> We heard all through the war that the army 'was eager to be led against the enemy,' . . . The truth is, when bullets are whacking

against tree-trunks and solid shot are cracking like egg-shells, the consuming passion in the breast of the average man is to get out of the way. Between the physical fear of going forward and the moral fear of turning back, there is a predicament of exceptional awkwardness. [Despite such fears, when his regiment was ordered to advance, it did so.] In a second the air was full of the hiss of bullets and the hurtle of grape-shot. The mental strain was so great that I saw at that moment the singular effect mentioned, I think, in the life of Goethe on a similar occasion – the whole landscape for an instant turned slightly red.

(McPherson, 1988, p. 540)

Aftermath

According to Polybius, there had been some fighting between the Roman and Carthaginian camp garrisons while the main battle was going on. Hannibal apparently came to the assistance of his men once victory was assured on the field, 2,000 of the Romans being killed and almost 10,000 captured (Polyb. 3.117.7–11). Livy, on the other hand, makes no mention of this, leading Caven (1980, p. 138) to surmise that Polybius wrongly assumed that fugitives from the battle, later captured in the camp, were in fact a garrison, there all along. However, even if the figure of 10,000 prisoners is spurious, Caven's theory fails to explain why Polybius would have invented the fighting between the camps, and it should probably be rejected.

The day after the battle, the Carthaginian troops returned to the battlefield to loot the corpses, apparently spending much of the day doing so (Liv. 22.51.5, 52.1). As mentioned above, plunder was an important motive for ancient soldiers, as well as for more modern ones (see also Keegan, 1976, pp. 180–1). Troops would not simply have been looking for precious items for themselves – the Libyans at Cannae had been equipped with Roman armour and weapons looted after previous encounters, so it is likely that Roman equipment was also taken, to be added to the army's supplies.[104] Another motive for this somewhat ghoulish scavenging of the battlefield was to gather up the various dead soldiers from the Carthaginian forces, so that they could be buried together. The Romans, with the possible exception of Paullus, were left to rot where they lay (Liv. 22.52.6).

Livy's description of the state of the battlefield that day may seem fanciful, but it is probably quite accurate:

There lay those thousands upon thousands of Romans, foot and horse indiscriminately mingled, as chance had brought them together in the battle or the rout. Here and there amidst the slain there started up a gory figure whose wounds had begun to throb with the chill of dawn, and was cut down by his enemies; some were discovered lying there alive, with thighs and tendons slashed, baring their necks and throats and bidding their conquerors drain the remnant of their blood.

(Liv. 22.51.6–7)

The heaped corpses and pools of blood have already been discussed in some detail, and are quite believable. Equally plausible are the references to wounded soldiers being revived by the cold, only to be killed by those busy plundering the battlefield. Hanson points out that on the previous day the main concern of Hannibal's men must simply have been to cripple Romans rather than kill them, faced with the largest Roman army ever assembled; time was not on their side and crippled soldiers could be finished off later.[105]

Polybius' casualty figures for Cannae are self-contradictory and must be rejected. In one passage he claims that 370 of the 6,000 Roman cavalry escaped, and that 10,000 infantry were captured away from the battle, 3,000 escaped and about 70,000 were killed (Polyb. 3.117.2–4). However, he later claims that only 8,000 infantry, in addition to 2,000 cavalry, were captured away from the battle (Polyb. 3.117.7–12). While complete accuracy is not to be expected in this sort of thing, it is clear that Polybius' figures are in some sense flawed. Other writers give lower casualty figures,[106] Livy's being the most convincing. He claims that 45,500 infantry and 2,700 cavalry were killed (Liv. 22.49.15), 19,300 were captured, and 14,550 escaped.[107] The fact that two legions were later formed from the survivors of Cannae gives these figures a certain amount of credibility.[108]

Finally, Hannibal's army had also suffered at Cannae. Polybius states that Hannibal's losses consisted of 200 cavalry, 1,500 Spaniards and Africans, and about 4,000 Celts (Polyb. 3.117.6). According to Livy, about 8,000 of Hannibal's men were killed in the battle (Liv. 22.52.6). There is little to choose between these figures, but it is striking that the brunt of Hannibal's losses were among his Celtic troops, those who had been driven back so ferociously by the Romans in the early part of the battle. In addition to those troops who were killed in the battle, it is quite likely that the majority of Hannibal's men had been wounded,[109] and many of them would have succumbed to infections in their wounds in the days following the battle. Sabin (1996, p. 67) points out that Hannibal's losses at Cannae amounted to the high figure of about 11 per cent of total troops involved, but it is possible that this figure may be too low. Unlike the Romans, Hannibal's army could not sustain losses on this scale, and it is hardly surprising that his invasion of Italy was to achieve nothing.

7

CONCLUSION

The disaster at Cannae entered the Roman national consciousness as one of the darkest days in Roman history, joining the defeat at the Allia and subsequent sack of Rome by the Celts under Brennus. Hundreds of years later the poet Juvenal would write of how schoolboys would discuss as rhetorical exercises whether Hannibal ought to have followed his victory at Cannae by marching on Rome (Juvenal, *Satire* 7.160–4), and twenty lines of his tenth satire are devoted to the futility of Hannibal's ambitions (*Satire* 10. 147–67). Juvenal presents Hannibal himself as a one-eyed, elephant-riding maniac, and the fact that he took his own life with a poisoned ring is seen as a humiliating punishment for the bloodshed at Cannae. Juvenal may have seen Hannibal's campaigns as pointless, serving no purpose except as subjects for schoolboy orations, but almost 300 years after he wrote, Ammianus Marcellinus, in attempting to convey the scale of the Roman defeat at Adrianople, sadly declared that no Roman army had ever suffered so heavily in battle, save that which was destroyed at Cannae (Amm. 31.13.14).

In this book I have tried to give a full-scale analysis of the battle of Cannae along the lines pioneered by John Keegan in *The Face of Battle*, while not neglecting traditional methods of analysing battles in terms of Grand Tactical manoeuvres. Victor Hanson and Adrian Goldsworthy have argued that there is not enough evidence to examine any one battle in Greek or Roman history in detail using Keegan's methods, but I hope that I have succeeded in doing just that.

Polybius' account of the battle has rightly been the foundation for all modern studies of Cannae. The earliest extant account of the battle, it is clear, straightforward, and devoid of fanciful details. It is, however, incomplete in some important respects. It says very little about what it was actually like to be at Cannae, and fails adequately to explain why the attacks on the Roman flanks and rear proved so catastrophic. This may be because his audience was quite aware of what battles involved, and did not need to be told about the mechanics of battle, or it may simply be because he was not fully cognisant himself of such matters, for his military experience has frequently been overrated. Furthermore, the objectivity of his account suffers somewhat from the fact that Cannae clearly has immense symbolic importance in his narrative of Rome's rise to world conquest. For him, Cannae is the absolute nadir of Roman fortunes, and is consequently made to seem an even greater disaster than it was in reality.

One of the major tasks of this book has been to penetrate in some sense beyond Polybius' account, in order to recover the experience of battle at Cannae. It is impossible to be certain of the actual nature of the battle, and second-guessing Polybius is a risky business, owing to his proximity to events. However, attempting to delve beyond his account has yielded some interesting conclusions, which, if not definitive, at least may help to explain what happened at Cannae.

Polybius' account is particularly useful in demonstrating how important the opposing commanders were in such a battle. He concentrates on Grand Tactical manoeuvres in order to show that the most important factor in the Carthaginian victory was Hannibal himself.

The initial period of skirmishing was probably more important than it is made out to have been. Its significance lay, however, at the level of morale rather than tactics. The cavalry conflicts were probably much as Polybius and Livy describe them, save that the Roman citizen cavalry broke and fled quite quickly, rather than putting up a dogged and protracted resistance against the Celtic and Spanish cavalry under Hasdrubal. Polybius' description of the Roman successes against Hannibal's Celtic and Spanish troops is convincing, but his account of the attacks on the Roman flanks is unsatisfactory. If, as seems likely, the Roman maniples deployed with the best troops at the front and rear of each century, the Libyan assault's power would have lain in the fact that it concentrated on the weaker troops in the middle of the centuries, as well as shattering the Romans' rather rigid command system. It is not the fault of Polybius that most modern writers have failed to understand why the cavalry assault on the rear was so decisive, when cavalry assaults on disciplined line infantry were almost futile. Polybius' audience would presumably have realised that such an attack would have focused upon the light-armed troops who had been withdrawn through the ranks. Finally, Polybius' description of the battle is highly simplified with regard to the final stages of the battle, presenting the Carthaginian forces as simply surrounding the Romans with a thin ring of steel and executing them, when the reality was, as ever, far more complicated.

NOTES

PREFACE

1 Lazenby, 1996b, p. 47 points out that most of the 57,470 British casualties on the first day of the Somme were wounded but survived; 19,240 were killed or died later as a result of wounds received in the fighting. Maga, 2000, p. 307 gives a total of 58,178 Americans who died in the Vietnam War. However, 10,798 of these were not combat fatalities: 5,242 died as a result of wounds inflicted in combat, and 3,523 went missing in combat, 38,505 were killed in combat, presumably dying later, giving a total figure of 47,386 combat deaths. Considering the scale of the slaughter at Cannae, it is not surprising that the very word 'Cannae' became a byword for slaughter on a colossal scale: for example, Weinreich, 1999 (original publication, 1946) quotes Goebbels' declaration that 'the Jews at the end of this war are going to experience their Cannae'.

2 Scullard, 1970, pp. 74–5, 94–5, 130–1. Scipio probably hoped to use similar tactics at Zama, but Hannibal's tactics were specially devised to prevent this; in any case the battle was won when Scipio's cavalry returned from pursuing Hannibal's cavalry and fell upon the Carthaginian rear in a manner reminiscent of Hasdrubal's cavalry at Cannae. See also Scullard, 1970, pp. 143–4 and Santosuosso, 1997, 184 ff.

3 Lazenby, 1996b, p. 40; Hanson, 1992, pp. 42–3. For Schlieffen, see Burne, 1950, p. 26 and Keegan, 1998, p. 35. For Eisenhower, see D'Este, 1996, p. 704.

1 INTRODUCTION: ROME AND CARTHAGE

1 In general, for Carthage's growth and government see Lancel, 1995 and for a somewhat more dated view, Picard, 1964. The most accessible general account of the rise of Rome is probably still Scullard, 1980, though this should be supplemented by Cornell, 1995. Plutarch's *Life of Pyrrhus* is the most important source for the Pyrrhic Wars, while Polybius Book 1 gives the best ancient accounts of the first war between Rome and Carthage and the subsequent war between Carthage and her mercenaries. Lazenby, 1996a is a very detailed, sensible, and readable account of Rome's first war with Carthage; other useful modern accounts of the war can be found in Goldsworthy, 2000a, pp. 65–133 and Bagnall, 1990, pp. 49–107. Lancel, 1998, pp. 10–24 is a good modern account of Carthage's war with her mercenaries.

2 Henceforth, all dates are BC unless otherwise noted.

3 Polyb. 1.72.2 notes that during the First Punic War half the Libyans' grain was required as tribute, and since the townsmen's taxes had been doubled, it is likely that the Libyan grain tribute had also been doubled.

4 Polybius gives no date for this treaty, but Liv. 7.27.2 and Diod. 16.69.1 believe there was a treaty signed with Carthage in 348, although Diodorus identifies this treaty as the first between Rome and Carthage. Had Polybius' second treaty been signed after 343 it would surely have specified Campania as a coastal area under Rome's influence. See Scullard, 1989a, pp. 528–30.

5 Scullard, 1989a, pp. 532–6 argues that the fact that Polybius could find no documentary evidence of the Philinus treaty is not proof against its existence, and that with both Rome and Carthage doing well against the Samnites and Timoleon respectively in 306, they may easily have wanted a treaty to recognise their growing power. Scullard may be arguing from silence here, but then so is Polybius. Against this, Walbank, 1957, pp. 354–5 says that 'it is impossible that at so early a date the Romans claimed Italy as their sphere of influence, with Tarentum untouched and the Samnites not yet finally defeated; still less was it necessary to warn them off Sicily.' Instead he suggests that, if genuine, the Philinus treaty may have represented an unpublished agreement from near the end of the Pyrrhic War.

2 THE ROAD TO CANNAE

1 Polyb. 3.9.6–10.6, however, presents the Spanish project as having been undertaken with a view to providing Carthage with a platform from which to fight a war of revenge with Rome, as Hamilcar was filled with wrath over Carthage's defeat in 241 and the immorality of Rome's behaviour towards Carthage over Sardinia during the Mercenaries' War. Polyb. 3.11.5–7 records the story of how in 193, while at the court of Antiochus, Hannibal told how his father made him, when a child, swear never to befriend the Romans. Walbank, 1957, pp. 314–15 gives full references to the story and points out that although Hamilcar's resentment towards Rome may have been genuine enough, this is not evidence for the claim that the Spanish project was undertaken to prepare for a war of revenge. See Lazenby, 1978, p. 19; Kagan, 1995, pp. 254–5. The whole concept of the 'Wrath of Hamilcar' is part of a general anti-Barcid tradition which seems to have originated with Carthaginian aristocrats eager to clear themselves of any blame for the Second Punic War. See Hoyos, 1994, pp. 258 ff.

2 Rich, 1996, p. 17 argues that the fact that Spain proved such a valuable source of manpower for Carthage is evidence for the authenticity of the 'Wrath of Hamilcar' as a primary cause of the Second Punic War.

3 Massilian links with Rome: Kramer, 1948, pp. 1–26; Badian, 1958, pp. 47–9; Sumner, 1967, p. 208. Massilian interests in Spain: Scullard, 1989b, p. 24; Kagan, 1995, p. 257. Authenticity of 231 embassy: Sumner, 1972, pp. 474–5; Scullard, 1989b, p. 24; Rich, 1996, p. 19; but see Errington, 1970, pp. 32–4 which argues that it is an annalistic fabrication.

4 Polyb. 2.13.5–7 implies that the embassy was sent shortly before the Celtic *tumultus* of 225.

5 Walbank, 1957, p. 169 argues that the treaty must also have limited Roman expansion, but if so, the Roman sphere of influence would appear to have been far greater than that of Carthage.

6 The date and nature of this alliance are disputed. See Walbank, 1957, pp. 170–1; Badian, 1958, pp. 49–51; Astin, 1967, pp. 589, 593–4; Errington, 1970, pp. 41–4; Kagan, 1995, pp. 261–2; Sumner, 1967, pp. 212–14; Harris, 1979, pp. 201–2; Rich, 1996, pp. 25–6.

7 Polyb. 3.20.6–21.8, 33.1–4; Liv. 22.18. The Roman response has probably been accelerated by Polybius. See Walbank, 1957, p. 334; Scullard, 1989b, pp. 36–7; Kagan, 1995, p. 268; Rich, 1996, pp. 30 ff.; Lancel, 1998, pp. 51–2.

8 Roman manpower: Polyb. 2.24; Walbank, 1957, pp. 196 ff. believes that Polybius' figures are a 'slight overestimate'. For analyses of the census figures see Brunt, 1971, pp. 44 ff. and Baronowski, 1993, pp. 181–202.

9 Shean, 1996, pp. 161–2 unconvincingly criticises the general consensus that this was Hannibal's strategy and argues that Hannibal was quite capable of capturing Rome if an opportunity arrived; Lazenby, 1996b, pp. 39–48 persuasively argues in favour of the traditional analysis; Peddie, 1997, p. 196 points out that a proper siege train, whatever that meant, would have slowed Hannibal down; Bagnall, 1990, pp. 168–9 supports this as a lengthy siege of Rome would have led to Hannibal becoming 'bogged down' in positional warfare, which would have allowed the Romans to concentrate their far more extensive resources against him.

10 Rankov, 1996, p. 53; Keegan, 1993, pp. 63 ff. on the need for warships to stay close to land.

11 Bagnall, 1990, p. 172 points out that the Carthaginians may not have enjoyed significant numerical superiority over the Romans, as Liv. 21.45.2 refers to 500 Numidians being sent out to ravage the crops of Rome's allies just prior to the battle; Bagnall suggests that other Numidian squadrons may have been otherwise engaged, but though this is certainly plausible, there is no evidence for it.

12 On the importance of military glory for Roman aristocrats, see Harris, 1979, pp. 17 ff. It is not unknown for Roman aristocrats to have put their own interests before those of the state; e.g., according to Liv. 30.40.7–8, the opposition to Scipio's treaty with Carthage in 202 was led by the incoming consul, Gnaeus Cornelius Lentulus, who wished to claim the victory for himself.

13 Polyb. 3.72.3 says it took place near the Winter Solstice. Briscoe, 1989, p. 49; Lancel, 1998, p. 85; Lazenby, 1978, p. 56.

14 Liv. 21.55.2–4 gives the Roman figures, omitting cavalry, as 18,000 Romans and 20,000 Latin allies, along with contingents from the loyal Cenomani Celts; App., *Hann.* 4 says that there were thirty-seven elephants in the army that left Spain, but even if this is correct, it is impossible to tell how many fought at the Trebia.

15 Erskine, 1993, pp. 58–62 argues that Polybius is merely interpreting Hannibal's actions through a Hellenistic filter and that Hannibal probably did not pose as a liberator.

16 Nep., *Hann.* 4.3 says that Hannibal's vision was damaged rather than destroyed entirely in his right eye.

17 Shean, 1996, p. 180 argues that Hannibal's campaigns in 217 were driven more by a need to feed his army than to goad Flaminius into pursuing him.

18 Derow, 1976, pp. 274–6 suggests 9 May. Walbank, 1957, pp. 412–13 and Lancel, 1998, pp. 93–4 accept the date of 21 June at face value.

19 Connolly, 1998, pp. 172–5 places the battle east of modern Tuoro, on the north shore of the lake; Lancel, 1998, pp. 93–4 spreads the battle over a slightly wider area; Walbank, 1957, pp. 415–18 and Lazenby, 1978, pp. 62–3 follow Kromayer in placing the battle on the eastern shore of the lake, between Passignano and Torricella.

20 The number of prisoners cannot be safely ascertained. See Walbank, 1957, pp. 419–20; Lazenby, 1978, p. 65.

21 For this alternative interpretation, see Erdkamp, 1992, pp. 127–47.

22 Polyb. 3.106.1–2 holds that the dictator held office until the new consuls were elected, with Servilius and Regulus being given proconsular commands until the new consuls arrived, but this is unlikely as it implies that Fabius was dictator for nine months rather than six.

23 Liv. 22.33.10–35.4, 38.1 ff. has the consuls join the armies some time before this and describes an attempt by Hannibal to defeat them through cunning, but Polybius' silence on the matter makes this seem unlikely. See Lazenby, 1978, p. 76.

24 Peddie, 1997, pp. 88–90. For the strategic significance of Cannae, see Kromayer in Kromayer and Veith, 1912, pp. 301–2, which identifies Canusium as the second-largest city in Apulia, and Cannae as its port, in a relationship analogous to that between Rome and Ostia. Brunt, 1971, p. 369 comments on the importance of Apulia for grain production.

25 Rosenstein, 1990, p. 84, n.100 points out that this day followed the Calends, and so was unsuitable for battle. It would not be surprising if this date was an annalistic invention, designed to explain the Roman defeat.

26 Walbank, 1957, pp. 440–1 lists the sources as follows: Polyb. 3.106–18; Liv. 22.40.5–49.14; App., *Hann.* 19–25; Plut., *Vit. Fab. Max.* 15–16; Cass. Dio fr. 57.23–9; Zon. 9.1; Nep., *Hann.* 4.4; Polyaen. 6.38.3–4; Frontin., *Strat.* 2.2.7, 2.3.7, 2.5.27, 4.5.5–7; Flor. 1.22.15–18; Eutrop. 3.10; Oros. 4.16.1–5; Val. Max. 3.2.11, 5.6.4, 7.4 ext. 2.

27 Polyb. 3.26. 1–2 (treaties preserved on bronze tablets in Rome); 33.17–18, 56.4 (a bronze tablet on the Lacinian promontory erected by Hannibal to record his achievements); 7.9 (text of the treaty between Hannibal and Philip of Macedon); 10.9.3 (letter from Scipio Africanus to Philip of Macedon). Walbank, 1957, p. 32 also points out that the *annales* of the Pontifex Maximus would have been available for consultation, and were doubtless used. See Walbank, 1957, pp. 27 ff. for Polybius' literary sources.

28 Plut., *Vit. Philop.* 21.5 describes Polybius as a *pais* at Philopoemen's funeral; Walbank, 1957, p. 2 notes that this term would hardly have been used for an adult.

29 Polyb. 28.13.1–3 makes it clear that Polybius had joined the Romans before the capture of Heracleium; Polyb. 28.11 and Liv. 44.9.6–9 describe the capture of the town using the *testudo* formation. See Liv. 44.1–10 for a continuous account of Roman activity in Rome and Macedon during this period.

30 Polyb. 9.20.4; Arr., *Tact.* 1. Such handbooks on generalship were common in the ancient world. See Campbell, 1987, pp. 13–29; Goldsworthy, 1996, pp. 120–1.

31 See Walbank, 1957, p. 29 for Polybius' Roman sources in general.

32 *OCD*, p. 1427. Cass. Dio fr. 55.1–9 and Zon. 8.22 include accounts of the debates. See Kagan, 1995, p. 268; Lancel, 1998, pp. 51–2; Rich, 1996, pp. 30 ff.; Scullard, 1989b, pp. 36–7; Errington, 1970, p. 53; Astin, 1967, p. 579 ff.

33 Suggested by Marsden and Walbank in the discussion of Marsden, 1974, pp. 298–9.

34 For Polybius' view of pragmatic history, see Walbank, 1972, pp. 66 ff. Keegan, 1976, p. 47 contrasts the differences between the generals' and soldiers' conceptions of battle.

35 Polyb. 3.9.6–10.5: Hamilcar's wrath, which was passed on to Hannibal, according to Polybius. Polyb. 3.34.3: Polybius claims he described the war with the Celts in the 220s to explain the Celtic hatred for Rome.

36 Polyb. 15.11.8 has Hannibal list his major victories over the Romans; this list stops with Cannae. Livy records several further Carthaginian victories, which Lazenby, 1996, p. 46 regards as historical, but they clearly had no symbolic value for Polybius.

37 Tuchman, 1995, p. xviii. Brunt, 1971, p. 695 notes that chroniclers could sometimes 'multiply the heaps of the slain' for dramatic effect, and that Roman authors were proud of their ability to recover from disasters, and could accordingly exaggerate casualty figures. Interestingly, Polybius' casualty figures for the Celts at Telamon resemble his figures for Cannae: Polyb. 2.23.4 describes the Celtic army as having 50,000 infantry and 20,000 cavalry and charioteers; Polyb. 2.31.1. notes that, the cavalry having fled, about 10,000 infantry were captured, and over 40,000 were killed, which resembles the fate of the 80,000 Roman infantry at Cannae, as described at Polyb. 3.117.3–4. Deliberate stylisation with regard to numbers was a feature of Roman writing: Scheidel, 1996, pp. 222–38 argues that many large figures, when cited as financial data by Roman authors, are not even rough approximations of real amounts; instead, he argues, they are merely conventional figures, almost wholly symbolic in nature.

38 Briscoe, 1996, p. 877; Walsh, 1961, pp. 1–19. It is possible that the dates for both birth and death have been post-dated by about five years.

39 Livy mentions Coelius ten times in his third decade, unlike Polybius, who is only referred to by name at 30.45.5, although there is a clear reference to him at 22.38.2. Coelius: 21.38.6, 46.10, 22.31.8, 23.6.8, 26.11.10, 27.27.12, 28.46.14, 29.25.3, 35.2.

40 Liv. 26.49.1–6 features perhaps his most damning criticism of his sources, discussing their tendency to exaggerate figures.

41 Walsh, 1961, pp. 68–73, 167. It is intriguing to compare Livy and Polybius with regard to these individuals. Walbank, 1957, pp. 192–3 notes that Polybius does display a strong anti-Flaminian tone, and suggests that this probably derives from Fabius Pictor, reflecting the hostility of Flaminius' senatorial opponents. While Polybius' account of the rivalry between Fabius and Minucius is substantially the same as Livy's, it is significant that Liv. 22.29.7–30.6 dramatises the reconciliation between the two commanders in order to degrade Minucius, in a scene which is absent from Polybius' narrative. Polyb. 3.110.3 describes Varro as inexperienced, and 3.116.13 describes his fleeing the battlefield as disgraceful, but, unlike Livy, he does not disparage his background.

42 See Rosenstein, 1990, p. 35 for the senate's treatment of Varro after Cannae.

43 Walsh, 1961, pp. 151–2. Although, curiously, the treatment of the *legiones Cannenses* indicates that the senate attempted to lay the blame for the disaster squarely at the feet of the troops. See Rosenstein, 1990, pp. 102–3.

44 For a particularly good example of this, compare Polyb. 3.84.1–13 with Liv. 22.4.6–22.6.11 on the battle at Lake Trasimene.

45 The claim, at Polyb. 3.109.4 and Plut., *Vit. Fab. Max.* 15.1, that the Roman army was more than twice the size of the Carthaginian one is clearly hyperbole, but does suggest that the Roman army was indeed significantly larger than that of the Carthaginians.

46 De Sanctis, 1968, pp. 126–30. Brunt, 1971, p. 419 follows De Sanctis, adding a fourth reason for disputing Polybius' figures. Polybius' figures are sensibly defended by Walbank, 1957, pp. 439–40 and Lazenby, 1978, pp. 75–6; their arguments are followed here.

47 Liv. 22.49.15 gives a total of 48,200 Roman and allied dead. He also accounts for 19,300 troops being captured by Hannibal: Liv. 22.49.13 refers to 2,000 troops being taken prisoner at the village of Cannae, and 22.49.18 mentions 4,500 prisoners captured in the battle itself; 7,000 troops had escaped to the smaller Roman camp (Liv. 22.49.13), of whom 600 reached safety in the larger (Liv. 22.50.11), the remaining 6,400 soon being captured (Liv. 22.52.1–2); 10,000 troops had reached the larger camp from the battlefield (Liv. 22.49.13), where they were joined by the 600 fugitives from the smaller camp (Liv. 22.50.11), 4,200 escaping (Liv. 22.52.4), leaving 6,400 to be captured. Livy also gives far more precise figures than Polybius for fugitives from the battle, allowing for about 14,550 free survivors: fifty cavalry fled with Varro to Venusia (Liv. 22.49.14), being later joined by a further 4,500 troops (Liv. 22.54.1), while about 10,000 survivors took refuge in Canusium (Liv. 22.54.4). In addition to the general casualty figures, Lazenby, 1978, p. 76 points out that Liv. 22.49.16 mentions twenty-nine military tribunes having been killed in the battle; in itself, this indicates that there were at least five legions present, as there were six tribunes per legion, but Livy in fact names seven surviving tribunes, as is discussed in Chapter 5 (p. 123), which means that Livy's account presupposes that the Roman forces at Cannae included at least six legions.

48 Delbrück, 1990 [1920], pp. 325–7 and Kromayer and Veith, 1912, pp. 344–5 are in rare agreement on this point.

49 Walbank, 1957, p. 29 states that Acilius' work was probably published about 142, by which time Polybius had completed his account of the battle of Cannae.

50 Sosylos of Lacedaemon is perhaps an obvious suspect, as according to Polyb. 3.20.5 his history ranked with barbershop gossip, and his Carthaginian connections might have led him to glamorise Hannibal by describing him defeating an army with 'countless' recruits. Conversely, patriotic Roman historians using Sosylos' account might have been inclined to interpret *murioi* as '10,000' in order to diminish the scale of the disaster at Cannae. Alternatively, it is possible that early Roman historians who wrote in Greek may not have been particularly proficient in their use of the language, leading to easy mistakes like this.

51 Most recent analyses of the battle accept this. See Lancel, 1998, p. 104; Peddie, 1997, p. 94; Hanson, 1992, p. 42; Bagnall, 1990, p. 192; Briscoe, 1989, p. 51; Lazenby, 1978, pp. 75–6.

52 Goldsworthy, 1996, pp. 12–13 on the difficulties in keeping armies at full

strength. For example, see Carlton, 1992, pp. 97–8 on the depleted unit-strengths of armies during the English Civil War. Liv. 23.17.8–9 notes how in 216 a 500-strong body of allies from Praeneste were levied late and consequently did not serve at Cannae.

53 But see Caven, 1980, p. 138 which argues that Polybius is here mistaking fugitives from the battle, as at Liv. 22.49.13, for a camp garrison.

54 Lazenby, 1978, p. 79, followed by Lancel, 1998, p. 105, believes that the camp guard was composed of a legion and an allied brigade. Connolly, 1998, p. 187 believes the camp guard was composed of *triarii*, and is followed by Healy, 1994, p. 73. Goldsworthy, 2000a, p. 382, n. 13 points out that although there are indeed references to the *triarii* guarding the baggage in Liv. 35.4 and 44.37, on neither of these occasions had their commander planned to fight a battle.

55 Polyb. 3.114.5; Liv. 22.46.6. Griffith, 1935, p. 222 goes so far as to say that there can be 'no question of statistics as far as Hannibal's mercenaries are concerned', but this seems too strong. Hannibal's army had to be fed and paid, and it is likely that some sort of records were kept. Whether camp historians would have had access to such information is an entirely different matter, however, as is the possibility that they might not have used it even it was available. A complicating factor would have been the presence of camp followers such as servants; Shean, 1996, pp. 168–9 suggests a ratio of one camp follower to three actual soldiers, based on Engels, 1978, pp. 11–14. Shean's estimate is perhaps too high, as Hannibal's army had to cross particularly hazardous terrain, notably the Alps and the Arno swamps, which may have discouraged potential camp followers. Incidentally, Liv. 21.45.7 actually has Hannibal refer to his men's slaves.

56 Dodge, 1995 [1891], p. 359. Although Dodge does not justify his claim it seems a reasonable estimate as the garrison which Hannibal left behind was evidently strong enough to hold out against the 10,000-man Roman garrison from the beginning of the fighting until Hannibal was clearly victorious in the main battle, allowing him to relieve them. See Polyb. 3.117.10–11, but again see Caven, 1980, p. 138 who doubts the authenticity of this entire episode.

57 Delbrück, 1990 [1920], pp. 326, 331 favours Silenos, presumably because Polyb. 3.20.3 scorns the reliability of Sosylos, but Polybius' criticisms of Sosylos may have been unfair; see *OCD*, p. 1427.

58 Lazenby, 1978, p. 81. Delbrück, 1990 [1920], p. 361, allows for 11,000 Africans and 7,000 Spaniards.

59 Connolly, 1998, p. 181; Warry, 1980, p. 120. Lancel, 1998, p. 107 follows this, favouring 4,000 Numidians and about 6,000 other cavalry. Lazenby, 1978, p. 82 suggests 3,500 Numidians and a total of 6,500 Celtic and Spanish cavalry, while Dodge, 1995 [1891], p. 367 suggests only 2,000 Numidians and a combined Celtic and Spanish force of 8,000 cavalry.

60 E.g., David Harrison, 'British soldiers ready to deal with revenge attacks', *Daily Telegraph*, 25 March 1999, p. 4 claimed that there were 10,000 NATO troops in Macedonia on the same day that Alec Russell, 'Leaders fear war engulfing Balkans', *Daily Telegraph*, 25 March 1999, p. 4 claimed that there were 12,000 such troops there. While this may simply have been a typographical error, it aptly demonstrates the scope for error when dealing with figures on this scale.

61 See Walbank, 1957, pp. 435–8 and Scullard, 1980, p. 498 for a summary of

the various views. Kromayer, and Veith, 1912, pp. 280–307 is still the most detailed and sensible discussion of this topic.
62 Kromayer and Veith, 1912, pp. 281–93 thoroughly refutes such hypotheses.
63 Walbank, 1957, p. 438. See Polyb. 3.112–13 for the Carthaginian and Roman challenges.
64 E.g. Polyb. 5.105.10; Liv. 22.58.1. Despite the many objections to placing the battle on the river's left bank, De Sanctis, 1968, pp. 131–8 locates it here; his claims are decisively refuted by Walbank, 1957, pp. 436–8.
65 Kromayer and Veith, 1912, pp. 293–4 is scathing in dismissal of this idea, and is followed by Walbank, 1957, p. 436. See also J. Kromayer and G. Veith, 1922, Röm. Abt. i, Blatt 6.
66 Connolly, 1998, pp. 183–4; Healy, 1994, pp. 71–2. Goldsworthy, 2000a, p. 201 follows Connolly's basic idea that the river lay further north when the battle was fought than it does today, and places the probable site slightly north-west of Kromayer's site, straddling the modern course of the river. Oddly, Goldsworthy, 2000b, pp. 66–7 in attempting to illustrate the battle's Grand Tactical manoeuvres does not appear to locate the battle at this point.
67 Lazenby, 1978, p. 79; Onas. 21.3 advises generals to deploy next to rivers in order to block encircling movements.
68 Fussell, 2000, p. 13 describes how the extremely obvious small-unit tactics used by the British army at the Somme were largely a result of staff officers being convinced that the newly trained recruits were too stupid to use more sophisticated tactics. Needless to say, as at Cannae, the combination of crude tactics and fairly recently recruited troops proved disastrous.
69 Goldsworthy, 1996, p. 178. Against this, du Picq, 1987, pp. 170–1 argues that panic tends to begin at the rear, though this may not have been so much of a problem in the Roman army, with the seasoned *triarii* at the very back, and with the rear lines of each maniple being composed of particularly steady individuals, as discussed earlier (p. 158). Goldsworthy, 2000a, pp. 204–5 discusses reasons for the peculiarly deep formation adopted at Cannae. One of the reasons he advances is simple lack of space, but he locates the battle within a much narrower area than Kromayer does. If Kromayer's theory is correct, the lack of space was probably not a significant factor influencing the Roman deployment.
70 Walbank, 1957, p. 445. Kromayer's echelon formation is described in Kromayer and Veith, 1912, pp. 314–15, and represented in Kromayer and Veith, 1922, Röm. Abt. i, Blatt. 6; Delbrück's 'horseshoe' formation is described in Delbrück, 1990 [1920] pp. 316–17.
71 Plut., *Vit. Fab. Max.*16.3 describes the Libyans wheeling in to attack the flanks, but Polybius' terminology refutes such an interpretation.
72 Polybius' account of the battle is not entirely clear, which has given rise to some dispute over the precise nature of the Carthaginian turning manoeuvre. See Thompson, 1986, pp. 111–17; Walbank, 1957, pp. 142–3.
73 Connolly, 1998, p. 168 argues that the Numidians actually ambushed the Romans rather than outflanking them, and that Polybius disguises this fact in order to whitewash Scipio's failure in reconnaissance. This seems unlikely, since the Numidian attack on the Roman rear is consistent with their actions in other battles.

74 Liv. 22.43.10–11, 46.8–9; App., *Hann.* 20, 22; Plut., *Vit. Fab. Max.*16.1; Flor. 1.22.16; Zon. 9.1, summarising Cassius Dio and recording the story, which is surely fantastic, that Hannibal actually ploughed up the battlefield to further loosen the soil, thereby creating more dust.

75 Enn., *Ann.* fr. 264 (Skutsch edition): *Iamque fere puluis ad caeli uasta uidetur.* Skutsch, 1985, pp. 443–4.

76 Liv. 23.31.2–4, 24.18.9, 25.5.10–7.4, 26.28.10–12, 27.7.12–13, 22.9, 28.10.13, 29.1.12–13, 13.6, 24.11–14.

77 Lazenby, 1996b, p. 45. Brunt, 1971, pp. 419–20 estimates that Roman losses were significantly less than this.

78 Liv. 22.51.1–4 names the officer as Maharbal; Plut., *Vit. Fab. Max.* 17.2 refers to him as Barca. The story appears to derive from Cato's *Origines* 4.13 (Chassignet edition) where the cavalry officer is not identified by name: *Igitur dictatorem Carthaginiensum magister equitum monuit: 'Mitte mecum Romam equitatum; diequinti in Capitolio tibi cena cocta erit'.*

79 Proctor, 1971, pp. 26–34; Shean, 1996, p.165. Lazenby, 1996b, p. 41 claims, based on Polyb. 3.50.1, that the army marched less than 14.5 km a day when travelling up the Rhone.

80 Lancel, 1998, p. 96; Lazenby, 1996b, p. 41. Shean, 1996, p. 166 underestimates the difficulties in actually taking the city since Plut., *Vit. Marc.* 13.2 only claims that it was thought that there was a manpower shortage in Rome, not that such a shortage actually existed; on the difficulties of holding the city see Strauss and Ober, 1992, pp. 154–5.

81 Liv. 34.50.3–7 notes that in 194 there were 1,200 Roman citizens in slavery in Achaea alone, and many more Roman slaves throughout Greece. Apparently these were captured by Hannibal during the Punic War, and sold when the Romans refused to pay their ransom; the reference would appear to be to Cannae.

82 Lazenby, 1996b, p. 44, citing Polyb. 2.24, 3.118; Liv. 27.21.6 ff., 27.24, 28.10.4–5.

83 Feig Vishnia, 1996, pp. 100 ff. An alternative view is put forward by Scullard, 1973, pp. 56–74 which argues that the most significant effect of Cannae was the political victory of the 'Fabian faction' in the senate, as the more aggressive strategy favoured by the 'Aemilian–Scipionic group' had proven disastrous. The more conservative aristocrats, led by Fabius Maximus, dominated Roman politics to a greater or lesser degree from 216 to 207, and the Fabian strategy of attrition was adopted and maintained for much of this period, coming to an end after Nero's victory over Hannibal's brother Hasdrubal at the Metaurus. However, this 'factional' view of Roman politics, however attractive it may be to historians, has no foundation in the ancient evidence, and must be rejected. See Millar, 1984, p. 10; Goldsworthy, 2000a, pp. 42–3.

3 THE ROMAN ARMY

1 Rich, 1983, p. 287 argues that arms were supplied by the state in Polybius' day, inferring this from Polyb. 6.21.6–7. However, Polyb. 6.26.1 says that recruits were ordered to arm themselves, and Polybius nowhere mentions the state supplying or refunding the cost of such equipment. Furthermore, if the state were supplying equipment there would be no reason for the poorest

citizens to serve only as *velites* and never as heavy infantry; they must have supplied their own weapons. Payment: Liv. 4.59–60. See Cornell, 1995, p. 188.

2 See Walbank 1957, p. 722. Crawford, 1985, pp. 146–7 discusses this issue, and believes that Polybius is referring to the Attic rather than the Aeginetic drachma, the currency of the Achaean League, in which case an infantryman was paid one-third of a denarius a day, with centurions receiving two-thirds of a denarius and cavalrymen receiving one whole denarius per day.

3 Walbank, 1957, p. 722: an Attic *medimnus* equalled 40.36 litres, and a Roman *modius* equalled 8.58 litres.

4 Harris, 1979, pp. 46 ff. Brunt, 1971, pp. 391 ff. and Nicolet, 1980, pp. 98–102 discuss the punishments for disobeying the summons to attend the *dilectus* and circumstances under which exemptions could be obtained. Brunt, 1988, pp. 255–6 points out that conscription was certainly unpopular among peasants during the first century, and that there is some evidence that the *dilectus* was not always welcome in the second century; this may have been related to the harsh discipline of legionary life.

5 On the importance of military experience and success to Roman aristocrats, see Harris, 1979, pp. 10–41.

6 For armies of the late Republic and early Empire, see Goldsworthy, 1996, pp. 251–61; MacMullen, 1984, pp. 440–56.

7 Nicolet, 1980, p. 104; Lee, 1996, p. 207. See Holmes, 1985, pp. 32–4 on military oaths in the USSR, Nazi Germany, and the USA.

8 Smith, 1990, p. 157. Muir, 1998, pp. 201–3 describes how officers of the Napoleonic era 'liked to implicate their men in the punishment of such offenders, thus strengthening the bonds within the unit rather than creating a divide between authority and its victims'. On the *bastinado*, see Walbank, 1957, pp. 719–20.

9 Muir, 1998, p. 73 notes that drill is nowadays justified as 'inculcating instinctive obedience and encouraging group cohesion', but that its most important practical purposes in Napoleonic times were to 'carry soldiers through the complicated evolutions necessary to change formation and to load and fire their weapons, amidst the noise, confusion and fear of battle'. The tactical manoeuvres performed by Roman troops were generally far less complicated than those performed by Napoleonic troops, so the primary role of drill must have been the development of group identity.

10 Lee, 1996, p. 20; Holmes, 1985, pp. 42–3. Onas. 10.1–6 discusses the need to drill troops, suggests ways of doing so, and describes the subsequent benefits of such training.

11 Proctor, 1971, p. 17 notes that troops tended to move to new quarters around the new year, and that spring officially began in early February, although the cold could persist for some time afterwards.

12 See Scullard, 1980, pp. 186–95 for brief descriptions of the *tumultus* and the Second Illyrian War.

13 MacMullen, 1984, p. 446 discusses the century as a focus of loyalty, albeit primarily with evidence from the Imperial period.

14 Lee, 1996, p. 208. Polyb. 6.24.6 points out that there were two *signiferi*, but Varro, *Ling.* 5.88 indicates that there was only one *signum* per maniple. Walbank, 1957, p. 707 suggests that one of the *signiferi* was a substitute, in case anything

should happen to the other. Connolly, 1989, p. 153 believes that two standard-bearers implied two standards, presumably one per century, and Goldsworthy, 2000b, p.45 explicitly states that each century had its own standard.

15 Rawson, 1971, pp. 14–15. Polyb. 6.20.9 notes the obsolete practice of recruiting cavalry before infantry; 6.25.3–11 compares the obsolete and contemporary equipment of the cavalry; 6.39.3 points out that although the contemporary reward for a cavalryman who had slain an enemy in a skirmish was horse-trappings, it had previously been a spear.

16 Rawson's belief that the main source for Polybius' description was an obsolete handbook for tribunes is largely derived from the remarkable prominence of military tribunes in Polybius' account. However, considering that Polybius is thought to have composed much of his history during the 160s, when his friend and patron, Scipio Aemilianus, was probably serving as a military tribune, this is hardly surprising.

17 Polyb. 31.24.1 states that Scipio was 18 years old when Polybius first began to associate closely with him in 168; Scipio would therefore have been about 26 when Polybius wrote his description of the Roman army, assuming Polybius wrote it around 160.

18 Sumner, 1970, p. 69 declares that 'the whole farrago appears as an antiquarian reconstruction, concocted out of scattered pieces of information and misinformation'. Keppie, 1998, p. 20 admits that 'its very incongruities may lend it a certain measure of authority'. Connolly, 1998, p. 127 argues that the description is essentially accurate as Livy has resisted his usual tendency towards modernisation.

19 Walbank, 1957, pp. 703–5. The earliest authentic mention of the *pilum* is Polyb. 1.40.12 (he uses the term *hyssos*), referring to 251, but Liv. 10.39.12 mentions *pila* being used in 295 during the Third Samnite War, and Plut. *Vit. Pyrrh.* 21.9 claims that Pyrrhus was wounded with a *pilum* at Ausculum in 279.

20 The legion of the mid-Republic is usually described as 'manipular', as the maniple was its basic tactical unit. Before this the legion operated as a hoplite phalanx. The legion of the late Republic is normally referred to as the 'Marian' legion, after the reforms of Gaius Marius, who is traditionally held to have replaced the maniple with the cohort as the basic tactical unit at the end of the second century. See Keppie, 1998, pp. 17, 19, 63 ff. On the manipular reform in general, see Oakley, 1998, pp. 455–7.

21 Elsewhere Polybius refers to a standard complement of 4,000 infantry and 300 cavalry (1.16.2) and of 4,000 infantry and 200 cavalry (3.107.10), which is supported by Liv. 22.36.4. It seems likely that on these occasions Polybius is simply rounding down his figure of 4,200 infantry, although Polyb. 6.21.10 suggests that there were sometimes fewer than 4,000 infantry per legion. Legions even larger than those used at Cannae, having 5,200 infantry and 300 cavalry each, had been raised less than a decade earlier to deal with the Celtic threat in northern Italy (Polyb. 2.24.3); see Walbank, 1957, pp. 702–3 for further references to oversize legions.

22 Liv. 1.43.8–11: the *equites*, the wealthiest citizens from whom the cavalry were drawn, were formed into eighteen centuries under the Servian constitution.

23 Lazenby, 1978, p. 79, for instance, works on the basis of a simple average of 1,466 men.

24 Polyb. 6.19.1–2, 8–9. Cavalry background: Harris, 1979, p. 13 argues that the post of military tribune was almost exclusive to *equites*, though Keppie, 1998, p. 40 suggests that potential tribunes may sometimes have served in the ranks.

25 Keppie, 1998, p. 40; Garlan, 1975, p. 157; Suolahti, 1955, pp. 40, 44. As was usual in Rome, patronage and family connections doubtless played a vital role in their appointment.

26 Keppie, 1998, p. 40; Suolahti, 1955, pp. 29–33 on the opening stage of the *cursus*, pp. 50–1 on the military and civilian privileges of military tribunes.

27 Enrolment: Polyb. 6.20. Oath: Polyb. 6.21.1–3 and Liv. 22.38.2–5. Organisation of infantry: Polyb. 6.21.6–10. Training: Polyb. 10.20.1. Camps: Polyb. 6.33. Pairs: Polyb. 6.39.3. Duties: Liv. 40.39.8, 24.15.3. After the Second Punic War, experienced tribunes may have had a certain degree of independence in command, e.g. Polyb. 18.26.2. See Suolahti, 1955, pp. 46–9.

28 Cornell, 1995, p. 188. The names for the first two lines are apparently anachronistic, as the *hastati* of Polybius' day were not armed with the *hasta*, the long thrusting spear, and the *principes* formed the second line of troops, even though their name suggests that they may once have formed the first line. Veg. 2.2. 15–17, 3.14 indicates that the order of the first two lines was indeed switched at some point, but it seems unlikely that Polybius' account is inaccurate in this respect as he frequently describes the mid-Republican army as deployed on this pattern. See Rawson, 1971, pp. 17–18; Adcock, 1940, pp. 8–9; Walbank, 1957, p. 702.

29 Delbrück, 1990 [1920], p. 275; Santosuosso, 1997, p. 150 ff. adopts this concept of a 'phalanx with joints' to describe the manipular system.

30 Walbank, 1957, pp. 707–8; Warry, 1980, p. 112. Polyb. 6.24.8 improbably suggests that neither centurion outranked the other and that each independently led his century, the maniple only working as a unit if either centurion was killed, the other being thus forced to take control of the whole. This would have been impractical, as Walbank points out, as the legion's tactical structure would then have relied solely upon chance.

31 Polyb. 6.35.12; 15.12.2; Liv. 1.43.7. See Adcock, 1940, p. 11; Connolly, 1998, pp. 129–30. Warry, 1980, p. 112 assumes that one of the two standard-bearers of Polybius' account was in fact a musician whose main purpose was to pass signals and draw attention to the actual standard-bearer.

32 E.g. Connolly, 1989, p. 162 suggests it was about 200 m, while Warry, 1980, p. 111 estimates it as being anything less than 76 m.

33 J. Kromayer in Kromayer and Veith, 1912, pp. 358–60. Adcock, 1940, pp. 8–12, followed by Walbank, 1967, p. 454. Goldsworthy, 2000a, pp. 53–62, and 2000b, pp. 49–55 proposes a model of battle, closely related to the ideas discussed in Sabin, 2000, pp. 1–17, which at first sight appears to allow the Romans to have fought with large gaps in their line.

34 Zhmodikov, 2000, pp. 67–78 argues that missile fighting was far more important in Roman battles than is generally realised. His point is very valid, but unfortunately his use of evidence is highly questionable. Many of his examples are drawn from Livy's first decade, the battle scenes in which are of extremely dubious authenticity. Numerous examples refer to the deaths of Roman commanders in battle, but the references cited can hardly be said to illustrate a general principle. In the first place, the fact that enemy troops were using missiles does

not automatically mean that the Romans must also have been relying on missiles. Second, Livy's descriptions of how Roman commanders were killed in battle may have been altered, if not wholly invented, for patriotic purposes. Individual cases are cited in a misleading manner: Aemilius Paullus' death, it is implied, was due to missiles thrown by infantry, despite the fact that Livy explicitly says that he was struck down by Numidians, and Livy is quite clear that the Numidians at Cannae were mounted; Zhmodikov also says that Livy claims that Flaminius was killed at Lake Trasimene by a Celt armed with a *lancea* – indeed he does, but he also makes it clear that the consul was run through at close range. Other examples of missiles being used in ambushes or siege may well be correct, but are hardly relevant.

35 The capabilities of ancient weapons are discussed in Chapter 6.

36 Sumner, 1970, pp. 66–7; Connolly, 1998, p. 142; Keppie, 1998, p. 39 argue for the Romans fighting in relatively solid lines. The battle of Zama is an exception, as on this occasion the gaps between maniples were indeed maintained, but this was for the express purpose of creating 'elephant lanes' rather than to facilitate line replacement. See Polyb. 15.9.12; Liv. 30.33.

37 Sabin, 1996, p. 71; Goldsworthy, 1996, p. 179. For the claim that Vegetius' source is ultimately Republican, quite possibly Cato, see Milner, 1996, pp. xvii ff.

38 Connolly, 1998, p. 142. Adcock, 1940, p. 11 suggests that the front rank of whichever line was being replaced may have had to sacrifice themselves to enable this to happen; this seems unlikely as the front rank were usually the best troops, but their casualties must indeed have been very high if they attempted line replacement during combat.

39 Goldsworthy, 1996, p. 199; Connolly, 1989, p. 162. Greek hoplites were known to carry two spears into battle, but this was facilitated by the vertical grip on their shields. See Anderson, 1991, p. 19.

40 According to the 'Caeso's Speech' tradition it was originally a Samnite weapon, and fourth-century frescos in the Giglili tomb in Tarquinia appear to depict it. See Cornell, 1995, p. 170; Bishop and Coulston, 1993, p. 50; Walbank, 1957, pp. 704–5.

41 Walbank, 1957, p. 208 suggests that this innovation may have been fictional, invented to show the tribunes, who allegedly initiated it, as being responsible for victory despite the reckless tactics of Flaminius.

42 Bishop and Coulston, 1993, p. 53. See Polyb. 3.114.3 on the Celtic swordsman's need for space.

43 Bishop and Coulston, 1993, p. 60. Connolly, 1998, p. 133 cites an example found at Canosa di Puglia, ancient Canusium near Cannae, and dating to about the time of the Second Punic War.

44 11,000 *asses*: Liv. 1.43.7. 4,000 *asses*: Polyb. 6.19.2. See Gabba, 1976, pp. 5–6. Gabba is followed by Brunt, 1971, pp. 402–4, dating the reform to 214. Walbank, 1957, p. 698 finds Gabba's argument unconvincing, and Rich, 1983, pp. 294–5, 305–12 convincingly refutes the notion of a reduction in the property qualification for military service.

45 Samuels, 1990, pp. 12–13. Military servants in ancient armies: Anderson, 1970, p. 40; Engels, 1978, pp. 12–13. Polyb. 3.82.3 notes that there were fewer soldiers than camp followers in Flaminius' army in 217.

46 Dion. Hal. 4.16 says that the fourth *classis* were armed with a *scutum*, a spear, and a sword.

47 Liv. 8.8.5–6, 8. Connolly, 1998, p. 128 believes that the last two groups, which Livy clearly associates with the *triarii*, were spearmen from the fourth and fifth *classes*, the fifth *classis* also supplying the *leves*. Rawson, 1971, p. 30 notes that Livy's specific identification of the *leves* as light armed implies that he regarded neither *rorarii* nor *accensi* as light troops. Liv. 8.9.14 has the *rorarii* support the heavily armed *hastati* and *principes* in battle, and Liv. 8.10.2–4 describes the *accensi* impersonating the *triarii*.

48 Varro, *Ling.* 7.57–58. Lucilius, 7.290 (*rorarius veles*), 10.293 (*pone paluclatus stabat rorarius velox*). Head, 1982, p. 39; Rawson, 1971, p. 29; Walbank, 1957, p. 701.

49 Cornell, 1995, pp. 181–2, based on Fraccaro's theory that the centuriate structure corresponded to the legion. See Sumner, 1970, p. 70.

50 Size of legion: Liv. 8.8.14. Number of *accensi*: Liv. 8.8.7–8 (15 *vexilla* of 60 soldiers each).

51 Liv. 26.4. This innovation may have been unique, and certainly did not last for long. Bell, 1965, pp. 420–1 discusses the use of combined forces of cavalry and light infantry, noting the disadvantage that if the cavalry were forced to retreat the infantry would have to be abandoned.

52 Connolly, 1998, p. 133. Polyb. 12.18.2–3 argues that cavalry should, as a rule, not be deployed more than eight files deep. This is merely his opinion, however, and should not necessarily be interpreted as being the standard depth of cavalry formations.

53 Walbank, 1957, pp. 707–8 describes the maniple as a single tactical unit based on the same principle, as in a maniple the *centurio prior* outranked the *centurio posterior*.

54 Scullard, 1980, pp. 141–6 briefly summarises Rome's Pyrrhic Wars. Plut. *Vit. Pyrrh.* 16 claims that Pyrrhus had 3,000 cavalry, some of them Thessalian.

55 Samuels, 1990, p. 13. Rawson, 1971, p. 21 cites the defeat of Centenius' 4,000 cavalry (Polyb. 3.86) as an example of the weakness of Roman cavalry, but her analysis is flawed as the 4,000 cavalry were defeated by a combination of Carthage's spearmen, of whom there were at least 6,000, and an unspecified number of her 10,000 cavalry.

56 Bar-Kochva, 1976, p. 74 also notes that these troops were eventually turned into heavily armed cataphracts. See Polyb. 16.18.6.

57 Connolly, 1998, p. 133. Snodgrass, 1999, p. 122 describes Hellenistic cuirasses as being plated, but with mail shoulder-flaps which fastened at the front.

58 Zhmodikov, 2000, p. 75 suggests that the Romans may have mutilated the corpses with the deliberate intention of causing fear and horror. However, there is nothing in the previous passage describing the encounter between Macedonian and Roman cavalry (Liv. 33.6–10) which supports such a hypothesis.

59 Goldsworthy, 2000b, p. 45 suggests that *gladii* with blades longer than 50.5 cm were probably used by cavalrymen or mounted officers. Connolly, 1998, p. 236 points out that the long sword, or *spatha*, of the early Empire was derived from the Celtic long sword; he points out that this is hardly surprising, since Celts were the Roman army's main source of cavalry during the early Empire.

60 Harris, 1979, p. 14. Holmes, 1985, pp. 54–5 is useful on comparative grounds, as he seems to directly refute Samuels' criticism by examining the importance

of sport in public schools for achieving just this. Carlton, 1992, p. 75 notes
that sports such as fencing and hunting were good training for the gentry who
made up cavalry units in the British Civil Wars, as they provided useful skills
for charging broken units and pursuing routed infantry.

61 Sherwin-White, 1973, p. 98. See Liv. 22.37.7, where Hiero of Syracuse reportedly observes that the Romans employed only Roman citizens and Latin allies
as heavy infantry and cavalry; this, while obviously an exaggeration, nevertheless indicates the importance of the Latins in the Roman forces. Presumably the
proportion of Latins in the army of Cannae was lower than in more normal
Roman armies, owing to the losses of the previous two years and the size of the
army of Cannae. Polyb. 2.24.10 states that that according to the census of 225
there had been 80,000 Latin infantry eligible to serve in Rome's forces that year;
they could hardly have contributed a high percentage of the 40,000 allied infantry
in the army of Cannae.

62 Lazenby, 1978, p. 10; Salmon, 1982, p. 64. Sherwin-White, 1973, p. 99 claims
that the greater part of Latin manpower was actually Roman.

63 Sherwin-White, 1973, pp. 119 ff. Lazenby, 1978, p. 11 cites the example of
Camerinum in Umbria.

64 Lazenby, 1978, p. 13 notes that the cohorts from Praeneste and Perugia serving
together at Casilinum in 216 were respectively 500 and 460 men strong.

65 Bell, 1965, pp. 404–19 discusses the development of the cohort as a tactical
unit rather than a purely administrative one, suggesting that the organisation
of citizen troops into cohorts may have been initially a temporary formation
adopted in Spain.

4 THE CARTHAGINIAN ARMY

1 Gsell, 1928, pp. 331–435 is a notable exception.

2 See Gsell, 1928, pp. 390–1 for unit organisation in the Carthaginian army.

3 Polyb. 3.72.8 divides the light infantry into slingers from the Balearian Islands
and *longchophoroi*, spearmen of unspecified nationality.

4 Diop, 1986, p. 69; Oliver and Fagan, 1975, pp. 47–8. Mattingly and Hitchner,
1995, p. 172 point out that the Numidians appear to have practised trans-
humant pastoralism rather than being strictly nomadic.

5 Picard, 1964, p. 28; O'Meara, 1954, pp. 20–1. But see Desanges, 1981, p.
427, which points out that Negroid remains are not uncommon in Carthaginian
burial grounds.

6 These last two references may be unreliable. See Griffith, 1935, pp. 223–5.

7 Although Greek mercenaries, for example, normally supplied their own equipment, some employers of mercenaries in the Greek world such as Dionysius I
(Diod. 14.43.2–3) and Timoleon (Plut., *Vit. Tim.* 13.3) sometimes purchased
large quantities of arms for their men. See Whitehead, 1991, p. 13; McKechnie,
1989, p. 82; Anderson, 1970, pp. 59, 286.

8 Caven, 1980, p. 73 goes so far as to suggest that this was why Carthage lacked
a citizen militia – such a force would have given the general populace political power, threatening the primacy of the aristocracy. However that may be,
it would certainly have been unwise for Carthage to have obliged her subject
Libyans to provide their own weapons. A useful parallel would be medieval

Egypt, where Kipchak Turks were used as slave-soldiers, called Mameluks. It was only a matter of time before the Mameluks themselves took power. See Riley-Smith, 1987, pp. 200–1; Keegan, 1993, pp. 34–5.

9 Head, 1982, p. 144 suggests that they used short, broad-bladed thrusting spears; Samuels, 1990, p. 18 believes that they used long thrusting spears, probably between 2.1 m and 2.4 m long, like those of the classical Greek hoplites or the Roman *triarii* (see Anderson, 1991, pp. 22–4 and Bishop and Coulston, 1993, pp. 52–3 for these weapons); Connolly, 1998, p. 148 assumes they were armed with long pikes like conventional Macedonian-style phalangites; Snodgrass, 1999, p. 118 notes that such weapons could be up to 6.4 m long.

10 For developments in infantry equipment and tactics in the Hellenistic period, see Hanson, 1995b, pp. 32–49; Warry, 1980, pp. 54–99; Garlan, 1984, pp. 353–62; Tarn, 1930, pp. 1–49. Although unlikely, it must be admitted that it is possible that Carthage's citizen militia were armed and fought in this increasingly obsolete fashion. The changes in Mediterranean warfare had been brought about largely because of specialisation and professionalisation, things which would have been mostly irrelevant to an infrequently assembled citizen militia in North Africa. The traditional phalanx was a simple system requiring little training and might therefore have been perfectly suited to such a militia. On the simplicity of the phalanx, see Hanson, 1989, pp. 31–2.

11 Bagnall, 1990, p. 10; De Beer, 1969, p. 98; Bradford, 1981, p. 41. For a more restrained analysis of Xanthippus' actions see Marsden, 1974, pp. 278 ff.

12 This has been the assumption of modern novelists writing about the period. See Leckie, 1995, p. 9; Flaubert, 1977, p. 45.

13 App. *Pun.* 93 refers to the standard Carthaginian arms as *longche* and *saunion*, *xiphos*, and *thyreos*. See Head, 1982, p. 142.

14 App., *Hann.* 4.93, though according to his problematic account 500 Celtiberians, apparently corresponding to the 500 Numidians of Liv. 22.48, pretended to desert to the Roman side, enabling them to turn on the Romans and arm themselves with Roman swords, shields, and spears.

15 Greaves and helmets might have been taken from dead or captured Romans, but this need not have been the case; bronze greaves were probably all alike whereas the *Montefortino*-style helmet of the third-century Roman infantryman was common throughout the western Mediterranean. See Head, 1982, p. 152.

16 Lazenby, 1978, p. 14; But see Bagnall, 1990, p. 170, who seems to see no difficulty in retraining experienced soldiers.

17 Asclep. 5.1; Plut. *Vit. Cleom.* 11.12; *Vit. Aem.* 19.1. Markle III, 1977, pp. 323 ff. argues that an 18-foot (5.5 m) *sarissa* probably weighed 14.5 lb (6.5 kg), compared to the 2.2 lb (1 kg) which an 8-foot (2.4 m) hoplite spear would weigh, and that phalangites required both hands for such a weapon, relying on a small, round shield slung from the neck to cover the left shoulder.

18 Lazenby, 1996a, p. 100 speculates that the Carthaginian commanders simply wished to avoid a setpiece battle with the Romans, but this is not entirely convincing, for if the Libyan and citizen infantry were close-order spearmen a setpiece battle on ideal terrain would have been essential for them if they were to stand any chance of defeating the Romans. Polyb. 18.31.5–11 explains that the pike phalanx is almost useless on any terrain other than clear, level ground.

For the importance of level terrain to classical hoplites, see Hanson, 1989, pp. 29–30.

19 E.g. Thuc. 4.96.1 on the Boiotian charge at Delium. See Goldsworthy, 1997, pp. 7 ff.; Hanson, 1989, p. 138.

20 Ferrill, 1985, pp. 176–7 discusses the nature of Alexander's heavy cavalry. Bar-Kochva, 1976, p. 74 describes Hellenistic cavalry in the Seleucid Empire. Snodgrass, 1999, pp. 119–20, 122–3 discusses Hellenistic cavalry equipment under Alexander and the Successors.

21 Polyb. 9.22.4 refers to him as Muttonos the Libyan, but Livy is convincingly precise as to his background. Lancel, 1998, p. 62 says that 'Muttines' is an attempt to render the Semitic name 'Mattan' in Latin; see Walbank, 1967, p. 150.

22 Warmington, 1960, p. 41 thinks Hannibal had 6,000 such cavalry, but presumably ignores the fact that the 6,000 cavalry brought to Italy in 218 included Spanish as well as African cavalry.

23 Brett and Fentress, 1996, pp. 24–5 say that the large Numidian kingdoms developed under Carthaginian influence. For smaller political units than the major kingdoms: Polyb. 3.33.15; App., *Pun.* 10, 33; Lancel, 1998, pp. 158–9; Gsell, 1928, p. 362. According to Plin., *Nat. Hist.* 5.1, 463 Numidian tribes gave allegiance to Rome.

24 Griffith, 1935, p. 227. For references to Masinissa, see Gsell, 1928, p. 363. Law, 1978, pp. 176–7 notes that the sources usually refer to Numidian leaders as 'king' (*basileos* / *rex*) or 'chief' (*dynastes*), in an attempt to render the indigenous title *gld*.

25 How many men Naravas could raise is unclear. Law, 1978, p. 179 points out that his relatively small contingent in the Mercenaries' War may suggest that his territories were not very extensive.

26 Gsell, 1928, p. 391 discusses possible references to Numidian units of 150 or 500 men each. App., *Pun.* 108 refers to Numidian *ilarchoi*, presumably commanders of sub-units of indeterminate size, in contrast to *hipparchoi*, apparently their Carthaginian superiors.

27 Hyland, 1990, p. 12; Connolly, 1998, p. 149; Dodge, 1995 [1891], p. 23. Desanges, 1981, p. 433 gives a detailed description of the small Barbary horse which would have been common in North Africa before the Arab invasions. Oliver and Fagan, 1975, p. 48, on the other hand, claim that Numidian horses were quite large.

28 Lazenby, 1978, p. 36; Head, 1982, p. 145; Connolly, 1998, pp. 149–50; but see Liv. 35.11.7 which describes shieldless Numidians. It is unlikely that all Numidians were armed in identical fashion.

29 The Gaetulians clearly considered themselves to be quite distinct from the Numidians, however, and may not have been nomadic. See Brett and Fentress, 1996, p. 42.

30 Wagner, 1989, pp. 145–56. Whittaker, 1978, pp. 71–4 argues, albeit with insufficient evidence, that Carthage lacked a system of provincial administration before the third century.

31 G.T. Griffith, 1935, pp. 225–6 points out that Iberians doubtless served as mercenaries as well as levies during the Hannibalic War.

32 Rich, 1996, pp. 1–38; Scullard, 1980, pp. 195–7. For further reading on the motives for Carthaginian expansion in Spain, see the bibliography to Rich, 1996, as well as Lancel, 1998, pp. 25–56.

33 Lancel, 1998, p. 34. It is uncertain to what extent these areas had remained loyal to Carthage during the First Punic War, and whether or not they had to be reconquered. See Scullard, 1989b, p. 21 and Schulten, 1928, p. 786.
34 Bagnall, 1990, p. 14. Schulten, 1928, pp. 783–4 claims that the organisation of Spaniards into small towns is a phenomenon more properly characteristic of the Celtiberians and Lusitanians, but see Diod. 25.10, 12 which describe Hamilcar and Hasdrubal conquering many cities throughout Spain.
35 10,000 infantry and perhaps 1,000 cavalry returned home at this point, Livy claiming that 3,000 of these were Carpetani deserters, the remainder being relieved of duty to maintain morale in the army by disguising the Carpetani desertion.
36 Hanson, 1989, pp. 121–5 discusses the similar influence of social ties on Greek hoplites in the classical period.
37 Samuels, 1990, p. 18. Liv. 34.14.11 describes Iberian infantry hurling metal and incendiary throwing spears before beginning close combat with swords.
38 See also Liv. 34.14.11; Gsell, 1928, p. 373.
39 Nicolini, 1974, p. 54, who goes so far as to suggest that the Iberians actually wore linen cuirasses which were mistaken for tunics.
40 Goldsworthy, 1996, p. 58; Samuels, 1990, p. 19. Rawlings, 1996, p. 90 notes that the Spaniards, as presented by Livy at any rate, 'have some striking similarities with Gallic military habits'.
41 Head, 1982, p. 150. Healy, 1994, p. 58 has reconstructions of troops wearing such armour, both infantry and cavalry.
42 Although this particular reference is suspect, Livy mentions Celtiberians serving in Carthaginian armies at several points during the Second Punic War, e.g. 24.49.7–8, 28.1–2, 30.7.10, 8.6–8.
43 Polyb. 3.44 deals with Magilius and other Celts inviting Hannibal to Italy. 3.66.7 mentions alliances with many of the Celts in Cisalpine Gaul. 7.9.6 is evidence that these were genuine alliances rather than informal arrangements, as Celtic and Ligurian allies are mentioned in Hannibal's treaty with Philip V of Macedon.
44 Classical prejudices against barbarians, especially Celts: Cartledge, 1993, ch. 3; Rankin, 1987, pp. 72–5; Shaw, 1982–3, pp. 5–32; Momigliano, 1975, ch. 3; Wiedemann, 1986, pp. 189–201.
45 Polybius describes the Celts as *gymnos*, which could also mean 'lightly clad'.
46 Although Polyb. 3.72.9 refers to the cavalry recruits as Celtic allies. See Griffith, 1935, p. 229; Delbrück, 1990 [1920], p. 361.
47 For Hellenistic cavalry being paid more than hoplites and peltasts see Griffith, 1935, p. 302.
48 Goldsworthy, 1996, p. 58; Head, 1982, pp. 154–5. Liv. 22.6.3–4 describes a Celtic trooper spurring his horse on through the troops surrounding the Roman consul Flaminius.
49 Polyb. 3.84.6 notes merely that Flaminius was attacked and killed by certain Celts.
50 Polybius sometimes specifically identifies the Balearian slingers among the light-armed troops, e.g. 3.72.8, 83.3, 113.6. However, he normally refers to the skirmishers, or sometimes more precisely to the spearmen, regardless of nationality – *euzdonoi*: 3.73.1, 74.2, 94.6, 110.4, 115.1, 115.4; *psiloi*: 3.104.4; *longchophoroi*: 3.72.8, 73.7, 83.3, 84.14, 86.4, 93.9, 94.6, 101.5, 113.6.

51 Lazenby, 1978, p. 81 suggests 11,400 skirmishers, based on the possibility that the ratio of light troops to line infantry was the same at Cannae as it had been at the Trebia. This idea is more plausible than compelling, as it presumes that Hannibal's army at the Trebia was of ideal proportions, and ignores Polybius' clear distinction between *euzdonoi* and *pezdoi*.

52 Lancel, 1998, p. 61; Gsell, 1928, p. 375. Warmington, 1960, p. 27 describes the founding of the Phoenician colony at Ibiza as being merely a stepping stone from Sardinia to Spain.

53 Lancel, 1995, pp. 81–2 notes that the first Phoenician colony at Ibiza seems to have been established in the mid-seventh century, but it is far from certain that this colony was actually Carthaginian. In any case, this does not mean that Balearian mercenaries were employed from such an early date. Hdt. 7.165 does not mention Balearians in the Carthaginian army at Himera in 480, but they may have been categorised as Iberians. There were certainly Balearians in Carthage's armies by the late fifth century, according to Diod. 13.80.2. See Gsell, 1928, pp. 374 ff. for references to Balearians in Carthaginian armies.

54 Head, 1982, p. 150 refers to large, fist-sized slingstones found in Spain. Xen., *Anab.* 3.3 notes that Persian slingers also used fist-sized slingstones.

55 Connolly, 1998, pp. 148, 169–70, 187 confuses the spearmen with the African heavy infantry, believing the former to have been pikemen, perhaps because of the inaccurate translation of *longchophoroi* as 'pikemen' by both the Loeb and Penguin translators.

56 Head, 1982, p. 47; Warry, 1980, pp. 51, 61; Delbrück, 1990 [1920], p. 125. Anderson, 1970, p. 131 even suggests that some Hellenistic peltasts may have used the Iphicratid pike, which was 12 feet (3.6 m) long.

57 Gsell, 1928, p. 359; Lancel, 1998, p. 60. Str. 17.3.7 claims that the North Africans tended to be armed with short, broad-bladed spears, and small shields made from rawhide.

58 Delbrück, 1990 [1920], p. 364 identifies the spearmen as peltasts for this very reason. Samuels, 1990, p. 18 claims that Hannibal's spearmen, armed in this fashion, were the model for Rome's *velites*, but this seems unlikely.

59 Arist., *Eth. Nic.* 3.8.6–9 notes that while mercenaries can have an extremely high level of skill as soldiers, they have a tendency to flee in times of great danger. See also Machiavelli, 1908 [1513], pp. 97 ff. for the unreliability of mercenaries in general. However, Polyb. 11.13.3–8 notes that mercenary soldiers, while unreliable in the service of democracies, can be extremely useful for ambitious despots.

5 COMMAND AT CANNAE

1 Goldsworthy, 1996, p. 117. A useful summary of these principles can be found in Marsden, 1974, pp. 274 ff.

2 For different martial cultures see Keegan, 1993, pp. 3–60.

3 Polybius also wrote explicitly about tactical matters: Polyb. 9.20.4; Arr., *Tact.* 1.

4 Marsden, 1974, pp. 278–9 cites the example of Xanthippus to illustrate how Polybius was aware of the various skills involved in generalship.

5 Eckstein, 1995, p. 175 demonstrates how Hamilcar epitomises this quality in Polybius' account.

6 Varro in command at Cannae: Polyb. 3.113.1; Liv. 22.45.5; Plut., *Vit. Fab. Max.* 15. However, App., *Hann.* 19 says that Varro allowed Paullus to command the troops at Cannae though it was his turn to lead, and Polyb. 15.11.8 presents Hannibal as saying that the Romans at Cannae were led by Paullus.

7 Liv. 22.35.3 says he was not condemned, but Plut., *Vit. Fab. Max.* 14 says that he was.

8 The elections of 216 and the relationship between Varro and Paullus are highly controversial. Lazenby, 1978, pp. 74–5 follows Scullard, 1973, pp. 49–54, who discusses the election of both consuls, the relations between them, and the blackening of Varro's name by later writers; Scullard believes that Varro was supported by a prominent senatorial faction built around the powerful Aemilii and Cornelii families. See also Staveley, 1954–5, pp. 205 ff.; Gruen, 1978, pp. 61–74; Twyman, 1984, pp. 285–94. Dorey, 1959, pp. 249–52 does not believe that there was any alliance between Paullus and Varro, but thinks that Paullus was elected as a compromise between the Fabian and Scipionic factions, since he was not a member of the 'popular' wing of the Aemilian-Scipionic group. This, however, presupposes the existence of such factions, and there is no real evidence for this, which refutes Scullard's hypothesis. Sumner, 1975, pp. 250–9 argues that there is no evidence for any alliance at all between Paullus and Varro, and thinks that the analyses of Scullard, Lazenby, etc. are entirely wrong. Rosenstein, 1993, pp. 323–6 argues that Paullus was in fact a prestigious consensus candidate put forward by the *nobiles* to ensure that 'their' man would not be beholden to Varro for his election, as they feared the rise of another prominent maverick like Gaius Flaminius.

9 In general it is fair to say that the reputations of 'new men' were far more likely to suffer from defeat than were those of nobles. Tatum, 1991, pp. 149–52 and 1992, p. 24 examines the statistics cited in Rosenstein, 1990. Forty of the generals defeated between 390 and 49 had not reached the consulship. Of these, only thirteen were definitely nobles or patricians; eight of these later reached the consulship. Twenty-two were definitely not nobles, and only two of these reached the consulship. The background of the remaining five commanders is unknown, but none of them reached the consulship.

10 Lazenby, 1978, p. 75. Livy's contempt for 'populist' leaders is also noteworthy. See Walsh, 1961, p. 167.

11 Sabin, 1996, p. 69. Against this, Polyb. 6.24.8 notes that whenever both a maniple's centurions were present, the senior of the two, the *centurio prior*, would command the right half of the maniple, with the *centurio posterior* commanding the left. Why there should be such an emphasis on command from the right is uncertain, but it may be connected with the fact that weapons were held in the right hand, shields in the left; in other words, the right hand would be the more 'aggressive' hand, and consequently the commander would lead the attack from the right. It was perhaps also linked with the tendency of the Greek line of battle to drift to the right, as discussed by Hanson, 1989, p. 146. For references to Greek commanders on the right wing, see Wheeler, 1991, p. 162, n. 65, p. 167, n. 136.

12 Persian kings tended to command from the centre in order to ensure their own safety and to facilitate the issuing of orders: Xen., *Anab.* 1.8.22; Arr., *Anab.* 3.11.5.

13 It is possible that the number of centuries had been raised to 373, rather than maintained at 193. See Scullard, 1980, pp. 187, 492; Walbank, 1957, pp. 683–6.

14 Scipio's aedileship: Polyb. 10.4.5; Liv. 25.2.6–7; Harris, 1979, p. 12; Lazenby, 1978, pp. 132, 293; Walbank, 1967, pp. 199–200.

15 Harris, 1979, p. 15, although Keppie, 1998, p. 40 points out that the practice of serving as a legate was not common until after the Second Punic War.

16 Harris, 1979, p. 17.

17 Harris, 1979, p. 30. See Polyb. 6.53–4 for the role of aristocratic funerals in inspiring young aristocrats to live up to the reputations of their ancestors.

18 Broughton, 1951, pp. 250–1. Ridley, 1978, pp. 161–5 notes that although Scipio seems to have genuinely been present at Cannae, Polybius never mentions this fact, while other sources refer only to his actions after the battle, in what appears to be an attempt to whitewash his record by concealing his participation in one of the greatest disasters in Roman history.

19 Harris, 1979, pp. 54 ff. discusses economic motives for Roman imperialism.

20 Hoyos, 1994, pp. 246–74 argues that military success and Spanish wealth enabled the Barcids to dominate Carthaginian politics.

21 Marsden, 1974, p. 278 notes that the essence of Xanthippus' analysis of the Carthaginian army was that it was not at fault, and that Carthage's problems lay with her commanders.

22 Hoyos, 1994, pp. 271–2; Bagnall, 1990, p. 157. Mago: Polyb. 3.71.5–9, 114.7. Hanno: Polyb. 3.42.6, 114.7; Liv. 21.27.2; App., *Hann.* 20. Hoyos, 1994, p. 272 points out that 'Appian's sole word on this sort of item must be treated with caution'. Hasdrubal: Polyb. 3.66.6, 93.4, 114.7; Liv. 22.46.7.

23 Liv. 21.12.1 mentions him besieging Saguntum in Hannibal's absence. Liv. 21.45.2, 22.6.11, 13.9 describes him commanding cavalry, and Liv. 22.46.7, 51.2 describes him as the cavalry commander on the right wing at Cannae. Polyb. 3.84.14, 86.4 does not identify him as a cavalry commander and Polyb. 3.114.7 states that Hanno commanded the right wing, where the Numidians were stationed. Flor. 1.22.19 refers to him as the son of Bomilcar, but this may simply have arisen through confusing Hanno, son of Bomilcar, and Maharbal, son of Himilco, as Polybius and Livy respectively regard them as being in charge of the Numidian cavalry.

24 However, this is uncertain, as the story appears to be derived from Cato, fr. 4.13, which refers to neither speaker by name: *Igitur dictatorem Carthaginiensium magister equitum monuit . . .*

25 *Synedroi*: Polyb. 3.20.8, 71.5. *Gerousiastai*: Polyb. 7.9.1. See Walbank, 1957, pp. 334–5; 1967, pp. 44–5; Picard, 1964, p. 138.

26 Lancel, 1998, p. 62. See Walbank, 1984, pp. 68–71 for the importance of the king's 'Friends' in the Hellenistic court. This may support the possibility that the Barcid generals tended to present themselves as Hellenistic monarchs.

27 Liv. 22.43.10–11; Plut., *Vit. Fab. Max.* 16.1; App., *Hann.* 20. Zon. 9.1 is based on Cassius Dio and even records the surely fantastic story that Hannibal ploughed up the battlefield to further loosen the soil, thereby creating more dust.

28 Quoted in Engels, 1980, p. 333.

29 Goldsworthy, 1996, pp. 131–3 discusses the *consilia* in Caesar's army, concluding that these were not general debates between officers, but were

primarily an opportunity for the commander to explain his plan and issue orders.

30 Minucius' powers were enhanced following a minor victory against Hannibal, making him the effective equal of Fabius. Polyb. 3.103.3–4; Liv. 22.25–6; Plut., *Vit. Fab. Max.* 8; Walbank, 1957, p. 434; Lazenby, 1978, p. 72.

31 E.g. Plut., *Vit. Alex.* 27–8, 33.1–2; Arr., *Anab.* 7.8.3, 29. See Keegan, 1987, pp. 52–4; Bosworth, 1993, pp. 282–90.

32 For Scipio's use of religious symbolism, see Santosuosso, 1997, pp. 198–200.

33 Paradoxically, this may have given Hannibal a somewhat 'exotic' appeal. Africa, 1970, pp. 529–31 and Moeller, 1975, pp. 405–7 suggest that his blindness in one eye may have given him a 'shamanic' quality, which could have been crucial in ensuring the loyalty of his Celtic and Spanish troops.

34 Levene, 1993, pp. 39–42 notes that Flaminius' impiety helps to explain the Roman defeat at Trasimene, at least in Livy's account.

35 App., *Hann.* 18. See Levene, 1993, pp. 42, 48. The fate of Publius Claudius Pulcher, who defied the auspices and lost his fleet at Drepanum in 249, is discussed Linderski, 1986, pp. 2176–7.

36 Lancel, 1995, p. 193; see, for example, Hdt. 7.167, describing the Carthaginian general Hamilcar at the battle of Himera in 480.

37 See Pritchett, 1971, pp. 109–15 and Jameson, 1991, pp. 197–227 for pre-battle sacrifices in Greek warfare.

38 Pritchett, 1979, pp. 230–9 discusses the practice of military vows in Greek warfare.

39 Hercules (Herakles-Melqart) crossing the Alps: Liv. 1.7.3, 5.34.6.

40 Palmer, 1997, p. 61. For Roman attempts to win the favour of Carthaginian gods in general, see Palmer, 1997, pp. 53–72. Rosenstein, 1990, p. 55 explains that the Romans believed that victory was impossible without divine support.

41 This detail is absent from Polybius' account, possibly due to his contempt for superstition (Lancel, 1998, p. 83), although the Loeb translator notes the similarity of this act to a Roman ritual, described by Liv. 1.24.9, and suggests that Livy is merely including it at this point for dramatic effect. This seems unlikely, however, as he describes Hannibal as impious at 21.4.9, and the artificial introduction of a Roman ceremony would contradict his earlier presentation of Hannibal. Curiously, however, in the Roman ceremony that this resembles, the rock is intended to symbolise the thunderbolt of Jupiter; Hannibal's surname, 'Barca', may be derived from the Phoenician word for 'thunderbolt'. See Lancel, 1998, p. 6. Levene, 1993, p. 47 notes that this action helps to explain Hannibal's early successes in Livy's account, juxtaposed as it is with Rome's bad omens.

42 The identification of Greek names with the Carthaginian deities is uncertain. See Walbank, 1967, pp. 46–50; Lancel, 1995, pp. 208–9. For a full discussion, see Barré, 1983.

43 Liv. 30.33.12 says that Hannibal addressed the Carthaginians while the various national leaders addressed their own men.

44 Ehrhardt, 1995, p. 120. Polyb. 3.108.2–109.13: Paullus' speech took place on the day he joined the army, a week prior to the battle. Polyb. 3.111: Hannibal's speech was given a few days later, three days before the battle.

45 Nep., *Hann.* 13.3 records that he was taught Greek by Sosylos of Sparta and wrote several books in the language. However, Cicero, *De Oratore* 2.18.75 mentions the poor quality of Hannibal's command of Greek. See Rochette, 1997, p. 156.

46 App., *Pun.* 40 and Liv. 30.33.6 say that this line was made up of Italians, but if Polybius had been aware of this it is unlikely that he would have had Hannibal refer to them serving with him for so long. See Walbank, 1967, pp. 457–8.

47 Polyb. 3.71.11 describes Hannibal at the Trebia exhorting the officers before battle, prior to ordering the men to get ready.

48 Walbank, 1957, pp. 13–14 for Polybius' speeches.

49 See Thuc. 1.22 for the classic formulation of this principle. For a good analysis of Thucydides' speeches, see Hornblower, 1994, pp. 45–72. Polybius' use of speeches is discussed in Walbank, 1972, pp. 43–6.

50 Davidson, 1991, p. 13 argues that this speech is given to Paullus by Polybius in order to establish the symbolic importance of the subsequent Roman defeat: since it was the first battle of the Second Punic War where the Romans were at their peak, their defeat was inexcusable. Although the speech does have this effect in the context of Polybius' work as a whole, it is unnecessary to regard it as a Polybian invention with a primarily symbolic role. It seems likely that the sentiments expressed in the speech are the sort of things that Paullus would have said under the circumstances.

51 Goldsworthy, 1996, p. 147. See Polyb. 3.44.13, 62.14, 64.11, 11.31.8. See also Xen., *Anab.* 1.8.14–16, where the Greek mercenaries answer Cyrus' statement that the omens were favourable by giving a loud war-cry, invoking Zeus.

52 Plutarch says it was given at daybreak, but it is difficult to see whether he means first light or dawn proper.

53 App., *Hann.* 21 (Cannae); Polyb. 10.12.4 (Cartagena), 15.12.2 (Zama).

54 Goldsworthy, 1996, p. 150. Arr., *Tact.* 27 and Asclep. 27.10 distinguish between verbal, visual, and horn signals.

55 Horn signals could have been quite versatile. Griffith, 1989, p. 58 notes that individual brigades in the American Civil War had their own signals. Muir, 1998, p. 54 describes how the Prussian army settled on a repertoire of twenty-two different horn commands, having found eight commands too few, and more than twenty-two too confusing.

56 Keegan, 1987, pp. 329 ff. See Carlton, 1992, pp. 180–1 for the importance of commanders in the British Civil Wars being perceived as brave.

57 See Hanson, 1989, pp. 113–15 on the frequency of battlefield deaths among Greek generals, whether on the defeated side or even on the victorious one.

58 Liv. 22.49.12 features a highly dramatised account of his death, where, following a lengthy conversation with a passing tribune, Paullus is felled by a hail of javelins cast by a group of Carthaginians pursuing some Roman fugitives.

59 This was one of the reasons why it was normal for Persian kings to base themselves at the centre of their line. See Xen., *Anab.* 1.8.22; Arr., *Anab.* 3.11.5.

60 Liv. 27.49.3–4 describes Hasdrubal behaving in a similar manner at the Metaurus in 207.

61 Liv. 22.6.2 (Flaminius), 22.49.2 (Paullus); Polyb. 10.13.1–2 (Scipio). Polyb. 15.15.3 describes Hannibal escaping from Zama accompanied by a few horsemen who may have been his bodyguard.

62 See Goldsworthy, 1996, p. 160 for the vulnerability of commanders just behind the front line.

63 It is foolhardy to be dogmatic on matters such as this. As Wheeler, 1991, p. 152 notes of hoplite commanders: 'Some generals sought personal combat; others did not'.

64 See Rawlings, 1996, p. 86–91 for the warrior ethos among Hannibal's Celtic and Celtiberian troops.

6 CANNAE: 'THE FACE OF BATTLE'

1 Polybius' own contingent was probably composed only of a legion and an allied brigade, or perhaps two legions, as Polyb. 3.117.8 states that he left 10,000 troops, the equivalent of two legions, behind as a camp garrison.

2 See Hanson, 1989, pp. 118–19. Griffith, 1989, p. 93 comments on the difficulties of integrating experienced and inexperienced units in armies of the American Civil War.

3 Gaps between sub-units were necessary to enable armies to manoeuvre properly. See Goldsworthy, 1996, p. 176.

4 See Walbank, 1967, pp. 588–90 for a discussion of this passage.

5 See Pritchett, 1971, pp. 144–54 on the frontage per man in the phalanx.

6 Seven legions and seven brigades, each deployed sixty men wide.

7 Gabriel and Metz, 1991, pp. 69–70. See Asclep. 6.2 which points out that light infantry could deploy behind a phalanx which was itself sixteen men deep.

8 240 files, each 25 deep, would give a total cavalry force on the left wing of 6,000 horses, the lowest modern estimate.

9 Lazenby, 1978, p. 80. If the allied contingents, as assumed above, included 1,520 skirmishers per brigade, there could have been as many as 21,280 skirmishers $(1,520 \times 14 = 21,280)$ in the Roman forces at Cannae.

10 One of the basic problems of tactics. See Marshall, 1947, p. 51, who cites Xen., *Cyr.* 6.3.22–3 where Cyrus scorns excessively deep formations as containing many men who cannot play a part in battle through being unable to reach the enemy with their weapons.

11 Assuming that the Roman depth was 24 *hastati*, 24 *principes*, 10 *triarii*, and that the *velites* were no more than 26 deep after being withdrawn through the ranks, giving a total depth of 84 men, in addition to the gaps between each of the lines.

12 22,000 divided by 840. This calculation is obviously extremely crude, for apart from ignoring the problem of how big the gaps were between units, it also ignores the fact that both Celts and Spaniards probably occupied a broader frontage than individual Romans owing to their fighting styles, which are discussed below. However, it serves to make the point that the Celts and Spaniards would have had to deploy in a far shallower formation than the Romans if they were to match the width of their line.

13 That this was possible is demonstrated by Thuc. 4.93.4, which describes the Boiotian forces at Delium being drawn up in one line, which was broken up into different units of varying depths e.g., the Thebans were deployed twenty-five men deep. See also Griffith, 1995, pp. 189–94 which argues that in Viking warfare the linear battle arrangements described by the sources are really little more than literary conventions, whereas the reality may have been that each army deployed in accordance with its own internal structures, with individual units fighting in whatever formations they were accustomed to.

14 See Goldsworthy, 1996 p. 50 and Griffith, 1995, p. 189 which express similar theories for the ancient Germans and Vikings respectively.

15 Ardant du Picq, a French infantry officer in the mid-nineteenth century, wrote a number of innovative and perceptive studies on ancient and contemporary battle, some of which were published before his death at Metz in 1870. His analysis of Cannae is particularly useful. See Keegan, 1976, pp. 70–1.

16 Du Picq, 1987, p. 78. See Sabin, 1996, p. 75 for examples.

17 For the effects of lengthy marches shortly before battles, see Keegan, 1976, pp. 134–5.

18 Pre-battle apprehension is normal in armies. See Holmes, 1985, pp. 136 ff.

19 Pritchett, 1985, pp. 46–51 catalogues the duration of various battles reported by Greek historians.

20 Liv. 22.6.1 (about three hours), 23.40.9 (four hours), 24.15.3 (over four hours), 25.19.15 (over two hours), 27.2.7–8 (all day), 27.12.14 (over two hours).

21 Hanson, 1992, p. 42. $100 \times 60 \times 8 = 48,000$.

22 The Roman panoply would have weighed over 30 kg. See Hanson, 1989, pp. 56 ff. for the effects of similarly heavy panoplies on classical Greek hoplites.

23 Hanson, 1989, p. 101 notes that Greek warfare tended not to introduce soldiers to combat gradually, but instead generally threw them in at the 'deep end' of full-scale phalanx battles, which must surely have worsened pre-battle anxiety. It is difficult to ascertain how the soldiers at Cannae would have felt, owing to the fact that many of Hannibal's troops were hardened veterans, while of the Roman forces even the new recruits had engaged in skirmishes with enemy troops over the previous few months, according to Polyb. 3.106.4.

24 See for example Hdt. 8.65; Thuc. 4.34.2, 44.4; Xen., *Anab.* 1.8.8; Polyb. 5.85.12; Caes., *B Civ* 3.36; Onas. 6.8; Plut., *Vit. Eum.* 16.6, *Vit. Pomp.* 72.1; Amm. 16.12.37, 25.3.10.

25 See also Keegan, 1976, pp. 139–40; Carlton, 1992, p. 133 for the similar effects of smoke on vision during more recent periods of history.

26 Hanson, 1992, p. 46. Carlton, 1992, p. 133 notes that frightened soldiers tend to bunch together, further diminishing visibility.

27 Hanson, 1989, p. 148 cites Thuc. 3.22.2 as evidence for this, as lightly armed Plataeans made a point of keeping their distance from each other when trying to escape from their besieged city at night without being detected – had they accidentally collided their weapons would have made a noise which could have alerted the Spartan guards.

28 Xen., *Anab.* 4.3.29 refers to the ringing of stones upon the shields of his men. These shields may have been covered with a thin facing of bronze, and certainly had a bronze rim. See Snodgrass, 1999, p. 53.

29 Amm. 16.12.37 mentions the shouts and screams of the victors and vanquished.

30 Xen., *Anab.* 4.5.18 also mentions Greek troops raising a din through clashing their spears against their shields in order to frighten their enemies.

31 Hanson, 1989, pp. 71–2 notes that in classical Greek warfare the so-called 'Corinthian' helmet would have made this problem even worse, as it lacked orifices for the ears, thereby impeding hearing to a great degree. Kromayer in Kromayer and Veith, 1912, p. 379 argues that since there were no cannons or rifles on the ancient battlefield it would have been quite possible for soldiers to hear orders.

32 Amm. 31.13. 4 describes how the moans of the dying and wounded distressed other soldiers at Adrianople in 378 AD.

33 Hanson, 1989, pp. 198–200; Keegan, 1976, p. 107. According to Liv. 22.51.6,

thousands upon thousands of horses and men littered the battlefield at Cannae, mingled together in accordance with the various stages of the battle.

34 See Holmes, 1985, pp. 254 ff. for a description of 'battleshock' in general.

35 Hanson, 1989, pp. 192–3. This is certainly not to say that all stories of apparitions arose in this fashion. Fussell, 2000, pp. 11–16 explains that the First World War story of the Angels of Mons, who supposedly appeared in the sky and protected the British retreat, had its origins in a short story about how the shining ghosts of English archers who died at Agincourt struck down the hostile Germans. Within a week of this story's publication the archers had metamorphosed into angels and were believed to have been genuine. Similar situations could easily have arisen in ancient wars.

36 Best, 1969, pp. 17 ff. clearly demonstrates how dangerous sufficient numbers of light-armed missile troops could be to heavy-armed line infantry. See Thuc. 3.97–8, and especially 4.32–7, which describes the famous Spartan defeat at Sphacteria in 425. Muir, 1998, p. 58 describes Napoleonic-era skirmishers' main tasks in attack as being 'to drive back the enemy's skirmishers and seek to fire on the enemy's main body, picking off officers, unsettling the men, and if possible provoking a response which might disrupt and disorganise the enemy'.

37 Hanson, 1989, pp. 15–18; 1999, pp. 157–8. A useful comparison is with the crossbows of medieval Europe, as these powerful weapons could penetrate armour and kill mounted knights at no risk to their users, who in turn were regarded as pariahs, albeit well-paid pariahs. See Bartlett, 1993, pp. 63–4.

38 As may have been the case with Viking warfare, according to Griffith, 1995, pp. 162–3, 188.

39 Pritchett, 1985, p. 51 describes them as spectators.

40 Polyb. 6.22.3 notes how some of Rome's *velites* wore distinctive headgear so that their officers could single them out and judge how bravely they fought; it is striking that the emphasis here is on displaying their courage, not on their skill as soldiers.

41 At least in the case of the Romans, where the youngest and poorest of those eligible to fight served as *velites*.

42 Dodds, 1951, p. 18 refers to 'the tension between individual impulse and the pressure of social conformity characteristic of a shame-culture. In such a society, anything which exposes a man to the contempt or ridicule of his fellows, which causes him to "lose face", is felt as unbearable.'

43 Best, 1969, pp. 3–4 distinguishes between peltasts and light infantry, following Arr., *Tact.* 3.1–4. See also Asclep. 1.2.

44 Snodgrass, 1999, pp. 81, 108. Connolly, 1998, pp. 48, 50 describes the Cretan bow as 'segment shaped', and features a drawing of one, based on a vase in the Louvre.

45 Snodgrass, 1999, pp. 40, 81, 108 for large Cretan arrowheads, 82 for more typical small arrowheads.

46 Str. 8.3.33; Xen., *Anab.* 3.3. Veg. 2.23 suggests that archers and slingers using a 'sling-staff' ought to be able to hit a man-sized target at a distance of about 600 Roman feet (177 m or 580 modern feet). Gabriel and Metz, 1991, p. 76 argue that in theory heavier shot could be lobbed for distances of up to 600 feet (183 m) while smaller shot could be fired along a virtually flat trajectory up to a distance of 225 feet (69 m).

47 Although Lazenby, 1978, p. 81 suggests that there may have been as many as 11,400 skirmishers in the army of Cannae.

48 Unless they were able to have fresh ammunition brought to them, as were the Parthian archers at Carrhae in 55. See Plut., *Vit. Crass.* 25. This lack of ammunition may not have been as pressing a problem for the Balearians as it was for the spearmen, owing to the fact that they would have been able to carry more stones than their colleagues would javelins.

49 Similar behaviour can sometimes be witnessed during modern riots and street-fighting, with bottles and stones replacing javelins as the missiles of choice – rioters gather in bunches for security and individuals step away from the group to throw their missiles, frequently remaining separate from the group while watching the missile complete its trajectory.

50 Strictly speaking, slingshot is best described as 'hurled' or 'cast', arrows as 'loosed', and javelins as 'hurled', 'cast', or 'thrown'. 'Fire' is an admittedly anachronistic term in this pre-gunpowder age, but is a convenient one to describe the various ways in which ancient missile weapons were used.

51 This is the most important reason why men fight in battle. Marshall, 1947, pp. 148–9; Keegan, 1976, pp. 72–3.

52 Goldsworthy, 1996, p. 188 notes that Marshall's research and recommendations were taken seriously by the American army, and implemented in time for the Korean War, raising the rate of fire to over 50 per cent. However, no more than 20 per cent of troops aimed their weapons.

53 This model of light infantry combat is not unlike the the description of tribal warfare in New Guinea and the analysis of 'Homeric' warfare in Van Wees, 1994, pp. 1–9.

54 Budiansky, 1997, pp. 94–5 notes that nervous mares are usually at the front in stampedes of feral horses, but in more purposeful herd movements dominant mares or stallions take the lead. When a herd is threatened from the rear, however, a dominant stallion will usually position himself between the herd and the threat to drive the herd from behind.

55 Du Picq, 1987, p. 213 states, 'The trot permits that compactness which the gallop breaks up.' Muir, 1998, pp. 116–17 points out that in Napoleonic warfare cavalry appear to have been almost always impossible to control once they charged.

56 Budiansky, 1997, pp. 190 ff. discusses the mechanics of different gaits, pp. 204–5 explains the advantages of shifting gait from 'trot' to 'gallop'.

57 4,000 javelins with 5 per cent accuracy would give 200 hits. If only 2,000 javelins were thrown, with a reduced accuracy rate of 2.5 per cent, there would have been only 40 hits. The 2.5 per cent accuracy rate may seem incredibly poor, but Goldsworthy, 1996, pp. 187–8 points out that in certain conditions one hit in 40 may have been quite good.

58 Goldsworthy, 1996, pp. 236–7; du Picq, 1987, p. 87. Carlton, 1992, p. 135 describes cavalry in the early modern period riding close to the enemy lines, where the riders would fire at the enemy before withdrawing, reloading, and repeating the procedure.

59 Hanson, 1989, pp. 165–7, describing 'hand-to-hand' fighting between hoplites.

60 Du Picq, 1987, p. 88. Spence, 1993, pp. 43 ff. notes that this instability of ancient riders is often overemphasised, but it seems to have been a genuine weakness in this case. Plut., *Vit. Crass.* 23.8 describes how Celtic troops stationed on the ground were able to unseat Parthian cavalry at Carrhae in 55 by grabbing their lances and pushing them from their horses.

61 Gabriel and Metz, 1991, pp. 95–6, also noting that the most common injury to cavalrymen until the nineteenth century was a broken wrist.

62 Plut., *Vit. Crass.* 23.9 describes wounded Parthian horses trampling upon and crushing both their own riders and enemy troops. See also Carlton, 1992, p. 136 with reference to cavalry combat in the British Civil Wars.

63 Liv. 31.34.1–5 describes such wounds. Muir, 1998, pp. 108–9 points out how difficult British cavalrymen in the Napoleonic era found it to use their sabres effectively in battle, but when they actual struck an enemy they did so to horrific effect. He quotes the French captain Charles Parquin: 'they always cut with their blade which was three inches wide. Consequently, out of every twenty blows aimed by them, nineteen missed. If, however, the edge of the blade found its mark only once, it was a terrible blow, and it was not unusual to see an arm cut clean from the body.'

64 Carlton, 1992, pp. 144–5 notes that unbridled pursuit by cavalry could often prove costly for the army as a whole, by removing the cavalry from the field of battle for long periods, during which the tide of battle might turn. Goldsworthy, 1996, p. 239 explains that pursuing cavalry could easily lose all sense of cohesion during such pursuits, and valuable time would be lost attempting to re-establish discipline.

65 There was no room for such 'normal' tactics on the far side of the field: Polyb. 3.115.3; Liv. 22.47.2. See also Polyb. 12.18.3, explaining that gaps were needed between cavalry units to facilitate such manoeuvres.

66 Liv. 48.1–4 does not mention Hasdrubal's charge towards the allied cavalry, but records instead a spurious ruse whereby a party of Numidians pretended to desert as a manoeuvre to get behind the Roman lines and attack them from behind.

67 Liv. 22.48.5 initially has the Numidians join his cavalry in attacking the Roman rear, before deciding that they were ineffective when fighting face to face, and despatching them to deal with the fleeing Romans.

68 Spence , 1993, pp. 157–8. Liv. 22.15.8 describes Carthalo leading Carthaginian cavalry in a pursuit that lasted for almost 5 miles (8 km).

69 See also Carlton, 1992, pp. 75, 145. Marshall, 1994, pp. 26–8 discusses how Mongol hunting practices were developed into cavalry training and tactics.

70 Liv. 22.48.4 describes Romans being struck down in this manner at Cannae. See also Amm. 16.12.52, 25.3.5, 31.7.13.

71 Goldsworthy, 1997, p. 7. Arr., *Anab.* 2.10.1 records Alexander at Issus calling a halt to the advance of his troops at several points. This probably allowed him to ensure that his men were maintaining their formations.

72 This is an odd passage as Polybius says that the Romans clashed their shields with their *xiphesi*; the word *xiphos* is usually translated 'sword', but that can hardly be the case here. In the first place, Polybius normally describes the Roman sword as a *machaira*; e.g., Polyb. 2.30.8, 6.23.6, 18.30.7. Second, the Romans had not yet hurled their *pila*. It is probable that *xiphos* is being used in a very loose sense, meaning perhaps 'blade' or 'weapon'; it appears to refer to the *pilum*. Zhmodikov, 2000, pp. 67–8 accepts Polybius at face value here, and assumes that the Romans did not use their *pila* at Zama.

73 Goldsworthy, 1996, pp. 197–8 cites Caes., *B Civ* 3.93 as evidence that this was an ordered drill, although it may be somewhat anachronistic to apply this evidence to the army almost two centuries earlier.

74 The elaborate blades on such spears may not have been designed with this express purpose, though they could well have had such an effect. As the Celtic shields and helmets described by Diodorus were primarily ornamental, so too might these blades have been. Fussell, 2000, p. 117 describes how German soldiers in the First World War were thought to have been armed with bayonets with a serrated edge in order to inflict terrible wounds; such bayonets did exist, but they had a much less sinister purpose – they were designed for sawing branches.

75 Goldsworthy, 1996, pp. 201 ff. Du Picq, 1987, pp. 169 ff. argues that infantry forces never collide with each other.

76 Hanson, 1992, p. 48 argues that 'the idea of ancient battle as orderly mass duelling with measured blows is absurd', but his conception of hoplite battle as basically a giant shoving match, the rear ranks pushing the front ranks onwards, whether or not it is correct, is inapplicable to the fighting at Cannae. Goldsworthy, 1996, pp. 206–8 points out that the central boss of the Roman *scutum* made it particularly unsuitable for pushing with, as it would have applied pressure very unevenly.

77 While they wore helmets, protecting their heads, *hastati* were perhaps less likely to have cuirasses than the *principes* and *triarii*. The rear ranks were older than the *hastati* and may have been wealthier, making them more likely to be able to afford such an expensive item.

78 Gabriel and Metz, 1991, p. 96 argue that even a glancing blow to an unprotected shoulder was liable to fracture the clavicle.

79 Goldsworthy, 1996, pp. 217–19, rightly dismissing the pronounced crouch position postulated by Connolly, 1989, pp. 358–63 as absurd. Such a low crouch would have been extremely uncomfortable and difficult to hold for any length of time, apart from exposing the soldier to attack from above. For what it is worth, Connolly, 1998, p. 131 argues that most of the time the Roman soldier would rest his shield on the ground and fight from behind it, in a manner similar to that proposed by Goldsworthy.

80 Hanson, 1989, pp. 211–14 discusses chest and head wounds.

81 Hanson, 1989, p. 162 discusses the threat posed by leg wounds.

82 Sabin, 1996, pp. 72–3, discussed more fully in Sabin, 2000, pp. 1–17. See also Goldsworthy, 2000b, pp. 49–55; 2000a, pp. 56–9.

83 See Goldsworthy, 1996, p. 50, who makes a similar point about German infantry who apparently fought as a row of wedges. Liv. 22.50.9, 34.15.1 describes Romans in wedge formation.

84 Kromayer and Veith, 1912, pp. 318–19 postulate a brief but large-scale breakthrough.

85 Muir, 1998, p. 60 describes skirmishers in the Napoleonic era being used for the purposes of screening other movements.

86 Goldsworthy, 1997, p. 8 points out that a narrow, deep unit could move quickly while maintaining formation.

87 Keegan, 1976, p. 101 describes this effect at Agincourt.

88 Two centurions for the 24 *hastati*, two for the 24 *principes*, and two for the 10 *triarii*. The *velites* in the rear lacked such officers.

89 Culham, 1989, p. 199 notes that panic tended to produce 'entropy' in ancient armies, and that elaborate systems of training and indoctrination were largely designed to prevent armies collapsing into disorder through panic. Culham's

article is interesting but highly deterministic – although there are individual actions in Culham's analysis there are no individual persons or emotions. For example, the representation by Julius Caesar of his legionaries as unswervingly loyal and obedient is never questioned. A useful corrective to this intriguing if somewhat one-sided depiction of battle is Lendon, 1999, pp. 273–329, which considers two traditions of writing about battle in antiquity, one essentially tactical and one essentially psychological.

90 Connolly, 1998, p. 128 describes and illustrates *triarii* in this position. In order to explain away the fact that the *triarii* would probably have been able to stop the Carthaginian cavalry, he has the *triarii* guarding the Roman camp (p. 187).

91 Connolly, 1998, p. 142 points out these were the two standard positions for *velites* after the initial skirmishing.

92 Muir, 1998, pp. 130–4 discusses combat between cavalry and Napoleonic infantry, stressing the point that cavalry was 'essentially a weapon of fear'. Cavalry charges against infantry were unlikely to succeed unless at least some infantrymen were overcome by fear and tried to flee.

93 Hanson, 1992, p. 46. Cass. Dio 40.3 describes the Romans at Carrhae tripping over their fallen comrades.

94 See Liv. 34.21 for the effects of this.

95 Culham, 1989, p. 199 comments on how the deaths of commanders could cause their armies to collapse into disorder.

96 Cass. Dio. 40.24.2–3 describes Parthians at Carrhae allowing Romans to escape as they were too tired to stop them, and feared retaliation. Liv. 22.48.6 describes the Libyans as being exhausted more through slaughter than fighting.

97 App., *Hann.* 24 describes Hannibal exhorting his troops and rebuking them for not overcoming the last remnants of the Roman forces. See Hanson, 1992, p. 48.

98 Goldsworthy, 1996, p. 249; Keegan, 1987, p. 329. See Lee, 1996, p. 199 on Roman morale in battle in general. Curiously, Chesterton, 1993 [1925], pp. 137–50, in a chapter devoted to the Punic Wars, wonders why men fight, recognising that they hardly do so for the same reasons that governments call on them to do so.

99 Lee, 1996, pp. 210–11 cites Caes., *B Gall* 2.25 as evidence for the importance of leadership by example at sub-unit level, pointing to the high casualty rate among centurions.

100 See Hanson, 1992, p. 45. Rosenstein, 1990, pp. 172–3 discusses what he calls the 'myth of universal aristocratic competence'.

101 Smith, 1990, p. 157. Conversely, Polyb. 6.39 also describes rewards for courage in battle, but he is really referring to displays of courage in skirmishes rather than pitched battles.

102 Keegan, 1976, p. 115. Holmes, 1985, pp. 353–5 discusses this motive in slightly more detail, with evidence from more recent periods.

103 Quoted in Fussell, 1990, p. 141.

104 This practice was not unique to antiquity. Griffith, 1989, p.79 discusses how Union and Confederate soldiers in the American Civil War would often engage in battlefield salvage, taking footwear, money, and, above all, weapons.

105 Hanson, 1992, p. 48, noting that many of these soldiers would have received numerous compound fractures through trampling, in addition to their original wounds from swords or missiles. See Hanson, 1989, pp. 214–15.

106 Quintilian 8.6.26 gives a figure of 60,000 killed, while App., *Hann.* 25 and Plut., *Vit. Fab. Max.* 16 both give round figures of 50,000.

107 See Lazenby, 1978, pp. 84–5 for the necessary calculations based on various scattered references throughout Liv. 22.49–54.

108 Against this, De Sanctis, 1968, pp. 128–30 argues that Livy's figure for fugitives and Polybius' figures for prisoners should be accepted, claiming them to derive from accurate Roman and Carthaginian sources. This would mean between 20,000 and 25,000 Roman deaths, by his own calculation, or upwards of 61,000 if Polybius' figures for the size of the army are accepted. However, as Walbank, 1957, p.440 points out, Polybius' prisoner figures look very suspicious.

109 Engels, 1978, p. 151, in an analysis of the killed:wounded ratio for Alexander's battles, identifies 1 dead: 5 wounded as the casualty rate in battles which were not hotly contested. Applying this ratio to Hannibal's forces at Cannae would mean that there were at least 28,500 Carthaginian wounded.

BIBLIOGRAPHY

Translations of ancient sources

All translations are from the Loeb Classical Library, with the following exceptions:

Cato, *Les Origines* (Fragments), trans. with commentary M. Chassignet, Paris, 1986.

Ennius, *The Annals of Q. Ennius*, ed. with introduction and commentary O. Skutsch, Oxford, 1985.

Flavius Arrianus, *ΤΕΧΝΗ ΤΑΚΤΙΚΑ* [*Tactical Handbook*] *and ΕΚΤΑΞΙΣ ΚΑΤΑ ΛΑΝΩΝ* [*The Expedition against the Alans*], trans. and ed. J.G. DeVoto, Chicago, 1993.

Vegetius, *Epitome of Military Science*, trans. with notes and introduction N.P. Milner (2nd edn), Liverpool, 1996.

Modern works

Adcock, F.E., 1940, *The Roman Art of War under the Republic*, Cambridge, MA.

―― 1957, *The Greek and Macedonian Art of War*, Berkeley and Los Angeles.

Africa, T.W., 1970, 'The One-Eyed Man against Rome: An Exercise in Euhemerism', *Historia* 19.

Anderson, J.K., 1970, *Military Theory and Practice in the Age of Xenophon*, Berkeley and Los Angeles.

―― 1991, 'Hoplite Weapons and Offensive Arms', in V.D. Hanson (ed.), *Hoplites: The Classical Greek Battle Experience*, London.

Astin, A.E., 1967, 'Saguntum and the Origins of the Second Punic War'. *Latomus* 26.

―― 1989a, 'Postscript. The Emergence of the Provincial System', in F.W. Walbank, A.E. Astin, M.W. Frederiksen, and R.M. Ogilvie (eds), *The Cambridge Ancient History* (2nd edn), vol. 7, part 2, Cambridge.

―― 1989b, 'Sources', in A.E. Astin, F.W. Walbank, M.W. Frederiksen, and R.M. Ogilvie (eds), *The Cambridge Ancient History* (2nd edn), vol. 8, Cambridge.

Austin, N.J.E. and Rankov, N.B., 1995, *Exploratio – Military and Political Intelligence in the Roman World*, London.

Badian, E., 1958, *Foreign Clientelae, 264–70 BC*, Oxford.

―― 1966, 'The Early Historians', in T.A. Dorey (ed.), *Latin Historians*, London.

Bagnall, N., 1990, *The Punic Wars*, London.

Bar-Kochva, B., 1976, *The Seleucid Army: Organisation and Tactics in the Great Campaign*, Cambridge.

Baronowski, D.W., 1993, 'Roman Military Forces in 225 BC (Polybius 2.23–4)', *Historia* 42.2.

Barré, M.L., 1983, *The God List in the Treaty between Hannibal and Philip V of Macedon*, Baltimore.

Bartlett, R., 1993, *The Making of Europe: Conquest, Colonization and Cultural Change 950–1350*, Harmondsworth.

Bell, M.J.V., 1965, 'Tactical Reform in the Roman Republican Army', *Historia* 14.

Bernstein, A.H., 1994, 'The Strategy of a Warrior-State: Rome and the Wars against Carthage, 264–201 BC', in W. Murray, M. Knox and A. Bernstein (eds), *The Making of Strategy: Rulers, States, War*, Cambridge.

Best, J.G.P., 1969, *Thracian Peltasts and their Influence on Greek Warfare*, Groningen.

Bishop, M.C. and Coulston, J.C., 1993, *Roman Military Equipment*, London.

Bosworth, A.B., 1993, *Conquest and Empire: The Reign of Alexander the Great*, Cambridge.

Bradford, E., 1981, *Hannibal*, London.

Brett, M. and Fentress, E., 1996, *The Berbers*, Oxford.

Briscoe, J., 1989, 'The Second Punic War', in A.E. Astin, F.W. Walbank, M.W. Frederiksen, and R.M. Ogilvie (eds), *The Cambridge Ancient History* (2nd edn), vol. 8, Cambridge.

—— 1996, 'Livy', in *OCD*, p. 877.

Broughton, T.R.S., 1951, *The Magistrates of the Roman Republic*, vol. 1, New York.

Brunt, P.A., 1971, *Italian Manpower, 225 BC–AD 14*, Oxford.

—— 1988, *The Fall of the Roman Republic and Related Essays*, Oxford.

Budiansky, S., 1997, *The Nature of Horses*, London.

Burck, E., 1971, 'The Third Decade', in T.A. Dorey (ed.), *Livy*, London.

Burne, A.H., 1950, *The Art of War on Land* (2nd edn), London.

Campbell, J.B., 1987, 'Teach Yourself How to be a General', *JRS* 77.

Carlton, C., 1992, *Going to the Wars*, London.

Cartledge, P., 1993, *The Greeks*, Oxford.

Caven, B., 1980, *The Punic Wars*, London.

Chesterton, G.K., 1993 [1925], *The Everlasting Man,* San Fransisco.

Clark, M., 1995, 'Did Thucydides Invent the Battle Exhortation?', *Historia* 44.3.

Clausewitz, C. von, 1993, *On War*, trans. M. Howard and P. Paret, London.

Connolly, P., 1989, 'The Roman Army in the Age of Polybius', in Gen. Sir John Hackett (ed.), *Warfare in the Ancient World*, London.

—— 1991, 'The Roman Fighting Technique Deduced from Armour and Weaponry', in V.A. Maxfield and B. Dobson (eds), *Roman Frontier Studies 1989*, Exeter.

—— 1998, *Greece and Rome at War* (rev. edn), London.

Cornell, T.J., 1995, *The Beginnings of Rome*, London.

——, Rankov, N.B. and Sabin, P. (eds), 1996, *The Second Punic War: A Reappraisal*, London.

Crawford, M.H., 1985, *Coinage and Money under the Roman Republic: Italy and the Mediterranean Economy*, London.

Culham, P., 1989, 'Chance, Command and Chaos in Ancient Military Engagements', *World Futures* 27.

Davidson, J., 1991, 'The Gaze in Polybius' *Histories*', *JRS* 81.

De Beer, G., 1969, *Hannibal*, London.

Delbrück, H., 1990 [1920], *History of the Art of War, Volume 1: Warfare in Antiquity* (3rd edn), trans. W.J. Renfroe, Lincoln, NB.

Derow, P.S., 1976, 'The Roman Calendar, 218–191 BC', *Phoenix* 30.

—— 1979, 'Polybius, Rome, and the East', *JRS* 69.

—— 1996, 'Polybius', in *OCD*.

De Sanctis, G., 1968, *Storia dei Romani*, vol. 3, part 2 (2nd edn), Florence.

Desanges, J., 1981, 'The Proto-Berbers', in G. Mokhtar (ed.), *General History of Africa*, vol. 2, London.

D'Este, C., 1996, *A Genius for War: A Life of General George S. Patton*, London.

Devijver, H. and Lipinski, E. (eds), *Studia Phoenicia X: Punic Wars*, Leuven.

Diop, C.A., 1986, 'Formation of the Berber Branch', in UNESCO, *Libya Antiqua*, Paris.

Dixon, K.R. and Southern, P., 1992, *The Roman Cavalry*, London.

Dodds, E.R., 1951, *The Greeks and the Irrational*, Berkeley and Los Angeles.

Dodge, T.A., 1995 [1891], *Hannibal*, New York.

Dorey, T.A., 1959, 'The Elections of 216 BC', *RhM* 102.

—— (ed.), 1966, *Latin Historians*, London.

—— (ed.), 1971, *Livy*, London.

—— and Dudley, D.R., 1968, *Rome against Carthage*, London.

Drummond, A., 1989, 'Rome in the Fifth Century II: The Citizen Community', in F.W. Walbank, A.E. Astin, M.W. Frederiksen, and R.M. Ogilvie (eds), *The Cambridge Ancient History* (2nd edn), vol. 7, part 2, Cambridge.

Du Picq, A., 1987, *Battle Studies*, trans. J. Greely and R. Cotton, repr. in Stackpole Books, *Roots of Strategy*, Book 2, Harrisburg, PA.

Eckstein, A.M., 1995, *Moral Vision in the Histories of Polybius*, London.

Ehrhardt, C.T.H.R., 1995, 'Speeches Before Battle?', *Historia* 44.3.

Engels, D., 1978, *Alexander the Great and the Logistics of the Macedonian Army*, Berkeley and Los Angeles.

—— 1980, 'Alexander's Intelligence System', *CQ* 30.

Erdkamp, P., 1992, 'Polybius, Livy and the "Fabian Strategy"', *Ancient Society* 23.

Errington, R.M., 1970, 'Rome and Spain Before the Second Punic War', *Latomus* 29.

—— 1971, *The Dawn of Empire: Rome's Rise to World Power*, London.

Erskine, A.W., 1993, 'Hannibal and the Freedom of the Italians', *Hermes* 121.

Feig Vishnia, R., 1996, *State, Society and Popular Leaders in Mid-Republican Rome 241–167 BC*, London.

Ferrill, A., 1985, *The Origins of War*, London.

Flaubert, G., 1977, *Salammbo*, trans. A.J. Krailsheimer, Harmondsworth.

Fuller, J.F.C., 1954, *The Decisive Battles of the Western World*, vol. 1, London.

—— 1960, *The Generalship of Alexander the Great*, New Brunswick.

—— 1965, *Julius Caesar: Man, Soldier, and Tyrant*, New Brunswick.

Fussell, P., 1990, *Killing, in Verse and Prose and Other Essays*, London.

—— 2000, *The Great War and Modern Memory* (25th anniversary edn), Oxford.

Gabba, E., 1976, *Republican Rome, the Army and the Allies*, trans. P.J. Cuff, Oxford.

Gabriel, R.A. and Metz, K.S., 1991, From Sumer to Rome: The Military Capabilities of Ancient Armies, New York.

Garlan, Y., 1975, *War in the Ancient World: A Social History*, trans. J. Lloyd, London.

—— 1984, 'War and Siegecraft', in A.E. Astin, F.W. Walbank, M.W. Frederiksen, and R.M Ogilvie (eds), *The Cambridge Ancient History* (2nd edn), vol. 7, part 1, Cambridge.

Goldsworthy, A.K., 1996, *The Roman Army at War, 100 BC–AD 200*, Oxford.

—— 1997, 'The *Othismos*, Myths and Heresies: The Nature of Hoplite Battle', *War in History* 4.1.

—— 2000a, *The Punic Wars*, London.

—— 2000b, *Roman Warfare*, London.

Green, P. (ed.), 1993, *Hellenistic History and Culture*, Berkeley and Los Angeles.

Griffith, G.T., 1935, *The Mercenaries of the Hellenistic World*, Cambridge.

—— 1979, 'The Reign of Philip II', in N.G.L. Hammond and G.T. Griffith, *A History of Macedonia*, vol. 2, Oxford.

Griffith, P., 1989, *Battle Tactics of the American Civil War* (rev. edn), Ramsbury.

—— 1995, *The Viking Art of War*, London.

Gruen, E.S., 1978, 'The Consular Elections for 216 BC and the Veracity of Livy', *California Studies in Classical Antiquity* 11.

Gsell, S., 1928, *Histoire Ancienne de l'Afrique du Nord*, vol. 2 (3rd edn), Paris.

Hackett, Gen. Sir John (ed.), 1989, *Warfare in the Ancient World*, London.

Hammond, N.G.L., 1988, 'The Campaign and the Battle of Cynoscephalae in 197 BC', *JHS* 108.

—— 1989, *Alexander the Great: King, Commander, and Statesman* (3rd edn), Bristol.

—— 1993, 'The Macedonian Imprint on the Hellenistic World', in P. Green (ed.), *Hellenistic History and Culture*, Berkeley and Los Angeles.

Hansen, M.H., 1993, 'The Battle Exhortation in Ancient Historiography: Fact or Fiction?', *Historia* 44.2.

Hanson, V.D., 1989, *The Western Way of War: Infantry Battle in Classical Greece*, London.

—— (ed.), 1991, *Hoplites: The Classical Greek Battle Experience*, London.

—— 1992, 'Cannae,' in R. Cowley (ed.), *Experience of War*, New York.

—— 1995a, 'Genesis of the Infantry 650–350 BC', in G. Parker (ed.), *The Cambridge Illustrated History of Warfare*, Cambridge.

—— 1995b, 'From Phalanx to Legion 350–250 BC', in G. Parker (ed.), *The Cambridge Illustrated History of Warfare*, Cambridge.

—— 1999, *The Wars of the Ancient Greeks*, London.

Harris, W.V., 1979, *War and Imperialism in Republican Rome, 327–70 BC*, Oxford.

Head, D., 1982, *Armies of the Macedonian and Punic Wars, 359 BC to 146 BC*, Groving-by-Sea.

Healy, M., 1994, *Cannae, 216 BC*, London.

Holmes, R., 1985, *Firing Line*, London.

Hornblower, S., 1994, *Thucydides* (2nd corrected impression), London.

—— and Spawforth, A. (eds), 1996, *The Oxford Classical Dictionary* (3rd edn), Oxford.

Hoyos, B.D., 1994, 'Barcid "Proconsuls" and Punic Politics, 237–218 BC', *RhM* 137.

Hyland, A, 1990, *Equus: The Horse in the Roman World*, London.

Ignatieff, M., 2000, *Virtual War: Kosovo and Beyond*, London.

Jameson, M.H., 1991, 'Sacrifices before Battle', in V.D. Hanson (ed.), *Hoplites: The Classical Greek Battle Experience*, London.

Kagan, D., 1995, *On The Origins of War and the Preservation of Peace*, London.

Keegan, J., 1976, *The Face of Battle*, London.

—— 1987, *The Mask of Command*, London.

—— 1993, *A History of Warfare*, London.

—— 1998, *The First World War*, London.

Keppie, L., 1998, *The Making of the Roman Army*, London.

Kramer, F.R., 1948, 'Massilian Diplomacy before the Second Punic War', *AJP* 69.

Krentz, P., 1985, 'Casualties in Hoplite Battles', *GRBS* 26.

—— 1991, 'The *Salpinx* in Greek Battle', in V.D. Hanson (ed.), *Hoplites: The Classical Greek Battle Experience*, London.

Kromayer, J. and Veith, G., 1912, *Antike Schlachtfelder in Italien und Afrika*, vol. 3, part 1, Berlin.

—— 1922, *Schlachtenatlas zur Antiken Kriegeschichte*, Gotha.

Lancel, S., 1995, *Carthage: A History*, trans. A. Nevill, Oxford.

—— 1998, *Hannibal*, trans. A. Nevill, Oxford.

Law, R.C.C., 1978, 'North Africa in the Period of Greek and Phoenician Colonisation, c. 800 to 323 BC', and 'North Africa in the Hellenistic and Roman Periods', in J.D. Fage (ed.), *The Cambridge History of Africa*, vol. 2, Cambridge.

Lazenby, J.F., 1978, *Hannibal's War*, Warminster.

—— 1985, *The Spartan Army*, Warminster.

—— 1991, 'The Killing Zone', in V.D. Hanson (ed.), *Hoplites: The Classical Greek Battle Experience*, London.

—— 1994, 'Logistics in Classical Greek Warfare', *War in History* 1.1.

—— 1996a, *The First Punic War*, London.

—— 1996b, 'Was Maharbal Right?', in T.J. Cornell, N.B. Rankov, and P. Sabin (eds), *The Second Punic War: A Reappraisal*, London.

Le Bohec, Y., 1996, *Histoire Militaire des Guerres Puniques*, Paris.

Leckie, R., 1995, *Hannibal*, London.

Lee, A.D., 1996, 'Morale and the Roman Experience of Battle', in A.B. Lloyd (ed.), *Battle in Antiquity*, London.

Lendon, J.E., 1999, 'The Rhetoric of Combat: Greek Military Theory and Roman Culture in Julius Caesar's Battle Descriptions', *Classical Antiquity* 18.2.

Levene, D.S., 1993, *Religion in Livy*, Leiden.

Liddell, H.G. and Scott, R., 1940, *Greek–English Lexicon* (9th edn, revised by H.S. Jones, assisted by R. McKenzie), Oxford.

Liddell Hart, B.H., 1994 [1926], *Scipio Africanus: Greater than Napoleon*, New York.

Linderski, J., 1986, 'The Augural Law', *ANRW*, II 16.3.

Luce, T.J., 1977, *Livy, the Composition of his History*, Princeton, NJ.

Luttwak, E., 1999 [1976], *The Grand Strategy of the Roman Empire*, London.

Machiavelli, N., 1908 [1513], *The Prince*, trans. W.K. Marriott, London.

McKechnie, P., 1989, *Outsiders in the Greek Cities in the Fourth Century BC*, London.

MacMullen, R., 1984, 'The Legion as a Society', *Historia* 33.4.

McPherson, J.M., 1988, *Battle Cry of Freedom: The American Civil War*, Oxford.

Maga, T.P., 2000, *The Complete Idiot's Guide to the Vietnam War*, Indianapolis.

Markle III, M.M., 1977, 'The Macedonian Sarissa, Spear, and Related Armor', *AJA* 81.

Marsden, E.W., 1974, 'Polybius as a Military Historian', *Entretiens XX: Polybe*, Geneva.

Marshall, R., 1994, *Storm from the East*, Harmondsworth.

Marshall, S.L.A., 1947, *Men Against Fire*, New York.

Mattingly, D.J. and Hitchner, R.B., 1995, 'Roman Africa: An Archaeological Review', *JRS* 85.

Millar, F., 1968, 'Local Cultures in the Roman Empire: Libyan, Punic and Latin in Roman Africa', *JRS* 58.

—— 1984, 'The Political Character of the Classical Roman Republic, 200–151 BC', *JRS* 74.

Milner, N.P., 1996, *Vegetius: Epitome of Military Science*, Liverpool.

Moeller, W.O., 1975, 'Once More the One-Eyed Man Against Rome', *Historia* 24.

Momigliano, A., 1975, *Alien Wisdom: The Limits of Hellenisation*, Oxford.

Montgomery of Alamein, Field Marshal Viscount, 1968, *A History of Warfare*, London.

Muir, R., 1998, *Tactics and the Experience of Battle in the Age of Napoleon*, New Haven, CT.

Nicolet, C., 1980, *The World of the Citizen in Republican Rome*, trans. P. Fallon, London.

Nicolini, G., 1974, *The Ancient Spaniards*, trans. J. Stewart, Farnborough.

North, J.A., 1989, 'Religion in Republican Rome', in F.W. Walbank, A.E. Astin, M.W. Frederiksen, and R.M. Ogilvie (eds), *The Cambridge Ancient History* (2nd edn), vol. 7, part 2, Cambridge.

Oakley, S.P., 1985, ' Single Combat in the Roman Republic', *CQ* 35.

—— 1998, *A Commentary on Livy, Books VI–X*, vol. 2, Oxford.

Ogilvie, R.M., 1965, *Commentary on Livy, Books I–V*, Oxford.

Oliver, R. and Fagan, B.M., 1975, *Africa in the Iron Age*, Cambridge.

O'Meara, J.J., 1954, *The Young Augustine*, London.

Palmer, R.E.A., 1997, *Rome and Carthage at Peace*, Stuttgart.

Parke, H.W., 1933, *Greek Mercenary Soldiers*, Oxford.

Parker, G., 1995, 'Dynastic War 1494–1660', in G. Parker (ed.), *The Cambridge Illustrated History of Warfare*, Cambridge.

Peddie, J., 1997, *Hannibal's War*, Stroud.

Picard, G.C., 1964, *Carthage*, London.

—— and Picard, C., 1961, *Daily Life in Carthage*, trans. A.E. Foster, London.

—— and Picard, C., 1968, *The Life and Death of Carthage*, trans. D. Collon, London.

Pleiner, R. and Scott, B.G., 1993, *The Celtic Sword*, Oxford.

Pritchett, W.K., 1971, *The Greek State at War*, vol. 1, Berkeley and Los Angeles.

—— 1974, *The Greek State at War*, vol. 2, Berkeley and Los Angeles.

—— 1979, *The Greek State at War*, vol. 3, Berkeley and Los Angeles.

—— 1985, *The Greek State at War*, vol. 4, Berkeley and Los Angeles.

—— 1991, *The Greek State at War*, vol. 5, Berkeley and Los Angeles.

Proctor, D., 1971, *Hannibal's March in History*, Oxford.

Rankin, H.D., 1987, *Celts and the Classical World*, London.

Rankov, N.B., 1996, 'The Second Punic War at Sea', in T.J. Cornell, N.B. Rankov, and P. Sabin (eds), *The Second Punic War: A Reappraisal*, London.

Rawlings, L., 1996, 'Celts, Spaniards, and Samnites: Warriors in a Soldier's War', in T.J. Cornell, N.B. Rankov and P. Sabin (eds), *The Second Punic War: A Reappraisal*, London.

Rawson, E., 1971, 'The Literary Sources for the Pre-Marian Army', *PBSR* 39.

Rich, J., 1976, *Declaring War in the Roman Republic in the Period of Transmarine Expansion*, Collection Latomus 149, Brussels.

—— 1983, 'The Supposed Roman Manpower Shortage of the Later Second Century BC', *Historia* 32.3.

—— 1996, 'The Origins of the Second Punic War', in T.J. Cornell, N.B. Rankov, and P. Sabin (eds), *The Second Punic War: A Reappraisal*, London.

Richardson, J.S., 1996, *The Romans in Spain*, Oxford.

Ridley, R.T., 1978, 'Was Scipio Africanus at Cannae?', *Latomus* 34.

Riley-Smith, J., 1987, *The Crusades: A Short History*, London.

Rochette, B., 1997, 'Sur le bilinguisme dans les armées d'Hannibal', *Les Etudes Classiques* 65.

Rosenstein, N., 1990, *Imperatores Victi: Military Defeat and Aristocratic Competition in the Middle and Late Republic*, Berkeley and Los Angeles.

—— 1993, 'Competition and Crisis in mid-Republican Rome', *Phoenix* 47.4.

Sabin, P., 1996, 'The Mechanics of Battle in the Second Punic War', in T.J. Cornell, N.B. Rankov, and P. Sabin (eds), *The Second Punic War: A Reappraisal*, London.

—— 2000, 'The Face of Roman Battle', *JRS* 90.

Sage, M.M., 1996, *Warfare in Ancient Greece*, London.

Salmon, E.T., 1982, *The Making of Roman Italy*, London.

Samuel, A.E., 1993, 'The Ptolemies and the Ideology of Kingship', in P. Green (ed.), *Hellenistic History and Culture*, Berkeley and Los Angeles.

Samuels, M., 1990, 'The Reality of Cannae', *Militärgeschichtliche Mitteilungen* 47.

Santosuosso, A., 1997, *Soldiers, Citizens, and the Symbols of War*, Oxford.

Scheidel, W., 1996, 'Finances, Figures and Fiction', *CQ* 46.1.

Schepens, G., 1989, 'Polybius on the Punic Wars: The Problem of Objectivity in History', in H. Devijver and E. Lipinski (eds), *Studia Phoenicia X: Punic Wars*, Leuven.

Schulten, A., 1928, 'The Carthaginians in Spain', in S.A. Cook, F.E. Adcock, and M.P. Charlesworth (eds), *The Cambridge Ancient History*, vol. 7, Cambridge.

Scullard, H.H., 1970, *Scipio Africanus: Soldier and Politician*, London.

—— 1973, *Roman Politics, 220–150 BC* (2nd edn), Oxford.

—— 1980, *A History of the Roman World, 753 BC to 146 BC* (4th edn), London.

—— 1989a, 'Carthage and Rome', in A.E. Astin, F.W. Walbank, M.W. Frederiksen, and R.M. Ogilvie (eds), *The Cambridge Ancient History* (2nd edn), vol. 7, part 2, Cambridge.

—— 1989b, 'The Carthaginians in Spain', in A.E. Astin, F.W. Walbank, M.W. Frederiksen, and R.M. Ogilvie (eds), *The Cambridge Ancient History* (2nd edn), vol. 8, Cambridge.

Shaw, B.D., 1982–3, 'Eaters of Flesh, Drinkers of Milk; The Ancient Mediterranean Ideology of the Pastoral Nomad', *Ancient Society* 13–14.

Shean, J.F., 1996, 'Hannibal's Mules: The Logistical Limitations of Hannibal's Army and the Battle of Cannae, 216 BC', *Historia* 45.2.

Sherwin-White, A.N., 1973, *The Roman Citizenship* (2nd edn), Oxford.

Skutsch, O. (ed.), 1985, *The Annals of Q. Ennius*, Oxford.

Smith, F.W., 1990, 'The Fighting Unit: An Essay in Structural Military History', *L'Antiquité Classique* 59.

Snodgrass, A.M., 1999, *Arms and Armor of the Greeks*, Baltimore, MD.

Spence, I.G., 1993, *The Cavalry of Classical Greece: A Social and Military History with Particular Reference to Athens*, Oxford.

Starks, J.H. Jr., 1999, '*Fides Aeneia:* The Transference of Punic Stereotypes in the *Aeneid*', *CJ* 94.3.

Staveley, E.S., 1954–5, 'The Conduct of Elections during an Interregnum', *Historia* 3.

Strauss, B.S. and Ober, J., 1992, *The Anatomy of Error: Ancient Military Disasters and their Lessons for Modern Strategists*, New York.

Sumner, G.V., 1967, 'Roman Policy in Spain before the Hannibalic War', *HSCP* 72.

—— 1970, 'The Legion and Centuriate Organization', *JRS* 60.

—— 1972, 'Rome, Spain, and the Outbreak of the Second Punic War: Some Clarifications', *Latomus* 31.

—— 1975, 'Elections at Rome in 217 BC', *Phoenix* 29.

Sun Tzu, 1993, *The Art of War*, trans. Y. Shibing, Ware.

Suolahti, J., 1955, *Junior Officers of the Roman Army during the Republican Period*, Helsinki.

Tarn, W.W., 1930, *Hellenistic Military and Naval Developments*, Cambridge.

Tatum, W.J., 1991, 'Military Defeat and Electoral Success in Republican Rome', *AHB* 5.

—— 1992, 'Military Defeat and Electoral Success – Two Corrections', *AHB* 6.

Thompson, W.E., 1986, 'The Battle of the Bagradas', *Hermes* 114.

Toynbee, A.J., 1965, *Hannibal's Legacy: The Hannibalic War's Effects on Roman Life*, 2 vols, London.

Tuchman, B.W., 1995, *A Distant Mirror: The Calamitous Fourteenth Century*, London.

Twyman, B.L., 1984, 'The Consular Elections for 216 BC and the *Lex Maenia de Patrum Auctoritate*', *CP* 79.

—— 1987, 'Polybius and the Annalists on the Outbreak and Early Years of the Second Punic War', *Athenaeum* 75.

Usher, S., 1969, *The Historians of Greece and Rome*, London.

Van Crefeld, M., 1985, *Command in War*, Cambridge, MA.

Van Wees, H., 1994, 'The Homeric Way of War: The *Iliad* and the Hoplite Phalanx', *Greece and Rome* 41.

Wagner, C.G., 1989, 'The Carthaginians in Ancient Spain from Administrative Trade to Territorial Annexation', in H. Devijver and E. Lipinski (eds), *Studia Phoenicia X: Punic Wars*, Leuven.

Walbank, F.W., 1957, *A Historical Commentary on Polybius*, vol. 1, Oxford.

—— 1966, 'Polybius', in T.A. Dorey (ed.), *Latin Historians*, London.

—— 1967, *A Historical Commentary on Polybius*, vol.2, Oxford.

—— 1972, *Polybius*, Berkeley and Los Angeles.

—— 1979, *A Historical Commentary on Polybius*, vol. 3, Oxford.

—— 1984, 'Monarchies and Monarchic Ideas', in A.E. Astin, F.W. Walbank, M.W. Frederiksen, and R.M Ogilvie (eds), *The Cambridge Ancient History* (2nd edn), vol. 7, part 1, Cambridge.

Walsh, P.G., 1961, *Livy: His Historical Aims and Methods*, Cambridge.

Warmington, B.H., 1960, *Carthage*, London.

Warry, J., 1980, *Warfare in the Classical World*, London.

Weinreich, M., 1999 [1946], *Hitler's Professors: The Part of Scholarship in Germany's Crimes against the Jewish People*, New Haven, CT.

Whatley, N., 1964, 'On the Possibility of Reconstructing Marathon and Other Ancient Battles', *JHS* 84.

Wheeler, E.L., 1983, 'The *Hoplomachoi* and Vegetius' Spartan Drillmasters', *Chiron* 13.

—— 1991, 'The General as Hoplite', in V.D. Hanson (ed.), *Hoplites: The Classical Greek Battle Experience*, London.

Whitehead, D., 1991, 'Who Equipped Mercenary Troops in Classical Greece?', *Historia* 40.1.

Whittaker, C.R., 1978, 'Carthaginian Imperialism in the Fifth and Fourth Centuries', in P. Garnsey and C.R. Whittaker (eds), *Imperialism in the Ancient World*, Cambridge.

Wiedemann, T.E.J., 1986, 'Between Men and Beasts: Barbarians in Ammianus Marcellinus', in I.S. Moxon, J.D. Smart, and A.J. Woodman (eds), *Past Perspectives; Studies in Greek and Roman Writing*, Cambridge.

Zhmodikov, A., 2000, 'Roman Republican Heavy Infantrymen in Battle (IV–II Centuries BC)', *Historia* 49.1.

INDEX

Baecula, battle of xii
Baga 94
Bagradas, River, battle of 7, 39, 42
Balearians 31, 83, 85, 94, 106–8, 112, 142,
 170, 173, 177, 197
Balearic Islands 1, 107
Baniurae 94
Barcids: 82, 86, 90, 92–3, 95, 112, 125,
 127, 135, 137, 141; position in Spain
 126; see also Hamilcar Barca, Hasdrubal
 (Hamilcar Barca's son-in-law), and
 Hannibal
Barmocar 128
Bastinado 52
'Battle madness' 200–1
'Battleshock' 171–2
Bayonet charge 186
Beneventum 4
Blasto-Phoenicians 96
Blood 171
Bodyguards 151, 154
Boii 14, 102–3
Booty 51,103, 109, 126, 138, 144–5, 199,
 201
Bracchiati 169
Brennus 201
Brundisium 76
Bruttians 4
Bruttium 128
'Bullfrog Effect' 19
'Bunching' 175, 178
Burial 201

Caetra 97, 100–1
Caetrati 97, 101
Calabria 43
Callisthenes 19
Camerina 6
Camp Garrisons 25, 26, 29, 32, 101, 201
Campania 16, 47
Cannae, as Roman Nightmare 28
Cappadocia 111
Carnyx 170
Carpetani 96
Carrhae, battle of 196
Cartagena 2, 53, 148
Carthage: foundation of 1; territories of
 1–2; government 2; treaties with Rome

3–4, 6–7, 9; support for Hannibal 10;
alliance with Boii 14; population of 86;
fall of 82;
Carthaginian Army: Polybius' view of 82;
 Carthaginian officers 82–4, 93, 140, 143;
 generals 124–6, 135; military council
 127, 133, 152; chain of command
 127–8; citizen militia 82, 87;
 mercenaries xi, 82–7, 90, 92, 94–5, 100,
 102, 105, 107, 109, 112, 199; subject
 and allied levies xi, 83–4, 86, 92, 95–6,
 100, 102, 109,112, 165; national
 subdivisions 83–4, 112, 164; officers
 from national groups 83, 92–3, 102,
 128, 140, 142–3; light troops of mixed
 nationalities 106–11; military standards
 83; weapons during Third Punic War 89;
 manpower at Cannae 29–32; tactics
 39–43; speed of march 46
Carthalo 128
Casilinum 94
Casualties xi, 15, 23, 28, 32, 44, 182, 184,
 201–2
Cavalry 10, 13–16, 21, 25–7, 29, 30, 32,
 33, 38, 39, 42, 44, 45, 50, 51, 55–8, 65,
 72–3, 76–7, 79–80, 84–5, 87, 89–93,
 95, 97, 100–1, 103, 105–6, 123–4, 127,
 148–9, 152, 156–7, 161–3, 178–84,
 195–6, 198, 204
Celeiates 106
Celines 106
Celtiberians 43, 95, 100–1, 109, 195
Celts 4, 7, 9, 12, 14, 21, 22, 30, 32, 35,
 39, 47, 49, 54, 65, 67, 68, 70, 76, 82–4,
 88, 95, 101–6, 109–10, 112, 115, 127,
 141–2, 145, 148, 150, 152, 154–5,
 160–1, 163–5, 167, 170, 178, 180,
 182–6, 189–93, 195, 198–9, 202, 204
Cenomani 76
Centenius, Gaius 15
Centuries 49, 50, 54, 60, 61, 72, 80
Centurions 58, 60, 63, 80, 122–3, 133–4,
 159, 194
Cerdiciates 106
Chaereas 20
Cicero x
Cincius Alimentus, Lucius 20, 29, 30
Cisalpine Gaul 7, 9, 76, 170